DATE DUE

OC 1			
DE 18 99			
DE 7 00			
NO 5 '02			
OC 1 04			
DE 1 7 '05			
NO 2 7 06			
JA 2 5 07			

Family Man

12

Family Man

FATHERHOOD, HOUSEWORK, AND GENDER EQUITY

Scott Coltrane

New York   Oxford

OXFORD UNIVERSITY PRESS

1996

University Press

Oxford   New York
Athens   Aukland   Bangkok   Bombay
Calcutta   Cape Town   Dar es Salaam   Delhi
Florence   Hong Kong   Istanbul   Karachi
Kuala Lumpur   Madras   Madrid   Melbourne
Mexico City   Nairobi   Paris   Singapore
Taipei   Tokyo   Toronto

and associated companies in
Berlin   Ibadan

Copyright©1996 by Oxford University Press, Inc.

Published by Oxford University Press, Inc.
198 Madison Avenue, New York, New York 10016

Oxford is a registered trademark of Oxford University Press

Library of Congress Cataloging-in-Publication Data
Coltrane, Scott.
Family man : fatherhood, housework, and gender equity
/ Scott Coltrane.
p. cm.   Includes index.
ISBN 0-19-508216-8
1. Family.   2. Fatherhood.   3. Sex role.   I. Title.
HQ503.C65   1996
306.85 — dc20   95-14414

1 3 5 7 9 8 6 4 2

Printed in the United States of America
on acid-free paper

Preface

When I became a father for the first time in the late 1970s, I had no idea it would launch me into a career as a sociologist of fatherhood. I was awkward with newborn babies and knew little about infant care, but my initial curiosity quickly developed into a passion for learning about parents and children. For many years I would wander into bookstores, head for the parental advice shelves, browse through the many manuals addressed to mothers, and become disgusted with the lack of quality offerings for fathers. Most parenting books for men were written for expectant fathers and rarely moved beyond personal stories and humorous anecdotes about pregnancy and the birth experience. The few books that gave advice on what to do once the baby arrived assumed that men would be peripheral parents. The most popular books were the most troubling, with their stereotypical portrayals of bumbling dads who had trouble figuring out which end of the baby to diaper.

After getting annoyed with the how-to books for parents, I would find myself drifting over to the sociology, anthropology, and women's studies sections where authors asked provocative questions about the complexities of family life and the reasons for gender inequality. Most of these books were also about women and mothers, but here I found an intriguing blend of personal experience and critical insight that inspired me to undertake a serious study of fatherhood. In 1979, as Wendy Wheeler and I haltingly began to share the care of our newborn son, I discovered Dorothy Dinnerstein's *The Mermaid and the Minotaur* and marveled at the perversity of our society's gender arrangements. In 1981, when Wendy was pregnant with our daughter, I turned to Nancy Chodorow's *The Reproduction of Mothering* to understand the sociological and psychological roots of American parenting practices. Both of these psychoanalytic books focused on the importance of mothers, but each had a subtext on the social and psychic cost of father absence, and, by implication, the potential redeeming features of father involvement. As a result of these experiences and discoveries, I entered graduate school to study sociology with Nancy Chodorow at the University of California, Santa Cruz. I have been studying fathers ever since.

Riverside, Calif.   S. C.
May 1995

Acknowledgments

I am extremely indebted to the many people who opened up their homes and their hearts to me by agreeing to participate in the studies that form the basis for this book. They willingly and repeatedly let me probe sensitive areas and unflinchingly answered my boldest questions. I hope they can appreciate the sense I have made of their personal stories, even as they realize that I have just touched the surface of their lives. I am also thankful to the many survey researchers, sociologists, psychologists, historians, and anthropologists who provided the raw material for the analyses in the later chapters of this book. Without such willing participants and thorough researchers, we would be much further from understanding the realities of everyday life and the possibilities for social change.

I owe special thanks to Michael Kimmel, who sometimes had more faith in my abilities than I, and who encouraged me to undertake this project. His pioneering research on men and masculinity laid the foundation for this book. I was also inspired by pathbreaking studies of two-job families conducted by Linda Haas, Arlie Hochschild, Jane Hood, and Lillian Rubin. Their words of encouragement buoyed me when my dedication faltered. Similarly, Robert Griswold, Bill Marsiglio, Ross Parke, and Joseph Pleck showed how to study fathers in a balanced and thoughtful way and their kind words reassured me that I was on the right path. My work was made considerably easier because colleagues like Harry Brod, Michael Kaufman, and Michael Messner offered unqualified support and showed that it was possible for a man to study gender from a pro-feminist perspective.

My colleagues at the University of California, Riverside, helped focus my efforts and refine my thinking. I am especially grateful to Randall Collins and Edna Bonacich who supported me and provided models of how to be an effective sociologist. The backing of UCR scholars like Lynda Bell, Vivian Nyitray, Linda Stearns, Barbara Tinsley, and Virginia Vitzthum gave me a much-needed sense of local academic community. Through their research and actions, more distant colleagues like Terry Arendell, Rae Lesser Blumberg, Francesca Cancian, Janet Chafetz, Bob Connell, Riane Eisler, Paula England, Myra Marx Ferree, Kathleen Gerson, Judith Howard, Miriam Johnson, Judith Lorber, Patricia MaCorquodale, Barbara Risman, Pam Roby, and Barrie Thorne showed me it was possible to seek truth and fight for gender justice at the same time.

My professors and fellow graduate students at the University of California, Santa Cruz were particularly helpful in encouraging me to pursue questions that mattered. Nancy Chodorow and Candace West deserve special thanks, for they not only shared their elegant theoretical models, but also challenged me to develop my own thinking about gender and inequality. Bob Alford, John Kitsuse, and Tom Pettigrew taught me to question the obvious and sharpen my analytical skills. Dane Archer, Bill Domhoff, Marcia Millman, and Norma Wikler showed me how diligence and intuition could be combined in the service of principled inquiry. Among my fellow graduate students and staff members at UCSC who gave me support and bolstered my courage to pursue nontraditional research topics were Susan Curtis, Danny Faber, Bristow Hardin, Angela Garcia, Michael Goldman, Hulya Gurtuna, Karen Hossfeld, Peter Ibarra, Amanda Konradi, Theresa Montini, Shunti Mori, Donna Rae Palmer, David Peerla, Carol Ray, Cathy Reback, Garry Rolison, Ken Shaffer, Lee Stork, Lynet Uttal, and Margaret Villanueva. Mike Webber, Nick Vecchione, and Kirstie McClure deserve special thanks because they continually reminded me that life was more than just books and that ideals should not be compromised.

I am also appreciative of the enthusiasm and support of my editors at Oxford University Press. David Roll was very encouraging in the early stages of the work, Rosemary Wellner corrected my faulty grammar, and Gioia Stevens and Paul Schlotthauer were instrumental in shepherding the manuscript through its final stages. Research assistants and graduate students including Kenneth Allan, Patricia Domingues, Neal Hickman, Karen Pyke, and Elsa Valdez contributed more than they know to the insights developed during the course of our joint research. Over the years, people such as Timo Cruz, Seth Ellner, Mark Neenan, Paul Niebanck, Keith Rolle, David Steinberg, and Billy Warters showed me it was manly to be thoughtful and sensitive. Suzun Brackenbury, Christine King, Candi Penn, and Phyllis Shulman taught me about the depths of care and helped me to trust myself. Other students, colleagues, and friends inadvertently omitted from this list have similarly contributed to my developing understanding with a thoughtful piece of research, a quizzical look, or a well-timed question.

Finally, the love and support of my family has been invaluable. My mother, Bonnie Evans, taught me the importance of perseverance and unconditional love, and my mother-in-law, Priscilla Wheeler, demonstrated the value of quiet inner strength. Though they cultivated invincible public images, my father, Roland Coltrane, and my father-in-law, Don Wheeler, showed me that fatherly love can include vulnerability. My children continue to inspire me in profound ways. Shannon and Colin endure my endless hours in front of the computer, draw me out with their playfulness, and ground me through the immediacy of their everyday lives. I owe the most to my life-long friend and partner, Wendy Wheeler, who supports and challenges me in loving ways, and continues to amaze me with her capacity to cut through the nonsense of the world. Without the love and encouragement of all these special people, this book would not have been possible.

Contents

Family Man

1

Parenting in Transition

While shopping for groceries a short time ago, I ran into Terry, a bright and vibrant attorney friend I hadn't seen in several years. As we stood in front of the produce bins, Terry used car keys to entertain a fidgety two year old and described the difficulties of balancing family and career: "I'll bet you can't imagine me as the domestic type, but things have changed since we had Megan. Now all I want to do is stay home and take care of her, and everyone at the office is questioning my commitment to the firm."

Listening to a monologue on the joys of baby care, I marveled at how this fast-track attorney had softened and slowed since we'd last seen each other. I found myself musing about some primal parenting instinct that had caused a profound reordering of priorities. As the conversation went on, I learned that Terry's new domestic commitments carried a steep price. According to colleagues, Terry was no longer considered "serious" about work and had been subtly relegated to a slower and less prestigious career track. The dilemmas Terry was facing are now commonplace for working mothers, but what makes this story unique is that Terry is a father.

When women sacrifice careers to have children, we consider it normal or even natural. So deep is our belief that mothers ought to value family over paid work, that we hardly give it a second thought when new mothers quit their jobs or cut back their hours of employment. When women approaching 30 still consider their careers to be more important than having babies, they tend to be chastised and labeled selfish. When employed mothers (which is most mothers these days) leave their young children in someone else's care during the work day, neighbors and in-laws still shrug their shoulders and wonder if there isn't something wrong with her. If mothers put their kids in child care to do something for themselves—like take a walk, go to a movie, or socialize with a friend—they are especially vulnerable to attack. As sociologists and psychologists have noted, our culture holds unrealistically high expectations that mothers will sacrifice their own needs for their children.[1]

Compared to the complete self-sacrifice expected of mothers, being a father in our culture carries far fewer burdens. Whereas nineteenth century fathers in Europe and North America were expected to be family patriarchs and stern moral teachers, twentieth-century fathers have been relatively uninvolved in the daily routines of family life. In common English language usage, to father a child means to provide the seed, to donate the biological raw material, to impregnate. Of course, people also expect fathers to be providers, which in the modern context means earning the money to pay the bills. But compare this to our unspoken and taken-for-granted expectations of mothers. To speak of *mothering* implies ongoing care and nurturing of children. *Fathering*, on the other hand, has typically implied an initial sex act and the financial obligation to pay.

Looking at the meaning of common parenting terms alerts us to the fact that mothering and fathering are gender-laden activities. What it means to be a woman or a man in our culture has been tied up with, and in a sense created by, what it is that mothers and fathers do within and for families. A woman who spoon feeds an infant, unceremoniously wipes a toddler's runny nose, or tenderly comforts a crying child is seen as exhibiting "motherly" love. In contrast, "fatherly" love is suggested by very different activities: perhaps playing catch on the front lawn; a suppertime lecture about the importance of hard work; or a tense evening chat with a teenage daughter's prospective date. We assume that mothers and fathers are very different, that they do different things with their children, and that these differences are fixed and natural. These assumptions mask the fact that ideas about parenting, and the actual practices of parenting, are constantly changing.

What parents do with and for children, like all forms of human activity, responds to the shifting demands of life within specific social and economic contexts. As the world around us evolves, so do our parenting practices. The simple fact of change is more "natural" than any supposed underlying genetic or spiritual reasons for mothers or fathers to act differently. Despite all the political and religious rhetoric about a mythical past when "family values" were secure, parenting and family life have always been subject to change and are going to continue changing as we move forward into the future. Instead of wringing our hands and trying to recapture some idyllic bygone era, we ought to pay more attention to why the changes are occurring and begin exploring how we can better adapt to them as we struggle to meet the needs of all family members. As the following analysis reveals, the family changes we are facing will be neither easy nor uniformly positive, but they do carry the potential of richer lives for men, more choices for women, and more gender equality in future generations.

New Fatherhood Ideals

At least in the ideal, modern fathering is no longer just procreation and bill paying. For contemporary fathers like Terry, becoming a father means reordering priorities and making a commitment to physically and emotionally care for children. The things Terry talked about in the supermarket—providing routine care for his baby daughter, feeling emotionally connected to her, and wanting to spend more time with her—are the sorts of things we have expected from women when they become parents. In fact, Terry created a stir at his office only because he was the "wrong" gender: he was a father acting like a mother.

According to recent media imagery, Terry is no longer an oddity. Single fathers and male nannies populate TV situation comedies as never before, and muscular men cuddling cute babies are used to sell everything from life insurance to fast food. While there are reasons to be skeptical about some of these idyllic portrayals, the line between fathering and mothering is beginning to blur. Even large scale government surveys are reporting substantial increases in the numbers of fathers who take care of children while mothers work.[2] It is becoming fashionable for fathers to act more like mothers; to shed their privileged outsider status and assume an active role in the routine care of their children. In short, it seems that American fathers are increasingly likely to be nurturing family men rather than the distant providers and protectors they once were.

This book is about men's involvement in families: what its been, how it's evolving, and where it might lead. Is the "new fatherhood" really new? How do men become involved in daily family work and what implications might this hold for the future? To explore these issues, I delve into the intimate details of family life derived from interviews and observations with fathers and mothers in two-job families. I explore who does what, how it feels, and why couples divide work as they do. I also look at survey questionnaires from people all across the country to see which patterns are typical and how much things are really changing. Do current trends represent a passing fad or a fundamental realignment of family roles? Tracing historical developments and using information from different cultures, I also explore why and how larger shifts in the culture and the economy shape families and how divisions of family work shape and are shaped by gender relations. Along the way, I raise issues about gender equity and address questions that have emerged in recent debates about American family values. Have we lost some primordial gender compass that kept families functioning efficiently for eons, or are we on the threshold of replacing oppressive patriarchal families with more democratic ones? These questions have no easy answers, but we can begin to understand the issues involved by looking at what family scholars have been saying about fathers for the past few decades.

Why Study Men in Families?

Men's involvement in families, or lack of it, is a relatively new topic of concern for researchers and is part of a renewed interest in women's lives led by feminist scholars. My interest in these issues coincided with my own children's births over a decade ago. Unsatisfied with a peripheral role in their upbringing, I changed jobs several times, and eventually returned to graduate school to study sociology. While at the University of California, I studied with Nancy Chodorow, who recently had written The Reproduction of Mothering, an influential book on why women mother (and coincidentally, why men do not). Her complex neo-Freudian theory placed much emphasis on the establishment of gender identity within families where mothers do all the child care. She described an unconscious process wherein male children compensate for a deep and painful sense of betrayal by the mother through their rejection of things feminine, including the feminine parts of their own psyches.[3]

Superficially, my own case seemed to contradict Chodorow's theory, insofar as I was raised by a nurturing stay-at-home mother and a distant breadwinner father. If the capacity and motivation for nurturing children is dependent on early childhood experience, then why was I, having been raised almost exclusively by my mother, so interested in being a nurturing caregiver to my own kids? With further study, I learned that Chodorow was suggesting that the capacity for nurturing exists in both boys and girls as a result of early experiences with a parent—usually the mother. It's just that men tend to suppress and devalue the soft and vulnerable parts of their psyches in an unconscious effort to maintain a firm sense of masculinity. But that sense of oppositional masculinity seemed so fragile and insecure to me that it appeared to be an oppressive trap. From my own experiences of personal growth as a child care worker in college, I wondered if caring for children might not provide other men with opportunities for fuller emotional lives. Could men reclaim a more complete sense of manhood that was not based on rejecting the softer or more "feminine" sides of themselves? That question led me on a search for the reasons why men might be drawn to caring for their children and into the realm of the sociology and social psychology of gender and families.

I was impressed by Chodorow's idea that gender socialization and the formation of masculine and feminine selves, with accompanying patterns of gender inequality in the larger society, were perpetuated through the organization of parenting. I became interested in the social forces that promoted men's assumption of family work and began to study the potential outcomes of involved fathering. I soon discovered that scholars had paid scant attention to fathers before the 1970s. Most psychologists and sociologists had assumed that fathers were peripheral to family functioning, even if their presence was usually deemed desirable. More recently, researchers have begun to help us understand how fathers directly and indirectly influence children and other family members, and how men's family involvements intersect with other aspects of their lives.[4] The few studies that have been conducted with men who are highly involved with their children suggest that fathers can "mother" in the sense that they can interact with and care for infants much like women do. What's more, the children of fathers who share responsibility for the everyday details of their upbringing tend to exhibit enhanced intellectual, cognitive, social, and emotional skills.[5] But a puzzle remains. Despite the potential payoffs of fathers taking a more active role in the family, large-scale surveys still show that most men avoid doing routine child care or housework. What's going on? Why is family work obligatory for women and mothers, yet still optional for men?

Regrettably, most of the popular books on men's changing family roles don't move us very far in answering these questions. With only a few exceptions, books on American fathers have been naively optimistic or bitterly reactionary.[6] In books like *Daddy's Home* and *Good Morning, Merry Sunshine,* we learned the intimate details of what it feels like for a reporter to take a leave of absence from his newspaper job to care for his infant daughter — lampooned in the comic strip *Doonesbury.*[7] We also have a few books by psychologists and social workers who present personal accounts from nurturing fathers struggling to become single parents or attempting to share parenting with their wives.[8] Although these advocates of the "new father" give us a glimpse into the innner lives of nurturing men and provide some useful advice to men who want to care for children, their analyses typically leave women out altogether. By focusing only on the men, and by ignoring most of the larger social, political, and economic contexts and consequences of their actions, these authors fail to give us a complete picture of men's family roles.[9] At the other end of the spectrum, we have men's authors like Robert Bly, who tell us to toughen up and reconnect with our absent fathers through all-male initiation rites.[10] These reactionary approaches, discussed more fully in Chapter 7, are best understood as a backlash against women's modestly expanding opportunities.[11]

Family Life and Social Change

Looking back over the past few decades in the United States, we see rapid shifts in women's employment and slower, though still significant, shifts in men's family roles. Although the everyday routines of family life appear to be timeless and natural (as well as somewhat trivial), they reveal and foreshadow some of the most dramatic social changes of this century.[12] In 1960, hardly anyone questioned why women did nearly all of the child care and housework. Most women were not employed and three out of four mothers were housewives. During the 1970s, more women entered the labor force, and some began to question why they should continue to do all the domestic chores. Researchers conducting studies in the 1970s were surprised to find that men were still doing little around the house or with children, even when their wives were working outside the home.[13] In the 1980s, about half of mothers with children under 18 had entered the paid labor force, and many observers continued to expect the division of household labor to equalize. Some slight shifts in the allocation of domestic responsibilities did occur during the early 1980s, with women putting in fewer hours than they had a decade earlier. As researchers like Arlie Hochschild documented, however, wives in two-job families continued to remain responsible for the *second shift* of raising children and running households.[14] Has anything changed since the 1980s? Yes and no. Mothers continue to enter the labor force in record numbers and women still do most of the family work. Nevertheless, important economic and social transformations are underway that will have profound implications for men's involvement in families. In the following chapters, I describe some of these changes, show how they are affecting mothers and fathers, and make some predictions about the future. Before beginning that analysis, however, let's take a glimpse into the life of a couple attempting to share the care of their two children.

Reluctant Pioneers

Gary and Susan Carter would not strike most people as radical innovators or social pioneers. In dress, appearance, and demeanor, they are virtually indistinguishable from other couples in this quiet neighborhood of young families on the edge of suburbia.[15] The landscape is dotted with trees, swing sets, and horse corrals, and Gary Carter's pickup truck with knobby tires and lumber racks sits in the driveway of their ranch style house. Gary is a 34-year old building contractor who has worked in construction since he graduated from high school in a neighboring town. He looks and acts like most of his "hang-loose" carpenter buddies; walrus mustache, healthy tanned face, casual Hawaiian shirt, and a ready smile. Susan Carter recently earned a Masters' degree in psychology and has been working toward certification as a marriage counselor and divorce mediator. She, too, blends in with her co-workers, though her dress and demeanor are more reserved than Gary's. They have two children, eight-year-old Jennifer, and five-year-old Jason.

For the past four years, Gary and Susan have been sharing the routine care of Jennifer and Jason while they work part-time at their jobs. This is an increasingly common pattern among parents with preschool-aged children. Thirty percent of fathers and over 40 percent of mothers with children under five now work non-day shifts, allowing them to share the care of their children. When the mother works part-time or a non-day shift, the father is now the most common child-care provider for the children.[16] This was the case in the Carter family.

Why Did They Share?

The reasons Gary and Susan gave for sharing child care and employment were typical of those heard from other parents I interviewed for this book. Most said they were simply focusing on what was good for the kids and what was economically feasible. Like many fathers, Gary talked about wanting to "bond" with his kids but worried about earning enough money to support his family. He and Susan worked out an arrangement where they both worked about half time, though both felt that it was a constant struggle to balance their work and family commitments.

Although Gary had been financially successful as a carpenter and contractor, he came to realize that having two earners in the household could be a kind of insurance policy for him and for the family.

> From the business standpoint, it started looking down. We were coming off a real unstable economy and it was long-term guess work for me. I wanted to be realistic about it: the next bad times I wanted help financially. So that, at least, was one of my trade offs. The other thing is that, physically, construction is real hard on the body and, I figured I could last longer if I worked three days a week, although it's real tough when everyone else is building five or even seven days a week.

As a result of adopting a three day work week, Gary lost some contracting jobs, was forced to rely exclusively on self-employment, and reduced his income by almost half. Nevertheless, he rationalized his short work week by comparing himself to his contractor buddies who never saw their families and to a few whose marriages "went sour" because they were never home. Gary also admitted that he was motivated to share child care and employment because of his commitment to his wife, Susan. After years of talk and schooling, Gary had come to realize that Susan's desire to become a counselor was not just a passing fancy, but was necessary to her happiness.

Susan wanted to pursue a fulfilling career of her own and talked about feeling limited when she had been the only one with the children on a regular basis. She was adamant in her support for women and men choosing their own paths in life: "People should be whatever and whoever they want and need to be." She referred to women who were forced to be only housewives and men who were forced to be sole breadwinners as "halves." For Susan, the only way for both spouses to become "whole" was to share the family work and the paid work: for mother and father simultaneously to be homemakers and breadwinners.

A major impetus for the Carters' sharing was a belief that many would call "conservative" or "old fashioned." Both Gary and Susan believed strongly that their kids should not be left with "strangers" during the day; that children needed to be with their parents on a regular basis. Gary talked about people abusing child care by "dumping the kids there for ten hours a day" and vowed that he would never do that. He admitted it was difficult to forego regular contracting work to perform child care, but he called his time with his children "precious." When I asked him how it felt to know that he could be earning many times what it would cost to pay a child-care worker to care for his children, he answered, "I wouldn't trade this time with the kids for anything." Saying "they're only small once," he commented that within the year they would both be in school until 2:00 P.M. everyday and that he would "gradually get my work time back." Similarly, Susan commented that she felt her children could have "handled day care just fine," but that she preferred that they be with her or with their father. She made a point of mentioning that many parents had no choice but to rely on day care, but she felt that children fared better in their own parents' care. She attributed their ability to avoid using outside child care to the flexibility of her and Gary's schedules and their strong commitment to be with their kids.

Ambivalent Reactions

The reactions that Susan and Gary got from most of the people around them were discouraging. Their decision to share breadwinning and homemaking was described as "a little odd" by many friends, and Gary commented that many friends "bet against" them. Gary also felt that Susan's parents, though usually silent, thought less of him because he had relinquished the sole provider role. Gary was seen as less of a man because he cut back on his time at work, and Susan's "maternal instinct" was called into question because she left the kids with Gary rather than "allowing" him to go to work. Gary and Susan also reported ambivalent reactions from neighbors and co-workers, even if most never mentioned the subject directly. According to Gary, most simply "scratched their heads in disbelief."

In discussing how others reacted to their situation, Susan suggested there was a "profound lack of understanding" about their efforts at sharing paid work and family work: "They either don't believe it, or they do believe it and it changes how they relate to us. People are really threatened. Reactions were negative for a really long time, and it took a track record before it started getting more positive." After they initiated their sharing routine, Gary was likely to be at school meetings or other child-centered activities where numerous mothers were present. He soon discovered that most mothers were reluctant to believe he really performed a full range of family work.

> At first they'd ask me, "Is this your day off?" And I'd say, "If it's the day off for me, why isn't it the day off for you?" They'd say, "Well, I work 24 hours a day!" And I'd say, "Yeah, right, I got my wash done and hung out, and the beds made, and the shopping done." It would take the mother a couple of times to realize that I really did that stuff.

After repeated contact, however, some mothers began to include Gary in their conversations and occasionally approached him for advice about how to deal with a problem child, usually a son. Gary also reported that he received more attention than he deserved simply for watching his own children. More than Susan, his actions were noticed and praised, even though he considered her the more adept parent. Susan commented, "I can bust my butt at that school, and all he has to do is show up in the parking lot and everybody's all ga-ga over him."

When couples like the Carters share family work and paid work, you might expect that the wife would get similar attention and praise for assuming half of the breadwinner role. Not so, according to Susan. Reactions to her career ambitions were mostly mixed, and she said Gary's parents did not readily accept her as a co-provider.

> In the beginning there was a real strong sense that I was in the space of Gary's economic duty. That came from his parents pretty strongly. The only way that they have been able to come to grips with this in any fashion is because Gary has also been financially successful. If he had decided, you know, "Outside work is not for me, I'm going to stay home with the kids and she's going to work," I think there would have been a whole lot more flak than there was. I think it's because he did both and was successful that it was okay.

Although others in their circle of friends were more supportive of their efforts, Susan reported that many still couldn't quite figure out what was going on with them.

> It's funny because we both talked about child care plans in terms of, "well you have to ask Gary—that's his day with the kids" or "you better check it out with Susan because the kids will be with her." At school, especially, a lot of people thought we were divorced and were sharing these kids, you know, since we were rarely together because the other person was always at work. So it got to be sort of a joke, "Are you guys really together or are you not?"

Others reported that they admired Susan and Gary's arrangements, but couldn't understand how they ever got there. The reactions the Carters received are similar to reactions other role sharing-couples have reported.[17] As we will see in subsequent chapters, social networks of close-by friends and relatives can easily discourage couples from raising children and doing housework differently from their own parents.

According to Susan, most people assumed it was her fault that Gary was "sacrificing" his career, and since she was still in training and not yet making much money, she felt especially vulnerable to attack. Friends and co-workers saw his contracting business as a huge success and couldn't understand how he could give up that earning potential to "babysit." Susan commented, "I became the bad guy in a lot of circles, and it took Gary a long time to convince people that he really wanted it this way." When I last talked to the Carters, the children were about ready to attend school every day, but Gary still had no plans to go back to work full time. Susan reported that most people had "finally gotten it" that Gary wasn't just going along with her demands, but that he was now fully committed to sharing the family work with her.

Sharing the Worry of Child Care

One of the most interesting findings about families that share child care is that the men go through some personal and emotional changes as they perform more of the mundane child-tending tasks. These changes are not the same for all men, but, for many, the process of routine caregiving fosters more intimate relationships with their children and provides them with opportunities for developing emotional sensitivities. In the Carter family, most of the child care tasks were shared about equally—including awakening their two children, helping them dress, bathing them, putting them to bed, supervising them, disciplining them, chauffeuring them, taking them to the doctor, caring for them when they were sick, arranging for babysitters, playing with them, and planning outings for them. When they began sharing the daily chores associated with raising children, they found that the experience initiated some subtle changes in Gary and the marriage.

Gary began by talking about some initial difficulties he had in watching his children. In the beginning, when he was "on duty," he had some trouble accepting that "just" being with the kids was important work.

> It was real hard to learn to sit down and hold them when they were sick. I had to keep telling myself that this is important, you need to be here with them doing nothing. (laughs) Which is the feeling I had—I'm not doing anything—but I was. Eventually those things really paid off with the trust the kids developed in me.

Not only did Gary learn how to "really be there" with the kids, but he also learned how to anticipate potential problems. For example, he talked about how his level of concern for child safety was heightened after he rearranged his work schedule to do half of the parenting.

There's a difference in being at the park with the kids since we went on this schedule. Before it was, like, "Sure jump off the jungle bars. Go for it!" But when you're totally responsible for them, and you know if they sprained an ankle or something, you have to pick up the slack, it's like you have more investment in the kid, and you don't want to see them hurt, and you don't want to see them crying. I find myself being a lot more cautious with them.

Although Susan initiated the child-care sharing plan, she was surprised by Gary's developing competence as a parent. Gary came to the marriage with little knowledge of child development and limited expertise as a caregiver. Nevertheless, Susan described how Gary began to notice subtle cues from the children as a result of being with them on a regular basis. She saw some changes in him that she had not anticipated, and her reaction to sharing the nurturing role with him was sometimes mixed. In part, this was because he became more sensitive and caring than she had expected, and his new-found skills intruded on her previous monopoly over the attentive and intuitive parts of parenting.

I used to worry about the kids a lot more. I would say in the last year it's evened itself out quite a bit. That was an interesting kind of thing in sharing that started to happen that I hadn't anticipated. I suppose when you go into this your expectations about what will happen — that you won't take your kids to daycare, that they'll be with their dad, and they'll get certain things from their dad and won't that be nice, and he won't have to worry about his hours — but then when it starts creeping into other areas that you didn't have any way of knowing it was going to have an impact on. When he began to raise issues about the kids or check in on them at school when they were sick or troubled, I thought, "Where did he get the intuitive sense to know what needed to be done? It wasn't there before." A whole lot of visible things happened.

Talking about Gary's parenting, Susan made it clear that she had to take some risks in the beginning to trust him with the kids. At first, his parenting style was all rough and tumble play and wild excitement, but it didn't take long for him to figure out that there were many other ways that he could interact with the children. Eventually, he developed a full range of parenting skills, including clear limit setting, frequent talks, anticipating needs, and enjoying quiet times. Susan's ability to "let go" and not hover over Gary when he was with the children contributed to his developing competence as an everyday father. Susan summed up her current attitude about Gary's parenting by saying, "I trust him totally with the kids, I don't have to worry about it at all."

The transformation that Gary underwent was significant to all members of the Carter family, but perhaps most of all to Gary himself. He commented that being a father was the top priority in his life right now, and that when people asked him what he did, he would reply "I'm a father." He focused on how the details of caring for Jennifer and Jason had helped him establish a special bond with them. Like many involved fathers I interviewed, Gary said that after he was "on duty" with the kids for a day or more, they would call for him in the middle of the night (rather than their mother). He noted that everyday child care could be a drudgery, but that it led to a sense of fulfillment when he could comfort them after a nightmare or after some other emotional crisis: "It's a good feeling to really know your kids and to have them trust you."

Susan reflected on how Gary had recently even come to share some of her characteristic reactions about leaving the kids. It used to be that when they went away for a weekend before they started splitting the child care, she would have a difficult time leaving the children, and would feel guilty about it. At those times, Gary used to give Susan a "hard time" by saying things like, "Good grief, you go away once a year for two days and you can't even have a good time!" After spending significant amounts of routine time with the children for about a year and half, however, the tables turned. Susan reported that when they tried to go away for a weekend, "He was really antsy about leaving the kids. He had a really hard time saying goodbye."

Even though Gary began to interact with the children in a style that was more sensitive than his earlier behavior, he reminded me that the way he took care of the kids was "like a man." For instance, he talked about enjoying being playful with the kids, and loved going on spontaneous adventures with them. This he attributed to a basic difference in parenting styles between men and women.

> For some reason, I really feel that women aren't that flexible with kids. And men seem to be able to say, "Okay if you want to go to the beach, grab your suits and a towel and lets go." Like I'll grab some snacks (laughs) — gotta have food — and we're off. With women, it's like you can't do it without making a big chore out of it: you've gotta plan it all out and take a few changes of clothes, and all this extra stuff, and by the time you get in the car, it's all packed down and it's this big production. I like being able to do that with the kids — just grab a couple of things and go.

Susan also commented that Gary was able to provide the children with a type of love and care that balanced her parenting style. "I've always been the one who's worried about them physically and mentally. Gary tends to be with them, you know, just however they are. It's sort of a more open naive approach, just accepting, which is really nice for the kids." Susan described herself as tending to worry about the "business stuff" — like practicing piano regularly and making sure their homework was done right. About herself, she said, "I don't play as well with them in terms of just getting into whatever they want to do. He's really good at that." She went on to praise his ability to "really be with them," rather than focusing on what else they should be doing or what needed to be done next.

Gary and Susan had worked out a division of child-care labor that left more of the fun activities to Gary. I wondered what impact this might have on their relations with each other and with the children and how they felt about it. Whereas Susan explained this division on the basis of personality differences, Gary relied on assumed generic differences between men and women. Like the other couples I interviewed, the Carters were continually negotiating unique arrangements that fit their specific personalities and drew on their notions of the way things should be. Since most people gain a profound sense of purpose and belonging from their family membership, and because their family identities are tied up with what they do for the family, negotiations over who does what often carry symbolic meanings far beyond the surface content of the tasks involved.

In the Carter household, Susan justified the expense of her training, the hours away from her children, and Gary's foregone earnings, because they enhanced her future earning potential. Perhaps to allay some guilt, she also mentioned that she and her husband played different roles as parents and that her children would benefit from having both of them intimately involved in their upbringing. She was grateful that Gary was able to assume many of the hours of child care and she appreciated that he was now sharing some of the worry. On balance, she did not feel that her role with the children had been displaced: "I'm still the mom." Gary agreed that Susan had a special and irreplaceable relationship with the children and gave her credit for being the "better communicator." He still relied on her occasionally to solve sibling disputes or to help him talk through an issue so that he could figure out his feelings. The child care was the easy part, according to the Carters, for that is what motivated their attempts at sharing in the first place. For housework, on the other hand, things did not evolve quite so effortlessly.

Sharing the Burden of Housework

Like most women in America today, Susan Carter reported that she had to frequently instruct and remind Gary before he began to notice and take care of the basics of running a home.

> Initially, when it all started out, I think part of him felt like he was doing me a big favor, that he was making this all possible for me. Bottom line was: if I got home and the house was trashed, dinner wasn't made, and the kids were filthy, then it would be easier for me to take my kids to day care somewhere, so that when I went and picked them up they would have been fed and the house would still be clean. All I'd have to do is bring them home, give them a bath, and put them to bed. So I said, "There's a missing piece here, maybe it's time to talk about what it is you do all day when you're at home with the kids." For a long time it was, "Well, I do the kids." "Well, okay, you can only do so much of that and there's other things have to get done." It took a good year for us to fine tune the fact that the wash still had to get done, the dishes still needed to be cleaned up, meals still had to be made; that if we really wanted this to work so that when I got home from

work I could have some good time with the kids too, other things needed to be accomplished during the day.

Gary acknowledged that it took him some time to notice what needed doing, and said that there were still disagreements about cleaning standards and timetables. He described himself as "more relaxed about clutter," and said that Susan's housecleaning standards were higher than his. He claimed that "when I get into a cleaning mode, I clean better than she does," but also admitted that she cleaned more consistently. Susan agreed, sort of.

Like most couples I interviewed, Gary's and Susan's descriptions of their task allocation, and their explanations for how their division of labor evolved, differed somewhat. Each spouse sorted cards listing household and child care tasks into five piles according to who most often performed them. Although the overall portrayal of task allocation was fairly similar for both spouses, husbands tended to claim more credit than their wives were willing to grant them. By averaging the responses between spouses, I came up with a middle-ground estimate of who did what for 64 routine household chores.[18]

In the case of the Carters, Susan did more of the housecleaning, including dusting, mopping, tidying, and cleaning bathrooms. Nevertheless, Gary did more of the vacuuming, and tasks like sweeping and making beds tended to be shared about equally. Susan was rated as doing slightly more of the total kitchen work, and more of the menu planning and shopping, but tasks like making breakfast, cooking dinner, washing dishes, and wiping counters were shared about equally with Gary. While the Carters rated Susan as doing more of the ironing and mending, both spouses mentioned that Gary did some of the ironing, and both rated the time-consuming task of laundry as equally shared. Thus, when it comes to the most frequent and repetitive housework tasks like cooking, washing, and vacuuming, we can see that the Carters shared more than most couples, though their sharing was not an even 50–50 division. During the interviews, when Susan was asked what she liked best about Gary's housework, she replied, "That he does half of it."

Unlike most couples we interviewed, the Carters also shared many of the outside chores and other miscellaneous household and family tasks. For instance, while Gary was more likely to fix something on a broken car, Susan was more likely to wash the cars and take care of routine auto maintenance, such as arranging for periodic tune-ups. Susan did more general yard work and gardening, but Gary mowed the lawn. Susan paid the bills and handled the taxes, but both took care of insurance and investments. Also unlike most couples we interviewed, the Carters were equally likely to perform "kinkeeping" — writing, phoning, and visiting relatives or friends — as well as initiating and planning couple dates and social get-togethers.

How did these task divisions come about? Was it an easy process or a constant struggle? According to Susan, it took months, and sometimes years of effort to reallocate the household chores in this manner, but once they had a system in place they gained more appreciation for what the other had to do. For instance, Gary talked about how assuming more responsibility for housework motivated him to encourage Susan to buy whatever she needed to make housecleaning easier.

> It was real interesting when I started doing more housework. Being in construction, when I needed a tool, I bought the tool. If I needed to work on a table saw, I went out and bought a good table saw. And I really realized—and I think I enjoyed it—that when most women buy a house cleaning tool or whatever, I mean, like when they go to buy an iron, they shop and shop and get the $5.95 model. I mean it's the cheapest thing they can get. But when I vacuum floors, I looked at this piece of shit, I mean I can't vacuum the floor with this and feel good about it. It's not doing a good job. So I got a good vacuum system. If I'm going to vacuum, I'm going to vacuum right. So I have more appreciation for the details of house cleaning. When I clean the tubs, I want something that is going to clean the tubs; I don't want to work extra hard. You know, I have a special kind of sponge to use for cleaning the tubs. So I have more of an appreciation for what she had to do. I tell her, "If you know of something that is going to make it easier, let's get it."

One of my colleagues who was reading interview excerpts commented that Gary's attitude toward housework was a bit on the macho side. Nevertheless, his comments show he was redefining housework in terms he could understand and accept. He was starting to "own" it. As I discuss more fully in Chapter 3, housekeeping and child care often remain within the province of the wife, even if the husband begins to help out by performing some tasks. If the wife is always making lists for the husband and must continually remind him to do chores, she retains responsibility for being the household manager. In some areas, the Carters had begun to transcend such manager-helper dynamics. Gary began to assume full responsibility for the tasks that were mutually designated as primarily his. Rather than being forced to accept lower standards in return for "help," Susan Carter was quite satisfied with Gary's efforts, at least on the two chores mentioned above. For vacuuming and cleaning the tubs, he may even have increased the previous standards in the Carter household. Significantly, Gary Carter tackled them in a fashion that was comfortable for him—"using the right tool for the job."

The Impacts of Sharing on the Marriage

The Carters also demonstrate how sharing the family work can affect the husband–wife relationship. Just as Susan observed that Gary had become more sensitive since he began doing more child care, Gary talked about changes in Susan since she had gone back to school and was now committed to pursuing her career.

Ya know, it's hard to relate to the other side until you're there. I would come home and be dead tired and probably cranky, and when the phone rang and I had business, when I was on the phone it was [very animated] "Oh hi! How are you doing?" and when I put the phone down I was cranky again. It was funny the other day she did the same thing. She came home kind of down and out and somebody she had to perk up for was on the phone and I just kind of laughed and said, "Yeah, you've got that phone voice down too." It's hard not to worry about that, but I can accept it more because I've been there.

Such convergence of experience between spouses can have a beneficial impact on marriages, but it can also raise some uncomfortable feelings. Because it was previously "her job" to be the sensitive and intuitive one, Susan was occasionally ambivalent about Gary's developing intuition and his growing worry about the kids. At times it seemed as though Gary was ambivalent about Susan's commitment to her career, in part because he worried that she would become too involved outside the family. He talked about how switching to their split schedule was followed by "better talk around the dinner table," yet he sometimes expressed concern and dismay over how much of Susan's time and emotional energy her outside work was consuming.

Gary was eager to have Susan become a co-provider and the two were in the process of working out what future job sharing would mean in terms of their individual careers, their feelings of self worth, and their division of family labor. Gary hoped that when Susan started making more money they could hire someone to help once a week with the housecleaning. Susan talked at length about their shifting parenting and career issues, with each person alternately supporting and questioning what the other was doing.

Gary knows how wrapped up in his career he was when he decided to do this with me, and [as] he sees me doing more and more in my career he worries that I'm becoming like he was, that somehow I'm backing out of the family thing. . . . He sees that I'm physically not there as much for the kids and he wonders if maybe it's because I'm putting too much into my work. But nothing occupies my thoughts more than my kids. . . . So we both have a whole lot of concerns of not knowing why or how we're going to do this now. On the one hand, he's beginning to feel like maybe he doesn't want to keep building anymore, but on the other hand, he knows he's good enough, he can still do it. So I'm saying, "If I'm going to be making a fair amount of money, you go do what you want to do, or do something else." It's not like I want to be the total financial provider either — I would never want to take the role that he had, it didn't look like much fun. So now we're talking about how it is that we're going to do this in the future and it may open up some new possibilities.

Thus, while Gary was generally perceived as having made the greater financial sacrifice in the past, Susan was now approaching a position where she would provide some financial cushion and might even be able to give Gary more flexibility in his future career options.

The Carters were not forging a new balance between work and family because they were following some abstract political goals or dogmatic notions of gender justice. They were responding to an unstable economic climate and trying to raise their kids the way they thought was right. Because their actions were alternately scripted and improvised, and because each partner was continually adjusting to the other, their balancing act of shared parenting and economic providing resembled a kind of dance. When they went into their marriage, they both assumed that Susan would be the only one to stay home with the children. Neither entered it thinking they should share everything or try to create some egalitarian new-age gender-blending. In fact, they still disagree about the value of feminism and the women's movement. When asked if women were disadvantaged in our society, Gary answered with a simple "No." For emphasis, he added that he would definitely hire a woman contractor "but only if she was competent." Susan described herself as "no women's libber" in college, but explained that she was exposed to various ideas about sexism and gradually accepted a pro-feminist perspective.

The Impacts of Sharing on the Children

Despite their different attitudes toward feminism, after they gave birth to their first child, Gary and Susan Carter agreed that their daughter Jennifer should be able to do whatever she wanted. Susan commented,

> She was a real bright kid and Gary was proud of her, and it didn't matter that she was a girl. Coming from that place of pride, having people say to him "Weren't you disappointed you didn't have a son?" He'd look at them like, "What's that supposed to mean?" So he had some new awarenesses about it too, but they aren't anything like what mine are. Still, they seem to translate into the same kind of values and behavior.

Thus, although Gary did not embrace the political ideals that Susan did, nor use a language of disadvantage to talk about gender relations, he encouraged his daughter to set high goals for herself. In addition, he waxed eloquent when he talked about his kindergarten son's future capacities for fathering. The way he saw it, with a real-life involved father as a role model, Jason was "way ahead of the game" and would easily be able to handle the nurturing aspects of parenting when he grew up and had kids of his own.

Susan also had high hopes for her children, but since she was still somewhat ambivalent about the future fate of feminism, she worried that she was setting her children up for disappointment. In discussing how sharing parenting with Gary might affect her children, she mentioned some positive aspects, but focused on her fear that she might be encouraging unrealistic expectations in her children.

I think it has the potential of making their lives more fulfilling. Jennifer's very nurturing and could do that number, but she also has a real strong drive and she's bright and she ought to do something else in her life too. I think she's going to have a different picture about it than I did, and I worry that if she goes about looking for a mate who's going to be able to share in all that, chances are she's not going to find one; or if she gets a mate thinking she can make that happen, chances are it won't. My concern is that they'll go out there and they'll meet people that won't play by the new rules. It's not fair because it's really my fight. I worry about Jason, too; that I've laid this on him. I have these values that I really believe in, and I raise him to be kind and gentle, but then I send him out there into a tough world, unarmed. Poor kid.

Susan's worries about her children's future prospects raise some interesting issues. Recent research confirms her suggestion that involved fathering does have an impact on children's attitudes about gender.[19] In one study at the University of Michigan, Norma Radin and her colleagues compared children raised in families where couples shared parenting with children raised in more conventional families. Parents and children from various family types were interviewed and given a battery of psychological tests in 1977, when the children were preschoolers (3–5 years old). The parents were interviewed again in 1981, when the children were between 7 and 9 years old. In 1988, the researchers interviewed the children again (when they were 14–16 years old), asking about their views on future employment and family plans. Teenagers raised in families with greater father participation when the children were preschoolers, and those with greater father participation when children were aged 7 to 9, held less traditional views. Teens whose fathers had been involved in routine child care expressed more approval for spouses working full time and sharing childrearing and were more negative about only husbands work-ing with wives staying home to care for the kids. Teens raised almost exclu-sively by mothers, not surprisingly, had expectations for traditional parenting arrangements themselves.[20]

Although the Michigan researchers confirmed Susan Carter's hunch that her children would have higher expectations for sharing employment, house-keeping, and childrearing with a future spouse, they came to a different conclusion. Instead of worrying about the children raised in shared parenting families, they questioned the ability of children in conventional mother-does-it-all families to adapt to the changing realities of family life. It's likely that children from Ozzie and Harriet type families will be the ones with unrealistic expectations. With almost two-thirds of teenagers expected to be in two-earner families when they become parents, those with attitudes more favorable to sharing paid and unpaid work may be better prepared for the future. The gender flexibility of the shared parenting kids, along with the other benefits of having two involved parents, are likely to outweigh the negative impacts of high expectations for egalitarian relationships.

There is ample evidence that times are changing. Mothers are increasingly likely to be employed when they are pregnant, shortly after they give birth, and throughout their children's school years. Both men and women are waiting longer to have children and having fewer of them. Some women are beginning to make nearly as much money as men, and divorce continues to be common. As I describe in later chapters, these trends are likely to persist. Given these projections, it makes sense that men and women should divide the care of their homes and children more equally than they have in the past.

Nostalgia for the Past and Dreams for the Future

Recent defenders of "traditional family values" include Dan Quayle who ridiculed TV's Murphy Brown for deciding to have a baby without a husband, and Phyllis Schlafly, who tells married women to quit their jobs and devote their time to tending husbands, children, and homes.[21] This public rhetoric uses idyllic images of bygone days to argue for a return to "family values," but most critics agree that the underlying message is that we should reinstate old-style paternal authority. Popular feminist authors tend to focus on the potential benefits of an emerging democracy within families, contrasting recent developments with trenchant critiques of the patriarchal roots of "traditional" family practices.[22] Similar debates are played out in the pages of scholarly journals, as academics either celebrate or lament recent changes in American family life.[23]

Arguments about the state of American families and the future of family life frequently take on mythical proportions far beyond the facts at hand.[24] Often the debates are more about the relative power of men versus women, locals versus newcomers, whites versus blacks, or middle class versus working class. It's difficult to separate underlying political and social issues from the emotional heartstrings that such debates set resonating with uncanny frequency.

Throughout the past century, public fears about the demise of the family have surfaced with annoying regularity. Politicians and religious leaders tend to fan the flames of controversy in an effort to further their own agendas. Appeals to a bygone era regularly capture our attention and reinforce idyllic images from the past, however unrealistic. No one wants to argue with cultural icons like "mom and apple pie " or "good ol' dad." Unfortunately, mythical images of The Family and public displays of hand wringing rarely move us closer to understanding the changes and challenges faced by today's families.

If, like the Carters, fathers began to act like mothers by nurturing children, and mothers began to act like fathers by being breadwinners, what would happen? Would the family go extinct? You might think so, if you took political and religious fundamentalist rhetoric seriously, but this scenario is very unlikely. People today are just as concerned about raising happy and healthy children as they ever were, perhaps even more so, since society's problems are publicized more widely. With politicians lamenting the breakdown of "family values" and TV comedies offering similarly unrealistic images of family life, it is difficult to decide what is really happening to The American Family. Talking about The Family (with a capital T) obscures the fact that families have always varied from place to place and from time to time. There has always been a rich diversity of family types, it's just that the forms they take, and what people do within them, may be changing faster now than at other times in our recent history.

In our nostalgia for a mythical past, we tend to envision an ideal family that transcends time and place. In reality, families are very specific forms of human organization that continually evolve and change as they respond to various pushes and pulls. Since we all grew up in families, we have strong feelings about various family members, carry at least a few family-related emotional scars or unresolved issues, and tend to cling to romantic images of family life. In short, it is extremely hard to talk about family life or family changes objectively. The ideological baggage we bring to discussions about how families are, or should be, is so personally biased and emotionally charged that we probably would do better to drop any pretense of pure objectivity. Although we can never fully transcend our biases, we can draw on the available family research to help us understand what changes are underway and where they might lead. On the following pages I do this as a family sociologist, summarizing numerous studies on the history, psychology, economics, and politics of family life. With this scholarly research as a backdrop, however, I also attempt to capture the flavor of the many changes that contemporary couples are facing. By using the words and stories of real people, I hope to provide some brief glimpses into the everyday lives of normal people struggling to adjust to changing circumstances. By drawing on some larger perspectives from the social sciences and humanities, I hope to grasp the significance of recent developments and to offer some projections.

Organization of the Book

Before returning to the stories of couples like Gary and Susan Carter, I provide some historical background on marriage, parenting, and housework. In Chapter 2, I briefly review the development of the modern ideal of separate spheres for men and women. In the nineteenth and twentieth centuries in Europe and America, a gradual shift occurred away from family-based production on farms to market-based industrial production. Men began to leave their families each day to earn wages, and an ideology of separate spheres emerged, in which men were primarily viewed as economic providers and women came to be seen as uniquely qualified to raise children and tend homes. Drawing on the work of historians, sociologists, and political economists, I quickly trace the development of separate spheres from the eighteenth century up to the mid-twentieth century, documenting who performed what chores in American households during various time periods. Readers who are more interested in modern couples than the history or sociology of families might want to skip Chapter 2 and move on to the next chapters.

In Chapters 3, 4, and 5, I turn to the 1980s phenomena of dual-earner families and shared parenting. I use questionnaire responses to paint a picture of the typical division of labor in American families, and in-depth interviews with couples like the Carters to explore who does what when they attempt to share parenting. I present people's own words to capture how they feel about what they are doing as well as to illustrate typical patterns and isolate common dilemmas. I look at who manages the home and who helps out; how they think about their children; who they know and what they believe in; and why they are successful or unsuccessful in their efforts to share both homemaking and breadwinning. Because much of the research on dual-career couples has been based on white middle-class families, I include interviews with Chicano (Mexican-American) families in Chapter 4, and highlight some of the interviews with white working-class families in Chapter 5. By including some class and ethnic variations, we learn more about general underlying processes that govern the allocation of family work. Looking at different groups also sets the stage for generalizing to larger populations in later chapters.

In Chapter 6, I step back from the intimate details of individual families to summarize and extend some of the most important themes that emerged from the interviews. Placing people's stories in the context of previous social research, I develop some generalizations about family work: what are typical patterns of housework and child care and what factors seem to promote or discourage sharing? In presenting these findings, I evaluate several theoretical models of household labor allocation and set the stage for making predictions about the future in the closing chapter.

Chapter 7 considers the potential importance of recent and prospective changes by looking backwards and around the world. Returning to the theme of public rhetoric about family values, I challenge the claim that a so-called "traditional" division of labor, in which men provide resources and women perform all the domestic work, is more natural or proper than some other arrangement. Because biological and religious fundamentalist arguments about women's or men's "rightful place" are typically bolstered by reference to images of primordial families, I take a closer look at societies that are precursors to our own. Summarizing what we know about how men and women in different cultures have divided family work, I provide information that can be used to assess conservative claims about the naturalness of separate spheres or the importance of having fathers in the home. Using cross-cultural comparisons, we can also begin to estimate how the sharing of family work might influence the meaning of masculinity and the position of women in society. I conclude the chapter with a critical assessment of Robert Bly's ritual masculinist movement with its unrealistic mythopoetic celebration of gender difference.

Returning to the modern world in Chapter 8, I summarize recent social and economic trends and make some preditions about the future of fatherhood in America. A roller coaster U.S. economy and persistent individualism will continue to push some men away from family commitments, but we should not expect that most men will turn their backs on children. In fact, I think we are moving in the opposite direction. In the closing chapter I show how and why, in the coming decades, more fathers will choose to become family men by assuming at least a portion of the everyday tasks of nurturing children and running households. Although fathers will typically do less than mothers, an increasing number will choose a "daddy track" of parental leave at birth, job scheduling to accommodate child care, and the performance of most family work. Will these trends reflect the self indulgence of a few middle-class fathers or will they spread to all levels of society? Will they reinforce male privilege or signal the end of male dominance as we know it? Only time will provide answers to these questions, but my concluding remarks assess the potential costs and benefits to men, women, and children of the trend toward more involved fathering.

2

Separate Spheres

According to the so called traditional view, it is a man's duty to serve his family by being a breadwinner and protector, whereas a woman's duty is to be a good wife and mother.[1] More than any other cultural belief, this idealized notion of separate spheres for mothers and fathers shapes what it means to be a man or a woman in our society. Kind and gentle women are supposed to stay home to care for children and family, allowing bold and aggressive men to venture out into the competitive worlds of work, politics, and war. According to this widely held view, the rights and duties of men and women are separate but complementary, flowing directly from some underlying natural difference between mothers and fathers. Like all beliefs, however, the separate spheres ideal is shaped by one's culture, and is subject to change as the social and economic factors that produced it undergo changes of their own. In this chapter I explore some of the historical roots of the belief in separate spheres to see just how much change might be possible.

For most Americans the reality of family life never quite fit the ideal of separate spheres, but today most families are farther from it than ever. Although over half of all American families had a breadwinner father and a stay-at-home mother in the 1950s, by the 1990s only one in five families fit this profile.[2] With three out of four mothers of school-aged children now in the paid labor force, it is no surprise that the separate spheres ideal has lost some of its appeal. One recent national survey found that over 80 percent of Americans agreed that "it takes two paychecks to support a family," and only about one in four favored a return to one parent raising the children full time.[3]

As men's and women's work lives begin to look more alike, they are also more likely to share similar family concerns. Recent polls find that over 70 percent of American men and over 80 percent of American women feel torn between the demands of their job and wanting to spend more time with their family.[4]

Though we seem to be moving away from the separate spheres ideal, it still operates in many subtle (and not so subtle) ways. Few Americans admit that job discrimination against women is acceptable, yet most feel uncomfortable when confronted with a female mechanic or a CEO in a dress. More women have been elected to public office than ever before, but most of them still sit on local school boards and city councils. Most Americans say they would vote for a woman for president, but no woman has ever been nominated for that office by a major party. When it comes to marriage and family life, Americans are even more ambivalent about women's roles, wanting them to be generous self-sacrificing mothers even if they are also expected to be dedicated professionals. Although women are encouraged to go to college and pursue their careers as never before, they are still held accountable for what was once called "women's work." If their houses are a mess, or if their children are unkempt, women they are still subject to blame.[5]

Similar equivocal feelings emerge about fathers and jobs. Although eight out of ten Americans believe it is OK for women to work, half still think that men should be the real breadwinners.[6] Americans want fathers to be more involved with their children, but most feel uncomfortable if a man takes time off work "just" to be with his kids. Recent polls report that fathers value their families over their jobs, and most men say they would like to work fewer hours in order to spend more time with their families.[7] One 1990 poll by the Los Angeles Times reported that 39 percent of fathers said they would even quit their jobs to have more time with their children, and another survey found that 74 percent would rather have a "daddy-track" job than a "fast-track" job. But in real life, according to a *Time* magazine cover story, most men do not follow through on their desires to be more involved in family life. "When they are not talking to pollsters, some fathers recognize the power of their atavistic impulses to earn bread and compete, both of which often leave them ambivalent about their obligations as fathers."[8]

Employers, too, are ambivalent about men's desires to be home instead of at work. When men take advantage of parental leaves or part-time work, they are often considered unreliable or not serious. Although it runs counter to public relations rhetoric, most employers assume that "work-family" programs are designed only for working mothers.[9] As we will see in subsequent chapters, the underlying equation of men with work and women with home has been surprisingly impervious to the labor market changes that have occurred over the past few decades. Most Americans now expect wives to work, yet few employers consider fathers' family obligations to be as important as mothers'. And most people still evaluate men on the basis of their paid work. By definition, his job is supposed to be more important than her job, and most people get uncomfortable if a wife makes more money than her husband.[10] It seems that the ideal of separate spheres is still with us, even if the factors underlying it have begun to change.

Separate Spheres and Gender Inequality

Many argue that the cultural ideal of separate spheres is so persistent because it helps men maintain power over women.[11] Like most modern systems of social control, the separate spheres ideal perpetuates an image of the subordinate group (women) as fundamentally different from the dominant group (men). The ideology that accompanies the separate spheres ideal suggests that women are inherently suited to serve men; that they are naturally and happily prepared to perform unpaid labor for the men in return for protection and provision. Those who challenge the ideology of separate spheres do not necessarily claim that men and women should be the same, nor do they disparage cooperation or complementarity between them. Instead, they find that the problem lies in the ways that the separate spheres ideal has been used to further men's interests at the expense of women's.

As discussed below, historical studies show that a rigid public/private split is something of a myth, insofar as working-class women have always had to engage in some form of productive labor and middle- and upper-class women have also been involved in various activities outside the home.[12] Nevertheless, a belief in natural and unalterable distinctions between men's and women's aptitudes, obligations, and social roles has legitimated some profound inequalities during the past two centuries.[13] When daily activities are segregated into separate spheres on the basis of gender, men are able to exploit women's labor. Perhaps even more important, when the ideology of separate spheres permeates most of our institutions and governs our conduct of daily life, opportunities for women to achieve outside the home are severely limited.

A Brief History of Separate Spheres

In all known societies, some tasks have been the province of men and others the province of women. Nevertheless, divisions of labor in most ancient societies were probably much less rigid than popular myths would have it. Except for breastfeeding and the earliest care of infants, there appear to be no cross-cultural universals in the tasks that women do and men do.[14] As we will see in Chapter 7, in some societies, the worlds of men and women were so separated that they had little contact with one another and rarely performed the same tasks.[15] In other societies, however, women routinely undertook tasks such as hunting, and men routinely performed tasks like caring for babies. In fact, in most societies, the majority of tasks could be done by either men or women, and a great many tasks were performed jointly or cooperatively. This does not mean that these societies thought men and women were interchangeable in all matters, for most considered the sexes different from one another in at least a few important ways. But the cross-cultural record is very clear in revealing that the things men and women are supposed to do are not the same everywhere. This suggests that we need to turn our attention away from biology and toward our own social and economic history if we are to understand the development of separate spheres in America.

From Home Production to a Market Economy

How has the division of labor changed from ancient times to the present? The most important difference between older nonindustrial societies and modern industrial ones is that in the former, production was organized in and through the family household, whereas in the latter, production is generally separated from the household. According to historical accounts, the growth of industrial capitalism and market economies promoted the development of separate gender spheres. In the earlier household economies of the seventeenth and eighteenth century—exemplified by the family farm or the small artisan shop—a man's place of work was also usually his home. After the emergence of commercial markets and industrialization, however, increasing numbers of fathers left home each day to become breadwinners, leaving their wives to run the household and look after the children.[16]

Beginning in about 1800, the United States began shifting from a largely rural agricultural society to an urban industrial one. The pace of this change accelerated dramatically between 1870 and 1900 when centralized industrial production increased fivefold. As late as 1871, two-thirds of the American population was still self-employed, but, by the turn of the century, a majority of Americans depended on wage-labor to support their families. In the earlier model of family-based agricultural production, men, women, and children worked side by side, along with hired hands, servants, and apprentices. In the newer model of industrial production, family members left home to sell their labor for wages.

We tend to think that it was only men who joined the waged labor force under industrial production, while the women stayed home. In fact, at the beginning of this transition, from about 1820 to 1850, young farm women were the most likely to work in factories, and it was only later that this work was performed predominantly by men.[17] Black women, immigrant women, and poor white women continued to work for pay in factories and as domestic servants. A sizable minority of middle-class women also continued to combine family responsibilities with income-generating work by taking in boarders, tending gardens, or doing other productive work at home.[18] For the entire economy, however, home production steadily declined throughout the century, and the majority of married women were excluded from the emerging wage economy. Although the total number of U.S. women workers increased between 1870 and 1900, these were predominantly unmarried women, and by 1900 less than 5 percent of married white women worked outside the home.[19] This economic shift had a profound effect on assumptions about who should be responsible for tending homes and raising children.

Shifting Images of Fathers and Children

In the rural agricultural era, American fathers served as moral overseers, as well as masters, of their families. Even though mothers provided most of the direct caretaking of infants and young children, men were very active in training and tutoring the young. Before the nineteenth century, most parental advice was addressed to fathers rather than mothers, and fathers were thought to have far greater responsibility for, and influence on, their children.[20] During this time, children were considered inherently sinful, and since fathers were thought to have superior reason and moral authority, they were considered the ideal overseers of their children's spiritual development. Discipline was typically harsh. Mothers were seen as overly indulgent, and therefore considered less able to encourage sound reasoning or to restrain their children's sinful urges. Consistent with this view of fathers as the stronger parent, in the rare case of divorce or marital separation, children went with their fathers.[21]

In the earlier pattern, father-child relationships were ruled by duty, and though a father's association with his children was not devoid of emotion, it was characterized by obligation. Much like husband-wife relationships of the time, parent-child relationships were fundamentally instrumental, with children expected to do their part to keep the household running. Fathers were conceived of as very different from mothers, but they were an active part of family life and had significant contact with, and responsibility for, their children. Men were a visible presence in children's lives, primarily because their work, whether farming, artisanship, or trade, occurred in the household context.[22] Furthermore, most work in the household economy of the agricultural era was directed by the father. Men introduced sons to farming or craft work, oversaw the work of others, and were responsible for maintaining harmonious relations in the household. The home was thus a system of control as well as a center of production, and both functions tended to reinforce the father's authority.[23]

As America began the transition away from household production to a market economy, the stern authority of patriarchal fathers began to weaken.

The historian Robert Griswold describes how economic, religious, and political ideas promoting individualism contributed to emergent ideals about men's proper role in the family even before most men left the home to work for wages: "The paternal dominance and evangelical authority that infused Calvinist visions of family life in the seventeenth century eroded in the eighteenth century, as they were slowly replaced by an emphasis on more affective, less instrumental family relationships. Hierarchy and order, the watchwords of older forms of paternal dominance, gave way to a growing emphasis on mutuality, companionship, and personal happiness."[24] Although the ideal of companionate fathering was not widespread, Griswold notes that some wealthy eighteenth-century fathers "wrote and spoke affectionately of their children, lamented separation from them, frequently gave them gifts, worried about their health, delighted in their accomplishments, and even participated with gusto in their play."[25] As America moved into the nineteenth century, fathers still performed little of the routine child care, but more fathers began to treat their children as unique individuals, paid attention to their emotions, and were amused by their antics.[26]

Men's family roles did not change all at once, and those from different social classes, ethnic backgrounds, and regions of the country were subject to different sorts of changes. Middle-class fathers in the North continued to rely on conscience, guilt, and religious redemption in rearing their children, but as the occupational link between fathers and sons weakened, paternal authority became more negotiable. Southern planter fathers, in contrast, continued to rely on shame and humiliation to instill a sense of family honor and hierarchy in their children. Griswold notes that traditional Southern fathers in the nineteenth century distrusted maternal indulgence and felt responsible for instilling toughness and aggressiveness in their sons by teaching them to ride, hunt, fight, and even duel.[27]

This last example reminds us that fatherhood practices are tied up with cultural images of masculinity, which, in turn, are directly affected by changes in the economy. As noted above, the nineteenth century was marked by a huge influx of men into waged labor. Near the turn of the century, unprecedented numbers of (mostly unmarried) U.S. women also entered the waged labor force, swelling the ranks of formerly all-male occupations such as clerks, typists, bookkeepers, cashiers, and sales personnel. This influx of women into what were previously men's jobs created a masculinist backlash and helped to create the rigid Victorian era belief in separate spheres for men and women.[28]

During this time, fraternal orders like the Odd Fellows and Freemasons gained thousands of members in the United States by putting men through an elaborate sequence of masculine initiation rituals. Whereas gentlemen in an earlier era tended to avoid physical exertion, the late nineteenth and early twentieth century saw an enormous growth in outdoor sports and camping that were idealized for their contributions to masculine character. Popular magazine depictions of male heroes at the turn of the century shifted from earlier praise of piety, thrift, and industry to appreciation for vigor, forcefulness, and mastery. This was also the era in which the Boy Scouts, with their emphasis on turning boys into "red blooded, moral, manly men" grew to unprecedented size.[29] Fears of emasculation rose to new heights as fathers spent less time at home and as men's authority inside the family was being eroded by larger social and economic forces.

Shifting Images of Mothers and Children

As the nation was turning to a commercial economy and eventually to urban industrial production, we see a clear and persistent shift toward a greater role for mothers in moral responsibility for home and children. In the earlier era, fathers tended to get the blame or credit for how children turned out as adults, but now mothers began to be judged in this way.[30] This shift toward greater maternal responsibility was accelerated by the "cult of domesticity" that emerged in the nineteenth century. As men increasingly left the home to go to work for wages, the cult of domesticity glorified motherhood and re-assured women that their natural place was in the home. Motherhood was placed on a pedestal, and the contrast between the outside world and home came to be seen as a contrast between Man and Woman.[31] Later in the nineteenth and early twentieth centuries, maternal responsibility for home and children was further promoted by the rise of scientific mothering and the home economics movement.[32]

The growth of capitalism and the gradual shift from home-based production to waged labor, industrialization, and a market economy also encouraged changes in Americans' overall ideas about children and how they should be treated. In the earlier era, children were valued mostly for their economic contributions. They usually worked on farms or labored in their parents' trade, and, by maintaining such pursuits, provided a kind of insurance policy for their parents. Childhood was not considered such a special time of life, and children were not as sentimentalized as they are today.[33] Death was much more visible in those days, which probably limited intense emotional dependency between parents and children.[34] Many women died in childbirth, and those who survived tended to have many children. In addition, most families experienced the death of at least one child at birth or during early childhood. Under these conditions, emotional involvement was probably relatively limited, out of self-protection, though such things are difficult to measure.[35] In the elite upper classes, where death was a less constant threat, children had more sentimental value, though still much less than today. As noted above, religious teachings, particularly those of the American Puritans and Methodists, stressed the "corrupt nature" and "evil dispositions" of children. Fathers, in particular, were admonished to demand strict obedience from children and to use swift physical punishment to cleanse them of their sinful ways.[36]

In Europe and America before the nineteenth century, childrearing was also a more collective or communal enterprise. The entire community participated in virtually every aspect of an individual's life, including most of those things we now consider private family matters. In this older and more collective pattern, parent-child relations were constantly regulated and monitored by relatives and other community members, and what happened inside the home was relatively public. A micro-community of close-by adults and older children usually acted as surrogate parents, and there were always plenty of people around to offer advice on what to do in specific situations. The decline of home production and the coming of the Industrial Revolution reshaped the relationship between family and work, promoting the idea that the family and childrearing were separate from other aspects of life.

Although usually characterized as promoting the withdrawal of the family from the public realm, the advent of market capitalism also gave the state more control over children. Compulsory schooling, juvenile courts, labor regulations, and various state policies and programs increased some aspects of community control over children and weakened the absolute power of fathers. At the same time, the ideology of separate spheres promoted the idea that the nuclear family should be a nurturant child-centered haven set apart from the impersonal world of work, politics, and other public pursuits.[37] The home — previously the normal site of production, consumption, and virtually everything else in life — was slowly transformed into the only "proper" place to find emotional security and release.

Bolstered by the ideology of separate spheres, families gained in psychological and emotional importance at the same time they became identified with feminine virtue and moral purity. Arlene Skolnick notes that the development of the modern private family brought new burdens for women because they were supposed to create a wholesome home life, which, in turn, was seen as the only way to redeem society.[38] Under the previous agricultural economy, the community regulated most family functions and repaired any moral defects of families. In the newer industrial model, however, families (and especially mothers) were supposed to compensate for the moral defects of the larger society. This general belief in the moral purity of the domestic realm was used by suffragists to claim that giving women the vote would create stronger families and a more humane society.[39]

As women became closely identified with the family, and as the home became seen as a haven from the outside world, the sentimental value of children increased dramatically. This trend had begun earlier, but in the late nineteenth and early twentieth centuries, it blossomed. Relying on insurance company records and court cases, the historical sociologist Viviana Zelizer shows how the economically useful child of previous times was transformed into an "economically worthless, but emotionally priceless child" in the 60 years between 1870 and 1930. During this time, traditional forms of child labor came to be seen as harmful and inappropriate for those of "tender years." In 1870, if a child died in an accident and the courts concluded that another party was negligent, the parents were compensated for the value of the child's labor. By 1930, however, in cases of "wrongful death," the parents were compensated for incalculable emotional pain.[40] This period saw a particularly remarkable increase in the emotional value of younger children. In the earlier era, older boy orphans were the first to be adopted because of their productive labor power, but now very young children, and especially baby girls, were the first to be adopted. During this time, the family came to be idealized as the only place where innocent and pure children could and should be protected. No longer considered evil creatures whose will had to be broken by their fathers, children had become precious love objects who needed nurturing and support from their mothers. Women became even more closely identified with the private domain of the home because they were now supposed to realize their "true" nature by marrying, giving birth, and tending children.

The separate spheres ideal strongly encouraged women to bear children, especially if they were white and middle class. Motherhood for these women was elevated to a revered status, and wives' homemaking came to be seen as a calling and a worthy profession. The ideology of separate spheres set high standards for all women and mothers, even if they were attainable only by the more affluent middle and upper classes. The True Woman was supposed to be inherently unselfish and her moral purity, nurturant character, and gentle temperament were seen as uniquely qualifying her to rear young children. Mothers' moral virtue, instead of fathers' stern reasoning, now ruled the home.

Men's lives in the public domains of work and politics came to be defined as greedy and corrupt, and in need of redemption via the purity and grace of the womanly home. Domestic tasks assumed a spiritual importance as the home was transformed into a private place where women were expected to comfort and civilize both men and children. The field of home economics blossomed during this time and the domestic science movement taught women efficient housewifery based on time management techniques. Turning the home into women's exclusive domain, and treating homemaking as a profession, ensured that women's activities would be subordinated to the needs of their husbands and families.[41]

Twentieth-Century Fathers

As traditional sources of male identity in work, religion, and community declined during the twentieth century, increasing numbers of men began to seek meaning in the private realm of family relationships. The doctrine of separate spheres left little room for real paternal participation in the day-to-day lives of children, but men, as well as women, focused on the emotional importance of the family, and public images of the "new" father became popular.[42] During the 1920s and 1930s family experts began to promote the middle-class vision of a closer, more personal bond between fathers and children.

Fathers were still expected to be good providers who spent most of their time away from home, and manly men still did not change diapers, but men's monetary contributions and their symbolic presence began to carry a new emotional significance. As breadwinners, fathers underwrote the flourishing of a consumer culture in the twentieth century that equated personal happiness with increased consumption. Being the family breadwinner carried renewed moral and emotional significance, but expectations for men to lovingly interact with children also increased. A more companionate ideal of family relations gained prominence, as men were told explicitly to focus on love and involvement instead of on discipline and authority. Women remained responsible for running households, tending children, and enforcing everyday discipline, but more fathers tried to be "pals" to their kids.

In the period from about 1920 to 1940, family experts became especially concerned about the feminizing influence that the home might have on young men because the domestic sphere was seen as the woman's realm. This led to calls for fathers to interact with their sons and to teach them how to be real men. Even though fathers were spending less time at home, they were told to challenge and encourage their children in distinctly manly ways. As Griswold notes, during this era, "fathers' jobs were to foster creativity, individualism, and proper sex-role identification, not to do children's laundry, pick up their rooms, cook their food, nurse them, or chauffeur them. Most men considered such labor 'women's work' and therefore unmanly and beneath them."[43] With the old patterns of paternal authority unavailable, and in the face of contradictory messages about providing, achieving, consuming, and modeling masculinity, men's connections to family life remained tenuous. As America approached mid-century, popular images of kind and loving dads became more common, but most American fathers continued to feel like emotional outsiders in their own families.

Economic Change and Masculine Privilege

In the simplified history of separate spheres sketched out here, I suggest that beliefs about gender and family tend to follow changes in the economy. In the seventeenth and eighteenth centuries, agricultural production and the household economy maintained the father's authority. Men had frequent contact with children, but family relationships were governed by duty. As market economies grew, fathers came to be viewed as breadwinners, and individualism flourished. As traditional forms of authority weakened and men's direct partici-pation in daily family life decreased, women's "nature" came to be seen as pure and virtuous, and mothering was elevated to a revered status. Cultural ideals about the inherent natures of men and women shifted as families came to play different roles in the overall economy. In the new market economy, gender ideals also shifted in response to competition between men and women for jobs. In response to competition from women, men defended their privileged position by asserting their "inherent" ruggedness and suitability for "men's work."

Concern for American men's toughness and individualism can be traced throughout our history, but as noted above, men's fears of emasculation are especially strong during times when women have achieved gains in the marketplace and the legal arena.[44] At the end of the nineteenth century and the beginning of the twentieth, male unionists used the notion of separate spheres to argue for women's "protective" legislation and for a family wage system that would pay individual male workers enough to support an entire family. The effect of this strategy was to consolidate men's power over women both inside and outside families. The new protective laws reduced women's ability to compete for lucrative jobs and the institution of a family wage ensured that wives would be financially dependent on their husbands.[45] The concept of separate spheres rationalized these institutional controls by promoting the view that the sexes were naturally different, but equal, with each heading their own domain. Various versions of separate spheres have been revived whenever men fear competition by women for jobs, as in the Great Depression, and again just after World War II under the label of "the feminine mystique."[46]

Similar exclusionary employment practices have also been used against various ethnic minority men. For example, notions of "separate but equal" spheres were used to protect white men's jobs when high immigration rates meant competition for work in the late nineteenth century, and when jobs became scarce at various times during the early twentieth century.[47] Later in the twentieth century, the notion of separate but equal spheres was invoked to keep black Americans out of all-white establishments and women away from all-male colleges and social clubs.

Although the reasons for the development of beliefs in separate ethnic and gender spheres are complex and varied, historians suggest that such beliefs are usually a response to anxieties generated by periods of rapid economic and social change.[48] Common to most such beliefs, however, are attempts by more powerful groups to maintain their advantageous position over less powerful groups. However benign an ideology of natural differences may appear, such beliefs have most often been used to protect the economic advantages of more privileged groups.

The glorification of women's moral and emotional family roles by the separate spheres ideal masked the economic significance of the work that women did in the home. Running a home in the nineteenth and early twentieth centuries was especially hard work, because modern conveniences like indoor plumbing and refrigeration were not widely available. Even though most married women did not work for wages, in many working-class and some middle-class American households, women continued to contribute direct labor to their husband's enterprises, and in virtually all households, wives contributed to their husbands' productive capacity by performing domestic services for them and tending their children. Since the ideology of separate spheres conceived of women's tasks as a moral responsibility, however, the economic function of work in the home was rarely recognized. Although it is not fashionable these days to think about families in political and economic terms, looking at the practical significance of family work for the maintenance of the economy can help us understand how and why separate spheres have been so resistant to change.

The modern development of separate spheres is part of the larger trend toward labor specialization that has been promoted by the rapid growth of industrial capitalism. Men came to constitute the basic labor force in the factories and offices, but this male labor force also had to be maintained and reproduced. This required the hidden labor of women, including feeding, clothing, and caring for adult male workers, as well as bearing and rearing children. As men began to bring home wages from outside employment instead of working for themselves or for some wealthy landholder, women's work increasingly came to include the care and support of those workers and the transformation of wages into usable commodities. Families came to be seen as sites for consumption of products rather than producers of them, and women became the primary household consumers.

Housework and child care are essential for the economic workings of our society, but because domestic work is unpaid, it goes virtually unnoticed.[49] The employer who hires a male worker is actually buying the use of a human body that contains the concealed labor of women in the same way that a loaf of bread contains the concealed labor of farm and bakery workers. Employers benefited from the development of separate spheres, since the costs of reproducing and maintaining the labor force were taken care of by hidden female labor. In addition, women came to constitute a reserve labor force that could be used to substitute for male labor or called on to counteract male wage demands. When the labor market is tight, as during World War II, women are called out of homes to work in offices, stores, and factories. Since the ideology of separate spheres defines women's primary job as family work, employers are able to treat female employees differently from male employees. They have not had to consider women as regular, lifetime employees, and have been able to pay them low wages and lay them off when labor demand dropped.

Thus, we can see that women's disadvantaged position in the waged labor market is connected to the division of labor promoted by the separate spheres ideology. In a practical sense, men benefit, as well as employers, because women serve as unpaid household servants. At home, men receive services that would otherwise cost them a considerable sum.[50] On the job, this gives men relatively higher wages, less competition, and power over a whole class of women workers whose labor is less valued. Lower wages for women allows men leverage in romantic and marital relationships too, because they can use their superior economic resources to attract and keep marital partners, and to get out of doing the less pleasant household tasks. To maintain these advantages during the twentieth century, male workers and their unions have repeatedly attempted to keep women out of the paid labor market, placed restrictions on the kind of work they could do, or relegated them to temporary and subordinate positions.[51]

In spite of their lower wages and secondary status in the labor market, American women contributed in both direct and indirect ways to economic production during the transition to an industrial economy. Because some groups of women (such as unmarried women and African-African women) were likely to be employed even when middle-class women were not, the cult of domesticity was sometimes more ideal than real. Still, the notion of separate spheres enjoyed widespread popularity during most of the twentieth century and had profound influence on the entire society. The romantic ideal of women's domesticity encouraged both working-class and middle-class couples to aspire to the goal of the woman becoming a full-time homemaker.

"Labor-Saving" Inventions

Another important historical development influencing domestic life in America during the early twentieth century was the distribution of utilities such as sewage, gas, and electricity. The diffusion of these utilities, along with the dissemination of indoor plumbing and the invention and mass production of new appliances, changed the amount and type of physical labor required to run a household. For example, widespread availability of refrigerators meant that fresh food did not have to be bought or prepared daily. Production and mass marketing of gas and electric stoves, and later washing machines, dryers, vacuum cleaners, and dishwashers, also changed the ways that housework was performed.

Although we tend to assume that all these household inventions and conveniences should reduce the number of hours that women spend doing housework, studies have shown that, at least among full-time housewives, women were spending about as much time doing housework in the 1960s as they did in the 1920s.[52] This probably results from a variety of factors including increased expectations for home comfort and personal hygiene, higher standards of cleanliness, and more time spent in child care. Other important household changes from the nineteenth to the mid-twentieth century include slow but dramatic decline in the number of servants and boarders in middle-class homes, increases in household income, increasing urbanization and suburbanization, and the spread of compulsory education.[53] As a result of these and other social and technological changes, modern middle-class American housewives did the domestic work that used to be performed by several women in the nineteenth century. An ideology of separate spheres, dramatically revived after World War II, played a major role in all this because it promoted the idea that homemaking was women's natural profession. The earlier cult of domesticity and the newer "feminine mystique" provided the cultural impetus for women to judge their self-worth based on clean houses, proper children, and contented husbands.

The Legal Institution of Marriage

The cultural ideal of separate spheres has been an important historical force, but ideas alone do not shape family relations. In addition to the economic and social forces promoting separate spheres discussed above, American family life has been shaped by the legal institution of marriage. Most people do not think of marriage as a legal and financial contract, but the law has historically defined what marriage is, how spouses should relate, and what duties and obligations husbands and wives have to each other and to their children. Many people become aware of these laws only when they get divorced, but legal codes and the court system technically govern the marital relationship at other times as well. Today, marriage statutes are undergoing revision, but historical laws and customs provide a context for understanding our present marital arrangements and the ways family work is performed.

Our system of law is based on the English system, which in turn derives from legal traditions inherited from the Roman Empire and other ancient civilizations. Our modern word *family* comes from the Latin, but does not mean blood relations or kinship as one might think. Rather, the ancient Romans used *familia* to refer to household property—the fields, house, money, and slaves owned by a man. The Latin word *famulus* means "servant." In Rome, the plebian form of marriage consisted of a man buying his wife, and she became recognized by the law as part of his property, his *familia*. Not only have Western societies carried on the legal tradition of defining the family as the property of the male head of household, but most laws have also defined women as inferior beings who require the protection of a man. A modern vestige of this idea can be found in the ceremonial custom of a father "giving" his daughter away in marriage.[54]

In past times, women gave up legal rights when they married, and acquired a set of obligations that tended to be rather severe. The feudal doctrine of coverture held that the husband and wife became a unity upon marrying, and that unity was the husband. Symbolic merging of the identities of husband and wife is still evident today in the custom of the wife legally adopting her husband's name at marriage. In the conventional pattern, if Jane Smith marries John Jones, she becomes Jane Jones or, more formally, Mrs. John Jones. In contrast, the husband's legal identity remains exactly the same as it was before marriage.

One result of the legal tradition of merging the wife's identity into the husband's is that the courts have assumed that the husband's needs are synonymous with the family's needs. This was historically held to be true, even for some cases where wives were abused. For example, in a 1906 U.S. Supreme Court ruling, the judges reasoned that to allow wives to sue their husbands for physical abuse would destroy the "harmony" of the family.[55] Although modern laws typically no longer protect husbands from prosecution for things like physical abuse, some states still deny wives the right to file rape charges against husbands. The legal reasoning refers back to the idea that the marital contract implies a wifely obligation to provide the husband with sexual services and bear and raise his children.

Traditional marriage laws in England and Europe required wives to live with and serve their husbands in a variety of ways. Four essential provisions of traditional marriage laws were directly incorporated into statutes governing marital contracts in the United States:

1. The husband is the head and master of the household.
2. The husband is responsible for financial support
3. The wife is responsible for domestic services.
4. The wife is responsible for bearing and raising children.[56]

These legal rights and obligations carried harsh consequences for women, especially because divorce was rare and unmarried women were treated as social outcasts. As late as 1850, marriage laws in almost every American state recognized a husband's right to physically punish his wife, though the courts generally discouraged beatings.[57] One vestige of these laws is the so-called "rule of thumb" that allowed a husband to beat his wife if she did not fulfill her wifely duties, provided he used a rod or branch no thicker than his thumb.[58]

We should not assume that the legal traditions governing marital contracts are antiquated vestiges of some distant past. Before the 1970s, even courts in liberal states tended to treat wives and their earnings as the property of their husbands. For example, U.S. courts have refused to enforce contracts in which the husband agreed to pay his wife for housekeeping, entertaining, child care, or other related "wifely" duties. Even if the wife performed services considered to be "extra," such as working in the husband's business, the courts voided the contract that obligated the husband to pay his wife wages.[59] Today, most marriage laws treat husbands and wives more equally, but in some states married women still lose some legal rights to control property or enter into legal contracts on the same basis as men or unmarried women.[60]

The 1950s: Separate Spheres Revisited

Marriage laws, economic relations, and an ideology of separate spheres shaped divisions of labor in American families throughout the nineteenth and early twentieth centuries. As production shifted from households to markets, families became more private, wage-earning men limited their direct participation in family life, true womanhood became synonymous with the purity of the home, and children became objects of sentimental devotion. As noted above, these trends did not manifest themselves in neat linear fashion in all regions of the country. The process was different for various ethnic groups, had differential impacts according to social class, and exhibited enormous individual and cross-family variation. The middle-class ideal evolved into a single wage-earning husband with a full-time housewife to tend a suburban house and children. Up until mid-century, this ideal was realized by only a minority of American families.

By the 1950s, economic and demographic changes had enabled an ever larger number of American families to achieve the conventional ideal of having a breadwinner father and a stay-at-home mother. The country enjoyed unparalleled economic success, suburbs multiplied rapidly, homeownership became a reality for more working-class families than ever before, and cars and televisions proliferated. Most young women in the 1950s got married by the time they were 20 and quickly had two or three children. Almost 80 percent of all U.S. households were married couples in 1950, and more people than ever before attended church on a regular basis.[61] Although the female labor force participation rate rose steadily after World War II, it was predominantly older married women aged 45 to 64 who accounted for the increase between 1940 and the mid-1960s, so that most women with young children in the 1950s era were full-time housewives.[62]

The period around 1950 was marked by a striking reversal of several earlier family trends. For over 100 years, the fertility rate had been slowly dropping, and the divorce rate climbing steadily. During the 1950s, the marriage rate went up, people began marrying earlier in their lives, and the divorce rate dropped sharply. Fertility also went up dramatically, as women had more and earlier children, producing the so-called baby boom. All these trends were primarily economic in origin. In the 1950s, the United States was producing the highest standard of living that the world had known. In that era of affluence, working-class people and younger, less affluent members of the middle class were more able to do what they preferred to do; to marry as soon as possible and to raise large families.[63]

More than ever, the American family continued its transformation into an isolated unit with a monopoly on emotions, raising children, and filling leisure time. The ideal image of the average American father was now firmly entrenched: he was the "good provider," who "set a good table, provided a decent home, paid the mortgage, bought the shoes, and kept his children warmly clothed."[64] More than ever, women were expected to be consumed and fulfilled by their "natural" wifely and motherly duties. Isolated in suburban houses, mothers now had almost sole responsibility for raising children, aided by occasional reference to Dr. Spock. Television images like Ozzie and Harriet defined the happy family—beautiful, loving and subservient housewife; kindly, authoritative, breadwinner husband; suburban home with sprawling lawn; and at least two wholesome, intelligent, and well-meaning children. This model of family life enjoyed unparalleled popularity during the 1950s.

The 1950s family ideal included isolated, indulgent, and exclusive parenting by biological mothers who fulfilled themselves performing domestic services for their families. This style of parenting is an "all-your-eggs-in-one-basket" approach to childrearing that can produce unique stresses and strains for both mothers and children.[65] When mothers are responsible for all the child care, they have little opportunity for taking breaks and their feelings become overwhelmingly important to their children. Sole caretaker mothers have few opportunities to derive self-worth from alternate activities, and they are often judged by how their children turn out. This can set up a kind of "hothouse" environment in which mothers and children feel responsible for each others' actions and emotions, sometimes leading to confusion over ego boundaries, communication problems, and mental illness.[66]

The 1950s model of parenting, with its mother-centered isolation, is much more individualistic than childrearing was in the past. When each family decides how to raise its own children, it sets up a two-party conflict and creates a certain amount of anxiety that was not present in societies with more collective childrearing practices. Modern parents, especially mothers, now made up their own rules, with occasional advice from friends or family and regular reference to a popular childrearing manual or two. Because rules were set individually, breaking or resisting them could now easily be perceived as a threat to one's parental authority, and power struggles between parents and children seemed more personal. In the modern pattern, which gained symbolic prominence during the 1950s, parents have individualistic power insofar as they can decide to change the rules, but they generally lack a larger sense of institutional legitimacy because each decision is an individual choice.

In the micro-communities of earlier times, children could disobey or fail to do their assigned tasks, but since it was not up to individual parents to establish the rules, the conflict was seen as outside their control. They were simply enforcing a community standard. Not only that, but if the parent did not enforce the standard, someone else in the micro-community would, providing validation that the parents were not individually responsible for setting the standards. The earlier pattern could also be conflictual, but parents had much more institutional legitimacy, and the standards themselves were rarely challenged.[67] One of the important things about the more modern individualistic pattern of parenting and marital relationships is that they allow for social change. Because individual couples are not as frequently monitored by neighbors and kin, they can institute new ways of organizing family life, subject to the opinions of emerging experts and bureaucratic state controls. We'll explore some of these processes in the next chapters.

Fathers in the 1950s and 1960s

By mid-century, the vast majority of American fathers were routinely absent from the day-to-day activities of family life. The desire to increase fathers' involvement in families intensified in the 1950s, still primarily motivated by a desire to provide sons with appropriate models of masculinity. The underlying fear was that sons who rarely saw their fathers would be too feminine or, reflecting the homophobia of the time, that they might turn out to be gay. Joseph Pleck, a social psychologist who studies men's roles, suggests that the 1950s' concern about fathers' absence and passivity was linked to a perceived epidemic of juvenile delinquency. He illustrates this connection by recalling a powerful scene from the film *Rebel Without a Cause,* in which the delinquent son finally seeks out his father for advice during a crisis. When the son finds his father wearing an apron while washing dishes in the kitchen, he is visibly shaken and recoils in disgust.[68] Presumably, an apron-clad father performing housework was incapable of providing manly advice to a wayward son. During the 1950s and early 1960s, popular culture and scholarly research encouraged fathers to be more involved in family life, but in ways very different from mothers. The primary concern was that young boys, who spent most of their time under the control of their mothers and other women teachers, would not be able to learn how to be manly men.

Since men weren't supposed to be responsible for routine child care, studies of men as parents in the 1950s and 1960s were extremely rare. Ross Parke, one of the first psychologists to write about fathers, suggests "we didn't just forget about fathers by accident; we ignored them on purpose because of our assumption that they were less important than mothers in influencing the developing child."[69] We have few detailed studies of what father–child interactions were like during this period, and virtually no systematic data on the extent of father participation in various child care tasks. We do know that before the 1970s, the typical American father did very little. The popular image is of a cigar-dispensing expectant father pacing hospital corridors while his young wife gives birth in the next room. After babies came home, expectations for "hands-on" infant care by fathers were so low that if a father changed a baby's diaper, he was likely to receive unsolicited comments and good-natured ribbing, if not outright ridicule. Although some fathers were undoubtedly very involved in raising their children during this era, there was little cultural support or encouragement for fathers to assume the sorts of mundane and routine tasks that mothers did.

Before the 1970s, husbands were likewise little involved in housework, at least the type of housework wives typically performed. As noted above, homes are economic units, where work has to be performed every day just to keep things going. This is especially the case when couples have children, since they require so much more work than they are able to reciprocally contribute. Every home is a combination hotel, restaurant, laundry, child-care, and entertainment center. Each of these activities takes work that is often invisible when one is the recipient of these services, as most men were in the 1950s and 1960s, and as many men still are today.

To determine how household members spend their time, home economists, "domestic scientists," and, most recently, feminist sociologists, have studied divisions of household labor using a variety of methods. Early researchers left men out of these studies altogether, but some surveys included questions about who does what around the house. Sometimes survey researchers asked who is more likely to perform a particular task, others asked who did particular tasks "last week," and still others asked people to keep time-budget diaries, recording what they did repeatedly throughout a given day. Depending on the method and sample used, researchers have come up with different estimates of the absolute and relative amounts of time men and women have spent cooking, cleaning, shopping, doing home repairs, and so on. The few household labor studies that included men in the 1950s or 1960s found that husbands spent most of their household work time doing repairs, paying bills, or performing outside chores.

If men were involved in stereotypical "female" chores before then, it was usually meal preparation, where husbands averaged just over an hour each week compared to an average of over eight hours per week for wives.[70] Even when cooking, however, husbands tended to limit their contributions to gender stereotyped tasks like barbecuing, rather than contributing substantially to the more routine preparation of daily meals. In the mid-1960s, husbands contributed less than a tenth of the time spent in cleaning up after meals or washing dishes in an average week, and only about 5 percent of the time spent doing housecleaning. Married men were extremely unlikely to contribute to doing laundry or ironing during the 1960s, averaging about five hours per *year*, compared to over five hours per *week* for wives. Overall, husbands contributed only about two hours per week to the combined tasks of cooking, meal clean-up, housecleaning, and laundry in the mid-1960s, compared to an average of almost 25 hours per week for wives. This meant that women were doing over 90 percent of the inside domestic chores.[71] At the same time, fewer than 80 percent of mothers with children under six years old in the United States were in the paid labor force.[72] It is no exaggeration to say that the practice, as well as the ideal, of separate spheres was alive and well in the 1950s and 1960s. Nevertheless, changes were already underway that would begin to transform everyday family practices, and to challenge the ideology of separate spheres that had become so taken for granted.

Increasing Diversity of Family Types

One of the biggest changes since the 1950s has been the increasing diversity in the types of families and households that make up the communities of the United States. The tendency in much popular analysis is to focus on the model middle-class family since it has been considered "normal." However, the traditional family of breadwinner father, homemaker mother, and biological children is much less prevalent than it was in the 1950s, and is now a statistical minority. Most people still get married, and most couples who stay married eventually have children, but married couple households (with or without children) will constitute only about half of all U.S. households by the year 2000. From 1950 to 1970, the percentage of households that were married couples fell from 79 percent to 69 percent. Since then, the percentage has continued to fall, so that by 1990, only 55 percent of all households were married couples. This means that many other types of living arrangements are becoming more common, and what is considered normal is undergoing a dramatic transformation.

Significantly more single individuals, both young and old, live on their own or with roommates than ever before. More couples are also living together without getting married, though most of these "co-habitors" eventually marry. Because divorce rates remain high, there are also significantly more single parent households, most headed by women. Although single parents are still overwhelmingly female, the number of single father households increased faster than any other household type during the 1980s. At the same time, there are increasing numbers of fathers (and some mothers) living away from their biological children. Because most divorced people also remarry, blended or stepfamilies are also more prevalent. With the odds of a new marriage ending in divorce hovering around 50 percent, and the odds of remarriage between 70 and 80 percent, one out of every three Americans is now a stepparent, a stepchild, a step sibling, or some other member of a stepfamily. In addition, more women are deciding to have children without ever marrying, and an increasing number of married couples are deciding to stay childless altogether. Gay and lesbian couples, though still not recognized by the same legal protections as heterosexual couples, are also more prevalent. Various demographic trends, including the aftermath of the "baby boom," falling rates of marriage and fertility, delayed marriage and childbearing, more college attendance, greater female labor force participation, higher rates of divorce, and longer life, are all contributing to an unprecedented diversity of household types. In short, kinship has become more complicated since the 1950s, and the concept of a "normal" family is getting harder and harder to define.[73]

People are puzzled about how to interpret or respond to all these new family arrangements, but the experts are also confused. American family patterns are so fluid that even the U.S. Census Bureau has had difficulty measuring recent trends. Some leading demographers summarized the situation by commenting, "Most large-scale, nationally representative surveys cannot readily tell us what proportion of husband-wife families are stepfamilies; how adopted or foster-care children are faring; distinguish roommates from couples who are living together as unmarried partners; or measure the extent of family support networks for elderly persons who live alone."[74] Adding to all the confusion is the tendency of people with competing visions of the "real" American family to cite different figures. For instance, using census figures, one can say that married couples with children represent a full 37 percent of all families. Alternately, one can cite the same source, claiming that married couples with children now represent just 26 percent of U.S. households.[75] The reason for the difference between these figures is that households and families are not the same thing. The Census Bureau carefully distinguishes between a *household*, defined as all persons (including single persons) who occupy the same living quarters, and a *family*, which is two or more persons related by birth, marriage, or adoption who reside together. Some people cite figures about households and some refer only to families, so the numbers that are thrown around can be contradictory and confusing. The main point to remember is that nonfamily households and single parent households have increased at a rapid pace since the 1950s, whereas married couples, and especially those with children, constitute a shrinking percentage of the total U.S. population.

I will return to the significance of these demographic trends in later chapters, so I can make some predictions about what the future might hold. For now, however, it is sufficient to recognize that there is no one type of household or family that is more important than the others. Much public discourse, whether from politicians, academics, or religious leaders, nostalgically assumes that a married couple of breadwinner husband, homemaker wife, and several natural children, is THE standard against which all others should be judged. This notion preserves the sanctity of the separate spheres ideal despite of the fact that most women are now employed and about half of all families no longer have children living in the home. The rapid increase in the percentage of married women with children in the paid labor force is probably the most dramatic demographic shift of the past few decades. American mothers have followed single women, young childless wives, and older empty nesters into regular year-round paid employment. Most married couples now have two earners and almost three-quarters of mothers with school-age children are currently in the paid labor force. As we will see in future chapters, these trends show no signs of reversing.[76]

Because there is so much diversity among households, we cannot hope to understand the overall pattern of labor allocation and gender relations in America without reference to the many different family types existing today. What happens in single-parent households, in childless couples, or among co-habitors, subtly influences what goes on inside all households. Nevertheless, what goes on in married couple households with children (or some nostalgic vision of it) tends to shape public perceptions of how family life should be. When people discuss the state of the American Family, they are usually referring to married couples with children. Such families are the inheritors and perpetuators of the separate spheres ideology. In part, this is because divisions of labor in married-couple families with young children tend to be more gender-segregated than in those without children, and even relatively egalitarian couples often shift to modern versions of separate spheres when they have children.[77]

Family Work in the 1970s and 1980s.

Divisions of labor inside contemporary families have been surprisingly resistant to change. Studies conducted in the United States during the 1970s and early 1980s repeatedly showed that wives performed at least two-thirds of the total household labor, including both inside and outside chores, even when they were employed. Domestic tasks continued to be divided according to gender during this time, with women performing between 80 and 90 percent of the daily repetitive and routine tasks, including cooking, cleaning, and child care. Men, in contrast, continued to contribute to household labor by mowing the lawn, taking out the trash, maintaining the cars, or playing with the children. According to national survey data, husbands increased their hourly contributions to the inside domestic chores of cooking, cleaning, and laundry only slightly, but because working women were contributing fewer hours to housework, men's proportionate contributions to household tasks rose.[78] Because men's aggregate changes were small, and because husbands of employed wives did no more, on average, than husbands of nonemployed wives, some researchers remarked that the housework studies of the late 1970s and early 1980s were "much ado about nothing."[79]

Child-care patterns during the 1970s showed increased participation on the part of fathers, although most of men's time was spent in relatively conventional gender-typed activities. One consistent finding from this time was that mothers fed and cared for infants and older children much more than fathers did.[80] The typical pattern was for the birth of a first child to bring about a shift in the household division of labor toward more conventional patterns. Often, the new father would increase his time on the job, and the mother would begin performing more of the housework and child care even if she continued to be employed outside the home. This movement toward separate spheres in the allocation of tasks after children arrive was likely even for couples who had previously shared housework, and for those who expected to share infant care.[81]

One of the most consistent findings from family research conducted in the past 40 years is that marital satisfaction drops following the birth of a first child—especially for women. This is probably due to the isolation women have experienced when they first become mothers and to their assumption of almost total responsibility for the neverending tasks associated with raising a family. In the 1960s and 1970s, married women spent more than twice the time on housework that unmarried women did, and married women with children spent by far the most time in household labor.[82] Marriage and birth have traditionally increased wives' domestic labor, while men's domestic labor typically remains unchanged by these events. Many researchers in the 1970s and 1980s suggested that the presence of a man in the house contributed more to the need for housework than to its completion, and this appeared to be especially true if there were children involved.[83]

Researchers investigating divisions of family labor in the late 1970s and early 1980s also discovered that psychological distress was greatest among wives with husbands who did little to assist with household chores.[84] This was primarily the result of the amount and type of labor for which wives and mothers were assumed to be responsible. Not only did women spend many more hours performing household labor than men, but the nature of their involvement differed. Women's household work tends to be unrelenting, repetitive, and routine. Tasks such as shopping, cooking, cleaning, laundry, and child care are repeated over and over in a neverending cycle. The household tasks that men typically do, in contrast, are infrequent and irregular. Activities like household repairs, mowing the lawn, or taking out the trash may need to be repeated every so often, but the time between repetitions is much longer than for stereotypical "wifely" tasks. The endless aspects of women's household labor contrasts sharply with men's normal tasks, and probably contributes to housewives' increased risk of depression.[85]

Both women and men experience boredom, fatigue, and tension when they do household work alone but women are much more likely than men to perform household tasks in isolation. Whereas men tend to do much of their family work on weekends, women tend to do housework each day. Women also report doing an average of three household tasks at one time, which may help explain why they find household labor to be less relaxing and more stressful than men do.[86] In addition, men tend to do the tasks that are more enjoyable, or at least less onerous. Research from the 1970s and early 1980s showed that women almost always cleaned the bathrooms and did the ironing, two of the least popular household tasks. When men contributed to the inside chores, they would most often concentrate their efforts on the relatively fun activities.

For instance, some studies found that men were more likely to do child care than housework, and that they were more likely to watch the children or play with them than to feed or clean up after them. When in the kitchen, men were most likely to cook, followed by washing dishes.[87]

Researchers have found that most women in the 1970s and early 1980s considered their divisions of household labor to be fair. Most wives had low expectations for help and did not necessarily think that their husbands should do more around the house. In part, this was because it was not socially acceptable for men to do "women's" work. Although most mothers surveyed a decade ago wanted their husbands to spend more time with their children, this was usually conceived of as benefiting the children rather than reducing their own workload. Even though most wives experience repetitive domestic chores as boring, they also consider them part of important family work, and derive satisfaction from serving their loved ones. Women do not usually find housework to be enjoyable, but as wives and mothers, they tend to enjoy feeding and taking care of their families and continue to base their self-worth on meeting family members' needs. As discussed in the following chapters, since household labor is tied up with what it means to love and care for others, women have often had ambivalent and contradictory feelings about being responsible for so many of the routine household chores.[88]

Although mothers were primarily responsible for home and children in the 1970s, research also began to document wide variability among individual families. Studies during this time focused on men's interest in caring for infants and toddlers, their capacity or competence as caregivers, and differences between mothers' and fathers' styles of interacting with children. Although some biologically based social theories continued to suggest inherent limitations in men's abilities to nurture children, most researchers assumed that sex differences in responsiveness to children were socially constructed.[89] For example, developmental psychologist Ross Parke and his colleagues demonstrated how fathers were capable of executing infant care tasks, and discovered that men were skillful at bottle feeding, showing as much sensitivity to infant cues as mothers.[90] Even though fathers were found to be competent caretakers of infants and young children, studies during this time observed few fathers who actually assumed the majority of those tasks in two-parent households.

Studies conducted in the 1970s also focused on the distinctive play styles of fathers and mothers. Although both men and women were found to be active playmates for their infants and children, fathers devoted a much higher proportion of their time with children to play than mothers. In one mid-1970s study, fathers spent 40 percent of their time with infants in play, whereas mothers spent only about 25 percent.[91] Fathers and mothers differed in the style of play as well as the quantity of play time. Fathers were more likely to be energetic with both infants and older children, playing physical games and arousing them. Mothers' play, on the other hand, tended to be more verbal, educational, and toy mediated.[92]

As discussed in the next chapter, changes in medical practices during the 1970s both promoted and reflected a growing awareness that fathers should be involved in labor and delivery. In the 1960s, few fathers were admitted into delivery rooms, but in the early 1970s, fathers began demanding to be allowed to attend the births of their children. In 1972, only about one in four fathers was present at the birth of their children.[93] In 1974, the American College of Obstetricians and Gynecologists endorsed fathers' presence during labor, and by the end of the 1970s, fathers could be admitted to delivery rooms in approximately 80 percent of American hospitals.[94] By the 1990s, analysts were estimating that approximately 90 percent of fathers were in attendance at their child's birth.[95]

The decade of the 1970s was a time of contradictory trends for U.S. fathers. Although married fathers increased their time with children during the 1970s, an opposing pattern of father absence resulted from dramatic increases in divorce. Because mothers were almost always awarded child custody following divorce, an increasing number of fathers lived apart from their offspring. Most divorced fathers failed to pay the full amount of child support, and post-divorce father-child contact usually declined steadily after initial separation. Thus, while some fathers were spending more time with their children, others were spending less and failing to fulfill even the older obligation to provide financial support.[96]

Two divergent patterns in the timing of births also emerged in the 1970s, one early and the other late. There were marked increases in the number and percentage of births to teenagers during the 1970s, although the rise in early births has since subsided. At the same time, more and more women were waiting longer to have children. The number of first babies born to women between 30 and 34 years old doubled between 1970 and 1979, and fertility rates increased for women past their mid-twenties.[97] As discussed in Chapter 7, this upswing in delayed parenting persisted into the 1980s and 1990s and continues to play an important role in shaping divisions of labor between mothers and fathers.

Separate Spheres and Doing Gender

Although married couples with young children often perpetuate the separate spheres ideal, they can also resist it. With most mothers of infants and preschoolers now in the paid workforce, many couples are forced to create new patterns of labor allocation and, in so doing, they are giving new meanings to parenting and gender roles. We can understand this process with reference to the concept of "doing gender," discussed more fully in the next chapter. According to Candace West and Donald Zimmerman, sociologists at the

University of California, everyone must "do gender" to be classified as a man or woman and be judged competent members of society.[98] This is not an optional activity, but a requirement of everyday life. Doing gender consists of interacting with others in such a way that people will perceive one's actions as expressions of an underlying masculine or feminine "nature." Thus, one is not automatically classified as a man or a woman on the basis of biological sex, but on the basis of appearance and behavior in everyday social interaction.

Family work offers people a prime opportunity to "do gender" because of our cultural prescriptions about the appropriateness of men and women performing certain chores. Doing household chores or caring for children allows people to reaffirm their gendered relation to the work and to the world.[99] Thus, women can create and sustain their identities as women through cooking and cleaning house and men can sustain their identities as men by NOT cooking and cleaning house. With peoples' sense of self so tied up with doing separate gender-linked activities, it is no wonder that the dual spheres ideal has been maintained for so long. In a basic sense, the things we do in and for our families create gender: "doing" family work is also "doing" gender.

If we take people's talk seriously, then we can also see that family commitments and activities are the most important things in people's lives. Adult women and men in the United States routinely say that they are motivated to do what they do each day because it contributes to the well-being of the family.[100] Family life is no less important than it was in the 1950s, even though increasing numbers of Americans are likely to divorce or live in nonfamily households. Commitment to family is typically expressed as concern for children. Because most children still spend some time growing up in two-parent households, married couples with children — what we often think of as THE family — continue to provide the primary model of marriage for the next generation. By socializing children, families also shape gender-specific patterns of obligation and entitlement in the next generation. By building expectations and shaping personalities, gender segregated patterns of family labor help to structure life chances into the future.

Whether we focus on how the changing economy has affected family life, how parents "do gender" in families, or how families influence children, family work is not trivial. Who does what around the house and for the children shapes gender relations in the society at large. The symbolic division of daily life into a public world of men and a private world of women has been remarkably resistant to change, even as employment has shifted to include both women and men. Despite pressures for change in the domestic division of labor, we saw few changes until the late 1970s, and only limited assumption of housework and child care by men in the early 1980s. In the following chapters, I will explore the sorts of labor sharing, negotiations, and interpersonal dynamics that have been occurring since then within two-earner families in the United States.

3

Changing Patterns of Family Work

In *The Second Shift,* sociologist Arlie Hochschild presented compelling accounts of working parents trying to balance job and family responsibilities in the 1980s.[1] Not surprisingly, she concluded that what seems natural and fair to most people actually favors husbands' interests over wives'. According to Hochschild, American women put in fifteen hours more each week than their husbands on all types of work—both paid and unpaid—amounting to a full extra month of 24-hour workdays in a year.[2] Trying to understand how and why this second shift falls on women, Hochschild and her assistants interviewed and observed 52 couples over an eight-year period.

One of their most consistent findings was that women were "far more deeply torn" between the demands of work and family than their husbands. Since wives remained responsible for home management as well as performing the most time-consuming and repetitive tasks, Hochschild found that they tended to talk intensely about being overtired, sick, and emotionally drained. She labeled the common situation of men's favored position in the household economy as "the leisure gap," since most men enjoyed more free time than their wives and were less burdened by family obligations.[3]

Hochschild's study acknowledged that economics play an important part in determining who does what around the house, but she found no simple trade-off between wages earned and household labor performed. Something else besides the bold assertion of power is at work when people divide up housework and child care. By focusing on eight couples with unique approaches to family life, Hochschild illustrated that ideology is extremely

51

important to divisions of labor. Like West and Zimmerman's conception of "doing gender," Hochschild's analysis highlighted the symbolic significance of various routine household activities for the men and women who do them. Who makes the bed, feeds the dog, washes the car, or stays home with a sick child depends on who *ought* to do those tasks in each particular household. Who ought to do a specific chore is shaped by gender ideology and the ideal of separate spheres.

Hochschild used the term "gender strategies" to capture the interplay of ideology and practice that is continually and subtly negotiated as couples divide family labor and make assumptions about who should do which chores. The allocation of responsibility for family work and paid work is unquestionably patterned by cultural understandings of "appropriate" gender behavior, but it is also directly shaped by individuals making tacit and overt choices in their everyday lives.[4] The feelings of entitlement, guilt, obligation, or appreciation that are inevitably associated with the performance of certain activities reflect what Hochschild calls the "economy of gratitude." Variations in the economy of gratitude contribute to different bargaining strategies and different divisions of family and paid labor. As peoples' life circumstances and self-evaluations change, economies of gratitude also shift.[5] By considering such factors, we can see how and why most families perpetuate separate spheres, and we can also begin to understand how new patterns of family labor sharing might emerge.

Who Does What?

In general, the men in Hochschild's study did not consider the second shift to be "their issue." Nevertheless, about one in five shared housework roughly equally with their wives, and these men seemed to be just as pressed for time as the women.[6] The fact that 20 percent approached equal sharing is a significant development, considering that the division of household labor has a history of such extreme imbalance. Other researchers studying household labor in the late 1980s also reported that the leisure gap was shrinking, albeit more slowly than most working women wanted.[7] Recent studies have also begun to identify specific areas, such as child care, for which men's contributions have increased substantially. A few studies have even found that the total number of hours spent on all paid and unpaid labor (not including child care) is now about equal between husbands and wives.[8]

In general, American women are likely to spend fewer hours than men on the job, and American men are likely to put in fewer hours than women on domestic labor, but the total number of hours is converging. Compared to a decade ago, women are spending more time on the job and less time on family work. In contrast, men are spending slightly more time on family work and slightly less time on the job. The gender gap is still with us because women continue to do more than men, but at least things seem to be moving in the direction of more equality.

Studies conducted in the last decade show that the majority of men still make only minimal contributions to those tasks conventionally performed by housewives, such as cooking and cleaning.[9] Nevertheless, variation among couples is increasing, with some men now making much larger contributions to some forms of family work. For instance, men's average contributions to the so-called feminine chores of preparing meals, washing dishes, cleaning house, and laundry/ironing have roughly doubled since about 1970, whereas women's contributions have decreased by about a third. In the earlier period, men were doing only about two hours a week, or about 10 percent of these inside chores. By the late 1980s, men had more than doubled their contributions so that they were doing over 20 percent of the inside chores. Hourly estimates vary because different surveys use different measures, but we can say that the average husband is now doing about five to eight hours of indoor housework per week, whereas the average wife is spending about 20 to 30 hours on these tasks. In terms of the average number of hours spent, and in terms of the average percentage of the total in married couples, men have been doing more of the inside housework than they used to.

Husbands with employed wives do more housework than husbands with non-employed wives, especially if their wives have lucrative or high-status careers. But even single-breadwinner families have reported an increase in the husband's percentage of housework in the past two decades. These modest increases are interpreted as trivial by some researchers, because they continue to be driven, in large part, by women's reduction in time spent directly on family work.[10] The limited amount of change can thus be seen as evidence for the persistence of the old separate spheres pattern. Even when men do assume more of the housework, they rarely do half, and, on average, women still do about three times as much as the men.[11] In contrast, others interpret recent changes as evidence for the emergence of new patterns of gender equality.[12] Because men have doubled their household contributions, it does appear that some shifts have begun, even if things are not gender balanced.

Overall average changes in patterns of housework are noticeable, even though some men still do virtually nothing, while others do a considerable amount. We must remember that most surveys use large samples composed of different people each time, even if the different samples are intended to represent the same population. When we talk about changes in such large groups, we are not referring to specific individuals making decisions about how to allocate their household chores differently from before, but, rather, to changes in the average contribution by all men in the sample. This is useful information because it helps us isolate broad social trends, but it does not tell us about processes of change in individual families. For that, we need to follow couples over time and isolate what changes and what stays the same in various circumstances. Unfortunately, the separate spheres ideal is so deeply embedded in our culture that most large-scale family studies have not even considered why men might do more domestic work. Nevertheless, we are beginning to get a picture of where change is occurring using questionnaires and telephone surveys

The family tasks men are increasingly likely to share include child care, shopping, and, in some cases, meal preparation. The most recent studies of dual-earner couples using representative samples show men contributing between about 25 percent and 40 percent of the time devoted to these activities with an average of almost one-third. Meal clean-up and housecleaning continue to lag behind, with dual-earner men contributing somewhere between 15 and 30 percent and averaging almost one-quarter. Finally, men doing laundry is still relatively rare, but dual-earner husbands now contribute between 10 and 25 percent of the hours spent in clothes care, compared to the 2 to 5 percent they contributed in the 1960s.[13]

Although men are putting in more of the hours on housework tasks conventionally performed by women, responsibility for noticing when tasks should be performed or standards for their performance are still often exercised by their wives. Women in the late 1980s and early 1990s were likely to carry the burden of managing the household as well as performing the most unpleasant tasks. For example, women continue to clean bathrooms and mop floors in the vast majority of American homes.

As we will see later in this chapter, even in families where much of the child care and housework is shared, wives are more likely than husbands to notice when chores need doing and to make sure that someone does them correctly. Interviews show that, in most families, husbands notice less about what needs to be done, wait to be asked to do various chores, and require explicit directions if they are to complete the tasks successfully. In line with this division of responsibility for management of household affairs, most couples continue to characterize husbands' contributions to housework or child care as "helping" their wives. In this chapter, I explore how some couples develop and justify such manager-helper divisions of family work, but I also report on couples who are successfully challenging them.

Women in most American households also worry more about the planning and scheduling of family social activities and about the emotional well-being of family members.[14] For example, mothers often say that they attempt to facilitate positive father-child interactions more for the benefit of the children than to reduce their own burden of work. Studies continue to report that most women in two-parent families are responsible for organizing, delegating, and scheduling the children's activities, even when they are not physically present.[15] Women are also likely to perform the most repetitive and less pleasant child-related tasks while simultaneously acting as overseers when others take care of their children.

Although mothers are still usually in charge, child care is the area marked by the most apparent change in men's family activities. Studies conducted since the mid-1980s show that men are now contributing close to a third of the child-care hours in dual-earner couples.[16] Results are contradictory here as well, but most studies show that parents are increasingly likely to work different shifts, and to alternate child care between them. When the mother is on the job, the father often stays home to watch the children.[17]

Because assumption of responsibility for child care is difficult to measure with simple surveys, household labor studies have tended to reduce parenting to the number of hours spent directly caring for children. The amount of time allocated to feeding, bathing, dressing, or putting children to bed comes to stand for parenting, even though a portion of tasks like laundry, shopping, housecleaning, and meal clean-up are also necessary for raising children and often occur at the same time as more direct forms of child care. Yet parenting is more than just direct care and various associated household chores. Effective parenting also entails setting countless limits, tending to the emotional needs of children, anticipating any communication or self-esteem problems, and working to provide children with optimum learning environments. Few recent studies are sensitive enough to explore these sorts of issues, but, when they are, most demonstrate that mothers are primarily responsible for the psychological support of children.[18] Nevertheless, we are beginning to see more men taking on at least a portion of this role, and most American couples now report that mothers and fathers share socioemotional aspects of child care such as teaching and discipline.

Parenting is a complex and contradictory endeavor for both men and women. As noted above, mothers, more than fathers, have assumed responsibility for the day-to-day feeding and supervising of younger children, and have more often provided them with emotional and physical comfort. Whoever does these "mothering" activities, however, is likely to find them somewhat monotonous and irritating. At the same time, most parents report a profound sense of fulfillment as a result of taking responsibility for children in this way. What happens when both husbands and wives attempt to share all aspects of child care? What impact does it have on family dynamics and how successful are couples at sharing parenting? To answer these questions, I turn to interviews with dual-earner couples who are struggling to adapt to the changing circumstances of their lives as parents.

Interviews with Shared Parenting Families

From 1987 to 1992, my research assistants and I interviewed parents who said they shared at least some aspects of parenting.[19] To aid in making later comparisons, for the first interviews I selected only dual-earner couples (i.e., both mother and father employed at least half time) with two or more school-aged children.[20] Locating couples who shared parenting was easier than anticipated because virtually everyone I approached knew of at least one highly participant father.[21] Unlike larger polls and surveys, selecting informants for the interviews was based on an informal "word-of-mouth" strategy (called snowball sampling because it builds from small to large as it gets rolling).[22] We asked school teachers, day care workers, and all the families we interviewed if they knew of couples with school children who shared child care.[23] The resulting group of informants tended to be in their late thirties, with two children and moderate rather than high or low incomes.[24]

Fathers and mothers were interviewed separately — usually at the same time in different rooms of their own house. Interviews lasted about two hours each, and as we were talking to the parents we also observed and informally interacted with the children. When we discovered something unique in an interview, or if we couldn't cover everything in one sitting, we often scheduled another meeting and returned to interview that person again. We tape-recorded the interviews and later transcribed them for more detailed analysis.[25] I was impressed with the warmth and hospitality of the couples who invited us into their homes, and I remain grateful for their willingness to discuss sensitive matters and for their thoughtful answers to some probing questions.

As described below, the parents said they shared most aspects of child care, though the extent of sharing for other household chores varied considerably. Parents offered different accounts of how and why they tried to be both breadwinners and homemakers. The interviews provide more detail than the survey studies reported above and help us to understand the personal struggles and joys that people were experiencing. I include frequent excerpts from the interviews in this and later chapters because the parents' own words capture the unique reality of their lives much better than I could.[26]

Deciding to Share

Most parents described falling into current divisions of labor by making minor practical adjustments to what they perceived to be relatively balanced domestic arrangements. A common sentiment was expressed by one father who commented, "Since we've both always been working since we've been married, we've typically shared everything as far as all the working — I mean all the housework responsibilities as well as child-care responsibilities. So it's a pattern that was set up before the kids were even thought of." Instead of divisions of labor becoming more traditional after having children, as other studies have found, most of the men in this study maintained their proportionate share of family work after becoming fathers or began to take on more.

Couples reported that mothers performed most of the early baby care. Like most mothers, the women reduced their hours of employment after the birth of their first or second child. Following the conventional breadwinner pattern, about a third of the fathers increased their employment hours to compensate for the loss of income resulting from their wife taking time off work around the birth. About half of the fathers, however, reported that they also took time off work near the birth to participate in newborn care.

Most fathers stressed the importance of getting involved early. This early involvement included men's participation in the decision to have children, their consultation on issues of prenatal care, their active involvement in the birth process, and their participation in newborn care. Most couples planned the births of their children jointly and intentionally, though in a few cases the wife desired children more than the husband and in a few others the husband was more eager than the wife to become a parent. In Chapter 5 I discuss more fully how some parents came to feel more eager for children than others, and how this affected their divisions of family work.

For many families, the men agreed to be active parents before the couple decided to have children. One mother described how she and her husband made their decision.

> Shared parenting was sort of part of the decision. When we decided to have children, we realized that we were both going to be involved with our work, so it was part of the plan from the very beginning. As a matter of fact, I thought that we only could have the one and he convinced me that we could handle two and promised to really help (laughs), which he really has, but two children is a lot more work than you realize (laughs).

By promising to assume at least partial responsibility for childrearing, most fathers influenced the mother's initial decision to have children, the subsequent decision to have another child, and the decision of whether and when to return to work. Almost all the mothers indicated that they had always assumed that they would have children, but most also assumed that they would return to paid employment before the children were in school. Like new mothers throughout the country today, half of the women did return to work within six months of the birth of their first child.

The Birth Experience

Most of the parents attended childbirth preparation classes and most births were natural, rather than surgical (i.e., cesarean sections). The births were about equally likely to occur in a normal hospital delivery room, a hospital alternative birthing center, or at home with either a doctor or midwife attending. In part, the tendency for home birth is greater than in many other studies because the mothers we interviewed had healthy pregnancies, wanted to be in control, and hoped to experience the birth in a nonmedical setting. All but one of the fathers were present at the births of their children and most talked about the importance of the experience, using terms like "incredible," "magical," "moving," "wonderful," and "exciting."

A lab technician, who was in his early thirties when his two children were born, described how excited he was to be a part of the births and how his participation helped him feel close to his children.

> I really participated in it. When I say we did the breathing together, I mean we really worked together and I really felt like I was understanding of how she felt, and really knew what she was going through, at least in the sense that I was in a rhythm with her. The second birth was a little harder. He was over ten pounds when he was born, so she was more uncomfortable. But, in that case too, I cut the cord which was symbolic, you know, a special thing to do, and particularly that first time the whole thing was very exciting and incredible, to hold the new baby right at first.

Many fathers marveled at how lucky they were to become parents at a time when men could be present and join in the birth experience rather than being relegated to a hospital waiting room. For example, one teacher talked about how being at a birth was a once-in-a-lifetime experience that contributed to a deep understanding of life and brought him closer to his wife.

> Both births were just wonderful, incredible experiences that made me realize how sad it would be to go through a whole lifetime and not be part of a birth. You realize how it's a part of life that so many people — so many men especially — have never had the opportunity to experience. And I think that's sad. It seems to me, for my life, it's a tremendously important part of understanding human experience. I think in both births I learned an enormous amount and they were both important parts of our relationship with each other.

A carpenter who was 30 when his first child was born described how his two children's births were quite different, but how being there helped him form a connection to each of them.

> I felt an immediate bond with Michael when he was born. I had been waiting for him and it was an important thing and I felt this sort of spiritual umbrella go from me to him when he was born. I think it's important that I was in that room. I mean, I didn't really have too much to do with the birth, as far as I wasn't allowed to get involved after the forceps delivery was gonna have to happen . . . but I was happy to be there. And Jennifer's birth was in some ways more important because, prior to her birth, I wasn't too excited. I was almost indifferent and I felt guilty about that. She was the second child and I wanted to be excited, but in my heart of hearts, I wasn't. So then, the minute she came out, that all changed. It was amazing.

For first births, in particular, but for subsequent births as well, the fathers talked about the importance of "bonding" with their newborns. Several fathers also commented that preparing for and participating in the births were important to their sense of involvement and to the creation of a close working partnership with their wives.

While some fathers waxed eloquent about their birth experiences, others were far less dramatic, even if they performed many of the same rituals. Some, like this 39-year-old father of three, poked fun at themselves as they described what they did to "bond" with their newborns.

> When the kids were born we did all the corny stuff to bond to the father too. There was a lot of physical contact between me and each of them as infants. Well, you know, within 5 or 10 minutes of the birth, having the child on my chest, naked, me and them, I mean, bare skin, so they have a sensory experience of the father right after the birth.

Some fathers referred to the peripheral role they played in the birth of their children, and a few indicated that they struggled with feeling useless during the process. For those who talked about it, the lack of centrality appeared to be a profound learning experience. Many men avoid putting themselves in situations where they are not central to what is happening. Since they were not part of the birth process in an immediate physical sense, if they wanted to be involved, they had to participate in a helping role. For some, this was difficult. Most midwives and doctors, however, made it easy for fathers to be there, and made sure that the fathers got to hold the newborn infant, even if they were of limited help to their laboring wives. One postal clerk who was 31 when he had his first child summarized his marginal status at the birth by saying, "I felt a little bit necessary and a lot unnecessary, but she was pretty good to me. I didn't bug her too much and I might have helped a little."

Early Infant Care

Three-quarters of the fathers reported that they were "very involved" with their newborns, even though mothers provided most of the daily care for the first few months. Most mothers breastfed their infants, and several fathers discussed feeling "left out." Arguments over whether to feed the baby formula in addition to breast milk sometimes surfaced, with fathers the more likely advocates of supplemental bottle feeding. Some mothers who did not want to turn to formula expressed milk using a breast pump, so that they could have longer breaks and so the father could experience feeding the infant. In general, however, fathers structured their newborn involvement in other ways. Many reported that they got up in the night to soothe their babies, and many described their early infant care experience in terms that mothers typically use to describe their postpartum experiences. The intensity of father–infant interaction was discussed by fathers as enabling them to experience a new and different level of intimacy and was depicted as "deep emotional trust," "very interior," "drawing me in," and "making it difficult to deal with the outside world."

Some fathers volunteered that the experience of being involved in the delivery and in early infant care was a necessary part of their assuming later responsibility for child care. Many described a process in which caring for their children provided them with the self-confidence and skills to feel that they knew what they were doing. They said their time alone with the baby in the beginning was especially helpful in building their sense of competence.

> I felt I needed to start from the beginning. Then I learned how to walk them at night and not be totally p.o.'d at them and not feel that it was an infringement. It was something I *got* to do in some sense, along with changing diapers and all these things. It was certainly not repulsive and in some ways I really liked it a lot. It was not something innate, it was something to be learned. I managed to start at the beginning: if you *don't* start at the beginning, then you're sort of left behind.

This father, like almost all the others, talked about having to learn how to nurture and care for his children. He also stressed how important it was to "start at the beginning." While all fathers intentionally shared routine child care as the children approached school age, only half the fathers attempted to assume a major share of daily infant care, and only one in four described themselves as equal caregivers for children under one year old.

Both husbands and wives described how they had to work hard at including the father in newborn care. One, however, was "forced" into this role because the baby was delivered by cesarean section and the mother recovered slowly from the surgery. Such "forced" participation can actually increase fathers' involvement with their babies. Psychologists have found that fathers of cesarean-delivered infants engage in more caregiving during the first year than fathers whose babies are vaginally delivered. Fathers of cesarean-delivered infants tend to show more soothing behaviors toward infants and to participate in infant care on a more equal basis than those in natural birth comparison groups. Investigators suggest that when mothers are unable to assume a fully active role in caregiving during the first weeks, fathers increase their involvement and, as a result, tend to develop competence and continue taking care of the child even after the mother has completely recovered. This is not to suggest that fathers of vaginally delivered infants don't catch up, because studies have also found little difference in father–child interactions between cesarean-delivered babies and others after 12 months.[27] These studies do show, however, that when fathers are involved in early infant care, they are more responsive to cues from the child. Our interviews indicate that early and extensive involvement in infant care can raise the father's confidence in his abilities to nurture his children and may also increase his commitment to be actively involved in later care.

As noted above, most of the mothers we interviewed had nonsurgical births, recovered quickly, and breastfed their babies, so those couples who shared early infant care did so as a result of explicit planning and scheduling. Early caregiving fathers described their involvement in infant care as deliberate, requiring continuous negotiation and adjustments between mother and father.

> She nursed both of them completely, for at least five or six months. So, my role was—we agreed on this—my role was the other direct intervention, like changing, and getting them up and walking them, and putting them back to sleep. For instance, she would nurse them but I would bring them to the bed afterward and change them if necessary, and get them back to sleep. . . . I really initiated those other kinds of care aspects so that I could be involved. I continued that on through infant and toddler and preschool classes that we would go to, even though I would usually be the only father there.

This man's wife offered a similar account, commenting that "except for breastfeeding, he always provided the same things that I did—the emotional closeness and the attention."

Another early caregiving father, who was laying tile in his bathroom as I interviewed him, described how he and his wife "very consciously" attempted to equalize the amount of time they spent with their children when they were infants. Looking up from his work, he said, "we made the decision that we wanted it to be a mutual process, so that from the start we shared, and all I didn't do was breastfeed. And I really would say that was the only distinction." His wife also described their infant care arrangements as "equal," and commented that other people did not comprehend the extent of his participation.

> I think that nobody really understood that Amy had two mothers. The burden of proof was always on me that he was literally being a mother. He wasn't nursing, but he was getting up in the night to bring her to me, to change her poop, which is a lot more energy than nursing in the middle of the night. You have to get up and do all that, I mean get awake. So his sleep was interrupted, and yet within a week or two, at his work situation, it was expected that he was back to normal, and he never went back to normal. He was part of the same family that I was.

This was the only couple that talked about instituting, for a limited time, an explicit record-keeping system to ensure that they shared infant care equally.

> [FATHER]: We were committed to the principle of sharing and we would have schedules, keep hours, so that we had a pretty good sense that we were even, both in terms of the commitment to the principle as well as we wanted to in fact be equal. We would keep records in a log—one might say in a real compulsive way—so that we knew what had happened when the other person was on.
>
> [MOTHER]: When the second one came we tried to keep to the log of hours and very quickly we threw it out completely. It was too complex.

Child-Centered Families and Equity Ideals

As I analyzed the interviews for patterns of similarity between couples, I was struck by the powerful symbolic meanings that they assigned to sharing parenting. There were two major ideological underpinnings to their current divisions of labor that I came to label "child-centeredness" and "equity ideals." While those who attempted to share early infant care tended to have more elaborate vocabularies for talking about these issues, later sharing couples also referred to them. For instance, all couples provided accounts that focused on the importance of childhood and most stressed the impossibility of mothers "doing it all."

Couples were child-centered in that they placed a high value on their children's well-being, defined parenting as an important and serious undertaking, and organized most of their non-employed hours around their children. Talking to most of the parents, I got the feeling that their children were their number one priority. For instance, one father described how his social life revolved around his children, commenting "they are the central driving force in my life."

Three-quarters of the parents we talked with regularly used some form of paid child care, and about half sent their children to day care centers or family day care homes for at least a few hours each day. Nevertheless, most of the parents said that they spent more time with their children than other dual-earner parents in their neighborhoods. Another father commented that he and his wife, like Gary and Susan Carter, had structured their entire lives around personally taking care of their children.

> An awful lot of the way we've structured our lives has been based around our reluctance to have someone else raise our children. We just really didn't want the kids to be raised from 7:30 in the morning 'til 4:30 or 5:00 in the afternoon by somebody else. So we've structured the last ten years around that issue.

Not only did most of the parents structure their lives around their kids, but many were also likely to give their children considerable power in other ways. Some parents advocated treating children as inexperienced equals or "little people," rather than as inferior beings in need of authoritarian training. For example, an Air Force veteran now employed in computer research stated, "We don't discipline much. Generally the way it works is kind of like bargaining. They know that there are consequences to whatever actions they take, and we try and make sure they know what the consequences are before they have a chance to take the action." Another father described a similar moral stance concerning children's rights.

> I'm not assuming—when I'm talking about parent–child stuff—that there's any inequality. Yes, there are a lot of differences in terms of time spent in this world, but our assumption has been, with both children, that we're peers.

And so that's how we are with them. So, if they say something and they're holding fast to some position, we do not say, "You do this because we're the parent and you're the child."

About half the parents talked directly about similar sorts of equity ideals for children, voicing opinions that might be labeled democratic or indulgent. The other half, in contrast, talked about valuing their children, but espoused more conventional and authoritative styles of parenting that did not treat children as equals.

Concerning women's rights, a complex and somewhat ambivalent portrait emerged. Most mothers and fathers agreed that women were not treated as equal in our society, but the women were much more likely than the men to use terms like discrimination or disadvantage. Nevertheless, few men or women used such ideals to justify their attempts at sharing parenting. Only two mothers and one father mentioned equal rights or the women's movement when asked about their motivations for sharing family work. Few made links between political movements and what they were doing with their children. Few saw housework as a form of gender politics. Most did not identify themselves as feminists, and some even volunteered derogatory comments about "those women's libbers."

Despite the lack of an overt political perspective on their household arrangements, most husbands and wives indicated that no one should be forced to perform a specific task just because they were a man or a woman. As discussed below, this implicit belief in gender equity and family democracy was followed by mothers and fathers when they relied on time availability to assign most household tasks. It was also followed by making direct comparisons between husbands and wives when couples were asked if their division of family work was fair.

Divisions of Labor

We assessed contributions to 64 household tasks by having fathers and mothers sort chore cards into five piles indicating who most often performed them. Frequently performed tasks, such as meal preparation, laundry, sweeping, or putting children to bed, were judged for the two weeks preceding the interview. Less frequently performed tasks, such as window washing, tax preparation, or car repair, were judged as to who typically performed them.[28] Because husbands and wives don't always agree on who does what, I took the average of the two spouses' reports.[29] Some differences occurred between mothers' and fathers' accounts of household task allocation as discussed below, but there was general agreement on who did what.[30]

As expected, both men and women reported sharing many more tasks than typical married couples with children in the United States. As can be seen in

Table 3.1, a majority of the tasks, including all direct child care, most household business, meal preparation, kitchen clean-up, and over half the other house cleaning tasks were shared about equally. Still, almost a quarter of the tasks were performed principally by mothers, including most clothes care, meal planning, kin-keeping, and some of the less pleasant repetitive house-cleaning. Just under one-fifth of the tasks were performed principally by the fathers. These included the majority of the occasional outside chores such as home repair, car maintenance, lawn care, and taking out the trash.

The couples in this study thus shared an unusually high proportion of housework and child care, but still conformed—in some respects—to a conventional division of household labor. Couples were pioneers in that they shared many more household tasks than their own parents, significantly more than most others in their age cohort, and more than the typical American family studied in time-use research in the 1970s and 1980s.[31]

Practicality and Flexibility

Couples talked about various difficulties associated with simultaneously ful-filling employment obligations and caring for home and children, but all described their arrangements as practical and flexible solutions to common everyday problems. Almost no one considered their family arrangements exceptional, and many were puzzled when we asked why they were sharing child care and housework. For example, one mother said, "It's the only logical thing to do," and in a separate interview, her husband said, "It's the only practical way we could do it." Like most of the other couples, they said they were responding to shortages of time and money by sharing the child care and housework, but they did not think they were doing anything out of the ordinary.

They first talked about the limitations imposed by their jobs. A 48-year-old newspaper delivery man with three children focused on how his work schedule allowed him to be home more often than his wife, and hence available to do both inside and outside household chores. "Making the beds and doing the laundry just falls on me because I've got more time during the day to do it. And the yardwork and cuttin' all the wood, I do that. And so I'm endin' up doin' more around here than her just because I think I've got more time." His wife, a nurse who worked about 50 hours each week, also described their division of household labor as practical and flexible. She said their assignment of tasks was "ad hoc" and that their current arrangements "just happened."

> Things with us have happened pretty easily as far as what gets done by who. It happened without having to have a schedule or deciding—you know—like cooking. We never decided that he would do all the cooking; it just kind of ended up that way. Every once in a while when he doesn't feel like cooking he'll say

Table 3.1 Household Tasks by Who Most Often Performs Them

	Mother More	Father and Mother Equally	Father More
Clean			
	Mop	Vacuum	Take out trash
	Sweep	Clean tub/shower	Clean porch
	Dust	Make beds	
	Clean bathroom sink	Pick up toys	
	Clean toilet	Tidy living room	
	Hang up clothes		
	Wash windows		
	Spring cleaning		
Cook			
	Plan menus	Prepare lunch	Prepare breakfast
	Grocery shop	Cook dinner	
	Bake	Make snacks	
	Wash dishes		
	Put dishes away		
	Wipe kitchen counters		
	Put food away		
Clothes			
	Laundry	Shoe care	
	Hand laundry		
	Iron		
	Sew		
	Buy clothes		
House			
		Run errands	Household repairs
		Decorate	Exterior painting
		Interior painting	Car maintenance
		General yardwork	Car repair
		Garden	Wash car
			Water lawn
			Mow lawn
			Clean rain gutters

(continued)

Table 3.1. Household Tasks by Who Most Often Performs Them (*continued*)

	Mother More	Father and Mother Equally	Father More
Miscellaneous			
	Write or phone relatives/friends	Decide major purchases Pay bills Prepare taxes Handle insurance Plan couple dates	Investments
Children			
	Arrange babysitters	Wake Help dress Help bathe Put to bed Supervise Discipline Drive Take to doctor Care for sick Play with Plan outings with	

Tasks were sorted separately by fathers and mothers according to relative frequency of performance: (1) Mother mostly or always, (2) Mother more than father, (3) Father and mother about equal, (4) Father more than mother, (5) Father mostly or always. For each task a mean ranking by couple was computed with 1.00 - 2.49 = Mother More, 2.50 - 3.50 = Shared Equally, 3.51 - 5.0 = Father More. If over 50 percent of families ranked a task as performed by one spouse more than the other, the task is listed under that spouse, otherwise tasks are listed as shared.

"Would you cook tonight?" "Sure, fine." But normally I don't offer to cook. I say, "What are we having for dinner?"

Like the family described above, most couples reported that they did not spend much time talking or arguing about who was going to do what around the house. One father commented, "Patterns have pretty much just developed, we haven't really consciously discussed things." About a third reported that they rarely or never talked about allocating the housework or child care. Another third said they talked frequently about parenting but not about housework, and the remaining third said they regularly discussed both parenting and housework. Mothers were more likely than fathers to report that explicit negotiation was an important part of sharing household labor, but even couples who discussed housework said they spent little time arguing about it. Like results from national surveys, few of the men and women we interviewed admitted to having arguments about housework, and most thought their divisions of family work were "fair."

When I began the interviews, I expected to find that couples who shared family work would use elaborate scheduling and complicated procedures for checking to see if chores were evenly divided. Instead, I found that domestic labor was loosely structured and taken for granted. The most common tacit assumption about assigning tasks was that whatever needed doing would be done by "whoever has the most time" or "whoever is home first." For example, a postal carrier whose work schedule was less demanding than that of his wife said he did most of the cooking in their household. "An awful lot of what gets done, gets done because the person is home first. That's been our standing rule for who fixes dinner. Typically, I get home before she does so I fix dinner, but that isn't a fixed rule. If she gets home first, then she fixes dinner." Although some of the women noticed more need for work than their husbands did, I was surprised at the extent to which a loose allocation procedure seemed to work in these families.

Time availability seemed to be the most important factor in dividing family work, almost without regard to the type of work entailed. A school teacher mother, whose husband worked a part-time maintenance job, said, "Our basic operating procedure is whoever gets to it first; whoever can work it into their schedule." To illustrate, she used the example of laundry. "If I come home and I have time to get the laundry in, I'll do it, but basically he does laundry." She went on to talk about how there is an underlying trust between them.

Periodically I get fed up, like with the mess, or with something, so I say, "We've got to do this." But other than that it pretty much just gets done whenever. I guess we both kind of feel like the other one's doing the best they can, cuz I'm working and he's working—although he's employed part-time, he works almost full-time on his job—so we both support each other's work and support what we're doing with our lives and our family.

Many couples said that support and trust were essential to this flexible household task sharing. They assumed they would cooperate because both wanted to take responsibility for the care of the children and the upkeep of the house. Such assumptions were not enough to achieve equitable divisions of labor, but couples were usually happy to live with unbalanced tasks if they could maintain an image of cooperation and trust as underlying their efforts. In this sense, willingness to share sometimes substituted for actual sharing, provided there were enough visible signs of the husband's desire to participate.[32]

Two teachers talked about issues of trust as they described how they managed to arrive at an equitable division of labor that sometimes looked like "chaos" to outsiders. They operated without formal systems, although they, like many families we talked to, kept a big calendar by the telephone to record their own and the children's away-from-home activities. The husband described how dinner preparation and clean-up happened in their family.

> We switch; whoever cooks doesn't have to do the dishes. If for some reason she cooks and I don't do the dishes, she'll say something about it certainly. Even though we've never explicitly agreed that's how we do it, that's how we do it. The person who doesn't cook does the dishes. We don't even know who's going to cook a lot of the time. We just get it that we can do it. We act in good faith.

He then explained why he prefers unstructured or informal systems of allocating household tasks, focusing on how impromptu solutions feel more "creative," and allow their hectic lives to feel less regimented.

> We live extremely busy lives and don't have very formal systems. It's very interesting, because I think a lot of people who are as busy as we are feel they have to have formal systems in order to survive. We've gone the other way. It hasn't even been that conscious . . . if we don't find a certain level of creativity in the occasion and context, then our lives are going to become too mechanized. I have a feeling, too, that formal routines would just be a burden for us. But it means you've got to count on each other then. You have to trust.

Most couples had been together for a decade when we talked to them, so their routines for domestic labor had been negotiated over many years and their standards had adjusted slowly to accommodate to their spouse. Most also altered their arrangements when their employment situations changed or if one of them felt dissatisfied. When I asked how they divided family tasks, one father said, "We don't consciously talk about it: The only time it comes up is when one of us gets tired of doing something too much and wants a better way to do it." Others reported similar informal and flexible procedures. As the circumstances of people's lives changed, they made incremental adjustments to existing arrangements. One mother talked about how these routine adjustments in task allocation were satisfying to her. "Once you're comfortable in your roles and division of tasks for a few months then it seems like the needs change a little bit, and you have to change a little bit and you have to regroup. That's what keeps it interesting. I think that's why it's satisfying."

Because most American families assume that mothers will do almost all the housework, I expected that if men were going to make substantial contributions, the couple would use explicit bargains and contracts. Instead, most mothers and fathers said things like "we don't make lists" or "we don't pre-decide on who needs to do things." Contrary to my expectations, overt bargaining and explicit scheduling were *not* necessary precursors to sharing family work.[33]

The couples talked about a "natural evolution" of chore allocation that seemed almost too good to be true. The more I talked to them, the more I realized that they had subtly "negotiated" divisions of household labor over the course of many years. Chains of hundreds of small negotiations and bargains had occurred over time, even though the present patterns appeared to have "just happened."[34] Often the bargains and negotiations that occurred in their everyday lives were not seen, because to acknowledge them would change their romantic perceptions about marital harmony. Acknowledging conflict in the marriage can be considered an admission of failure, especially for women who have traditionally been held responsible for making the relationship work.[35] Portraying their relationships as free from overt conflict could make them feel good about the success of their marriages, and could also protect husbands from taking responsibility for doing more work. For that reason, I worried that peoples' stories about their easy and natural divisions of labor could be a gloss, but I was surprised that some of the most equal divisions of labor appeared in the couples with the fewest explicit systems for balancing the work.

Although many couples did not have fixed schedules or rules for allocating tasks, when queried, most did report that they had implicit agreements about certain specific tasks being the province of one spouse or the other. In addition, many wives, when pressed, voiced resentment that their husbands needed to be reminded to do certain chores. As I discuss in the next chapters, many of the most important negotiations in this area revolve around which tasks needed doing, how often they should be performed, whose standards should be followed in doing them, and coincidentally who was seen as "good at" doing which tasks.

Too Little Time

Virtually everyone we talked to complained that they did not have enough time: for themselves, for each other, to do the housework, to be with the kids, to advance their career, to relax. The "time crunch" was the paramount issue for these families, and may be the newest problem for families throughout America.[36] Lack of time motivated many couples to consider seriously sharing tasks, served as the basis for the allocation of household responsibilities, and sometimes even justified conventional gender-based divisions of labor.

The time that each spouse felt they had available for doing housework or child care was dependent on the number of hours employed, the scheduling of those hours, and on the amount of take-home work that their jobs required. Often, the allocation of family work was based on such time availability, though changes in job hours were also influenced by family demands. A lab technician husband described how he and his teacher wife divided household tasks in response to employment demands. "Her work schedule is more demanding and takes up a lot of evening time, so I think I do a lot of the everyday routines, and she does a lot of the less frequent things. Like I might do more of the cooking and meal preparation, but she is the one that does the grocery shopping. How that works out, I don't know, but it's similar with other things like child care too." In a separate interview in the next room, his wife described their arrangements in similar terms. "I think he probably does more with the children and everything on Monday through Friday, but my job's more demanding than his."

In most American families, the wife has more "free" time, since husbands are likely to be employed more hours. This was also the case in this select sample of two-job couples, but the differences in hours employed were less than the national average. Among the couples we interviewed, the husband was employed an average of eight hours more per week than the wife. The difference in hours employed was strongly related to the sharing of housework and child care in these families. If a wife's employment hours approached or exceeded those of her husband, his contribution to child care and housework approached hers. In other words, the more she worked at her job, the less she worked in the home, and the more housework and child care he did.

Over half of the women we interviewed were employed part time (20 to 35 hrs/wk). These women were much more likely than those working full-time (35 + hrs/wk) to perform the bulk of the cleaning and cooking. Only one of 11 husbands whose wives worked part time contributed equally to cleaning and cooking, whereas eight of nine husbands whose wives worked full time did so. These findings contradict some earlier research on household labor and indicate that time availability can be an important criterion in the allocation of domestic tasks. Because most of these couples thought either spouse was capable of performing most family work, the spouse with the most "free" time did what needed doing.

The number of hours per week that wives were employed can be said to "predict" the amount of housework shared among these couples, but it is not simply that more "free" time "caused" wives to do more domestic chores. In many cases the women who worked part time did so purposely to enable them to be home with their children. Several men made similar choices to work less and spend more time at home. Decisions to work part time were influenced by the overall income of the couple, the availability of jobs with good pay and scheduling flexibility, and attitudes toward the use of paid child care. If one parent took part-time work, the relative amount of time available to that person for performing housework increased, and he or she typically ended up doing more of the work and becoming the "expert" for those chores. A choice to go to part-time work early in a child's life also tended to influence later decisions about allocating paid and unpaid labor between spouses.[37]

The relative number of hours employed by each spouse is a useful measure of time availability, but it is only part of the picture. As national surveys have found, the scheduling of those hours, and their relation to a spouse's work schedule, are equally consequential.[38] In our study, the ability to schedule one's employment hours around children's schedules was extremely important to the sharing of both housework and child care. This was true even if both spouses were employed more than 40 hours per week.

Five of the men and four of the women we interviewed worked irregular hours—early morning shifts, evening shifts, or weekend shifts. In three couples, both spouses worked irregular shifts, and in three others, one spouse worked a shift schedule. Although large-scale surveys have found that shift work tends to encourage the sharing of child care, we were talking only to those who shared significant amounts of child care. Consequently, the division of household labor and the perceived quality of attachment between father and children did not vary systematically according to the utilization of irregular shifts of employment. Nevertheless, we were able to learn about how shift work affected the couples and discovered that the shift-work families were less likely to use outside child care than others.

Fathers whose wives worked irregular shifts commented on both the negative and positive aspects of having sole responsibility for their children. While solo care helped to build the father's confidence, it was experienced as stressful. One father likened his performance of child care when his wife was working evening shifts to being a single parent because he knew he had to do everything on his own. Other men described the forced responsibility of solo care as an "opportunity to be close" to their children. One father, a business administrator married to a nurse who worked a swing shift, commented on how the quality of his time with his children was different because he had to be "totally in charge" and "more in touch": "When she was gone working, whether it was a dirty diaper or a bath or a feeding or just sitting in a rocking chair with a bottle—you know, to me, I felt fortunate to have that opportunity. Some men just don't have a chance to spend time like that with their kids." He went on to talk about how the "forced" quality of his wife's absence could also work to his advantage.

> Sometimes I think it's a blessing that she works evenings and that I, on the nights that she works—five o'clock or five thirty at night, when there are a lot of people

that are still going to be at work for an hour or two more — I go "Adios!" (laughs) I mean I CAN'T stay, I've gotta pick up the kids. And there are times when I feel real guilty about leaving my fellow workers behind when I know they're gonna be there for another hour or so . . . About a block away from work I go, "God, this is great!" (laughs)

Husbands and wives with shift-worker spouses appreciated that their partner could be with the children during normal working hours, and this was often the rationale for taking an irregular shift in the first place. Nevertheless, they regretted that alternating child care limited the amount of time they had to be together as a couple or as an entire family. For instance, one mother talked about how hard it was for her when her husband first started going to work at 2:00 in the morning. "I used to be real irritated with his present job, especially when he first started it, because I never saw him. All we'd talk about was logistics, kids, and money. He worked seven days a week; he went to bed at 8 o'clock at night. There just wasn't enough time; I was highly irritated." She went on to describe how things have been better since he has been taking regular days off, and that they had instituted a routine of spending regular time together apart from the children, sometimes at one in the morning.

The ability to schedule flexibly one's work hours was especially important to the successful implementation of task sharing in the families we interviewed. Fully half the subjects exercised substantial control over the timing of their work hours. These included 20 percent who were self-employed and could regulate the amount of work they did to match their desired workload. A few of the self-employed worked primarily at home, allowing them to easily combine child care and employment. The remaining 30 percent with schedule flexibility had set work hours, but could change them with minimal trouble, like the nurses who could easily trade shifts with others, or the delivery man and the salesman who could vary their starting times by an hour or more. Another 25 percent worked regular hours, but could, with advance notice, occasionally alter their days or hours of work. The remaining 25 percent had no control over their work scheduling, and had to take sick time or vacation time if unexpected child care needs arose. It was this last group that complained most bitterly about the difficulties of balancing work and family.

As noted above, the spouse with the fewest employment hours did more of the household labor. The spouse with the most flexible hours also tended to do more of the housework and child care. Not incidentally, the two tended to coincide among this sample of dual-earners. As discussed in following chapters, differential earning capacity, along with differential investment in career, helps to determine who works more and who is most often home to do the housework and child care.

Financial Need and the Necessity of Two Jobs

Virtually all the couples vehemently stated that both spouses needed jobs for financial reasons. This was true for the upper-middle-income couples as well as the low-middle and lower-income couples. Most families had little disposable income, and over half owned their own homes. Most admitted that accumulating money was not a major goal. The highest paid husband we interviewed commented, "People who make a lot of money die with a lot of money . . . and they don't live a whole lot better than people with a little less money." Similarly, one of the lowest paid husbands commented, "You can always make more money, but, what the hell, who needs it! I mean, what good is it gonna do you if you're miserable. That's why I'm not crazy about goin' out and makin' a bunch of money. I've done it before and I was a lot unhappier than I am now." Couples thus characterized themselves as more concerned with family well-being than with material gain.

Financial need was cited by most couples as the primary motivation for the wife taking a job in the first place. In almost every family, there was also a taken-for-granted attitude about the wife's continued employment. Even though both spouses talked about the timing of the wife's return to work, or her choice of a particular job, they rarely felt compelled to justify the need for her employment or to frame the discussion in terms of a "decision" to work. Rather, it was assumed that mothers would be employed for both financial and personal reasons. I return to issues about the meaning of breadwinning and homemaking in the next chapter.

Managing versus Helping

Divisions of household labor in these families looked relatively balanced when we asked each spouse to sort household task cards into piles according to who performed the tasks. Compared to most American households, fathers were making substantial contributions. It took further questioning to determine who took responsibility for planning and initiating various domestic activities. In every family there were at least six frequently performed household chores over which the mother retained almost exclusive managerial control. That is, mothers noticed when the chore needed doing and made sure that someone performed it according to her standards. In general, mothers were more likely than fathers to act as managers for cooking, cleaning and child care, but over half the couples in this select sample shared responsibility in these areas too. Because we selected families on the basis of sharing child care, it was not too surprising that all the fathers were responsible for initiating and managing at least a few chores traditionally performed by mothers.

Based on the couples' descriptions of their strategies for allocating and performing household labor, I classified 12 as sharing the responsibility and eight as reflecting "manager-helper" dynamics. Helper husbands often waited to be told by their wives what to do, when to do it, and how it should be done. While they invariably expressed a desire to perform their "fair share" of housekeeping and childrearing, they were less likely than other fathers to assume responsibility for anticipating and planning these activities. Husbands of manager wives often referred to their contributions as "helping," symbolically indicating that the task remained in the mother's domain, even if the father occasionally performed it.

When asked what they liked most about their husband's housework, the sharing mothers focused on their husband's self-responsibility: voluntarily doing the work without being prodded. They commented, "He does the everyday stuff" and "I don't have to ask him." Other mothers praised their husbands for particular skills with comments such as "I love his spaghetti" or "He's great at cleaning the bathroom." In spite of such praise, many of both sharing and managing mothers said that what bothered them most about their husband's housework was the need to remind him to perform certain tasks. Many also complained of having to "train him" to correctly perform the chores, even if he eventually began to take responsibility for the task. Before assuming that this is always a gender-linked pattern, consider that a third of the fathers I interviewed also complained that their wives either didn't notice when things should be done or that *their* standards were too low.

Some mothers found it difficult to share authority for household management. For instance, one mother said, "There's a certain control you have when you do the shopping and the cooking and I don't know if I'm ready to relinquish that control." Another mother, an elementary school teacher who shared most child care and housework with her husband, admitted that "in general, household organization is something that I think I take over." In discussing how they divide housework, she commented on how she noticed more than her husband did. "He does what he sees needs to be done. That would include basic cleaning kinds of things. However, there are some detailed kinds of things that he doesn't see that I feel need to be done, and in those cases I have to ask him to do things. . . . He thinks some of the details are less important and I'm not sure, that might be a difference between men and women." Like many of the mothers who maintained a managerial position in the household, this mother attributed an observed difference in domestic perceptiveness to an essential difference between women and men. By contrast, mothers who did not act as household managers were unlikely to link housecleaning styles to essential gender differences.

Many mothers talked about adjusting their housecleaning standards over the course of their marriage and trying to feel less responsible for being "the perfect homemaker." By partially relinquishing managerial duties and accepting their husband's housecleaning standards, some mothers reported that they were able to do less daily housework and focus more on occasional thorough cleaning or adding "finishing touches." This fits with some researchers' findings that wives with lower standards have husbands who do more housework.[39] In my study, the nurse married to the newspaper delivery man said,

> He'll handle the surface things no problem, and I get down and do the nitty gritty. And I do it when it bugs me or when I have the time. It's not anything that we talk about usually. Sometimes if I feel like things are piling up, he'll say, "Well, make me a list," and I will. And he'll do it. There are some things that he just doesn't notice and that's fine; he handles the day-to-day stuff. . . . He'll do things, like for me cleaning off the table—for him it's getting everything off it—for me it's putting the tablecloth on, putting the flowers on, putting the candles on. That's the kind of stuff I do and I like doing that, it's not that I want him to start.

This list-making mother illustrates how responsibility for managing housework can stay in the mother's domain, even when the father does more of the actual tasks. In this case, she was concerned with what she labeled "a woman's touch." When she did things like arranging flowers or putting out candles, it helped her to feel like she "was still the mom," that she was performing special tasks for the family that only a woman could provide.

Responsibility for managing child care, in contrast to housework, was more likely to be shared among couples we interviewed. Planning and initiating "direct" child care—including supervision, discipline, and play—was typically an equal enterprise. Sharing responsibility for "indirect" child care—including clothing, cleaning, and feeding the children—was less common, but was still shared in over half the families. That fathers tended to assume responsibility for routine childrearing contrasts with findings from other studies showing that mothers, regardless of whether they are employed, carry 90 percent of the burden of responsibility for child care.[40] When they cooked, cleaned, or tended to the children, the fathers I interviewed did not talk of "helping" the mother. Instead, they considered the tasks and the worry as equally their burden. For example, one father described how he and his wife divided both direct and indirect child care. "My philosophy is that they are my children and everything is my responsibility, and I think she approaches it the same way too. So when something needs to be done it's whoever is close does it. Whoever it is convenient for. And we do keep a sense of what the other's recent efforts are, and try to provide some balance, but without actually counting how many times you've done this and I've done that."

Despite efforts to relinquish total control over managing home and children, mothers were more likely than fathers to report that they would be embarrassed if unexpected company came over and the house was a mess. When asked to compare themselves directly to their spouse, both mothers and fathers tended to report that the mother would be more embarrassed than the father. Some mothers reported emotional reactions to the house being a mess that were similar to those they experienced when their husbands "dressed the kids funny." The women were more likely to focus on the children "looking nice," particularly when they were going to be seen in public. Mothers' greater embarrassment over the kemptness of home or children can be seen as reflecting the extent to which mothering is viewed as part of women's essential nature.[41]

Some of the mothers reported that relinquishing control over the management of home and children made them uncomfortable because it entailed accepting their husbands' "looser" standards. Since other people continued to assume that the home was the woman's responsibility, these mothers feared negative judgments and reported feeling guilty if the house was "too messy." Those who relinquished full control over household management, in contrast, often reported that their husbands already had similar housekeeping standards. Alternately, mothers reported that through negotiations with their husbands, one or both of them adjusted their standards so that an agreed-on level of cleanliness was mutually maintained.

Adult Socialization Through Childrearing

Parents were engaged in creating and sustaining a shared world view through the joint performance and evaluation of childrearing.[42] Most reported that parenting was their primary topic of conversation, exemplified by one father's comment, "That's what we mostly discuss when we're not with our kids—either when we're going to sleep or when we have time alone—is how we feel about how we're taking care of them." Others commented that their spouse helped them to recognize unwanted patterns of interaction, often inherited from their own parents, and to work to change them. For instance, one father remarked,

> I'm not sure I could do it as a one-parent family, cause I wouldn't have the person, the other person saying, "Hey, look at that, that's so much like what you do with your own family." In a one-parent family, you don't have that, you don't have the other person putting out that stuff, you have to find it all out on your own, and I'm not sure you can.

Like the couple above, many parents we talked to were self-consciously trying to improve their parenting and their marital interaction. Many used popular psychological jargon to describe how they were "getting in touch with" their emotions, "transcending dysfunctional communication" patterns, and "working on" various aspects of their relationships with spouse and children.

The men often talked about significant personal changes that were brought about by becoming active fathers. Like Gary Carter, the contractor described in the first chapter, many fathers described how hands-on parenting experiences helped them to develop increased sensitivity. Gary talked about learning how to pay more attention to the details of his children's lives and to anticipate when they might get cranky or encounter difficulty with another child. This was accomplished, according to many shared parenting couples, when fathers were left alone with their children on a regular basis.

Recognition of increased sensitivity on the part of the fathers, and their enhanced competence as parents, were typically evaluated with reference to adopting a vocabulary of motives and feelings similar to the mothers'. This vocabulary of caring and concern was created and sustained through an ongoing dialogue about the children, which, in turn, grew out of the practice of routine child care. For example, one father recounted how when he spent little time with his children, he wasn't "tuned in."

> I didn't always hear the kids calling right away, it would maybe take two or three times before I actually noticed what was going on. But more and more, I think that's changed. It used to be I never heard, or I might not notice what they were doing, or I might not understand what the broader implication of whatever they were doing was, you know, at the time it was happening. I didn't even notice that. And now, I've become more in tune with what they're actually — you know how we should feel about it or how we should react to it. Before I tended to not put together certain things and now I try to focus more on what's going on.

This father's reflections show how the definition of "what's going on" is dependent on interaction with his wife. In the above passage, he starts to focus on his increased capacity to pay attention to his children and become "in tune with what they're actually [doing]." Before finishing the sentence, however, he substitutes "how we should feel" and "how we should react" for a more direct description of his children's behavior. In so doing, he measures his parental perceptiveness in his wife's terms. His talk reveals that his growing competence as a parent depends on his wife's definition of the situation. To the extent that he could learn to see what she saw, to react as she would, he judged himself and was judged by her to be a full and competent parent. This is another example of men "helping" their wives, insofar as this father had not moved beyond almost rote learning of his wife's parenting vocabulary and techniques. As we will see, however, other fathers we talked to had moved beyond the helper role and were espousing their own unique ways of parenting.

Another mother described how her husband had "the right temperament" for parenting, but had to learn how to notice the little things she felt her daughters needed.

> When it comes to the two of us as parents, I feel that my husband's parenting skills are probably superior to mine, just because of his calm rationale. But maybe that's not what little girls need all the time. He doesn't tend to be the one that tells them how gorgeous they look when they dress up, which they really like, and I see these things, I see when they're putting in a little extra effort. He's getting better as we grow in our relationship, as the kids grow in their relationship with him.

Of particular note in this account is the link between the couple relationship and the father–child relationship. Like many fathers in this study, this one was portrayed as developing sensitivity to the children by relying on interactions with his wife. She "sees things" that he has to learn to recognize. Thus, while he may have "superior" parenting skills, he must learn something subtle from her. His reliance on her expertise suggests that his "calm rationale" is insufficient to make him "maternal" in the way that she is. Her ability to notice things, and his inattention to them, serves to render them both accountable: parenting remains an essential part of her nature, but is a learned capacity for him. This example illustrates how the couples talked about fathers being socialized, as adults, to become nurturing parents. Sharing routine child care, and talking about it with their wives, helped to construct and sustain images of the father's competence.

As the men became more sensitive parents, their marital relationships often improved. As a result of learning how to care for their kids, some fathers also paid more attention to emotional cues from their wives and engaged in more reciprocal communication. One father exemplified a common pattern by noting that the sensitivity and vulnerability he learned from caring for his children on a regular basis enhanced his ability to "operate on a feeling level." By spending so much time talking about parenting together, couples were maintaining a positive focus on family life and sustaining their commitments to each other. The "spillover" effect of men's parenting on the couple relationship was not uniformly positive, however, as some of the men voiced complaints similar to those that housewives have made for years. For example, some men talked about the frustrations of being trapped in the house all day with no adult contact or the oppressive monotony of doing the same household task for the tenth time in the same day. Still, the couples tended to value the men's exposure to the hassles of daily family work because it gave them some insight into women's lives.

Both fathers and mothers also indicated that the mother's employment enhanced the marriage, in part because it, too, made their lives more similar than they would be if only the man worked away from home. Recall how Gary Carter could appreciate the effort it took for his wife to put on her "telephone voice" after an exhausting day at work. He understood the toll of balancing paid and family work, because he'd "been there" many times before. As other researchers have noted, similarity of wives' and husbands' daily worlds when both have extrafamilial jobs can promote understanding and solidarity in the marriage.[43] My interviews indicate that we should begin to focus on the potential impacts of similarity in family roles as well. When fathers and mothers both perform routine child care and housework, it can promote mutual understanding and enhance marital solidarity.

Putting oneself in another's position can increase one's understanding and acceptance of the other's predicaments, as evidenced by fathers like Gary

Carter who described the finer points of scrubbing bathtubs before he told me he feels like he never has enough time to do everything on his lists. Doing the housework helped most of the fathers understand what wives have faced by themselves in the past. Taking responsibility for routine family work also helped the men understand their mothers' lives. One involved father who did most of the housework suggested that he could sometimes derive pleasure from cleaning the bathroom or picking up a sock if he looked at it as an act of caring for his family.

> It makes it a different job, to place it in a context of being an expression of caring about a collective life together. It's at that moment that I'm maybe closest to understanding what my mother and other women of my mother's generation, and other women now, have felt about being housewives and being at home, being homemakers. I think I emotionally understand the satisfaction and the gratification of being a homemaker.

More frequently, however, sharing child care and housework helped fathers understand its drudgery. Most reported that they were growing more tolerant of little messes and imperfect meals, because they were now aware of the neverending cycles associated with everyday cleaning and cooking.

I was surprised to discover from the interviews that doing child care encouraged the men to do more housework. Earlier studies had shown that men tended to do visible leisurely activities with children, whereas mothers did virtually all the invisible, unwitnessed, and more drudging work related to child care.[44] In this study, fathers reported that performance of direct child care (or simple babysitting) tended to increase their commitment to doing more of the indirect child care and housework. Solo time with children was especially effective in getting men to notice more and to anticipate what needed doing. All the fathers in the study had been involved in some housework before the birth of their children, but their awareness of, and performance of, routine housework increased in conjunction with their involvement in parenting. They reported that as they spent more time in the house alone with their children, they noticed more about how they contributed to messes around the house and became more aware of the many small activities that add to housekeeping. As they spent more time at home with their children, they began to assume more responsibility for cooking, cleaning, and other support activities.

As wives spent more time away from home, and as they relinquished total responsibility for housekeeping, the men became more aware of household tasks and slowly became more willing (or at least more likely) to perform them. This was conditioned by the amount of time fathers spent on the job, but most reported that they increased their contributions to household labor during the time that their children were under 10 years old. This did not always mean that fathers' relative proportion of household tasks increased, because mothers were also doing more in response to an expanding total household workload when the children were young.

Gender Attributions

Approximately half of both mothers and fathers volunteered that men and women brought something unique to child care and many stressed that they did not consider their own parenting skills identical to those of their spouse. One woman whose husband had recently increased the amount of time he spent with their school-aged children commented, "Anybody can slap together a cream cheese and cucumber sandwich and a glass of milk and a few chips and call it lunch, but the ability to see that your child is troubled about something, or to be able to help them work through a conflict with a friend, that is really much different." Another mother who worked two nursing jobs explained that doing fewer hours of child care and housework than her husband did not change the fact that "she was the mother." As noted above, she enjoyed setting out flowers and candles after cleaning off the table, in contrast to her husband, who did more routine surface cleaning. She described herself as "more intimate and gentle," and her husband as "rough and out there." Like many parents, she emphasized that mothers and fathers provide "a balance" for their children. She said she came to terms with her expectation that her husband would "mother" the children by realizing that he was different.

> One of the things that I found I was expecting from him when he started doing so much here and I was gone so much, I was expecting him to mother the kids. And you know, I had to get over that one pretty quick and really accept him doing the things the way he did them as his way, and that being just fine with me. He wasn't mothering the kids, he was fathering the kids. It was just that he was the role of the mother as far as the chores and all that stuff.

Another mother who managed and performed most of the housework and child care used different reasoning to make similar claims about essential differences between women and men. In contrast to the mother above, this mother suggested that men could probably nurture as well as women, but that they might not be able to perform the routine everyday activities of parenting.

> Nurturance is one thing, actual care is another thing. I think if a father had to, like all of a sudden the wife was gone . . . he could nurture it with the love that it needed. But he might not change the diapers often enough, or he might not give 'em a bath often enough and he might not think of the perfect food to feed. But as far as nurturing, I think he's capable of caring. . . . If the situation is the mother is there and he didn't have to, then he would trust the woman to do it.

This mother went on to conclude that "the woman has it more in her genes to be more equipped for parenting." By defining women as inherently more capable of specific parenting behaviors, many of the manager-helper couples legitimated their conventional divisions of labor. These couples reaffirmed the "naturalness" of essential gender differences through their parenting practices and their talk about what the children needed and what each parent was "good at."

Parents who equally shared the responsibility for direct and indirect child care, on the other hand, were more likely to focus on the comparability of their parenting skills and similarities in their relationships with their children. For instance, they all reported that their children were emotionally "close" to both parents. When asked who his children went to when they were hurt or upset, one early and equal sharing father commented:

> They'll go to either of us, that is pretty indistinguishable. In fact it has long been the case that they'll address us and confuse us in addressing us. They'll say "Dad, I mean Mom," or "Mom, I mean Dad," and it has more to do with who they've been with for the last twenty-four hours. So they're hardly conscious of which one it is, in most cases.

Mothers and fathers who equally shared most of the child care commented that their children frequently addressed the mother "daddy" or the father "mommy" without realizing that they had done so. Children typically called for the parent they had most recently spent time with, using the gendered form to signify "parent." Almost all the responsibility-sharing couples (non-helpers) also reported that their children would go to either parent for comfort. Most often, parents indicated that their children would turn to "whoever's closest" or "whoever they've been with," thus linking physical closeness with emotional closeness. In-home observations of family interactions confirmed these reports, as we observed many of the shared parenting fathers comforting their children because of a scraped knee or hurt feelings.

Shared activities provided the basis for emotional connection between parent and child. If fathers spent substantial time alone with children, they became central emotional figures to them. Substantial "on-duty" time also contributed to the image of fathers as competent nurturing caregivers. Two-thirds of both mothers and fathers we talked to said that men could care for children's emotional needs as well as women.

When asked whether men, in general, could nurture like women, mothers frequently used their husbands as examples. One mother who had initially been reluctant to return to school because she had been the primary parent for the first few years was surprised at how she now thought that her husband was just as good a "mother" as she.

> I think, without a doubt, that men can nurture like women. In my case that's obvious. That's saying something because I trust him totally with the kids and I trust that whatever they need they could go to him and he could handle it. That's real different from just going through the motions. . . .

Other mothers, especially those who shared most child care, talked about how parenting was also something that women had to learn. One summarized a common view by saying, "I don't necessarily think that nurturing comes with a sex-type. Some women nurture better than others, some men nurture better than other men. I think that those skills can come when either person is willing to have the confidence and commitment to prioritize them." Not surprisingly, the parents who were most successful at sharing all aspects of child care were the most likely to claim that men could nurture like women. Those who sustained manager-helper dynamics in child care, in contrast, tended to invoke images of "maternal instincts" and alluded to natural differences between the parenting abilities of men and women.

What explains the link between parenting attitudes and behaviors and why was more sharing accompanied by an ideology of gender similarity? Based on the interviews, there are two likely explanations: (1) Those who believed that men could nurture like women seriously attempted to share all aspects of child care, and (2) Sharing child care facilitated the development of beliefs that men could nurture like women. In other words, it is too simple to claim that one thing simply caused the other. Instead, we ought to think of family work and gender ideals as mutually and simultaneously produced as people live their everyday lives.

Emerging Issues and Patterns

Interviews with this select group of families showed that some fathers can and do learn to perform duties traditionally ascribed to mothers. Previous studies of shared parenting used couples with younger children and found that even when fathers actively participated, they did not assume full responsibility for planning and initiating child care.[45] In contrast, my sample included families with school-aged children, and over half of the fathers assumed major responsibility for planning and initiating housework and child care. Like previous studies, however, I did find that most men also needed prompting and reminders from their wives. What accounts for the higher level of sharing in the couples observed for this study? I will explore various underlying causal forces in subsequent chapters, but the couples themselves identified many straightforward reasons for their sharing child care and housework.

All couples described flexible and practical task-allocation procedures that were responses to shortages of time. All families were child centered in that they placed a high value on their children's well-being, defined parenting as an important and serious undertaking, and organized most of their non-employed time around their children. Besides being well educated and delaying childbearing until their late twenties or early thirties, couples who shared most of the responsibility for household labor tended to involve the father in routine child care from early infancy. Those who shared the most were also the most likely to talk about men and women as essentially similar. Those who shared less, in contrast, tended to attribute special skills and intuitions to women and mothers.

Regardless of the extent of sharing or the timing of the fathers' assumption of domestic duties, both fathers and mothers reported that the practice of child care, in itself, transformed the men. Through interaction with their children and, in concert, plenty of talk with their spouse, parents constructed images of fathers as sensitive and nurturing caregivers. The couples were "doing gender" through direct and indirect child care.[46] As Sara Ruddick has noted, the everyday aspects of child care and housework help shape ways of thinking, feeling, and acting that become associated with what it means to be a mother.[47] My findings suggest that when domestic activities are shared equally, "maternal thinking" develops in fathers as well as mothers, and the social meaning of gender begins to change.

This social constructionist approach deemphasizes perceived differences in the personalities of men and women and locates gender in everyday practices and social interaction. What it means to "mother," or to be a "real man," is not fixed in stone, but slowly shifts as new patterns of household labor are negotiated in countless families. In the next chapters, I begin to explore how divisions of family work change in response to larger social forces and how individual choices help to transform the overall meaning of gender and family.

4

Providing and Caring

One of the most popular slang terms to emerge in the 1980s was "macho," used to describe men prone to combative posturing, relentless sexual conquest, and other compulsive displays of masculinity. Macho men continually guard against imputations of being soft or feminine and thus tend to avoid house-work and family activities that are considered "women's work." Macho comes from the Spanish "machismo," and although the behaviors associated with it are not limited to one ethnic group, Latino men are often stereotyped as especially prone toward macho displays.

To explore the possible impact of macho stereotypes on men's family partici-pation, and to add some diversity to our knowledge about fathers, I turn to Latino couples and their allocation of family work. Most of what we know about life in American families comes from studies of white middle-class couples and their children. When ethnic minority families were studied in the past, the focus was typically on their supposed shortcomings. More recently, social scientists have studied African-American, Asian-American, Native-American, and Latino families to understand their strengths as well as their weaknesses. Following this new trend, I decided to interview a group of Mexican-American couples in Southern California to see how they divided family work in the 1990s.[1]

Research on Mexican-American Families

Mexican-Americans (called Chicanos in many parts of the southwestern United States) are often stereotyped as living in poor farmworker families with many children. But popular images of Chicanos are changing, as diverse groups of people with Mexican and Latin-American heritage respond to the same sorts of social and economic pressures faced by families of other ethnic backgrounds. For example, most Chicano families in the United States now live in urban centers or their suburbs, rather than in rural farming areas. And the label "minority" will not even fit in a few years. Because of higher than average birthrates and continued in-migration from Mexico and Latin America, by the year 2015, Hispanic children will outnumber Anglos in many southwest states including California, Texas, Arizona, and New Mexico.[2]

In early research by social scientists, as well as in popular imagery, Mexican-American families were characterized as rigidly patriarchal. The father was seen as having full authority over mother and children, and wives were described as passive, submissive, and dependent.[3] William Madsen emphasized the destructive aspects of Mexican-American *machismo* by comparing the men to roosters. "The better man is the one who can drink more, defend himself best, have more sex relations, and have more sons borne by his wife."[4] According to such depictions, Chicano men were aloof and authoritarian, and rarely participated in the everyday tasks of running a household.

In contrast, some contemporary Chicano scholars reject such stereotypes as inaccurate and unfair. The sociologist Alfrédo Mirandé, for example, suggests that within the Chicano community, *machismo* can imply respect, loyalty, responsibility, and generosity, in addition to the term's more perjorative implications. Mirandé reports that Chicano fathers participate more actively in child care than the old macho stereotypes imply, even if they continue to do less family work than their wives.[5] Some recent research on marital interaction in Chicano families also supports the notion that gender relations are more egalitarian than the traditional model assumes. Studies of marital decision-making have found that a large percentage of Mexican-American couples, especially those in which both spouses are employed, regard their decision-making as relatively shared and equal.[6]

Most researchers agree, however, that marital roles are not truly equal in Mexican-American households, even when both spouses work outside the home.[7] (Neither are they equal in two-job Anglo-American households.) Because Mexican cultural ideals require the male to be honored and respected as the head of the family, Maxine Baca Zinn contends that Chicano families maintain a facade of patriarchy while mothers assume authority over day-to-day household activities.[8] Like other contemporary scholars, she warns against analyzing racial ethnic families using a deficit model that treats them as backward or culturally deviant. Instead, she suggests that families are not the product of ethnic culture alone and that social context and employment opportunities give rise to diverse family forms among Chicanos or any other ethnic group.[9]

Most of what we know about minority families is mixed up with social class. When family researchers study white couples, they typically focus on middle-class suburban households and highlight their strengths. Studies of ethnic minority families, in contrast, tend to focus on the problems of poor or working-class households. Research that includes both majority and minority families often attributes any observed differences to ethnicity, yet ignores important factors like the economic standing of the family, whether the wife is employed, and how recently they immigrated to the United States. Although many observers continue to rely on simple cultural stereotypes like "machismo" to explain Chicano family patterns, we have yet to understand how gender, employment, and cultural ideals combine to influence life in these families.[10]

We do know that Mexican-American families have higher than average birthrates and household size. Many researchers also suggest that they are more family focused than other households, using terms like "familism" to describe how collective family needs take precedence over individual or personal needs.[11] When compared to African-Americans and Anglo-Americans of various class levels, Mexican-American families in the United States also have the highest levels of co-residence between generations. Chicano couples with limited resources sometimes double up in houses or apartments with their own parents or with other relatives, although extended families are less common than stereotypes suggest.[12] Regardless of ethnicity, most married couples in the United States today choose to live in a household with just their children if they can afford to do so.

Few researchers have investigated how cultural ideals of family-centeredness or machismo might effect divisions of household labor in modern Mexican-American families. When I embarked on this research, I wondered how contemporary Chicano couples would talk about commitments to their families, and how wives' employment and other factors would shape parenting and housework. The interviews summarized in this chapter provide some insight into these issues and frame some larger questions about gender, resources, and family power that are discussed in later chapters.

Interviews with Two-Job Families

As in the earlier study, we contacted dual-earner couples through word-of-mouth referrals and interviewed mothers and fathers separately.[13] To correct for omissions in previous studies of dual-career or minority families, we recruited middle-class two-job Chicano couples with at least one school-aged child.[14] Since the majority of Latino two-job families in the United States comprise husbands and wives with service sector jobs, we began by interviewing white-collar workers (e.g., secretaries, clerks, social workers).[15] In addition, we interviewed some people who held jobs that were working class (e.g., mechanic, laborer, painter) or professional (e.g., attorney, teacher, administrator).[16] We screened potential couples on the basis of husband and wife both holding jobs, rather than on any statements they made about sharing domestic tasks.[17]

The Chicano husbands and wives tended to be in their mid-thirties with children of preschool and school age. Compared to those in the first interview study, these couples had younger children, more diversity in family size, earlier and longer marriages, and more church attendance.[18] Most lived in suburban neighborhoods, though a quarter lived in smaller rural towns. Few were first-generation immigrants and most had lived in southern California for their entire lives.[19] Virtually all considered themselves middle class, but almost all had parents who were working class.[20]

I used the same general interview, observation, and card sorting procedures as before, but added questions on extended family relations and ethnic identity. Elsa Valdez and I asked husbands and wives who initiated various tasks, who set standards for their performance, and whether they felt that their division of family work was fair. It was evident from the initial card sorting that wives were responsible for most housework and many child-care tasks, and that husbands did mostly outside work and shared some child care. These findings are not surprising. The Chicano couples shared somewhat less than the couples in the first study, in part because they had younger children and in part because they were not selected based on egalitarian self-identification. As in the first interviews, however, many more tasks were shared than in the hypothetical "average" family. Also like the families described in the last chapter, many domestic tasks were still allocated according to conventional gender expectations.

Table 4.1 shows wives' and husbands' perceptions of who did which family tasks. The two spouses' ratings are listed separately to illustrate how they saw things differently. For housecleaning, wives rated themselves as doing most of the vacuuming, mopping, sweeping, dusting, cleaning sinks, cleaning toilets, cleaning tubs, making beds, picking up toys, tidying the living room, hanging up clothes, and spring cleaning. Wives listed only cleaning the porch and washing windows as shared, and indicated that husbands most often took out the trash. Husbands also listed trash as their chore, but rated more tasks as equally shared than as being done by their wives.

A similar pattern was evident for meal preparation and clean-up. Wives listed all tasks in this area as being performed by themselves, with the exception of putting food away, which was listed as shared. Husbands again placed almost half the tasks in the shared pile, with many of the less time-consuming tasks being rated as being performed by husbands and wives about equally. Such tasks included putting food away, preparing lunch, making snacks, putting dishes away, and wiping kitchen counters. Both

Table 4.1. Wives' and Husbands' Perceptions of Domestic Task Performance

	Wife's Perception			Husband's Perception		
	Wife More	Both Equally	Husband More	Wife More	Both Equally	Husband More
House Cleaning	Vacuum Mop Sweep Dust Clean sinks Clean toilets Clean tubs Make beds Pick up toys Tidy living room Hang up clothes Spring cleaning	Clean porch Wash windows	Take out trash	Mop Sweep Dust Clean toilets Make beds Hang up clothes	Clean porch Wash windows Vacuum Clean sinks Clean tub Pick up Toys Tidy living room Spring cleaning	Take out trash
Meal Preparation and Clean-Up	Plan menus Prepare breakfast Prepare lunch Cook dinner Make snacks	Put food away		Plan menus Prepare breakfast Cook dinner Bake Wash dishes	Put food away Prepare lunch Make snacks Put dishes away Wipe kitchen counters	

Bake
Wash dishes
Put dishes away
Wipe kitchen counters
Grocery shop

Clothes Care

Laundry
Hand laundry
Shoe care
Sew
Buy clothes

Iron

Home Maintenance and Repairs

Redecorate

General yardwork
Water lawn
Mow lawn
Garden
Interior painting
Exterior painting
Clean rain gutters

House repairs
Car maintenance
Car repairs
Wash car

Grocery shop

Laundry
Hand laundry
Sew
Buy clothes

Iron
Shoe care

Redecorate
Clean rain gutters

House repairs
Car maintenance
Car repairs
Wash car
General yardwork
Water lawn
Mow lawn
Garden
Interior painting
Exterior painting

(continued)

Table 4.1. Wives' and Husbands' Perceptions of Domestic Task Performance (continued)

	Wife's Perception			Husband's Perception		
	Wife More	Both Equally	Husband More	Wife More	Both Equally	Husband More
Finances and Home Management						
	Run errands	Prepare taxes		Pay bills	Run errands	
	Pay bills	Make investments		Contact relatives/friends	Prepare taxes	
		Handle insurance			Make investments	
		Decide major purchases			Handle insurance	
		Plan couple dates			Decide major purchases	
		Contact relatives/friends			Plan couple dates	
Child Care						
	Put children to bed	Supervise children		Awaken children	Put children to bed	
	Awaken Children	Discipline children		Help children dress	Drive children	
	Help children dress	Play with children		Help children bathe	Supervise children	
	Help children bathe	Plan outings with children		Take child to doctor	Discipline children	
	Drive children			Care for sick child	Play with children	
	Take child to doctor			Arrange babysitting	Plan outings with children	
	Care for sick child					
	Arrange babysitting					

husbands and wives indicated that wives were primarily responsible for planning menus, preparing breakfast, cooking dinner, baking, washing dishes, and shopping for groceries.

The discrepancies between husbands' and wives' accounts were much smaller in the area of clothes care, primarily because both agreed that wives did almost all of it. Wives were rated as performing the laundry, the hand laundry, the sewing, and purchasing clothes. In an unexpected finding, both husbands and wives listed ironing as a shared activity. This was the only stereotypically "feminine" housework task that was consistently ranked as shared. Few of the Anglo men in the first study shared ironing with their wives, but among the Chicano couples, even the women considered this a shared activity. Wanting the entire family to appear well-dressed in public, especially on Sundays, motivated some men to iron their own clothes and sometimes also their children's and their wives' clothes. Ironing is also a task that some men reported they could do while watching sports on television.

The same general trend observed for housework was also evident for child care. Here, both spouses listed more tasks as shared, but husbands listed as many tasks in the equal column as in the wife's column. In contrast, wives listed only supervising, disciplining, playing with, and planning outings with the children as shared activities. Husbands said that putting children to bed and driving them places were also shared activities. Bodily care aspects of childrearing, including getting children up in the morning, monitoring bathing, helping them dress, taking them to the doctor, tending them when sick, and arranging for babysitters, were all listed by both spouses as the province of the wife.

Similar discrepancies were evident between spousal reports for tasks traditionally considered "manly" activities. Wives listed 7 of 12 home maintenance and repair tasks as performed equally by both spouses, and one — redecorating — as performed principally by themselves. Husbands, in contrast, listed only two tasks as shared, with all others listed as being performed principally by themselves.

In the area of finances and household management, both spouses listed 6 of 8 tasks as shared, and two in the wife's domain. Both spouses listed paying bills as being primarily the wife's task. Wives saw themselves as running errands more often, whereas husbands considered errands to be an equally shared activity. Wives indicated that spouses shared phoning and writing relatives and friends, but husbands saw wives as being primarily responsible for these social and "kin-keeping" activities. This was the only task that men listed as performed by wives more often than the wives themselves did. Perhaps because keeping contact with kin has been stereotyped as the wife's obligation in both Chicano and Anglo families, men overestimated their wife's efforts and underestimated their own.

To summarize, wives thought they had sole or primary responsibility for many more housework and child-care tasks than their husbands gave them credit for and husbands thought they had more responsibility for outside work than their wives gave them credit for. Disagreement was especially likely for frequently performed tasks of short duration that were stereotyped as being women's work or men's work.

Living in Separate Worlds

Looking at the patterns of disagreement described above, we could say that husbands and wives were living in different worlds.[21] In fact, this view might shed some light on what happens with family work in most families. The sociologist Jesse Bernard suggests that every marital union actually contains two distinct marriages—"his" and "hers."[22] Because the activities, rights, duties, and obligations of husbands and wives are so different, spouses often experience married life as two separate realities.

His marriage and her marriage are different because of historical conventions and power inequities as discussed in Chapter 2, but seeing family work differently also comes from some routine biases in perception. Social psychologists have documented how vivid and rare events are more likely to be recalled than common, everyday events.[23] What could be more mundane than wiping the kitchen counter or putting away the dishes? Routine housework activities are therefore not likely to be precisely attended to, stored in memory, or quickly retrieved. If, however, one rarely performs such activities, the tasks can become more salient. Thus, some men remember every housecleaning or child-related task they perform because these events are more vivid to them. Similarly, women might remember changing the oil or mowing the lawn precisely because these are relatively rare events for them. Whether one performs the tasks or not, however, both inside and outside household chores are relatively unremarkable, which makes them more difficult to recall precisely. This increases the chances that a second type of perceptual distortion might come into play.

Another cognitive tendency is for memory distortions or miscalculations to be ego-enhancing. That is, we are likely to remember those things that make us look good, and forget those that make us look bad.[24] For women, family work is routine, but they typically know what needs to be done and feel good about themselves when the work fulfills the needs of other family members. Depending on whether they feel better about being the only one who does the work, or having a husband who helps, they are subject to different bias in their estimates of who does what. For example, consider a hypothetical household in which the husband and wife spend equal time on cooking, but her efforts are concentrated on serving hot "sit-down" meals and his efforts are focused on shopping, washing and chopping vegetables, stocking the refrigerator with lunch and snack foods, and packaging leftovers for later consumption. If the woman's self-image is based on the caring and feeding that she performs during family meals, she is likely to "see" her cooking contribution as greater than her husband's. If, on the other hand, her self-evaluation is more dependent on being a woman who shares the kitchen work, she will "see" his contribution as equal to her own.

For men, doing family work is typically less routine than it is for women, so when they do it, it is likely to be relatively vivid or salient. If they are involved in smoldering chore wars and agree they should do more of it, they are even more likely to overestimate their domestic contributions, for it enhances their self-image as an involved and caring husband. Some of the wives we talked to complained that their husbands remembered every time they made a small contribution to kitchen clean-up, but hardly noticed the countless times the women shopped, chopped, cooked, cleaned, washed, and tidied the kitchen. In reporting who does what, men and women thus tend to focus more on their own activities, because these things are ego-enhancing and cognitively more available.

Men are likely to give extra weight to the rare housework tasks they perform, but what about those that they don't notice? Because men usually don't have reponsibilty for initiating housework and because their identity is not usually tied to doing it, they often don't pay much attention to it in the first place. The most common complaint heard from both Anglo and Chicano wives was that husbands "just didn't see" when things needed doing or take responsibility for initiating the important details of housekeeping. Most wives thus remained in control of setting schedules and generating lists for domestic chores. Unfamiliar with the details of running the household, men were likely to underestimate their wives' contributions and to escape the full range of tensions and strains that come with the second shift of family work. By "not seeing" what needed to be done, and missing the full extent of their wife's contributions, the men enjoyed a privileged position in many of the families we interviewd (even though most of them "saw" more than the average husband).

Although the Chicano couples did not agree on which tasks were shared, they independently reported that their current arrangements fell short of being fair. Because previous studies have found that even unbalanced divisions of labor are labeled "fair" by husbands and wives, I was surprised that these couples said things were unfair. After sorting the task cards, some of the men noticed that their wife's pile dwarfed their own, with one commenting, "Gee, I guess I don't do as much as I thought." Seeing many more cards in her pile did not fit with their ideal that things *should* be shared, so some men may have been encouraged to acknowledge that things were unequal. When asked directly, most wives did not think of their divisions of labor as fair, yet few expected much change in the future. Housework, in particular, was viewed as a mundane burden that they had to shoulder alone or seek help with, simply because they were women.

Ranking the Amount of Sharing

Though husbands and wives saw things differently and work was divided in relatively conventional ways, some noticeable shifts in work and family responsibilities were underway in these families. I averaged the husband-wife scores for each task so that I could compare across families and figure out why some couples shared more than others.[25] I combined the various tasks associated with housecleaning, meal preparation, meal clean-up, and clothes care into a single housework measure and used the 12 child-related tasks to form an overall measure of child care. Fathers uniformly spent more time in direct interaction with their children than their own fathers had with them, but fewer than half of the individual child-care tasks were ranked as shared when husbands' and wives' ratings were averaged. In the more traditional families, the wives still exercised control over all child care and reported that they were responsible for facilitating father–child interaction. In other families, however, the fathers themselves initiated and sustained regular contact with their children. In some cases, fathers' commitments to spend more time with their children created work/family conflicts that we typically associate only with mothers. At least some child-care tasks were shared in every family and a few families even divided responsibility for the children about in half.

Looking at housework, as well as child care, I focused the analysis on why some men were sharing more of the planning and performance of tasks conventionally assumed by women. One of the important issues that emerged was the extent to which wives were defined as sharing the economic provider role with their husbands. After presenting some theoretical ideas about how paid work and family work fit together, I turn to the interviews with the Chicano couples.

The families we interviewed did not think of themselves as having chosen to become two-job families. Like the couples in previous studies, they were simply responding to financial necessity. Few couples talked about the joys of sharing either market or household labor, and few mentioned that they were motivated to share family work because they wanted to change gender roles in the larger society. Most husbands talked as though they were coerced into their present arrangements with comments like "we were pretty much forced into it" and "we didn't really have any choice."

According to most social science explanations, paid work and family work should influence each other, yet we do not understand exactly how and why this is so. As discussed in Chapter 6, "new" home economics theories assume that family members allocate responsibility for various tasks based on "tastes" for certain types of work and the underlying desire to maximize benefits for the entire family unit. Efficiency is supposed to be the driving force behind why women do most of the housework, though there is some question why it is "efficient" to pay women lower wages for similar work in the wage-labor market.[26] Feminist and structural conflict theories assume that all family members' needs are not equally served by conventional task allocation, and that responsibility for housework can be seen as a measure of women's oppression.[27] Finally, most social role theories suggest that the boundaries between work and family are "asymmetrically permeable," with men's paid work excusing them from family obligations, but women's family commitments allowed to intrude on their work roles.[28] All three of these theoretical approaches assume that changes in paid work will promote shifts in family work, but most empirical studies have not been able to isolate how and why.

To understand the interplay of work, family, and gender, the sociologist Jane Hood suggests that we must accurately measure the economic provider role. Her assumption is that divisions of paid and unpaid labor are shaped by gender-linked notions of who is responsibile for providing financially for the family and who is responsible for direct care to family members.[29] According to Hood, only when wives are accepted as economic providers will husbands assume more of the parent/homemaker role.[30] We looked at this issue by asking husbands and wives how they felt about performing paid work and family work.

Although all the Chicano husbands and three-fourths of the Chicana wives we interviewed were employed full time, the couples varied in the extent to which they accepted the wife as a co-provider. By considering the employment and earnings of each spouse, along with each spouses' attitudes toward the provider role, I divided the twenty families into two general groups: main providers and co-providers.[31] As Hood predicts, this distinction, with minor variations, makes a big difference in who does what around the house.

Main Provider Families

In almost half the families, husbands made substantially more money than wives and assumed that men should be primary breadwinners and women should be responsible for home and children. Families were categorized as main providers because they generally considered the wife's job secondary and treated her income as "extra" money to be earmarked for special purposes.[32] One main provider husband said, "I would prefer that my wife did not have to work, and could stay at home with my daughter, but finances just don't permit that." Another commented that his wife made just about enough to cover the costs of child care, suggesting that the children were still her primary responsibility, and that any wages she earned should first be allocated to cover "her" tasks.

The main provider couples included all five wives who were employed part time, and three wives who worked in lower status full-time jobs. Wives in these families made substantially less money than their husbands, contributing an average of 20 percent to the total family income. In main provider households, wives took pride in the homemaker role and readily accepted responsibility for managing the household. One part-time bookkeeper married to a law clerk studying for the bar described their division of labor by saying, "It's a given that I take care of children and housework, but when I am real tired, he steps in willingly." Husbands typically remained in a helper role: in this case, the law clerk told his wife, "Just tell me what to do and I'll do it." He said that if he came home and she was gone, he might clean house, but that if she was home, he would "let her do it." Neither spouse questioned the underlying obligation of the wife to be in charge of making sure that daily family needs were taken care of. She was the household manager and he was a helper.

The lawyer-to-be was very conscious of the difference in occupational status between he and his wife, even though he had not yet reached his full potential earnings. He talked about early marital negotiations that seemed to set the tone for some smoldering arguments and resentments about housework that both he and his wife hinted were always present.

> When we were first married, I would do something and she wouldn't like the way that I did it. So I would say, "OK, then, you do it, and I won't do it again." That was like in our first few years of marriage when we were first getting used to each other, but now she doesn't discourage me so much. She knows that if she does, she's going to wind up doing it herself.

His resistance and her reluctance to press for change reflected an economy of gratitude that was as unbalanced as their household division of labor. When he occasionally contributed to housework or child care, she was indebted to him. She complimented him for being willing to step in when she asked for help, but privately lamented that she had to negotiate for each small contribution. Firmly entrenched in the main provider role and somewhat oblivious to the daily rituals of housework and child care, he felt justified in needing encouragement. When she did ask him for help, she was careful to thank him for dressing the children or for giving her a 10-minute break from them. While these patterns of family work and inequities in the exchange of gratitude were long-standing, tension lurked just below the surface. He commented, "My wife gets uptight with me for agreeing to help out my mom, [because] she feels she can't even ask me to go to the store for her."

Another main provider couple reflected a similar pattern of labor allocation, and claimed that the arrangement was fair to them both. The woman, a part-time teacher's aide, acknowledged that she loved being a wife and mother and "naturally" took charge of managing the household. She commented, "I have the say-so on the running of the house, and I also decide on the children's activities." Although she had a college degree, she described her current part-time job as ideal for her. She was able to work 20 hours per week at a neighborhood school and was home by the time her children returned home from their school. While she earned only $6,000 per year, she justified the low salary because the job fit so well with "the family's" schedule. Her husband's administrative job allowed them to live comfortably since he earned $48,000 annually.

This secondary provider wife sorted the household task cards in a conventional manner: Her piles contained all the cleaning, cooking, clothes-care, and child-care tasks, while his piles included yard work, home repairs, finances, and home management. Her major complaints were that her husband didn't notice things and that he created more work for her. "The worst part about housework and child care is the amount of nagging I have to do to get him to help. Also, for example, say I just cleaned the house; he will leave the newspaper scattered all over the place or he will leave wet towels on the bathroom floor." When asked whether there had been any negotiation over who would do which chores, the husband responded, "I don't think a set decision was made, it was a necessity." His wife's response was similar, "It just evolved that way, we never really talked about it."

His provider role was taken for granted, but occasionally she voiced some muted resentment. For example, she commented that she gets discouraged and upset when he tells her that she should not be working because their youngest child is just five years old. Additionally, she mentioned in passing that she was sometimes bothered by the fact that she had not been able to further her career, or work overtime, since that would interfere with "the family's" schedule.

Wives of main providers not only performed virtually all the housework and child care, but both spouses accepted this as "natural" or "normal." The wife's commitment to outside employment was generally limited, and her income was considered supplemental. The husbands' few domestic contributions were seen as aiding the wife and he took more credit for his housework contributions than his wife was willing to grant him. Another main provider husband admitted, "She tells me to do lotsa things, but whatever she tells me to do, then I do half." The husbands in main provider couples consistently failed to see most of the details of running the household, and since they were not "supposed" to be responsible for such tasks, they were rarely challenged by wives to redefine housework as their responsibility.

Main provider husbands assumed that financial support was their duty. When one man was asked how it felt to make more money than his wife, he responded by saying: "It's my job, I wouldn't feel right if I didn't make more money. . . . Any way that I look at it, I have to keep up my salary, or I'm not doing my job. If it costs $40,000 to live nowadays and I'm not in a $40,000-a-year job, then I'm not gonna be happy." This same husband, a small-town auto mechanic and shop manager, worked between 50 and 60 hours every week. His comments revealed how main provider husbands sometimes felt threatened when women began asserting themselves in previously all-male occupations.

As long as women mind their own business, no problem with me, you know. If you get a secretary that's nosy and wants to run the company, hey, well, we tell her where to stick it. . . . There's nothing wrong with them being in the job, but when you can't do my job, don't tell me how to do it.

The mechanic's wife, also a part-time teacher's aide, subtly resisted by "spending as little time on housework as I can get away with." Nevertheless, she still considered it her sole duty to cook, and only when her husband was away at military reserve training sessions did she feel she could "slack off" by not placing "regular meals" on the table each night.

The Impact of Failed Aspirations

Main provider couples allocated most of the family work to the wife, but a few of these couples—those with husbands who had unfulfilled career goals—tended to share more than the others. Using the combined measures for housework and child care, these couples were rated as sharing significantly more family labor. What appeared to tip the economy of gratitude away from simple male privilege was the wife's sense that the husband had not fulfilled his career potential. For example, one main provider husband graduated from a four-year college and completed two years of post-graduate study without finishing his Masters' thesis. At the time of the interview, he was making about $30,000 per year as a self-employed house painter and his wife was making $13,000 a year as a full-time secretary. His comments show how her evaluation of his failed or postponed career aspirations led to more bargaining over his participation in routine housework.

She reminds me that I'm not doing what we both think I should be doing, and sometimes that's a discouragement, because I might have worked a lot of hours, and I'll come home tired, for example, and she'll say, "You've gotta clean the house," and I'll say, "Damn I'm tired, I'd like to get a little rest in." But she says, "You're only doing this because it's your choice." She tends to not have sympathy for me in my work because it was more my choice than hers.

He acknowledged that he should be doing something more "worthwhile" and hoped that he would not be painting houses for more than another year. Still, as long as he stayed in his current job, she would not allow him to use fatigue from employment as a way to get out of doing housework.

I worked about 60 hours a week the last couple of weeks. I worked yesterday [Saturday], and today, if it had been my choice, I would have drank beer and watched TV. But since she had a baby shower to go to, I babysitted my nephews. And since we had you coming, she kind of laid out the program: "You've gotta clean the floors, and wash the dishes and do the carpets. So get to it buddy!" (Laughs).

Although this main provider husband capitulated to his wife's demands, she was the one to set tasks for him and reminded him to perform them. In responding to her "program," he used the strategy of claimed incompetence that other main provider husbands also used. While he admitted that he was proficient at the "janitorial stuff," he was careful to point out that he was incapable of dusting or doing the laundry.

> It's amazing what you can do when you have little time and you just get in and do it. And I'm good at that. I'm good at the big cleaning, I'm good at the janitorial stuff. I can do the carpet, do the floors, do all that stuff. But I'm no good on the details. She wants all the details just right, so she handles dusting, the laundry, and the things that I couldn't do, like I would turn everything one color.

By re-categorizing some of the housework as "big cleaning," and "janitorial stuff," this husband rendered it accountable as men's work. Thus, he continued to "do gender" as he did housework. While he drew the line at laundry and dusting, it is significant that there was at least some redefinition of tasks like vacuuming and mopping. He was complying, albeit reluctantly, to many of his wife's requests because they agreed that he had not fulfilled "his" job as sole provider. He still yearned to be the "real" breadwinner and shared his hope that getting a better paying job would mean that he could ignore the housework.

> Sharing the house stuff is usually just a necessity. If, as we would hope in the future, if she didn't have to work outside of the home, then I think I would be comfortable doing less of it. Then she would be the primary house care person and I would be the primary financial resource person. I think roles would change then, and I would be comfortable with her doing more of the dishes and more of the cleaning, and I think she would too. In that sense, I think traditional relationships, if traditional means the guy working and the woman staying home, is good. I wouldn't mind getting a taste of it myself!

A similar failed aspirations pattern was found in another main provider household, even though the husband had a good job as an elementary school teacher. While his wife earned less than a sixth of what he did, she was working on an advanced degree and coordinated a nonprofit community program. In this family, unlike most others, the husband performed more housework than he did child care, though both he and his wife agreed that she did more of both. Nevertheless, he performed these household chores reluctantly, and only in response to prodding from his wife. "Housework is mostly her responsibility. I like to come home and kick back. Sometimes she has to complain before I do anything around the house. You know when she hits the wall, then I start doing things. So I get out of the house on weekends."

This main provider husband talked about how his real love was art, and how he had failed to pursue his dream of being a graphic artist. The blocked occupational achievement in his case was not that he didn't make good money in a respected professional job, but that he was not fulfilling his "true" potential. His failed career goals increased her willingness to make demands on him, influenced their division of household labor, and helped shape feelings of entitlement between them. "I have talents that she doesn't have. I guess that's one of my strongest strengths, is that I'm an artist. But I have not done it. She's very disappointed in me in the sense that I have not done enough of it, and that I do not spend enough time helping my daughter be creative."

Another main provider household followed a similar failed aspirations pattern. He was a telephone lineman making $34,000 a year and she had recently quit an "outside" job, and was now running a family day care center in their home that earned about $10,000 per year. She regretted that he didn't do something "more important" for a living. He said, "She's always telling me, 'You're pretty smart, you're too smart for what you are doing.' " Like the other two failed aspirations husbands, he did more family work than other main providers, but resentment came through when he described what he didn't like about "the wife" working outside the home.

> What I didn't like about it was that I used to get home before the wife, because she had to commute, and I'd have to pop something to eat. Most of the time it was just whatever I happened to find in the fridge. Then I'd have to go pick up the kids immediately from the babysitter, and sometimes I had evening things to do, so what I didn't like was that I had to figure out a way to schedule baby watch or baby sitting when I had evening things.

Thus, even when main provider husbands began to assume some of the domestic chores in response to "necessity" or "nagging," they seemed to cling to the idea that it wasn't fully their responsibility. According to their accounts, this seemed to justify their resentment at having to do "her" chores. Not incidentally, most of the secondary provider wives reported that they received very little help unless they "constantly" reminded him. Wives didn't like their husband's reluctance to assume responsibility for family work, but the women also continued to accept the homemaker role. In addition, the wives appreciated their husband's substantial financial contributions. When performance of the provider role was deemed to be lacking in some way (as in failed aspirations or low occupational prestige), wives' resentment appeared closer to the surface and couples reported that the wives were more persistent in demanding help.

Co-Provider Couples

The remaining families were classified as co-providers, based on an evaluation of their employment, earnings, and ideology. Compared to main provider couples, co-providers tended to have more equal earnings and to value the wife's employment more highly. Among the 12 co-provider couples, wives averaged 44 percent of the family income compared to 20 percent for main provider couples. There was considerable variation among co-provider husbands, however, in terms of their willingness to accept their wives as equal providers, or to assume the role of equal homemaker or parent. Accordingly, I categorized these families into *ambivalent* co-providers (5 couples) and *full* co-providers (7 couples). The ambivalent co-provider husbands accepted their wive's jobs as important and permanent, but often used their own job commitments as justifications for why they did so little at home. I discuss both types of co-providers, considering variation between them in terms of earnings, job status, ideology, role attachments, and divisions of family work.

Ambivalent Co-Providers

Compared to their wives, ambivalent co-provider husbands usually held jobs that were roughly equivalent in terms of occupational prestige and worked about the same number of hours per week. All these husbands earned more than their wives, however, with average annual husbands' earnings of $39,000, compared to $30,000 for the wives. While both husbands and wives thus had careers that provided "comfortable" incomes, the husbands, and sometimes the wives, were ambivalent about treating her career as equally important to his. For example, few ambivalent co-provider husbands let their family work intrude on their paid work, whereas wives' family work often interfered with their paid work. Such asymmetrically permeable work/family boundaries are common in single earner and main provider families, but must be supported with subtle ideologies and elaborate justifications when husbands and wives hold similar occupational positions.

Ambivalent co-provider husbands remained in a helper role at home, perceiving their wives to be more involved parents and assuming that housework was also their wives' responsibility. Husbands used their breadwinner responsibilities to justify their absence, but most lamented not being able to spend more time with their families. For instance, one husband who worked full time as a city planner was married to a woman who worked an equal number of hours as an office manager. In talking about the time he put in at his job, he commented, " I wish I had more time to spend with my children, and to spend with my wife too, of course, but it's a fact of life that I have to work." His wife, in contrast, indicated that her paid job, which she had held for 14 years, did not prohibit her from adequately caring for her three children, or taking care of "her" household chores. Ambivalent co-provider husbands did not perform significantly more housework and child care than main provider husbands, and generally did fewer household chores than main provider husbands with failed career aspirations.

Not surprisingly, ambivalent co-provider husbands tended to be satisfied with their current divisions of labor, even though they usually admitted that things were "not quite fair." One junior high school teacher married to a bilingual education program coordinator described his reactions to their division of family labor.

> To be honest, I'm totally satisfied. When I had a first-period conference, I was a little more flexible, I'd help her more with changing 'em, you know getting them ready for school since I didn't have to be at school right away. Then I had to switch because they had some situation out at fifth-period conference, so that, you know, now she does it a little bit more than I do, and I don't help out with the kids as much in the morning because I have to be there an hour earlier.

This ambivalent co-provider clearly saw himself as "helping" his wife with the children, yet made light of her contributions by saying she does "a little bit more than I do." He went on to reveal how his wife did not enjoy similar special privileges due to her employment, since she had to pick up the children from day care every day, as well as take them to school in the mornings.

> She gets out a little later than I do, because she's an administrator, but I have other things outside. I also work out, I run, and that sort of gives me a time away, to do that before they all come here. I have community meetings in the evenings sometimes too. So, I mean, it might not be totally fair—maybe $^{60}/_{40}$—but I'm thoroughly happy with the way things are.

While he was "thoroughly happy" with the current arrangements, his wife thought that their division of labor was decidedly unfair. She said, "I don't like the fact that it's taken for granted that I'm available. When he goes out he just assumes I'm available, but when I go out I have to consult with him to make sure he is available." For her, child care was a given. For him, it was optional, as evidenced by his comment, "If I don't have something else to do then I'll take the kids."

Ambivalent co-provider husbands also tended to lament the way they saw their family involvements limiting their careers or personal activities. For instance, the school teacher discussed above regretted that he could not do what he used to before he had children.

> Having children keeps me away from thinking a lot about my work. You know, it used to be, before we had kids, I could have my mind geared to work—you know how ideas just pop in, you really get into it. But with kids it doesn't get as—you know, you can't switch. It gets more difficult, it makes it hard to get into it. I don't have that freedom of mind, you know, and it takes away from aspects of my work, like doing a little bit more reading or research that I would like to do. Or my own activities, I mean, I still run, but not as much as I used to. I used to play basketball, I used to coach, this and that.

Other ambivalent co-provider husbands talked about the impact of children on their careers and personal lives with less lament and more appreciation for establishing bonds with their children. Encouraged by their wives to alter their priorities, some reinterpreted the relative importance of career and family commitments. For example, another teacher and coach talked about how having a family changed his feelings about his job.

> I like the way things are going, let's put it this way. I mean, it's just that once you become a parent, it's a neverending thing. I coach my kid, for example, this past week we had four games and I'm getting ready to go out there, you know and I'm getting ready to change a door knob here. I just think that by having a family that your life becomes so involved after awhile with your own kids, that it's very difficult. I coached at the varsity level for one year and I was taking so much time away from it that I had to give that up. In other words, I had to give up something that I like to do, for my own kids' sake. I would leave in the morning when they were asleep, and I would get out of coaches' meetings at ten or eleven at night. My wife said to me, "Think about your priorities, man, you leave when the kids are asleep, come back when they are asleep," so I decided to change that act. So I gave it up for a year, and I was home all the time. And now I am going to coach again, but it's at lower levels, and I'll be home every day. I have to make adjustments for my family. So your attitude changes, it's not me that counts anymore.

Whereas family labor was not shared equally in this ambivalent co-provider couple, the husband, at his wife's urging, was beginning to accept and appreciate that his children were more important than his job. Like many other husbands, he was evaluating his attachment to his children on his wife's terms, but he was beginning to take on more responsibility for them. Unlike the main providers, ambivalent co-provider husbands were more conflicted about giving up job time to perform family work. Like the main providers, however, they did not relinquish the assumption that the home was basically the wife's domain.

Hiring Outside Help

Two of the ambivalent co-provider couples attempted to alleviate stress on the wife by hiring outside help. For instance, we asked a self-employed male attorney making $40,000 per year if he thought their division of household tasks was fair: "Do you mean fair like equal? It's probably not equal, so probably it wouldn't be fair. That's why we have a housekeeper." His wife, a social worker earning $36,000 per year, talked about how the household was still her responsibility, but that she now had fewer tasks to do. "When I did not have help, I tended to do everything, but with a housekeeper, I don't have to do so much." She went on to talk about how she wished he would do more with their five- and eight-year-old children, but speculated that he would as they grew older.

Another couple paid a live-in babysitter and housekeeper to watch their three children during the day while he worked full time in construction and she worked full time as a psychiatric social worker. Although she labeled the outside help as "essential," she noted that her husband contributed more to the mess than he did to its clean-up. He saw himself as an involved father because he played with his children and she acknowledged this, but she also complained that he competed with them in games as if he were a child himself. His participation in routine household labor was considered optional, as evidenced by his comment, "I like to cook once in a while."

Only one other family, a full co-provider couple who shared most of the housework, talked about paying for household help. In their case, as described below, they hired a gardener to do some of "his" chores, freeing him to do more of the child care and housework. This strategy reflected an assumption that the husband "should" share in family work, an assumption that most main provider and ambivalent co-provider husbands did not willingly make.

Full Co-Provider Couples

Over a third of the Chicano couples were classified as full co-providers. Husbands and wives in these families took the wife's employment for granted and considered her career to be just as important as his. Like the more ambivalent couples discussed above, full co-provider husbands and wives worked about the same number of hours as each other, but, on the whole, the co-provider couples spent a total of about 10 more hours each week on the job than their more ambivalent counterparts.[33] Despite working more hours, co-providers tended to have significantly lower incomes.[34]

The sharing of family work was substantially greater for full co-providers than for any other groups. (No co-provider couple had a mean husband-wife housework/child care score over 3.0 — the true midpoint of the combined scale — but five of the seven families had mean husband-wife scores of 2.5 or higher, indicating substantial sharing of these tasks.)[35] Since husbands tended to take more credit than their wives granted them, I also looked specifically at the wives' ratings in the co-provider couples. Six of seven co-provider wives rated child care as shared, and two of these wives also rated housework as shared. The co-provider families thus represent the most egalitarian families in this sample of dual-earner Chicano couples and show the direct link between accepting the wife as co-provider and the husband as a co-caregiver. On the following pages I explore some factors that the couples indicated led to sharing these roles.

Like the more ambivalent co-providers, husbands in full co-provider families discussed conflicts between work and family and sometimes alluded to the ways that their occupational advancement was limited by their commitments to their children. One husband and wife spent the same number of hours on the job, earned approximately the same amount of money, and were employed as engineering technicians for the same employer. When asked how his family involvement had affected his job performance, he responded by saying, "It should, because I really need to spend a lot more time learning my work and I haven't really put in the time I need to advance in the profession. . . . I would spend more time if I didn't have kids. I'd like to be able to play with the computer or read books more often." Nevertheless, the husband repeatedly talked about how such adjustments were not really sacrifices because he valued time with his children so highly. He did not use his job as an excuse to get out of family work like the ambivalent co-providers, and he seemed to value his wife's career at least as much as his own.

> I think her job is probably more important than mine because she's been at that kind of work a lot longer than I have. And at the level she is — it's awkward the way it is, because I get paid just a little bit more than she does, I have a higher position. But she definitely knows the work a lot more, she's been doing the same type of work for about nine years already, and I've only been doing this type of engineering work for about two and a half years, so she knows a lot more. We both have to work, that's for sure.

Because they recognized that they were equal providers, this couple shared more of the family work. In the interview and the card sorts, the husband indicated that he did more child care and housework than she did. In contrast, she gave her husband credit for doing a substantial amount of the child care, though less than she. She described his relationship with their seven-year-old son as "very caring," and noted that he helps the boy with homework more often than she does. She also said that he did most of the heavy cleaning and scrubbing, but, contrary to his classification, rated herself as doing many more of the total housework tasks. She also commented that he doesn't clean toilets and doesn't always notice when things are dirty.

The husband also raised issues about standards and styles for housework. Similar to some of the men in the first interviews, he suggested that he does more of the routine maintenance and general cleaning jobs but leaves the "little things" and major redecorating to her.

> Some of the things she does, I just will not do. I will not dust all the little things in the house. That's one of my least favorite things, is dusting. I'm more than likely to do the mopping and vacuuming and trying to make things fit. And she's more than likely to want to move something around that's going to require a new piece of furniture to make it work.

His comments reveal how arguments shift to differences over housework standards once both spouses accept that they should share responsibility for the housework. "She has high standards for cleanliness that you would have to be home to maintain. Mine tend to acknowledge that hey, you don't always get to this stuff because you have other things to do. I think I have a better acceptance that one priority hurts something else in the background."

Although this couple generally agreed about how to raise their son, standards for child care were also subject to debate. He saw himself as doing more with his son than she did, as reflected in comments such as "I tend to think of myself as the more involved parent, and I think other people have noticed that too." While she had only positive things to say about his parenting, he offered both praise and criticism.

> She can be very playful. She makes up fun games. She doesn't always put enough into the educational part of it, though, like exploring or reading. . . . She cherishes tune-up time [job-related study or preparation], and sometimes I feel she should be using that time to spend with him. Like at the beach, I'll play with him, but she'll be more likely to be under the umbrella reading.

Like many other husbands, he went on to say that he thought their division of labor was unfair. Unlike the others, however, he indicated that he thought their current arrangements favored *her* needs, not his. "I think I do more housework [and] it's probably not fair because I do more of the dirtier tasks. . . . Also, at this point, our solution tends to favor her free time more than my free time."

In this family, comparable occupational status and earnings, coupled with a relatively egalitarian ideology, led to substantial sharing of family work. The husband took more credit for his involvement than his wife gave him, but we can see a difference between their talk and that of some of the more conventional families discussed above. While other husbands sometimes complained about their wife's high standards, they treated housework, and even parenting, as primarily *her* duty. They often resented being nagged to do more around the house, but rarely moved out of a helper role to consider it *their* duty to anticipate, schedule, and take care of family and household needs. In this co-provider household, that unbalanced allocation of responsibility was not so taken for granted. Because of this, negotiations over housework and parenting were more frequent than in the other families. Since they both held expectations that each would fulfill both provider and caretaker roles, resentments came from both spouses — not just from the wife.

Sharing provider and homemaker roles seems to be easier, when, like the family above, the wife's earnings and occupational prestige equal or exceed those of her husband. For instance, in one of the couples reporting the most sharing of child care and housework, the wife earned $36,000 annually as executive director of a nonprofit group and as a private consultant, whereas he earned $30,000 as a self-employed general contractor. This couple shared most of the housework according to both, and although she rated him as doing fully half of the child care, he rated her as performing more than he did.

This couple started off their marriage with fairly traditional gender expectations and a conventional division of labor. While the husband's ideology had slowly changed, he still talked like most of the main provider husbands.

> As far the household is concerned, I divide a house into two categories: one is the interior and the other is the exterior. For the interior, my wife pushes me to deal

with that. The exterior, I'm left to it myself. So, what I'm basically saying is that generally speaking, a woman does not deal with the exterior. The woman's main concern is with the interior, although there is a lot of deviation.

In this family, an egalitarian belief system did not precede the sharing of household labor. The wife was still responsible for setting the "interior" household agenda and had to remind her husband to help with housework and child care. When asked whether he and his wife had arguments about housework, this husband laughed and said, "All the time, doesn't everybody?"

This couple was different from most others because she made more money than he did, and had no qualms about demanding help from him. While he had not yet accepted the idea that interior chores were equally his, he reluctantly performed them. In the card sorts, she ranked his contributions to child care equal to hers, and rated his contributions to housework only slightly below her own. While not eagerly rushing to do the cooking, cleaning, or laundry, he complied with occasional reminders, and according to her, was "a better cleaner."

His sharing stemmed, in part, from her higher earnings and their mutual willingness to reduce his "outside chores" by hiring help. Instead of complaining about their division of labor, he talked about how he has come to appreciate his situation.

Ever since I've known my wife, she's made more money than I have. Initially—as a man—I resented it. I went through a lot of head trips about it. But as time developed, I appreciated it. Now I respect it. The way I figure it is I'd rather have her sharing the money with me than sharing it with someone else. She has her full-time job and then she has her part-time job as a consultant. The gardener I'm paying $75 per week, and I'm paying someone else $25 per week to make my lunch, so I'm enjoying it! It's self-interest.

The power dynamic in this family, coupled with their willingness to pay for outside help to reduce his chores, and the flexibility of his self-employed work schedule, led to substantial sharing of cooking, cleaning, and child care. Because she was making more money and working more hours than he was, he could not emulate other husbands in claiming priority for his provider activities.

A similar dynamic was evident in other co-provider couples with comparable earnings and career commitments. One male IRS officer married to a school teacher now made more money than his wife, but talked about his feelings when she was the more successful provider.

It doesn't bother me when she makes more money than me. I don't think it has anything to do with being a man. I don't have any hangups about it, I mean, I don't equate those things with manhood. It takes a pretty simple mind to think that way. First of all, she doesn't feel superior when she has made more money. I guess if the woman felt that she could expect more because she was making more money, that's when the guy might feel intimidated.

This husband's statement implied that his wife did not use her equal or superior earnings as a basis for making demands on him. Contrary to his portrayal, however, she commented that he was "better" at housework than she was, and that she "nagged him" to get him to do it. Although only two wives in this sample of families earned more than their husbands, the reversal of symbolic provider status seemed to raise expectations for increased family work from husbands. Both of the husbands we interviewed who made less than their wives performed more of the housework and child care than other husbands.

Even when wives' earnings did not exceed husbands', some co-providers shared the homemaker role. A male college admissions recruiter and his executive secretary wife shared substantial housework according to mutual ratings and most child care according to her rating. He made $29,000 per year working an average of 50 hours per week, while she made $22,000 working a 40-hour week. Like the contractor/executive secretary couple above, she was willing to give him more credit than he was willing to claim for child care. In both cases this appeared to reflect the wife's sincere appreciation for her husband's parenting efforts and a desire to praise him for doing so much more than other fathers, an issue I will return to in the next chapter. For their part, the husbands placed a high value on their wives' unique parenting skills and seemed to downplay the possibility that they might be considered equal parents.

Like most men, the college recruiter husband was reluctant to perform many housecleaning chores. Like other co-provider husbands, however, he managed to redefine these routine household chores as a shared responsibility. For instance, when we asked him what he liked least about housework, he laughingly replied: "Probably those damn toilets, man, and the showers, the bathrooms, gotta scrub 'em, argghh! I wish I didn't have to do any of that, you know the vacuuming and all that. But it's just a fact of life." Even though he did more than most men, he still acknowledged that he did less than his wife. He also admitted that he had used his job to get out of doing more family work. "I think there might be room for a more equal distribution than in the past. But then, I also have always used my job as a justification, you know, for doing less. I'm on the road and stuff, that makes it kinda hard." Whereas other wives often allowed husbands to use their jobs as excuses for doing less family work, or assumed that their husbands were incapable of performing certain chores like cooking or laundry, the pattern in this family resembled that in the failed aspirations families. In other words, the wife did not assume that housework was "her" job, did not accept her husband's job demands as justification for his doing less housework, and sometimes challenged his interpretation of how much his job required of him. He commented, "Sometimes she's not always understanding of my work. I mean, it's like 'Why are you doing this, it's not even your job.' Because the typical thing is always like, you know, 'Well, this is my job, this is what I do for a living and you just have to accept it.' "

When he described who did what around their house, this husband provided some insight into how his wife was able to get him to do more.

> Sometimes she just refuses to do something. . . . An example would be the ironing, you know, I never used to do the ironing, hated it. Now it's just something that happens. You need something ironed, you better iron it or you're not gonna have it in the morning. So, I think, you know, that kinda just evolved, I mean, she just gradually quit doing it so everybody just had to do their own. My son irons his own clothes, I iron my own clothes, my daughter irons her own clothes, the only one that doesn't iron is the baby, and next year she'll probably start.

Hood describes this strategy as "going on strike," and suggests that it is most effective when husbands feel the specific task *must* be done.[36] Since appearing neat and well-dressed was a priority for this husband, when she stopped ironing his clothes, he started doing it himself. Because he felt it was important for his children to be "presentable" in public, he also began to remind them to iron their own clothes before going visiting or attending Mass.

Many co-provider couples said that sharing housework was contingent on continual bargaining and negotiation. Others focused on how the sharing of family work "evolved naturally." One co-provider husband, director of a housing agency, reported that he and his wife didn't negotiate; "we pretty much do what needs to be done." His wife, an executive secretary, confirmed his description, and echoed the ad hoc arrangements of many of the role-sharing couples in the first study. "We have not had to negotiate. We both have our specialties. He is great with dishes, I like to clean bathrooms. He does most of the laundry. It has worked out that we each do what we like best."

When both spouses assume that household tasks are a shared responsibility, negotiation can be less necessary or contentious. For example, a co-provider Chicano husband who worked as a mail carrier commented, "I get home early and start dinner, make sure the kids do their homework, feed the dogs, stuff like that." He and his wife, also an executive secretary, agreed that they rarely talked about housework. She said, "When I went back to work we agreed that we both needed to share, and so we just do it." While she still reminded him to perform chores according to her standards or on her schedule, she summed up her appreciation by commenting, "at least he does it without complaining." Lack of complaint was a common feature of co-provider families. Whereas many main provider husbands complained of having to do "her" chores, the co-providers did not talk about harboring resentments about contributing to housework or child care. Time was short and the work was often tedious, but they rarely assumed that they were being forced into it by their wives. Neither did co-provider husbands complain about not having the services of a stay-at-home wife like the main provider husbands sometimes did.

Getting Involved as Fathers

The Chicano and Anglo fathers who were the most involved used similar terms to talk about being with their children. In the Chicano sample, fathers tended to view their own contributions to parenting as less significant than those of their wives, but, like the Anglo men, they spoke of making explicit choices to become actively involved in their children's lives. One co-provider husband talked about the uniqueness of a mother's love, but focused on his decision to "invest" in his kids.

> Fathers are always going to be at a disadvantage in the whole nurturing thing simply because it can't be the same [as it is with mothers]. But I think that fathers can make it their choice to become as nurturing as they want to. I think that if they consider the relationship that they will have with them for the rest of their life they can see that it is the most important investment they can make.

Involved fathers in both groups characterized what they were doing as a decision to put their children's needs first. Main provider husbands, in contrast, tended to use their jobs as excuses for spending little time with their children. Ambivalent co-providers similarly lamented how children sometimes detracted from their careers. Co-provider husbands, on the other hand, even though they were employed as many hours as the others, talked about making a definite choice to spend time with and care for their children. None voiced regret over such a choice.

When asked whether fathers could provide the same type of nurturance that mothers did, the majority of co-providers said no, even while affirming that it was very important for fathers to be involved with their children. Most of the main provider husbands, in contrast, answered that men could nurture like women, but only if they were somehow compelled to do so by some unusual circumstance. For instance, one main provider said, "If it was necessary, yes I think a father could . . . you know, you can adapt to anything, so if their mother couldn't do it, their dad could." Ambivalent co-providers generally did not claim credit for men being able to parent like women, yet their answers resembled those of the main providers. One said, "Maybe men could provide the same nurturance if they were the only parent, but mother nurturance is more important." Another ambivalent co-provider answered, "Probably, I don't know about permanently, but they probably could if they had to, if they were left in a situation where they had to." Whereas main providers and ambivalent co-providers focused on how men could parent when they were forced to do it, co-providers stressed the fact that one had to choose it voluntarily.

Sharing and Reluctance

For these dual-earner Chicano couples, we found considerable sharing in several areas. First, as in previous studies of ethnic minority families, wives were employed a substantial number of hours and made significant contributions to the household income. Second, like some researchers, we found that couples described their decision-making to be relatively fair and equal. Third, fathers in these families were more involved in childrearing than their own fathers had been, and seven of 20 husbands were rated as sharing most child-care tasks. Finally, although no husband performed fully half of the housework, a few made substantial contributions in this area as well.

One of the power dynamics that appeared to undergird the household division of labor in these families was the relative earning power of each spouse, though this was modified by occupational prestige, provider role status, and personal preferences. When the wife earned less than a third of the family income, the husband performed little of the routine housework or child care. In two families, wives earned more than their husbands. These two households reported sharing more domestic labor than any of the others. Among the other couples who shared family work, we found a preponderance of relatively balanced incomes. In the two families with large financial contributions from wives, but little household help from husbands, couples had hired housekeepers to reduce the household workload.

Relative income thus makes a difference, but there was no simple or straightforward exchange of market resources for domestic services in these families. Other factors like failed career aspirations or occupational status influenced power differentials and helped to explain why some wives were willing to push a little harder for change in the division of household labor. In almost every case, husbands reluctantly responded to requests for help from wives. Only when wives explicitly took the initiative to shift some of the housework burden to husbands did the men begin to assume significant responsibility for the day-to-day operation of the household. Even when they began to share the family work, men tended to do some of the less onerous tasks like playing with the children or washing the dinner dishes. When we compare these men to their own fathers, or those of their mothers, however, we can see that they are sharing more domestic chores than the generation of parents that preceded them.

Acceptance of wives as co-providers and wives' delegation of a portion of the homemaker role to husbands were especially important to creating more equal divisions of household labor. If wives made lists for their husbands or offered them frequent reminders, they were more successful than if they waited for husbands to take the initiative. But remaining responsible for managing the home and children was cause for resentment on the part of many wives. Sometimes wives were effective in getting husbands to perform certain chores, like ironing, by stopping doing it altogether. For other wives, sharing evolved more "naturally," as both spouses agreed to share tasks or performed the chores they most preferred.

Economies of gratitude continually shifted in these couples as ideology, career attachments, and feelings of obligation and entitlement changed. For some main provider families, this meant that wives were grateful for husbands' "permission" to hold a job, or that wives worked harder at home because they felt guilty for making their husbands do any of the housework. Main provider husbands usually let their job commitments limit their family work, whereas their wives took time off from work to take children to the dentist, care for a sick child, or attend a parent-teacher conference.

Even in families where co-provider wives had advanced degrees and earned relatively high wages, women's work/family boundaries were more permeable than their husbands'. For example, one professional woman complained that her teacher husband was a "perpetual" graduate student and attended "endless" community meetings. She was employed more hours then he, and made about the same amount of money, but she had to "schedule him" to watch the children if she wanted to leave the house alone. His stature as a "community leader" provided him with subterranean leverage in the unspoken struggle over taking responsibility for the house and children. His "gender ideology," if we had measured it with conventional survey questions, would undoubtedly have been characterized as "egalitarian." He spoke in broad platitudes about women's equality and was washing the dishes when we arrived for the interviews. He insisted on finishing the dishes as he answered my questions, but in the other room his wife confided to Elsa in incredulous tones, "He *never* does that!"

In other ambivalent co-provider families, husbands gained unspoken advantage because they had more prestigious jobs than their wives, and earned more money. While these highly educated attorneys and administrators talked about how they respected their wives' careers, and expressed interest in spending more time with their children, their actions showed that they did not fully assume responsibility for sharing the family work. To solve the dilemma of too little time and too many chores, two of these families hired housekeepers. Wives were grateful for this strategy, though it did not alter inequities in the distribution of housework and child care, or in the allocation of worry.

In other families, the economy of gratitude departed dramatically from conventional notions of husband as economic provider and wife as nurturing homemaker. When wives' earnings approached or exceeded their husbands', economies of gratitude shifted toward more equal expectations, with husbands beginning to assume that they must do more around the house. Even in these families, husbands rarely began doing more chores without prodding from wives, but they usually did them "without complaining." Similarly, when wives with economic leverage began expecting more from their husbands, they were usually successful in getting them to do more.

Another type of leverage that was important, even in main provider households, was the existence of failed aspirations. If wives expected husbands to "make more" of themselves, pursue "more important" careers, or follow "dream" occupational goals, then wives were able to get husbands to do more around the house. This perception of failed aspirations, if held by both spouses, served as a reminder that husbands had no excuse for not helping out at home. In these families, wives were not at all reluctant to demand assistance with domestic chores, and husbands were rarely able to use their jobs as excuses for getting out of housework.[37]

The leisure gap, common among Anglo couples, is also clearly present in dual-earner Chicano families. Nevertheless, in couples where the economy of gratitude is more balanced, the leisure gap begins to shrink. It becomes much less significant, though it doesn't disappear entirely, when both spouses consider the woman's job as important as the man's. In subsequent chapters we will see that this tends to happen when wives' earnings approach those of husbands'.

The economies of gratitude in these families were not equally balanced, but many exhibited divisions of household labor that contradicted cultural stereotypes of male-dominated Chicano families. Particularly salient in these families was the lack of fit between their own class position and that of their parents. Most parents were immigrants with little education and low occupational mobility. The couples we interviewed, in contrast, were well educated and relatively secure in middle-class occupations. The couples could have compared themselves to their parents, evaluating themselves as egalitarian and financially successful. While some did just that, most compared themselves to their Anglo and Chicano friends and co-workers, many of whom shared as much or more than they did. As described in the next chapter, the couples had no absolute or fixed standard against which to make judgments about themselves. Implicitly comparing their earnings, occupational commitments, and perceived aptitudes, these individuals negotiated new patterns of work and family commitments and developed new justifications for their emerging arrangements. These were not created anew, but emerged out of the popular culture in which they found themselves. Judith Stacey labels such developments the making of the "postmodern family" because they signal "the contested, ambivalent, and undecided character of contemporary gender and kinship arrangements."[38] Our findings confirm that families are an important site of new struggles over the meaning of gender and the rights and obligations of men and women to each other and over each other's labor.

One of our most interesting findings has to do with the class position of Chicano husbands and wives who shared the most household labor: white-collar working-class families shared more than upper-middle-class professionals. Contrary to findings from some nationwide surveys, the most highly educated of our well-educated sample of Chicano couples shared only moderate amounts of child care and little housework.[39] Contrary to other predictions, neither was it the working-class women in this study who achieved the most balanced divisions of labor.[40] It was the middle occupational group—the executive secretaries, clerks, technicians, teachers, and mid-level administrators—who extracted the most help from husbands. The men in these families were similarly in the middle in terms of occupational status for this sample—administrative assistants, a builder, a mail carrier, a technician—and in the middle in terms of income. What this means is that the highest status wives—the program coordinators, nurses, social workers, and office managers—were not able to, or chose not to, transform their salaries or occupational status into more participation from husbands. This was probably because their husbands had even higher incomes and more prestigious occupations. The lawyers, program directors, ranking bureaucrats, and "community leaders" parlayed their status into extra leisure at home, either by paying for housekeepers or ignoring the housework. Finally, Chicana wives at the lowest end fared least well. The teacher's aides, entry level secretaries, day care providers, and part-time employees did the bulk of the work at home whether they were married to mechanics or lawyers. When wives made less than a third of what their husbands did, they were only able to get husbands to do a little more if they were working at jobs considered "below" them—a telephone lineman, a painter, an elementary school teacher.

These interviews with Chicano couples corroborate results from previous depth-interview studies of Anglo couples and suggest that the major processes shaping divisions of labor in middle-class Chicano couples are about the same as those shaping such divisions in other couples.[41] That is not to say that ethnicity did not make a difference to the people we talked with. They grew up in recently immigrating working-class families, watched their parents work long hours for minimal wages, and understood first-hand the toll that various forms of racial and ethnic discrimination can take. Probably because of some of these experiences, and their own more recent ones, our informants looked at job security, fertility decisions, and the division of family work somewhat differently than their Anglo counterparts. In some cases, this may give Chicano husbands in working-class or professional jobs license to ignore more of the housework, and might temper the anger of some working-class or professional Chicanas who are still called on to do most of the domestic chores. If our findings are generalizable, however, it is those in between the blue-collar working class and the upper-middle-class professionals who might be most likely to share family work.

Assessing whether my findings apply to other two-job Latino or other minority couples will require the use of larger, more representative samples. If the limited sharing we observed represents a trend—however slow or reluctant—it could have far-reaching consequences. More and more mothers are remaining full-time members of the paid labor force. With the "post-industrial" expansion of the service and information sectors of the economy as discussed in Chapter 8, Chicanos and other minorities will be increasingly likely to enter white-collar working-class occupations. As more minority families fit the occupational profile of those we studied, we may see more assumption of housework and child care by the men within them.

Regardless of the specific changes that the economy will undergo, we can expect ethnic minority men and women, like their white counterparts, to continue to negotiate for change in their work and family roles. Economic and institutional factors will undoubtedly play a major part in the shaping of these roles, but social and personal factors will also be important. Reluctant husbands will be unlikely to accept even partial responsibility for the homemaker role unless wives are accepted as co-providers. In the next chapter, I examine some of the social and personal issues that might promote such changes.

5

Why Do Couples Share?

In the last two chapters, I explored how couples divide family and paid work by focusing on how they talk about jobs, gender, and the practical realities of everyday life. In this chapter, I examine personal motivations and social forces that influence the division of child care and housework.[1] Why do some men want to become more involved in family life and why do their wives encourage them? Does it matter how old they are when they become parents? And what happens when other people see new fathers doing "women's work"? Do family, friends, and co-workers react with praise or criticism, and how do new parents respond? Even partial answers to these questions can help us determine why some couples attempt sharing and which ones might be the most successful. By placing these parents' personal stories in a social context, the larger economic and demographic factors shaping divisions of household labor come into better focus. In subsequent chapters, I estimate how widespread these social forces are, and predict whether they will grow stronger in the future.

Personal Motivations

When we interviewed couples about the intimate details of their home lives, they gave many reasons for dividing family work the way they did. Despite substantial differences among their stories, however, one theme emerged as common to all the men: Being a father carried great importance. For many, fathering offered a way to get in touch with their emotions and a rare opportunity to develop the sensitive, vulnerable, and caring parts of them-selves. Many talked about discovering a new form of love and experiencing the world in different ways since they became fathers. Some also talked about how being a parent was helping them to work through unresolved emotional issues with their own fathers.

I was initially surprised at the number of fathers who described child care as an opportunity to grow and mature. After all, most men are reluctant to admit that they are deficient in any way, and acknowledging a need to develop emotionally required them to show vulnerability. According to the fathers, however, family work literally forced them to deal with various personal and relational issues and most welcomed the opportunity.

Fathers said that the everday aspects of child care demanded that they tune into their own and their children's emotions. Men are not typically called on to attend to others in a kind and gentle way, nor are they usually confronted with the hundred minor crises that routine parenting presents. It can be very exasperating when a baby will not sleep or when a toddler vehemently shouts "no" at full volume. These little struggles challenge fathers (and mothers) to respond without using angry outbursts or physical shows of force. Most men need help in such endeavors, for the gentle perseverance demanded of parents is not often inculcated in boys as they are growing up. The fathers we talked to were slowly developing these subtle skills, but the road to effective parenting was more bumpy and demanding than they had initially anticipated.

One of the most consistent themes we heard from fathers was how watching and interacting with their children encouraged their own personal growth and development. The psychologist Erik Erikson was one of the first to note that parenthood provides the core experience of what he called "generativity," the seventh of eight stages in his hypothesized cycle of human development. He suggested that fatherhood could further a man's maturing by increasing his awareness of himself, his values, and his familial relationships, and by helping him to accept and integrate his emotional needs.[2] Psychologists and sociol-ogists studying parenthood have similarly noted that becoming fathers provides some men with an opportunity for personal development by bringing them in touch with their emotions and promoting self-disclosure.[3] Others have sug-gested that participation in the "father role" depends on the positive identity that men derive from it.[4]

Confirming these earlier findings, the men we interviewed reported that active fathering encouraged emotional expression and helped them develop positive self-images. In addition, we discovered that becoming involved in the intimate details of their children's lives allowed them to work on some unresolved issues from their own childhoods. In a less flattering view, our interviews might also be used to support Diane Ehrensaft's suggestion that some fathers become unrealistically enamored with their children in the service of narcissistic self-indulgence.[5] Whether we interpret these new fathers' stories as reflecting selflessness or selfishness, however, embracing fatherhood was a deeply felt emotional experience for them all, and almost every man we interviewed said that becoming a father was the most important thing that had ever happened to him.

Although most men initially described being a father in positive terms, as we asked more questions and got them talking, they described their relationships with their children as extremely challenging as well as fulfilling. For instance, one father, talked about the "opportunity" that building an ongoing caring relationship with his children provided him.

> I like the opportunity for us to communicate caring and information and insights, all at once. At its best, child care can be a reciprocal sort of dance, a feeling of being able to share the ordinary and the extraordinary all at the same time. Care is the key word there — the depths of the word care. "Care" isn't the same as "taking care of." Care is a quality that it seems to me can shape all of one's interactions with another person. That quality is what I think I like the best about being with my children. What I like *least* about it is, well, my inability sometimes to care, the restrictions I feel. It makes me aware of my own limitations. At various times I wish I were more able to be more sensitive, be more peace loving, etc. So I guess it's a big syndrome of things; it's an opportunity, but it's an occasion to recognize both potential and limits.

Other fathers mentioned that parenting allowed them to explore or "work on" parts of themselves that normally remained submerged. One termed child care a way to become "rounded out" because being with his children, unlike more conventional masculine pursuits, required his full loving attention and his constant "emotional presence." Most reported that they were not in the habit of putting themselves in emotionally demanding situations. Routine child care, it seemed, forced them to pay attention to their own and their children's feelings simultaneously. Several commented that being with their children as a routine caregiver prohibited them from taking things for granted, or, as one said, "you can't just leave it in automatic."

Learning to be attentive was one of the most common lessons the men got from fathering. Many related stories about having to learn how to tune into others' needs by picking up on subtle cues and anticipating problems. Few knew how to "read" children before they had their own, so they had to develop the necessary skills by interacting with their kids, and by watching their wives handle the inevitable problems of everyday family life. Most learned how to interpret signs of crankiness in their kids as hunger, tiredness, or hurt feelings, and how to deal with potential problems before they became full-blown crises.

Although most men said that parenting helped them to develop intuition and sensitivity, other forms of emotionality were also mentioned. For example, an outwardly easy-going mail clerk said that his relationship with his children brought out anger in him that he did not expect. It was difficult for him to control his temper when his children defied him, but he said he gained from being confronted with situations that exposed him to his "raw" feelings. He also commented that having children helped him to acknowledge and overcome his shyness.

> I often feel very shy around strangers and I see that in my kids and it helps me work on it too. They say, "Daddy, would you come with me to go up to Sarah's door?" and I feel embarrassed to go up to Sarah's door too, but I'm trying to get my kid to understand how to deal with people, so I do it. It's been very instructive for me, I mean I've learned a lot, not just in raising kids, but about myself, by having kids.

Several fathers talked about being put in situations like this, where they were required to overcome their own fears or anxieties. Already committed to being an involved father and wanting to set an example for his son, this man felt forced to deal with his own insecurities. His child's literal interpretations and innocent questions compelled him to act as he felt he should, rather than avoiding emotionally challenging situations as he had in the past.

Many fathers also said that parenting helped them be more patient, tolerant, and mature. The men talked about becoming less impulsive than before they were fathers, and about learning to consider a full range of possible consequences for their actions when they were with their children. For most of the men, developing this sensitivity and maturity was dependent upon identifying and accepting their own emotions. They learned that if they could first pay attention to their own feelings, they could do a better job of understanding and responding to the feelings of their children and to the others around them.

Even though parenting challenged the men on an emotional level, for most, the outcome was an increase in their self-esteem. Many came to rely more on fathering than anything else for their sense of self. I asked one father, a hard-working delivery man, how his involvement with his children had affected his self-image.

> I think if anything, it's enhanced it, I mean, how I feel about myself. The children, my relationship with the kids has been good for me because it's given me a sense of how I'm able to handle things that you question before you've done it. You know, it's like, when something comes up with the children and you actually do it or handle whatever the problem is, I feel better about myself. It makes me feel like I'm more positive about myself—being able to deal with the problem.

Many of the men talked about how coming to see themselves as fathers had been a "profound" transformation. One commented on how being actively involved with his children made him confront some underlying identity issues.

> It's made me think that I am my father. I see a lot of my father in myself. I think I understand him better. I mean the experience that he experienced. And really—I hate to say it, but I know it is true, 'cause I've thought about it for quite awhile—I don't really know how to retain myself if I wasn't a father. . . . I'm not sure who I am if I'm not a father.

Being a father had become so important to this man that he could not even imagine who he was without his children. Many men, when pressed, revealed similar vulnerable feelings. When asked to reflect deeply on parenthood, most intimated that being a father was by far the most important thing in their lives. One father commented that his relationship to his children was "absolutely central" and that he "experienced the world in many ways through my relationship with them." A few commented that when introducing themselves to others, instead of saying "I am a salesman," or "I am a builder," they would say "I am a father." In the following section, I explore how the relative absence of their own fathers contributed to these men's desire to be nurturing parents to their children.

Finding Their Own Fathers

Psychological explanations for men's preferred style of fathering are usually based on men's past relationships with their own fathers. Put simply, new fathers can either follow positive role models or compensate for negative ones. In modeling, the young father takes an active part in his children's lives because he learned how to do it from from watching and imitating his own involved father. Alternately, young fathers can attempt to compensate for a lack of involvement on the part of their own fathers by making a larger contribution to their children's upbringing.[6] The latter pattern was much more common among those I interviewed, though some men were simultaneously modeling aspects of their father's behavior that they appreciated and compensating for those they did not.

Most mothers, as well as the fathers, reported that they were attempting to raise their children differently from how they had been raised. This usually included reference to their own fathers' emotional or physical absence, and sometimes to harsh treatment received at the hands of their fathers. Some mentioned that they were providing their children with experiences that they had secretly wished for during childhood; and a few noted that sharing parenting helped to compensate for the things they had not received. As one mother of two commented, "Having children has helped me to heal a lot of my pain from my own childhood, because I am experiencing all the things I never had—like a father—through my husband, through watching him and being part of him and having the family that I never had before."

About two-thirds of the women in both interview studies reported that they wished their own father had been more involved when they were growing up. Most reported that their father was working all the time or gone for some other reason. Many described their father as a feared and respected figure in their lives, but someone who was peripheral to family life. Most expressed a desire for their father to have spent more time with them when they were little. Many indicated that they would have liked their father to be "more open," "more loving," "more verbal," "more playful," or in some way emotionally closer and more communicative. Many women also focused on what they didn't like about their own father, wishing that he had been "less rigid," "less uptight," "not so angry," "less of a disciplinarian," or "less abusive."

The men we interviewed were even more likely to report that their own fathers had been relatively uninvolved in family life when they were growing up. A few said that their fathers gave them plentiful attention, frequently played with them, or took them fishing or camping regularly, but these men were in the minority. Most of the men reported that their fathers were "not really there" when they were growing up. Many said they lacked a true connection or sense of intimacy with their father, even though they feared, respected, and sometimes played with him. Feeling dissatisfied with their own fathers in various ways, many of these new fathers vowed that they would "do it differently."

Besides wanting to provide their own children with a more full or complete father–child relationship, many of the men we interviewed also expressed a desire to overcome unresolved feelings from their own childhoods. As the clinical psychologist Samuel Osherson suggests, many men carry around a "wounded father" within their own psyches. The wounded father is an internalized image of an inadequate or out-of-reach father that, according to Osherson, most men sense only vaguely. He encourages men to heal the wounded father within themselves by nurturing their own children. Submerged dependency needs are awakened when men participate in childrearing, according to Osherson. "Men have much to gain from tolerating the discomfort of getting into their families: It may help the husband to work through his own anger and to let go of his fantasies of being perfectly taken care of by his wife-mother in a way that allows him to be more nurturing of others."[7]

Many men we interviewed were on a search to heal themselves through nurturing their children. For many, this meant recognizing how absent their own fathers had been from their lives and attempting to compensate. For instance, the father who said that being with his children taught him about anger remembered that he sometimes got mad at his mother. When asked if he got mad at his father, he replied, "My father wasn't there, so it is hard to think of any negative feelings toward him, because he just wasn't there. I always wanted to please my father, but looking back on it I realize he wasn't a factor. He came home, we sat around the dinner table, and that was pretty much it."

Most of the men and women described fathers who were rarely present, but even those who were around interacted with their children in conventional ways during the evenings and weekends when they were home. For example, both men and women noted that their fathers rarely performed routine child care or did inside housework. Although many remembered their fathers getting angry, few were described as openly showing other emotions. And most fathers were remembered as treating their sons and daughters very differently: they rough-housed and played ball with their sons but expected daugthers to please or serve them. This conventional pattern is exemplified by one of the men's comments about his father. "I don't think I've ever seen him to this day wash a set of dishes or do laundry. Basically my mother would do all the cooking and all the cleaning, all the housework, all the mending, sewing, clothes buying, everything in addition to holding a full-time job. And I think subconsciously I didn't want to repeat that pattern and subject somebody else to that kind of stress." This man went on to suggest that his father was frequently around, but that the nature of his participation in household activities—or lack of it—helped to reinforce conventional expectations about gender roles in the family.

> He wasn't a compulsive worker, so he would be home in the afternoons and on the weekends, and he did play ball with us and he did take us camping. So he was present as a father in ways that were probably supportive of my doing it. It was just as household domesticator that he didn't get involved. . . . Nor was he emotional. He was pretty private and shy, and as a result a cool and distant person. He never, for instance, got involved in discipline negotiations or in making difficult choices. He would either not make them or make them in isolation, he would not talk about them. So, it was hard for him to share emotionally. For instance, I don't think I ever saw him cry.

Like many of the men we interviewed, this one reported that he had consciously decided to counteract some of the patterns he saw in his own father. He acknowledged that his parenting was modeled, in part, on how his father had been with him, but he was attempting to change some of the more "stiffling" and "oblivious" aspects of his father's behavior. He recalled how much work his employed mother had to do around the house, and the stress it placed on their marriage, so he was now trying to do his fair share of the housework. He also confided that his children have seen him cry and that he tries to be open and vulnerable with them instead of being quiet and remote as his own father had been.

Other men were trying to change styles of father–child interaction from their own families, but found little to emulate in their father's behavior. For example, one man described how his father was more likely to express anger, frustration, and disappointment than any positive feelings. "Of course he took care of all the punishments and things like that, all of the beatings. . . . We used to have to count up our things [rule infractions] and wait 'til the end of the week and then take five or six straps for each infraction. So they were beatings, I mean there's no way you could call them anything else." This father went on to describe how he tries to be more positive with his own children and uses less punitive disciplinary techniques. He said he was so traumatized from his own harsh treatment at his father's hand that he found it difficult to administer even "light spankings" to his own children; "Having come from a whole lot more than that, I have some troubles with it. I make sure the kids know that I love them and that they're really sure what the spanking is for and I try to give it right away." Reacting to his own upbringing, this father explicitly tried to avoid giving his children the message he had internalized as a child — that since he sometimes broke the rules he was not worthy of his father's love. Because he still found it hard to express love and other emotions, he said he was compensating for his past and trying to be extra-affectionate with his children whenever he could.

Involved Fathers and Precious Children

The tendency of fathers to heal themselves and develop their emotional capacities through interacting with their children may not be as novel as it first seems. Many mothers also use parenting to fulfill themselves and gain identity, yet most also acknowledge that child care can be emotionally stressful, isolating, and monotonous. I noticed a tendency for first-time fathers to romanticize their relationships with their children more than their wives did, often doting on the children or worrying about being accepted by them. Fathers with older children who had been sharing parenting for years were much less likely to consider parenting a therapeutic self-actualization exercise, but even they tended to hold slightly idealized images of their children.

Why are romantic images of fatherhood and children so important to some men in the late twentieth century? The answer lies in larger social and economic trends and in the growth of what historians have labeled "affective individualism."[8] As we saw in Chapter 2, the "new" father actually dates back at least to the 1920s and is tied up with the expansion of the American middle class and the growth of mass consumerism. As children lost most of their immediate economic benefit, their sentimental value increased for both women and men. This romanticizing trend began many decades ago, but continues to this day, especially in the more affluent middle and upper classes.[9] The modern phenomenon of involved fathering is thus an extension of earlier economic and cultural processes that have increased the emotional value of children. Just as some profound contradictions were embedded in earlier romantic images of domestic wives and priceless children, the modern ideal of the New Father carries some interesting contradictions shaped by class and gender inequalities.

Although some children are being indulged more than ever, one of the most troubling issues facing the nation is our growing inability to care and protect all our children. In general, we are devoting less time to our children and providing them with fewer relative resources than we did just a few decades ago. Children make up a larger percentage of the nation's poor than at any time since we began keeping statistics on such things. With the need for most adults to be employed full time, fewer parents are around on a regular basis to care for children and there are many more dangerous situations confronting them. With continuing high rates of divorce, more biological fathers live away from their children than ever before. In many regions, we now spend more tax dollars on prisons than on schools. On the whole, things seem to be getting worse for children — at least for those living in families in the lower half of the income distribution.

At the same time, some children — especially the more privileged ones — seem to be more priceless than ever. Well-to-do infertile couples are paying tens of thousands of dollars to surrogate mothers to have babies for them; white couples are paying dearly to adopt third world babies; and upper-middle-class parents of all ethnicities are lavishing countless material possessions on their offspring.[10] As if to compensate for the lack of resources we give to the majority of children, we are providing a few with more than enough. To make up for the lack of time that parents can spend with their children, we coin terms like "quality time" so that we can feel better about the time we do spend with them. As if to compensate for the increasing numbers of childless couples and children who do not see their fathers, the ideal middle-class father now comes to resemble Dustin Hoffman in *Kramer vs. Kramer,* Steve Martin in *Parenthood,* or Robin Williams in *Mrs. Doubtfire.* In the overall picture, children may be becoming more symbolically precious to men precisely because father–child relationships are becoming more tenuous and optional, even among the middle class. Today's Mr. Mom could easily become tomorrow's Deadbeat Dad, so we develop elaborate cultural symbols to celebrate the joys of fatherhood.

In an era when outside social forces no longer require women to be subservient to men, romantic cultural symbols that give men reasons to stay involved with their children will have some positive consequences. But as long as gender, class, and ethnic discrimination remain widespread, emotional fulfillment through involved fathering will not be equally available to all and should not be considered a panacea for larger social ills. For example, some critics suggest that modern middle-class men who are unable to develop true intimacy with their wives are the ones most likely to romanticize and overindulge their children. Even if indulgent fathering is a personally fulfilling experience for a husband, from his wife's perspective, it can be a selfish attempt to achieve intimacy without risking vulnerability.[11] And as we saw in the last chapters, taking over some of the more fun parts of child care is not the same as equally sharing all aspects of domestic labor.

Sentimentalizing one's children and celebrating one's emotional involvement with them can be healing for some men, but it may be a privilege that can only be afforded by the more affluent. Mike Messner suggests that the image of the sensitive and involved father should be considered a new class icon because it sets middle-class fathers apart from working-class ones.[12] My research, and that of other sociologists, indicates that middle-class men's emphasis on self-fulfillment that accompanies involved fathering is a by-product of first being able to be an economic "good provider."[13] All the men we talked to expressed love for their children, but the most sentimental fathers had secure jobs and comfortable incomes. The marginally employed men I interviewed did not focus as much on the personal rewards of fathering, but rather on the mundane realities of managing home and children. As noted in the last chapter, those main providers with failed occupational aspirations, but steady work, tended to perform more household labor. Older studies showed that when some men became unemployed, they did less family work rather than more, probably because they lost the emotional security of a job-related masculine identity. Economic conditions and the ability to be a good provider, coupled with prevailing masculinity ideals, thus combine to influence whether a man will embrace fatherhood as emotional self-fulfillment.

Although we are just beginning to learn about the class basis of the New Father ideal, social scientists have long observed that middle- and working-class parents tend to differ in how they think about and attempt to raise their children in modern industrial societies.[14] Even though virtually all parents love their children and want them to be responsible and well behaved, childrearing styles and preferences vary according to one's position in the occupational hierarchy. In general, parents who hold similar kinds of jobs tend to hold similar childrearing values and practices.

Studies done in modern North America, Europe, and Asia show that middle-class parents are more likely than working-class parents to use rewards rather than punishments and to value self-expression and individuality over strict obedience. The theory is that these traits are required by middle-class occupations, and because parents are attempting to prepare their kids for the only type of work life they know, they instill the sorts of traits that will serve them best. For example, middle-class children are more often allowed to be loud because it is seen as healthy expression. At the same time, they are expected to regulate their emotions and attempts are made to get them to "buy into" or "own" specific courses of action (e.g., "Give the toy back to your cousin because you love him and you should want to share with him"). Such training probably helps to shape adult workers who can more easily identify with their job, be efficient emotional managers, and put in long hours in the service of "their" company or "their" profession.[15]

Working-class parents, in contrast, tend to use more direct punishments and place greater value on obedience and outward conformity in their children. In an oversimplified working-class style of parenting, it does not matter what the child feels, only that the child obeys and does not show disrespect (e.g., "Give the toy back or I will spank you"). Not surprisingly, the traits emphasized by working-class parents are thought to contribute to successful performance of routine job tasks, but the jobs themselves do not require that the worker invest a sense of self in the menial tasks performed. Childrearing values and practices thus serve to prepare and place children in the occupational hierarchy, and perpetuating similar differences in the next generation helps to maintain the class structure.[16]

We conducted interviews with people who were raised in families from different class backgrounds and talked to mothers and fathers who were working in both middle-class and working-class jobs (though, like the vast majority of Americans, most thought of themselves as "middle class" no matter what type of job they held). Virtually all the couples we talked to subscribed to a childrearing philosophy that corresponds more closely to the middle-class pattern than the working-class pattern. Some, particularly those who were more religious, demanded more obedience from thier children than others, but most also tended to acknowledge and value their children's expressiveness and individuality. One possible explanation for these parents subscribing to a more indulgent middle-class style of parenting has to do with when they married and became parents. In general, working-class people have experienced earlier transitions to marriage and parenthood than middle-class people. In the next section, I consider the timing of having children because it begins to show how larger social and economic forces help shape how people feel about work and parenting.

The Importance of Timing

Although I did not set out to investigate the timing of parenthood in these peoples' lives, I eventually came to focus on it. As the men and women described their personal histories and private motivations for sharing the care of their children, it soon became clear that having babies relatively "early" or "late" in one's life had important consequences. Age at first birth turned out to be a particularly good predictor of the amount of housework and child care that was shared in both sets of interviews.[17] If couples waited to have children until they were in their late twenties, they were likely to share most aspects of child care and many aspects of housework. In over two-thirds of families with women who were over the age of 27 when they first gave birth, the couples rated housework as relatively equally shared. In contrast, only about one in four couples in which women gave birth earlier shared housework with husbands relatively equally. Although there was wide variation among couples, husbands and wives who achieved the most equal divisions of household labor were also likely to have levels of education, hours of employment, and earnings that were similar to those of their spouse. As discussed below, such similarity between spouses is also related to later childbearing.

Many who wait longer to have children also delay getting married until at least their mid-twenties. Husbands and wives in both interview studies tended to marry later than national averages during the year of their marriage. The median age at marriage for the men was 25 years, and for the women, 23 years. Two-thirds of both men and women were married a year or more later than the national median, with almost a third of both men and women marrying at an age over three years older than the national median.[18] These couples thus married "late" with reference to other marriages in the 1970s, but, by the late 1980s, most people in the United States were similarly waiting until their mid-twenties to marry.[19]

The average age at first birth for the couples we interviewed was also considerably higher than national and state averages. Over a third of the men waited until they were in their thirties to have their first child, as did almost a quarter of the women. The median age at first birth for women was 27, compared to a national median of 23.[20] Three-quarters of the women waited until they were at least 25 years old to have their first child. The women were thus twice as likely to be over 25 when they gave birth to their first child as other women living in California who had children about the same time.[21] Although comparable data on men are not routinely collected by government agencies, we can safely assume that the men we interviewed were also older when they first had children than national and state averages.

What does it mean, in human terms, for couples to delay childbearing until their late twenties or early thirties? What impacts might such a course of action have on family processes and family divisions of labor? While the interview data do not allow for controlled comparisons between representative groups of early- and late-timed parents, they can help us identify some potential impacts of delayed birth. In general, delaying the transition to parenthood allowed women to develop employment-related identities, readied men for parenting, and encouraged the sharing of both child care and housework.

Birth Timing and Father's Role Attachment

Using Erving Goffman's terms to describe how people play different social roles, we can say that most men in this study were "attached" to the father role. Goffman described "role" as the activity expected of a particular position in some system of social relations, and used "role attachment" to describe a person's tendency to become emotionally and intellectually enamored with the self-image available for one entering or enacting a particular role.[22] We probably all know people who become so attached to a particular role identity that they have trouble dropping it. The overbearing coach who drills his own kids or the overindulgent mother who babies everyone are typical examples.

The key contribution of Goffman's formulation was to distinguish the content
or performance of a role from the self-identification that emerged from
enactment of the role. Role attachment thus implies that the individual desires
and expects to see oneself in terms of the enactment of the role, and that
performance of the role further bolsters the image of one's "being" the role.

Many men in this study became attached to the father role in ways that have
typically been associated with a male "mid-life crisis." Studies of mid-life
transitions or "crises" have usually focused on 40- to 50-year-old men and their
reassessment of previous life goals in light of occupational progress.[23] Vaillant
reported that in their middle years, "Men leave the compulsive, unreflective
busywork of their occupational apprenticeships and once more become ex-
plorers of the world within."[24] Other researchers have also described male mid-
life transitions as marked by ongoing self-evaluation, modification of aspirations, and shifts in self-esteem. The common recognition that middle-aged
men have little time left to achieve previous goals can lead to diverse outcomes,
including a substitution of more attainable goals, a career change, a sense of
despair, withdrawal from work, and typically a shift toward greater involvement in family and interpersonal relationships.[25]

Alice Rossi isolates an intriguing commonality among conceptions of male
mid-life transitions.

> [T]his shift from the high centrality of work to greater investment in family is a
> reaction to stress, age, failure in work, or some combination of the three.
> Fatherhood becomes important in the aftermath of dashed dreams, a life- or
> status-threatening experience, or as a component in the developmental reassess-
> ment of life choices during the mid-life transition. This means significant
> emotional accessibility of men to their children only when the children reach
> adolescence and to their wives only late in the second decade of marriage.[26]

Rossi claims that mid-life transitions have encouraged men to value family life
only after it is too late to establish close father–child relationships. In contrast,
delaying the transition to parenthood helped put the men we interviewed on a
different timetable. Many of the fathers made family a priority in ways similar
to those described by the mid-life transition researchers, but they adjusted
their priorities before they had children in the first place, or when their
children were relatively young, rather than waiting until they were adolescents.

Interviews with the fathers suggest that delaying childbearing played
an important part in becoming attached to the father role. For example,
one father of three commented on how being a dad was central to his definition of self:

> I'm definitely, I'm Katie's dad, you know. I'm used to that idea. . . . I think a lot of
> it has to do with the fact that our kids came pretty late in our lives. I'm going to be
> 42 next month — that's pretty old to have little kids the age they are — and I'd done
> an awful lot of things. By the time they came along, I'd gone through all that, I'd

worn out a lot of ideas, you know. I don't feel like I've missed that much. It's okay to be Katie's dad because that's just fine.

Delaying the transition to parenthood can help men avoid some of the financial and time strains that early-timed fathers face when they simultaneously launch a career and a family.[27] Some researchers label the clash between limited resources and increasing family costs at the time of a first birth as the "life cycle squeeze."[28] By first establishing themselves in their jobs, and often by limiting their work commitments in the face of parenthood, many of the late-timed fathers were able to minimize some hardships of the life-cycle squeeze. In addition, when describing the evolution of their divisions of labor, many couples alluded to an ongoing pattern of sharing established early in the relationship that was solidified by postponing marriage and childbearing. Asked why she and her husband shared child care and housework, one mother summarized a common explanation: "Some of it is just assumed from when we first started living together, before we were married or had kids. We each did our own laundry; we each helped in the kitchen though I tended to cook more than he did. We each had our own finances and we just pretty much kept them separate, so it just sort of kept on that way." Husbands used similar explanations to describe how they "naturally" came to share housework and child care with their wives. For instance, one commented that they began sharing household responsibilities before they even considered having children. "Since we've both always been working since we've been married, we've typically shared everything as far as all the working—I mean all the housework responsibilities as well as the child care responsibilities. So it's a pattern that was set up before the kids were even thought of."

Late-timed parents, those who waited until their late twenties or thirties to have children, stated that remaining childless allowed them to be fully ready for parenting and to consciously and jointly choose the parental role. One mother commented,

> We had these kids together; it was definitely a time we decided. When they came, they came to both of us. I think it was a real conscious decision, because we were together for seven years before we decided to have kids and it was definitely something we decided together. We always did things together anyway; it wasn't I did this, he did that and we met for a certain part of the day. We had a lot of time together. We had a pattern of how we ran our household and this extends out of that. And we both have worked all that time, or if we were not working we were going to school.

Similarly, many late-timed parents talked about the importance of experiencing other things in life before becoming parents. One woman noted that waiting several years before having children allowed her and her husband to get comfortable with each other and explore the world before "settling down."

We were real fortunate because we had free time before we had any children; about four years, the year before we were married and three years after that. Sophia was born in '76, so we had almost five years. We had a really nice relationship where we did just about anything we wanted to do. We did a lot of camping and took extended trips, and it just happened that Sophia came along when we were about ready to settle down or semi-settle down or whatever you want to call it.

Many of the late-timed fathers described relatively smooth transitions to parenthood. Asked if he felt competent when he first became a parent at 30 years old, one father talked about his readiness for parenting.

At various times when people would ask me that, closer to when my son was born, 12 years ago, it struck me and I would answer frequently by saying that I felt like my whole life was preparation, and that from the time I was a baby and how my father and mother were with me, everything was all a preparation. It felt like a real natural evolution to me to become a parent, so it didn't seem disruptive or like this big disjuncture. It seemed very much consistent with a pattern, a plan, not a plan but an evolution. So it did feel like my whole life up until then had been a preparation. I felt ready.

This father "felt ready," in part, because he did not enter parenthood soon after leaving the family in which he grew up. His transition to parenthood was an "evolution" rather than "disruptive" precisely because he delayed the childbearing decision. For many of the late timers we interviewed, the birth of the first child was planned and anticipated for a number of years. For early timers, on the other hand, the birth was typically unplanned, and sometimes disruptive.

In summary, the late-timed couples tended to talk about their transition to parenthood in terms of a general sense of readiness for the parental role and an assumed or "natural" sharing of parental responsibilities. Another study of first-time fathers found that three factors were particularly important to the development of a sense of readiness for the parental role: (1) stability in the couple relationship; (2) relative financial security; and (3) a sense of closure on the childless period of their lives.[29] The late-timed couples in our interviews explained their transitions to parenthood with reference to these three factors and also highlighted the notion that early sharing in the relationship established the basis of role sharing after the children arrived. The third criterion, a sense of closure on the childless portion of one's life, is probably the most critical in exploring men's readiness to embrace the father role. Willingness to share fully in child care and other domestic responsibilities typically comes when men have developed a sense of closure on the child-free portion of their lives.

The men we interviewed who shared the most housework were likely to have lived on their own for a number of years, to have attended college, and to have shared household chores with their spouse for several years before the arrival of children. In addition, the men tended to have been employed more continuously than their wives before deciding to have children. Most had increased their earning power and advanced their careers, but some felt confined by an overriding focus on employment. In the context of social approval for involved fathering, many experienced motivational dilemmas and personal re-evaluations similar to those described for mid-life crises. All placed a high value on close relationships and family ties, and some sacrificed financial success and career advancement for personal fulfillment or for their wife's career advancement. Those who delayed having children the longest seemed to be the most attached to the father role.

Mother's Autonomy and Job Attachment

Wives who shared most household labor tended to delay marriage and childbearing because of educational pursuits, commitment to employment, and other personal reasons, thereby enhancing their job prospects and increasing the likelihood of continuous employment after giving birth. With increased economic self-reliance and in the context of commonplace divorce, some of these women also altered traditional criteria for selecting a husband. Instead of seeking a mate on the basis of his ability to be a sole provider, many women sought compatible husbands who were also willing to take part in parenting and housework.

Along with educational and career development, role-sharing women typically developed an enhanced self-image and acquired skills in negotiation and assertion. Even though most fathers expressed a desire to share housework and reported a "natural" evolution of current arrangements, many mothers indicated that equitable divisions of labor were not forthcoming without ongoing reminders. Those women who waited longer to have children were eager to relinquish total responsibility for cleaning, cooking, and child care, and were somewhat more likely than others to bargain for their husband's participation. The ability to relinquish total responsibility for housework was also related to the mother's attachment to her job, which was higher when she had more education and work experience.

Most of the women who had children in their early twenties shared less household labor than late-timers. I found that career and work patterns differed between women who began parenthood in their early twenties or delayed parenthood into their thirties. Early-timed mothers were more likely to follow a sequential pattern in which work/career involvement was delayed, whereas late-timed mothers were more likely to pursue work/career and parenting simultaneously.[30] I also found that early-timed mothers were less autonomous than late-timed mothers, derived more of their identity from their mother role, and were less likely to recognize and talk about their own needs.[31]

In general, women we interviewed who had children in their early twenties were reluctant to demand help and had more difficulty getting their husbands to share child care and housework than women who waited until their late twenties or early thirties to have children. Even though the men in these early-timed families did more child care and perhaps more housework than most men, they tended to do less than most other husbands. Early-timed mothers had less education when they became parents than other women in the samples, and had a harder time defining child care and housework as an equal responsibility of their husbands.

One early-timed mother of two embraced the mother role from the start, but was struggling to find time to launch her own career. She talked about how becoming a mother helped shape her young adult identity: "I feel like my kids helped me grow up. I was 21 when I got pregnant; I was 22 when I had Jasmine. I realize now that I was young. It really helped me grow up; it just helped me with responsibility and I feel like it empowers me that I know I'm a good mom. I have this solid thing inside me that I know I feel good about." She described their household division of labor as being motivated by the fact that her husband made more money and worked longer hours than she did. She had primary responsibility for housework and children, and although she praised him for "helping out" when asked, she complained that she had to initiate conversations to increase his contributions. In describing the household division of labor, she showed her ambivalence.

> I think we work pretty well together on these things. He really does help out a lot. It's the kind of thing where if I ask him to help, he'll help. If I ask him "Please do the dishes," he'll do them. So I have to give him credit; he does help when I ask. But on the average I do things. . . . Sometimes I feel like I would love to just say, "Look, this is your day. You find the babysitter. You worry about everything." But we haven't done that. I mean he'll say he's going to do it, and then time ticks away and I have to do it. I'm not pursuing my work as much because I've got to deal with the kids.

This mother, like some of the other early-timed mothers, talked about their husbands "helping" and referred to women's "natural superiority" in parenting. While they commented that they sometimes requested assistance from their husbands, they did not attempt to redefine family work as a fully shared responsibility. In contrast, late-timed mothers tended to define paid work, housework, and child care as the equal responsibility of both spouses, even if they failed to achieve that ideal. On the whole, early entry into parenthood appeared to create barriers to future role sharing by contributing to women's exclusive reliance on the mother role for a sense of self-worth and by limiting women's earning potential. Delaying the transition to parenthood, on the other hand, changed the couple dynamics by allowing for firm establishment of a job-related identity in women and encouraging men to value the father role.

Birth timing was also related to patterns of relationships with family, friends, and co-workers. Those who delayed the transition to parenthood tended to have higher levels of education, more income, and a preponderance of individually chosen social contacts. Early birth, in contrast, was associated with remaining embedded in social networks from one's youth. For women, having a baby early in one's twenties meant more frequent contact with women kin and other young mothers from church or the local neighborhood, whereas for men it meant more association with family and male friends from high school or the workplace. As we will see in the next section, these different patterns of social contacts have implications for divisions of family work.

Social Networks and Household Labor

Before describing how the couples we interviewed talked about the influence of other people on their daily lives, it is useful to review some important findings about social networks from previous research. In a provocative study of London families in the 1950s, Elizabeth Bott showed how local social circumstances shape family interaction and household labor. In a typical working-class pattern, men and women remain in the community where they grew up, living in gender-segregated worlds much as their parents did. Men tend to socialize with other men, whereas women have frequent contact with women relatives and friends who structure their lives around home and children. Bott observed that this gender-segregated pattern of social interaction was also accompanied by a rigid division of marital roles. Bott contrasted this dense insular pattern with one in which couples had more loose-knit and individualistic social networks. In the latter pattern, husbands and wives were more likely to treat their spouse as a companion, and share both domestic labor and leisure activities with them.[32]

Other researchers have described these sorts of social network differences using the terms "social density" — the extent to which people are constantly in the presence of other people — and "cosmopolitanism" — the variety of people with whom they come into contact. Such factors are important because the higher the social density, the more people identify with their local group, distrust outsiders, and demand that other group members conform to conventional moral standards. In addition, the lower the cosmopolitanism, the more one's ideas tend to be concrete, rather than abstract, becoming crystallized into powerful local symbols. Randall Collins builds on the insights of the classic sociological theorist Emile Durkheim to show how these influences lead those in dense localistic social networks to think in terms of moral absolutes and adhere to rigid codes of behavior, including norms about appropriate gender roles.[33]

Close-knit, kin-based networks, with their high social density and low cosmopolitanism, provide emotional and practical support to women and exert pressure on both men and women to conform to conventional patterns of gender differentiation within families. Bott's study showed that wives in dense social networks share very few leisure or family work activities with their husbands. In contrast, the lack of social support and social sanctions in loose-knit cosmopolitan social networks allow for more sharing of both household duties and leisure activities among husbands and wives.[34]

In the past few decades, other researchers have supported and expanded Bott's notions about the impact of social networks on marital relations by looking at group size and the location of social gatherings. For example, rigid divisions of labor are associated with a collective patterning of social contacts, in which men and women socialize independently with members of the same sex in public settings, such as churches, social clubs, and pubs. Flexible and shared divisions of domestic labor are associated with more individualistic social contacts, in which husbands and wives tend to socialize together, interacting with one or two other couples in the privacy of their homes, as in the typical middle-class dinner party.[35]

American families typlify the same tendencies as the British families that Bott and others interviewed. For example, a study of Boston area working-class couples in the 1970s showed that men's collective social networks discouraged them from assuming most domestic duties. Men typically perceived their paid work to be their primary contribution to the family and had difficulty relinquishing the breadwinner role. Like most men of their day, they rarely assumed responsibility for housekeeping or parenting duties, and fathers were reluctant to display loving behavior toward their children in public settings. Noting that men's peer groups often explicitly ridiculed or ostracized men for doing women's work, Laura Lein suggested that men "down-grade the efforts of other men to contribute to homemaking and pressure them to spend more time and effort on the job or in the peer group."[36]

Studies of couples' embeddedness in larger patterns of social relations, like those noted above, conceive of men's and women's social networks as having different functions. For women, social networks are composed of other women who provide advice, substitute child care, and emotional or material support. Women's networks are often organized around mothering functions, center on kinship ties and almost always contain intergenerational linkages.[37] Even when many of the same people — such as kin or couple friends — are in both the women's and the men's social networks, women tend to be the "kinkeepers" and social organizers, keeping in touch with others, planning social get togethers, and talking more on the telephone.[38]

Men's social networks overlap with those of women, insofar as they are part of the same kin group that is maintained by their wife. Men's own social networks, however, tend to exclude women and are usually composed of men who share similar positions in organizational hierarchies. Because they are often job centered, men's social contacts provide them with informal information on "how the system works."[39] Lein notes that "for men it is more useful to know people who know other people. For women it is more helpful to have personal contact with people who can pitch in."[40] Similarly, Bott sums up social network differences by saying, "Men have friends. Women have relatives."[41]

Recent research provides support for this model of gender-segregated social networks, but also suggests that it may not apply to all families. Unlike the dense neighborhood-centered networks of London described by Bott, social networks in North America are typically more dispersed and less focused on kinship ties. And recent changes appear to be weakening community-based network ties even further. American families move around much more and travel farther to see friends and relatives than those in England, and generally more than they used to. Friends as well as kin still help with the daily hassles of life, and neighbors sometimes watch each other's children, but patterns of routine assistance and social contact are much more individualistic than in the past, especially with today's high rates of geographic mobility and divorce. Instead of the local community and extended family imposing its ideals and practices on individual couples, the modern pattern is based more on individual couples choosing which contacts they want to maintain, and from whom they will receive support.[42] Networks are becoming less kin centered, but most people still have contact with relatives who live nearby, and women still tend to maintain those contacts. Nevertheless, the trend is definitely toward shaping one's own networks rather than passively accepting one's local and kin ties.

Supporting Bott's idea that kin contacts shape marital relations, most studies show that marital roles are more segregated when the wife's parents help out and that sole breadwinner fathers play less frequently with children when other women relatives live nearby.[43] Having female relatives in close proximity encourages the view that child care is women's work, and is associated with lower levels of routine child care by fathers. One recent study found that women in all family types reported receiving more child care and household help from relatives than men did. Nevertheless, single fathers, like single mothers, are likely to maintain frequent contact with kin, and receive substantial support from them.[44] Having sole responsibility for children thus seems to promote kin network ties, regardless of whether the single parent is a man or a woman.

But what happens in the increasingly common situation of two-parent families having loose-knit social networks? One midwestern study suggested that fathers who performed significant amounts of routine child care were substituting non-kin bonds for extended family networks.[45] Thus, when fathers wanted to be more involved in the daily routines of family life, or when practical necessity forced them to do more family work, they were more involved with friends than with kin. Researchers looking at women's lives have also found that they rely on non-kin social networks instead of kinship networks if they are attempting nonconventional occupational pursuits.[46] Taken together, these findings support the notion that different types of social networks can have different impacts on divisions of family labor, and that individual families may have more control over shaping their social networks than earlier research implied.

In our interviews, we discovered that two-job couples were actively transforming their social relations at the same time that they were influenced by kinship, friendship, and job-related associations with others. They were not simply passive victims of their social situations, but were constantly making decisions about whom to spend time with, how to portray their family arrangements to others, and whose comments they should take seriously. When I talked to the couples about their family and paid work allocation I heard many different stories. As I analyzed the interview transcripts, I noticed wide variation in the ways that people talked about family and friends and about whether they even noticed others' reactions to their situations. Some people rarely saw anyone outside their immediate family, whereas others saw members of their extended families or close friends on a regular basis. Some seemed to be unaffected by responses from relatives, friends, and co-workers, whereas others tended to agonize over slight signs of disapproval from those they loved or respected.

People learn about themselves by comparing themselves with others, which is based, in part, on who they know, how often they see them, how they interact with them, and whether they value them.[47] Researchers studying reference groups, relative deprivation, and equity judgments look at who is chosen as a comparative reference, on which attributes they are compared, how evaluations are made, and what outcomes follow various evaluations. We know something about how people compare their rewards and efforts to others' in paid-work settings because most research focuses on employment and occupational promotions. People use others like themselves — in terms of education, training, and job skills — for making those comparisons. By seeing what other people do and receive, we tend to develop a sense of fairness, and evaluate our own job efforts and rewards accordingly.

Although people make social comparisons and invoke principles of fairness in discussing paid work, some suggest that in evaluating divisions of family work, neither mothers nor fathers use vocabularies of "deservingness."[48] Others speculate that people *do* compare their patterns of family work to those of other people, but that they only compare themselves to people of the same gender. For example, researchers interpreting national survey data suggest that dual-earner men with children "compare themselves to single-earner men and experience relative deprivation with respect to conventional gender expectations regarding the provider role and the services of a nonemployed wife."[49] Whether fathers experience "relative deprivation" or mothers invoke "principles of deservingness" concerning their performance of household labor depends on how people conceive of appropriate roles for themselves within their families, which, in turn, is strongly influenced by their placement and interaction in wider social networks. In the next section, I turn to a discussion of social factors that promoted or inhibited the sharing of family work for the couples we interviewed.

Friendship Networks

Like most new parents, the couples we interviewed reported that their social lives were sharply curtailed when they had children. This was explained in terms of the limited time they had for anything except the essential tasks of earning money, maintaining the household, and focusing on family relationships. Although the traditional pattern is for the mother's social life to be altered more than the father's, most couples reported that both men's and women's social networks contracted and came to be constituted around mutual concern for children. This was especially true of those couples who were sharing the most child care and housework. One father commented, "Basically if the other people don't have kids and if they aren't involved with the kids, then we aren't involved with them. It's as simple as that. The guys I know at work that are single or don't have children my age don't come over because we have nothing in common."

Parents also reported developing new social contacts based on their relations with children. Many of the older children participated in organized sports that became a focal point for adult interaction. A few mothers and many fathers helped coach their children's teams, and parents reported socializing with new friends during gymnastics lessons, soccer games, baseball games, and other organized athletic activities. A father of a 12-year-old boy and an eight-year-old girl reflected on how sports provided the closest thing to an extended family that he had experienced since childhood.

> It's strange. It's unlike anything I ever thought I would be involved in. It's the parents of the kids on my kids' teams meeting at the park on the bleachers, sitting in the school basketball courts, doing the sports. So we become observers of our children together and that defines our relationship as adults. We are the witnesses of our children's athletic talents.

Structuring social relations around their children's athletic, musical, school, or extracurricular activities provided many parents with opportunities for interaction not otherwise available to them. Some reported that they regularly interacted with people from a different social class, religion, race, or lifestyle, as a result of having children on the same team or in the same school classroom. With a few exceptions, parents claimed that this was a positive experience, both for them and their children.

A substantial minority of parents in both groups noted that many of their close parent-friends were divorced, with single-mothers far outnumbering single-fathers as close friends of both men and women. Virtually all families had some married couple friends who were more conventional in their divisions of labor, but many knew couples who were more egalitarian than they perceived themselves to be. Many couples indicated that divisions of labor in their single and married friends' families influenced how they related to them. One father commented on how his friendship with a less involved father suffered and how he felt judged by a more involved father.

> In one family where the husband has pretty much backed out of any responsibility that I can see — partially because of his employment situation and partially just because that's the way things were set up — I think my relationship with them and our relationship with that family has in some ways disintegrated. . . . That is, his relationship to his kids, his absence in my perception (even though I'm very aware that it's my judgment; it may not be his family's judgment at all) has affected me. On the other hand, I have another friend — they only have one child — and I've always felt slightly judged by him that I've not paid as much attention to my daughter as he has to his.

This example illustrates how social contacts with more conventional parents were often limited, in part because they failed to support these parents' view of the world. In feeling "judged" by a more involved father, this father also shows that friendship networks can work in the opposite direction from that usually predicted. His comments demonstrate that some social networks can encourage, rather than discourage, the sharing of parental duties.

Mothers and fathers reported that women friends who were in more conventional marriages or were single often idealized their situations. Many mothers said their women friends repeatedly told them that they were extremely fortunate to have such helpful husbands. The men were described as "wonderful," "fantastic," "incredible," and other terms suggesting that they were unusual. Some mothers reported that women friends were "jealous," envious," or "amazed," and most mothers we talked to had at least one acquaintance who held unrealistic appraisals of their husbands. One woman said that although she appreciated her husband's "willingness to help," friends who called him perfect were "a little out of touch."

Both mothers and fathers agreed that men received more credit for family involvement than did women, because it was expected that mothers would perform child care and housework. Since parenting was assumed to be "only natural" for women, fathers were frequently praised for performing a task that would go unnoticed if a mother had performed it. One mother who did more of the child care than her husband talked about resenting all the attention he got. "I think I get less praise because people automatically assume that, you know, the mother's *supposed* to do the child care. . . . And he gets a lot of praise because he's the visible one."

Fathers, too, talked about resenting certain types of comments from friends or co-workers, especially when they felt misunderstood. One said he bristled every time anyone characterized his parenting efforts as "helping" his wife.

> At the beginning of our relationship there was an assumption by everyone that my wife did all the woman or housework type of things, like she took care of the babies and played the nurturing role. There was sort of an expectation that I didn't do that. It would irritate me. . . . I think there is something within Latino culture or roles that if you do it, you're somehow different, you're exceptional. It bothers me when people make it sound like I'm doing something special, like "Oh, you're babysitting the kids, huh?" My standard reply is "No I don't babysit my own kids." That bothers me, because there's a perception that I don't care enough about my own kids to take care of them.

Although this Chicano father attributed the stereotype of mothers being solely responsible for family work to Latino culture, most of the other fathers we interviewed had similar feelings about reactions they received. One father, a teacher, said he resented all the special attention he received when he was out with his infant son.

> Constant going shopping and having women stop me and say, "Oh it's so good to see you fathers." I was no longer an individual; I was this generic father who was now a liberated father who could take care of his child. I actually didn't like it. I felt after a while that I wanted the time and the quality of my relationship with my child at that point, what was visible in public, to simply be accepted as what you do. It didn't strike me as worthy of recognition, and it pissed me off a lot that women in particular would show this sort of appreciation which I think is well-intentioned, but which also tended to put a frame around the whole thing as though somehow this was an experience that could be extracted from one's regular life. It wasn't. It was going shopping with my son in a snuggly or in the backpack. Shopping was what I was doing. [Having my son with me] wasn't somehow this event that always had to be called attention to.

Many fathers admitted that they enjoyed the praise they got for being actively involved with their kids, but most indicated that they did not take direct or second-hand compliments very seriously. One postal carrier said, "I get more credit than she does, because it's so unusual that the father's at home and involved in the family. I realize what it is: it's prejudice. The strokes feel real nice, but I don't take them too seriously." Another father, a part-time clerk, similarly commented, "I'm sort of proud of it in a way that I don't really like. It's nothing to be proud of, except that I'm glad to be doing it and I think it's kind of neat because it hasn't been the style traditionally. I kind of like that, but I know that it means nothing."

These comments reveal that fathers appreciated praise about their involvement with their children, but actively discounted compliments, especially if received from those in dissimilar situations. If the fathers participated in routine caretaking, their everyday experiences led them to view parenthood as drudgery, rather than as some special event or status that deserved special recognition. Many described their parental responsibility as taken for granted and did not want it to be considered out of the ordinary or something worthy of special praise. When I asked one father what kinds of reactions he got from his wife's friends when his children were babies, he summed up a typical one.

> They all thought it was really wonderful. They thought she'd really appreciate how wonderful it was and how different that was from her father. They'd say, "You ought to know how lucky you are, he's doing so much." I just felt like I'm doing what any person should do. Just like, "Shouldn't anybody be this interested in their child?" No big deal.

These accounts show how fathers discounted and normalized extreme reactions to their divisions of labor and interpreted them in a way that supported the "natural" character of what they were doing. By rejecting or discounting praise from people in dissimilar situations, fathers maintained consistency in their taken-for-granted reality.

A similar pattern was evident when fathers suspected that their friends might not approve of their family involvements. For instance, one Chicano father rejected imputations of being unmasculine from nonfathers and turned his focus to men who had children. "Most of my male companions, you know, are Chicanos, and to them I'm sure what I do, they probably see it as not too 'masculine.' To me that's a lot of crap. The ones who have children would probably understand."

In contrast to previous studies, only a few fathers indicated that men friends reacted negatively to their assumption of child care or housework duties. A few men were teased by friends for doing "unmanly" housework, but even they seemed to reject the implied comparisons, and chose to compare themselves to fathers in similar situations. Rather than internalizing humorous or derogatory comments from other men, they described a process of selectively discounting the ribbing and actively joining in the good-natured bantering. One commented,

> I don't know if they mean it literally or something, but, you know, a friend comes in and I'm ironing, and it's like a tease, you know, "Aieeeee, why are you married, man?" That kinda stuff. But that doesn't bother me, you know, because I just tease right back: "If you want it done right you have to do it yourself." The main thing is we tend to go out with other people who have kids, you know, who can relate to our situation.

Instead of taking every reaction to heart, the couples we talked to filtered the overt comments and subtle cues they received from those around them, discounting some and accepting others. The parents were not passive recipients of social judgments from those in their social networks, but were engaged in a process of selectively attending to or responding to reactions from others.

They were typically members of multiple social networks, and were not surprised by contradictory reactions from people in different situations. One mother commented on a pattern that was mentioned by the majority of parents: domestic divisions of labor were "normal" to those who were attempting something similar, and "amazing" to those who were not. "All the local friends here think it's amazing. They call him 'Mr. Mom' and tell me how lucky I am. I'm waiting for someone to tell him how lucky *HE* is. I have several friends at work who have very similar arrangements and they just feel that it's normal."

Although both mothers and fathers had some friends who shared parenting, most described other couples' situations as being somewhat different from their own. For example, some commented that the people they knew who divided child care most equally were divorced, and alternated child care between separate households. Friends in two-parent families were also typically described as being different in important respects. The scarcity of directly comparable referents encouraged fathers to filter and transform received praise or criticism, and to turn elsewhere for comparisons.

Because fathers were assuming traditional "mothering" functions, they often had more social contact with mothers than with other fathers, at least when they were not on their paid jobs. They talked about being one of the only fathers at children's lessons, parent classes and meetings, at the laundromat, or in the market.[50] As a consequence, the most involved fathers often compared their efforts to other mothers' efforts, as they saw themselves doing similar things. Even more typically, however, the fathers compared their child-care efforts directly to those of their wives. Previous researchers have assumed that men and women rarely use each other as comparison referents, especially for family work. In contrast, the couples we interviewed first compared their efforts to those of their spouse, and only secondarily used same sex others, provided that they were matched on some important issues like employment status, number of children, and level of commitment to the family.

Occupational Networks

All the couples we interviewed assumed that both parents would work to earn money, even though a few still hoped that they could change to a single earner arrangement when the husband began making more money. One 39-year-old father whose oldest child was 11 commented, "We made it right at the end of the time period when it was really a choice, and a conscious decision, whereas now almost everybody has two jobs and has to deal with this." The possibility of mothers not working, at least for the first year after the baby was born, was raised in almost all families. The complementary possibility that husbands would not work was infrequently discussed, and rarely considered feasible, though almost all the fathers took a few days off after the birth.

For most mothers, talking about their children to their co-workers was acceptable. This was true, in part, because the majority of their co-workers were also mothers. In a handful of cases, the mothers chose not to discuss their family lives because it interfered with their perceived occupational authority or impartiality. Others limited talk about their family because they felt co-workers could not relate to, or would be jealous of their family situations. Most, however, talked openly about their home life, and many indicated that their co-workers were in similar, if somewhat less supportive, relationships.

Although mothers were employed in occupations predominately composed of women, fathers tended to work for and with other men, and were sometimes discouraged from talking about family or children. Several fathers reported that people at their place of work could not understand their situation and a few mentioned that co-workers would be disappointed when they would repeatedly turn down invitations to "go out for a drink." Most fathers said that their sense of obligation to their families kept them from "hanging out" with the guys, and only a few admitted that they sometimes stayed late with friends after work. A 36-year-old mechanic commented, "I don't hang around with my friends at work because if I want to come home and spend time, I can't do both. Once you deviate from coming straight home, by the time you talk, have a beer, it might be two, three hours and I get home at nine."

Other fathers focused on the demands of the job, and worried that bosses, clients, or co-workers might consider them "flaky" if they left work to be with their children. One self-employed carpenter said that he would sometimes conceal that he was leaving work to do something with his children because he worried about negative reactions.

> I would say reactions that I've gotten, in business, like if I leave a job somewhere that I'm on and mention that I'm going to coach my son's soccer game, I have felt people kind of stiffen. Like I was shirking my job, you know, such a small thing to leave work for, racing home for. . . . It got to the point with some people where I didn't necessarily mention what I was leaving for, just because I didn't need for them to think that I was being irresponsible about their work, I mean, I just decided it wasn't their business. If I didn't know them well enough to feel that they were supportive, I would just say, "I have to leave early today" — never lie, if they asked me a question, I'd tell them the answer — but not volunteer it. And, maybe in some cases, I feel like, you know, you really have to be a little careful about being too *groovy* too, that what it is that you're doing is just so wonderful, "I'm a father, I'm going to go be with my children." It isn't like that, you know, I don't do it for what people think of me.

Another father, a self-employed computer systems consultant, also described how he made choices to reveal or withhold information about his family life.

With some of his business clients, he felt like he was "in the closet" about spending so much time with his kids.

> It is true that in my work only some people knew. . . . I mean I may be playing with my kids and they want a job done and some people understand that—no—most people don't know, of course, but some people know who are very supportive. Other people would say, "I'm concerned about you getting the job done, I don't care about this stuff." And in that way I'm a little bit in the closet—part of me would like to come out of the closet and say, "Listen, folks, this is who you've been dealing with all these years."

For some involved fathers, comments about spending time with their children were perceived as indications that they were not "serious" about their work. Particularly in occupations dominated by men, commitment to parenting was seen as evidence of an insufficiently strong commitment to the job. Fathers reported that they received indirect messages that providing for the family should be primary and that physically being with family should be considered secondary. Women are subject to some of the same pressures when they work in professions dominated by men, but they face a unique double bind: ignoring the children is a sign of maternal neglect, but spending time with the children is perceived as a lack of career commitment.[51]

Some of the men we interviewed also mentioned that if they talked about child care or family obligations on the job, co-workers teased them or told them that they were undermining men's privileged status. A utility lineman commented,

> Some of the guys at work resent me for it. Like they say, "You guys are too perfect, you always help out, you're always doing the chores." So I tend to not discuss too much with them, they don't understand, and they don't want to understand, they really don't care. . . . Besides, I hate people who brag about their kids, so I wouldn't talk too much about my kids at work, just little things every now and then.

Most men had not heard any overt comments from co-workers, but they sensed some unspoken criticisms, and a few worried that co-workers might not consider them "real men" if they admitted that they did "women's work." Even though most fathers rejected these labels as misguided, the fear of being labeled unmasculine by co-workers' prompted many to keep their family activities private.

Some fathers selected their current jobs on the basis of schedule flexibility or acceptance of their need to have time off to take care of their children. Joseph Pleck suggests that many more fathers would take advantage of such workplace policies and programs if we began assuming that fathers, as well as mothers, should take advantage of them.[52] One father we interviewed was employed at a large firm as a computer technician. He commented that he had consciously decided to accept the possible imputations of nonseriousness that came with admitting that his family came first.

I kind of tend to choose my jobs. When I go to a job interview, I explain to people that I have a family and the family's very important to me. Some companies expect you to work a lot of overtime or work weekends and I told them that I don't have to accept that sort of thing. I may not have gotten all the jobs I ever might have had because of it, but it's something that I bring up at the job interview and let them know that my family comes first.

Kin Networks

Only a small proportion of the people we interviewed reported having at least weekly contact with their parents, in-laws, or siblings. Few had parents who lived close by and none reported that they used "grandma" for routine child care. (Even if "grandma" lived in the neighborhood, she typically had her own job and a busy schedule.) Most couples indicated that their relatives "tolerated" or "put up with" their sharing of child care and housework. The older generation of parents were described as "confused," "bemused," and "befuddled," and it was said that they "lack understanding" or "think it's a little strange." Only a few reported outright hostility, but many people sensed that their parents were uncomfortable because they were raising their own children so differently from how they had been raised.

One mother reported that her parents and in-laws wouldn't "dare to criticize" their situation because "times had changed," but she sensed some underlying worry and concern, especially from older women relatives.

I think both sides of the family think it's fine because it's popular now. They don't dare—I mean if we were doing this 30 years ago, they would dare to criticize. In a way, now they don't. I think both sides feel it's a little strange. I thought my mom was totally sympathetic and no problem, but when I was going to go away for a week and my husband was going to take care of the kids, she said something to my sister about how she didn't think I should do it. There's a little underlying tension about it I think.

Other people reported that disagreements with parents were common, particularly if they revolved around trying to change childrearing practices their own parents had used. One mother related how her mother's "archaic" childrearing standards have created conflict in their relationship.

As far as my relationship goes with my mother, I feel like I have an adult relationship with her, but as far as she goes, I'm her daughter. So how my children work into that is, she often questions my decisions about my children. When I decided my children were not going to eat certain foods until certain ages, she did not respect those decisions and she questioned them and she even did things when I wasn't around, gave them certain kinds of foods and then when I came back, she would say, "See, I gave them corn and they didn't choke," you know, that kind of thing. Kind of a test of authority. So we've had a lot of discussions about that and still occasionally argue about my standards versus her standards.

As noted above, most couples mentioned that their own fathers were relatively uninvolved in family life when they were growing up. Many sensed that "grandpa" was troubled by the new ways they were trying to raise their kids, though few reported that they discussed it directly with them. One man said he had to counter his father's fear of boys playing with dolls.

> My son would pick up the dolls, and he was acting like a daddy to the doll. And I guess that I 'm mature, or whatever, because I didn't see anything wrong with it. Then my father came down and says, "Get that away from him," and I said, "Papa, it's nothing, it's just a toy." But he would equate it with being, you know, a little strange. If it's anything, it's caring.

Many couples reported that initial negative reactions from parents turned more positive over time as they saw that their grandchildren were "turning out all right." It helped that the couple was still together after an average of over 10 years of marriage and that the men, even if initially viewed as "a little strange," were still employed. This last point, that parents were primarily concerned with their son's (or son-in-law's) financial provider responsibilities, highlights how observers typically evaluated the couples' task sharing. Some of the study participants mentioned that their parents wanted the wife to quit work and stay home with the children and the husband to "make up the difference" by working more hours or getting a better job. Even when they approved of the couple sharing the family labor, the older generation was still concerned that the husband continue to be the major provider. When the wife made more money than the husband, or had a more prestigious job, they tended to treat his family involvement as somewhat degrading. If on the other hand, they could treat the wife's earnings as"extra money" and characterize the husband's family involvement as "helping out," then they were less threatened by their children's novel arrangements.

One mother, who earned almost as much money as her husband, talked about the reactions she got from his parents.

> In the beginning there was a real strong sense that I was in the space of my husband's *duty*. That came from his parents pretty strongly. . . . The only way that they have been able to come to grips with this in any fashion is because he has also been financially successful. If he had decided, you know, "Outside work is not for me, I'm going to stay home with the kids and she's going to work," I think there would have been a whole lot more flak than there was. I think it's because he did both and was successful that it was okay.

Another mother, a teacher who earned more money than her husband, noted that parental acceptance of shared parenting did not necessarily entail acceptance of the woman as an essential financial provider. "There is a funny dynamic that happens with our parents, but it's not about the child care. I don't get enough credit for being the breadwinner, [and] they're still critical of him for not earning as much money as I do. In a way they've accepted him as being an active parenting father more than they've accepted me being a breadwinner." The older generation assumed that the "essential nature" of men is to be providers. If their sons, or sons-in-law, continued to earn more money than their wives, they could still be seen as real men. Remaining a significant provider made it easier for others to accept their unusually active role in family work.

These examples illustrate that contact with kin creates pressure to conform to the elders' more conventional standards. If people had frequent contact with their parents, they were exposed to comments and subtle cues to allocate responsibilities differently. Most young parents said they were resisting such pressures and attempting to parent differently from how they had been raised. Most valued their relationships with their mothers and fathers, but were also trying to avoid the typical 1950s pattern of overinvolved mothers and emotionally absent fathers. Having infrequent contact with their own parents aided their efforts to change these inherited patterns.

Although their own parents pressured them to change, the siblings of those we interviewed rarely gave them any trouble. Brothers and sisters were as frequently supportive as critical or "tolerant," and many siblings were described as better at sharing family work than those with whom we spoke. Like parents, most siblings did not live close by, so were infrequently seen. If brothers, sisters, or other relatives lived near, they typically gathered together only for birthdays or special holidays.

The couples in the first interviews were of white European descent, with approximately equal numbers originally from Protestant, Catholic, or Jewish families. Most, however, did not now regularly attend church. They were generally mobile, middle-class, college-educated couples who lived far from the towns and cities where they were born and raised. As noted above, this tended to minimize contact with their own parents and gave them more freedom in forging new patterns of family life. Many acknowledged the positive aspects of being free from restrictive family networks, but some also lamented the fact that they and their children did not enjoy the benefits of a close-knit extended family.

> I regret that we don't have relatives nearby with whom we would function as a whole family. I think there's a way in which, when I compare my childhood to the childhood my children are having, there were many occasions where—with cousins and aunts and uncles—we were a family, and it was simply that was the way it was. You went to your cousin's house. That's just so absent from our lives. We have not replaced that by friends, by families of friends or friends of families—I don't know how to put it. We have the equivalent of the family structure in our lives; but we have a variety of other more atomized relationships. The kids have their friends, I have my friends and colleagues, my wife has her

friends, but it's very hard to say "We have *our* friends," in the same sense as we had our relatives when I was a kid.

A few of these couples commented that they were recreating a sense of extended family by choosing their own friends and creating institutions like babysitting co-ops or play groups. Despite attempts to recreate extended family networks, however, most study participants said their friendship networks did not satisfy their desire for a sense of family belonging. Most said they were too busy to cultivate and maintain close relationships on a voluntary basis. They had too little energy, or lacked the motivation to build a structure that would facilitate close and ongoing contact with other parents and children. For that reason, existing organizations, like schools, team sports, or occasionally churches, served as a "family-like" community. Because most people lacked a close-knit extended family network, they relied on the couple relationship and their immediate family to provide their primary source of entertainment, support, and interaction.

The interviews with Chicano couples revealed some interesting differences in social networks. Like the Anglo couples, they were mostly middle class and college educated, but a larger portion had been raised in families on the edge of poverty. Another important difference between the two groups was that the Chicanos were much more likely to be Catholic and attend church regularly. They were also more likely to have grown up in the local area and have relatives living nearby. In stark contrast to the Anglos, the Chicanos saw their parents several times each week. These different patterns of church membership and kin contact reflect more dense social networks.

Not surprisingly, the Chicano couples reported more resistance when they tried to change traditional patterns of labor allocation. Their dense social networks contributed to more conventional views about gender and cultivated contrasting perceptions between men and women. As noted in the last chapter, the men we interviewed did more family work than their peers, but they did less, on average, than men in the first group. The social pressure the couple felt was not perceived as oppressive because they could make their own decisions, but regular contact with parents and other kin was constraining. When a couple departed from conventional, gender-based allocations of work, there was more chance that some friend or relative would observe it and feel entitled to make some disparaging comment.

Interpreting Social Reactions

We discovered that most couples say they do not take mild disapproval or even outright criticism very seriously. Nevertheless, when they shrug it off, or even angrily reject it, they still have to justify their actions to others and to themselves. In the face of a rigid societal ideology of separate spheres, they are constantly called on to render themselves accountable as men and women. How can the husband, as a "real" man, afford to take time off from work to care for a sick child? Why is he at the park with his toddler during the middle of the day? How can the wife, as a "true" woman and mother, allow her children to be cared for every day by a man, even if he is the children's father? How can she let herself go to work when her child is home sick? The routine presence of kin and neighbors requires one to explain and justify any action that departs from the ideal of separate spheres. Couples in both groups were held accountable for their actions, but since couples in the second were "doing gender" in a more public arena, their actions were further constrained. Simple exposure to kin and others more conventional than themselves limited the extent to which they could be innovative in their distribution of family work and paid work.

These findings show that dense local kin networks can discourage husbands and wives from sharing family work. In contrast, high mobility, individualistic social networks, and heavy reliance on the couple relationship can encourage the sharing of both child care and housework. Previous research suggested that men's social networks are group oriented, typically derive from paid-work contexts, and are defined in opposition to cultural definitions of "femininity." The most involved fathers in our interviews avoided these types of social contexts. For practical reasons and personal preferences, the fathers did not usually spend their leisure time in all-men group settings, and most did not "hang out" with other men after work. Like mothers, fathers who performed the most child care and housework had little contact with adults apart from their interactions with co-workers or their spouse. The daily interactions of the most involved fathers occurred in child-centered small-group contexts, thus facilitating more intimate and personal expression than the larger all-men groups that have been assumed to shape men's behaviors.

According to previous studies, the job-related context of most men's social contacts and the kin-related context of most women's social contacts exert pressure to maintain conventional gender-based divisions of labor. For most of the couples we interviewed, however, these gender-differentiated network functions were beginning to blur. The mothers had many work-related friends and the fathers usually came into contact with friends and acquaintances only if they shared an interest in children. Among couples who shared the most, parenting functions came to dominate the fathers' social networks at least as much as they shaped the mothers'. Most "outside" activities were centered around the children and if other adults were included, they tended to be parents with children of similar ages.

Another assumption has been that men will be judged negatively by other men and will judge themselves only in relation to men. In the context of focusing on children, and with a contraction of kinship and friendship networks, many men we interviewed reported more social contact with mothers than with other fathers. They reported friendships with fathers too, and occasionally compared themselves to such men, but rejected most comparisons to men in more conventional marriages. As a consequence, they did not experience relative deprivation as suggested by other researchers.[53] They did not use men in single-earner families as referents, nor did they directly compare themselves to two-earner husbands who did little housework or child care. Instead, sample men most often compared themselves to their wives and secondarily to single and two-parent mothers or caretaking fathers in two-earner families.

Social scientists do not know much about selecting cross-gender referents for social comparison, but in this case, it had some important consequences. Comparing men's contributions directly to those of wives and other women significantly influenced implicit and explicit bargaining over the division of family work. Cross-gender comparisons allowed for more housework items to be negotiated, because couples were no longer considering certain tasks to be exclusively the province of men or women. These comparisons were made possible because of changing social networks and new ideas about what mothers and fathers should do. The couples we interviewed were actively and passively involved in the creation of their own social networks rather than relying on pre-established kinship networks.

These exploratory interviews were not designed to test competing hypotheses about the general relationship between social networks and divisions of household labor. We cannot say, for instance, that differences in the social networks of the first and second samples "caused" the observed differences in their divisions of family work. Neither can we predict with confidence that the observed processes would apply to most other families. The interviews with these 40 families are suggestive, however, and highlight some potentially fruitful areas for further inquiry. Clearly, social networks matter, and if men are to assume a more active role in parenting and housework, changing social networks will play a major role.

As noted above, delaying parenthood and a desire to compensate for the emotional absence of one's own father also appear to be important motivators for sharing child care. Late transitions to parenthood and seeking self-fulfillment through children are related to educational attainment, employment experience, and social network configurations, which, in turn are related to social class and opportunities and expectations for career advancement. All these elements, along with other individual and cultural factors, produce varying attachments to jobs and families, which influence family interactions and shape gender identities. We are just beginning to understand how these things fit together and how they change over time.

The couples we interviewed were constrained by economic, social, and psychological factors, but they had more influence over shaping their daily lives than most sociological theories have implied. The practice of daily paid and unpaid work, in part conditioned by financial necessity, and in part a reflection of personal priorities, was highly influential in forming and solidifying personal and family identities. The timing of the transition to parenthood, along with contraction in social networks and increased reliance on the marital relationship, provided many of these two-job couples with a high degree of autonomy. They tended to fit the middle-class pattern of a slower and more gradual assumption of adult roles with a significant emphasis on individuality and emotional self-fulfillment. They did not always feel in control of their lives, but they were consciously attempting to overcome personal limitations and social conventions, and were actively involved in shaping their own destinies.

The results presented above challenge the typical bifurcated model of job/family relations that posits separate networks and different social processes for fathers and mothers. Instead of primarily focusing on women's family commitments and men's job commitments as defined by an ideology of separate spheres, we need to pay attention to the explanatory power of men's family commitments and women's job commitments. This is not to say that men and women will behave in the same manner because their socialization, employment experiences, and social networks continue to differ in most cases. But we ought to acknowledge that the demands of family and employment can have similar impacts on men and women, even though these demands remain deeply gendered. One of our tasks might then be to specify the conditions under which a gender-neutral or a gender-segregated model of family work emerges. In order to do that, I turn to national survey data in the next chapter to see if the processes described in the last few chapters are representative of other American households.

6

Explaining Family Work

In the last three chapters I explored how some California couples talked about balancing paid work and family obligations. Focusing on personal motivations and social contexts, I was able to generate some ideas about why other couples might attempt to share various aspects of household labor and which couples might be most likely to succeed. My goals in this chapter are to broaden the previous analysis to include studies of families from throughout the United States, to identify the most promising explanations for why Americans share family work, and to test these ideas using a national sample of households. Results will provide the basis for making predictions about the future in the last chapter.

The research procedures and statistical analyses needed to test the different theories and untangle complicated relationships are a bit tedious, even for those trained in such endeavors. Consequently, I will only briefly introduce the major theories and specific hypotheses from past research, focusing on the most important or consistent empirical findings from studies using large representative samples. Readers interested in the technical details of previous studies should consult the endnotes for references to original published sources.[1] Readers less interested in theories and surveys can skip this chapter and get a condensed summary in the beginning of Chapter 8.

Theories of Household Labor Allocation

The most common reasons scholars offer for why and how family work is divided in American families include many of the explanations used by the couples we interviewed. Social scientists have transformed and enlarged many of these everyday accounts using complex conceptual schemes and elaborate causal modeling techniques, but the core ideas are still fairly simple. Theories, after all, are just interpretations of why things happen as they do, and we can explore their basic outlines by briefly reviewing some of their underlying premises. A thorough discussion of the merits and shortcomings of the major theories is beyond the scope of this chapter. Neither is there space to adequately test hypotheses derived from the theories, but we can at least begin to identify the main ideas and see which ones have the most empirical support.

Although a few scientists continue to argue for direct biological determinants of gender-segregated work, most scholars focus on the social processes that shape labor allocation. Two general theoretical frameworks have been proposed to explain how family work is divided: human capital theory and social-structural theory. Both approaches highlight the social and economic factors that constrain people's choices, with one very important difference: Human capital theory tends to accept and justify the status quo, whereas social-structural theory tends to challenge it.

Human Capital Theory

Human capital theory provides an economic explanation for how families divide responsibility for paid and unpaid work.[2] One of its major proponents, the Nobel Prize winner Gary Becker, based his arguments on classical economic theory, but applied the theory to aspects of family life that most economists ignore. According to Becker's argument, individual men and women trade off between spending time in market work and household work, basing their decisions on getting the most for the time invested (often dubbed "maximizing household utility"). In general, this approach assumes that couples make decisions for the good of the entire family unit, always deciding to do what will bring the maximum rewards for the least total effort.

Labor specialization is the key principle behind each family's cost-benefit calculation, according to human capital theory, as individuals decide to invest more time and effort in the activities at which they are most efficient. As Becker sees it, since women are biologically committed to bearing and rearing children, they are most efficient at household work and develop what economists call tastes or preferences for it. Men, on the other hand, are most efficient at market labor, in part, because they spend more time at it. According to human capital theory, this intrinsic difference in productive efficiency between men and women drives the unequal division of family work.[3]

Because the family is considered an efficient cooperative unit, human capital theory suggests that husbands and wives will substitute for each other's labor both on the job and at home. In a simplified form, this is a zero-sum model of energy and time investment that predicts that a decrease in one spouse's family work will be compensated for by an increase in the other spouse's family work. As one spouse's labor time becomes more valuable, it becomes more efficient for the other spouse to perform more family work. Because having babies or many children creates a large time demand for both family work and paid work, there are supposed advantages to each spouse specializing in one type of labor. To maximize efficiency, men in large families, or fathers with preschoolers, should invest more time and effort in market labor and do less housework and child care. Women in these families would maximize efficiency by taking on more responsibility for household labor. Based on the supposedly neutral concept of efficiency, human capital theory thus legitimizes separate spheres and promotes a gender-segregated division of family and market labor.

Human capital theory also contains some gender-neutral assumptions that could predict more sharing of household work. When women are more productive on the job, they are assumed to earn higher wages and work longer hours. Women "efficient" at market labor in this way are likely to take on less responsibility for family work than other women because the labor time they invest on the job is more valuable than it is for women who are employed fewer hours (i.e., when they are "less efficient"). By the same token, men who are less productive on the job are assumed to earn lower wages and work fewer hours. These less efficient men are supposed to be more involved in family work because their labor time is less valuable in the market than it is for men who are more efficient and are employed more hours. Within a specific couple, husbands' and wives' comparative efficiency should shape divisions of market and domestic labor.

Social-Structural Theory

Instead of focusing on market efficiency and the utility-maximizing decisions of harmonious family units, social-structural theory concentrates on inequitable access to market resources and the unequal institution of marriage.[4] Labor markets are assumed to be structured or stratified to exclude women from higher status jobs, thus rendering their market labor less valuable than men's. This forces women into the unequal bargain of marriage, within which they are expected to care for home and children. Like human capital theory, social-structural theory looks at peoples' responses to time availability and resources, but it also includes consideration of ideology and starts from a different set of assumptions.

According to social-structural theory, various economic, institutional, and ideological forces encourage couples to assume that women will handle most of the child care and housework. In this view, couples depart from a traditional division of domestic labor only when situational constraints in the home or the workplace demand it. For most couples, reducing the man's hours of paid employment is not a viable option, because the couple needs a minimum income on which to live, and the husband's wages are typically much higher than his wife's. When wives' hours of paid employment increase significantly, however, they begin to interfere with their participation in household labor, and women's responsibility for family work is expected to decline while men's rises. Social-structural theory thus parallels human capital theory in some respects, though it does not make the same assumptions about the need for efficiency, harmony in the family, intrinsic biological predispositions, or the inevitability of labor specialization.

Unlike human capital theory, social-structural theory argues that the time demands associated with large households or preschool children would increase the family labor time of both husbands and wives. When women have full-time jobs and the demands of household labor are high, men would be expected to take on more responsibility for domestic work, even if the men's "comparative efficiency" in market labor was still higher than their wives'.[5] In addition, structural constraints of jobs are hypothesized to encourage or discourage both men and women from taking more responsibility for child care, even if they have similar status jobs.[6] For example, in a couple with a male accountant working at a large firm that requires its salaried workers to put in 50 hours per week, and a female nurse working in a neighborhood clinic where people work fewer hours and have schedule flexibility, the husband would probably not do much of the housework and child care. If employment constraints were reversed, with the husband as the nurse and the wife as the accountant, social-structural theory predicts that the couple would share significantly more household labor, although this would still be modified by cultural assumptions about appropriate gender roles. Like human capital theory, social-structural theory includes some gender-neutral assumptions, insofar as it assumes that labor market factors will limit both mothers' and fathers' abilities to do family work. Unlike human capital theory, however, social-structural theory explicitly considers constraints imposed by gender segregation and discrimination in the paid labor market. In addition, it takes account of gender-biased social expectations instead of assuming that women and men occupy different spheres because of biological determinism or market efficiency.

Deciding whether human capital theory or social-structural theory explains more about family work is neither simple nor unambiguous. There is substantial overlap between predictions from the two, even if the reasons for them are assumed to be different. In fact, most attempted "tests" of the two general theories have been inconclusive, if not downright confusing. Before turning to results of those tests, however, I will describe some of the predictors used in less ambitious household labor research. Although empirical studies with specific predictors sometimes yield conflicting results, we are beginning to isolate some of the immediate factors associated with different levels of sharing family work. The three most common predictors from middle-range theories of household labor allocation are: (1) *relative resources,* often including consideration of imbalances in income or marital power; (2) *ideology,* usually conceived of as resulting from socialization into "traditional" or "nontraditional" gender roles; and (3) *time availability,* or "free time" apart from hours spent in market labor.[7]

Relative Resources

The basic idea in the relative resources approach is that the person with the most power will do the least domestic work. Resource and exchange theories, like most economic and rational choice interpretations of social life, assume that people are constantly engaged in relatively conscious trades and bargains, and that a person's hypothetical "market worth" determines how much unpleasant work one must perform. The root image is one of monetary exchange, though most theories of this type also assume that people exchange non-material things, like good looks, physical affection, or emotional support, as well as more tangible things like income, a new car, or a clean house. Thus, a young woman who ranks high on conventional beauty standards might "trade" that resource on the marriage market to gain an older, less attractive, but wealthy husband who would be expected to share his income with her.[8] Others who focus on the relative resources of husbands and wives do not make the same assumptions about fair trades and open markets as human capital theorists, instead focusing on the ways in which men routinely exercise power over women because of structural inequality in work, marriage and society.[9]

As applied to divisions of household labor, researchers have typically measured relative resources in terms of earning power. In early research, relative resources were measured with a single question, simply asking whether the wife was employed. Much of this research found that men in single-earner families did not do more housework than those in dual-earner families, leading to the misguided conclusion that differences in monetary or occupational resources had no impact on divisions of household labor. A more appropriate way of measuring resources is by looking at earned income, though this narrow definition of resources can also be misleading at times. Researchers sometimes ask both husbands and wives how much money they earn in a year, and then compute a relative income measure that includes both spouses' reports (such as the ratio of wife-to-husband earnings, percentage of household income earned by one spouse, or the dollar difference between spouses' incomes). These measures allow for the testing of resource theories because they capture the relative contribution of both husbands and wives to the family's resource base.

Resource and exchange theories predict that when the wife's relative income is higher, husbands will do more housework, and, in fact, this is what some researchers find.[10] In our small interview sample, wives' higher relative earnings were definitely associated with more sharing of domestic work. When wives earned nearly as much money as their husbands, they were more likely to demand that husbands do more around the house. Husbands whose wives earned as much as they did, paid more attention to what needed doing and were more willing to take on housework and child care. This pattern tended to be true for couples who earned the most and those who earned the least, but it seemed most true for those whose incomes were in the middle. Because of the types of families we interviewed, this suggests that relative resources, and assumption of provider responsibilities, might be less important in the lower-working-class and upper-middle-class families, and most important in the stable working class and the lower middle class.

Other researchers have argued about whether there is more or less sharing among working-class or middle-class couples. Because men at all class levels do relatively little, most researchers have reported no significant differences in domestic labor patterns between "dual-earner" (i.e., working-class) and "dual-career" (i.e., upper-middle-class) households.[11] This suggests that professional status, in itself, does not necessarily lead to more sharing of household labor. In general, middle-class men tend to *talk* about household labor in more egalitarian terms, whereas working-class couples are more likely to talk about certain activities as the exclusive province of women, regardless of who actually does what around the house. When assessing the amount of time people actually spend *performing* household tasks, however, studies produce conflicting results, with some showing that working-class men share more, and some showing that middle-class men share more. One source of the problem lies in the way that researchers measure the class position of the couple, with the man's job typically defining the class position of both spouses, even when the wife has a more middle-class job.[12] Contradictory results also stem from differences between samples, and from the ways that housework is measured, but may also reflect the fact that the earnings gap between wives and husbands differs by social class. Employed working-class wives make less than employed middle-class wives, but typically earn a larger proportion of their family's total income. How income or relative earnings are measured is thus important to the results obtained.

Some have found that just the wife's resources, measured as her labor force participation, level of earnings, or occupational prestige, are linked to more equal divisions of household labor.[13] In general, we did not find this to be true for those we interviewed, because many women with lower-status jobs shared significant amounts of child care and housework, and some women with higher-status professional jobs shared little. Professional women with higher earnings tend to be married to professional men whose income and occupational status still tend to outstrip their own, thus effectively offsetting any relative bargaining advantage they might realize through their own economic resources. The relatively lower earnings of women in most middle-class jobs, compared to their husbands, also encourages both husbands and wives to treat her employment as secondary or optional. Working-class women, in contrast, usually consider paid employment as an absolute necessity, even though they are more likely to talk about wanting to be stay-at-home housewives. Because working-class women earn closer to what their low-paid husbands earn, they might enjoy increased bargaining power and influence who does what around the house. For this reason, relative contribution to total household income, rather than the absolute dollar amount of women's income, is likely to be a better predictor of the extent to which wives can bargain for assistance from husbands.

In contrast to the results presented above, many researchers using large random samples have found that the wife's relative income is *not* related to the division of household labor.[14] Like the occasional finding that employed wives share no more than non-employed wives, the nonsignificant impact of relative earnings on housework suggests that couples may not divide domestic responsibilities according to a simple cost-benefit calculation. For example, the economy of gratitude in some of the couples that Arlie Hochschild interviewed explicitly contradicted a simple exchange process for allocating household labor. She found that some wage-earning wives married to underemployed husbands attempted to "balance" this counter-normative situation by not demanding that he do more around the house. Being dependent on a wife's earnings threatens some men's identity as the breadwinner, and can lead to more deferential behavior on the part of some wives and lower household contributions from husbands.[15] In general, however, such findings are rare, and if wives have more power and prestige, they are usually obligated to do less family work, though they may still choose to do it.

In my interviews, economies of gratitude could shape divisions of labor in ways not predicted by simple resource or exchange models. For instance, some couples had very unequal income ratios, but still shared substantial housework and child care. This may not mean that relative resources are unimportant, but it does suggest that simple exchange models do not capture the feelings of entitlement and gratitude that shape divisions of household labor.[16] The question remains, however, under what conditions, and for which women, might more equal earnings increase their bargaining power, and under what conditions might men's domestic labor be expected to increase?

Before moving on to consider theories other than relative resources, it is important to mention attempts to measure resources in other ways. Some economic approaches, like human capital theory, suggest that educational level would be valued in the job market and could be counted on to increase one's personal power. A spouse whose years of schooling far outstripped their partner's would be expected to do less housework. Nevertheless, studies fail to find a consistent and significant relationship between relative educational levels between spouses and contributions to household labor.[17] In contrast, many researchers have found a positive association between husbands' educational level — measured alone — and his assumption of more housework, and a few have found an association between wives' educational level and more sharing.[18] Most researchers suggest, however, that education in this case is really reflecting liberal attitudes, and that what is being measured is not resources or efficiency, but gender ideology.

Gender Ideology

A number of theories in this general area assume that people are socialized to adopt values and beliefs about the appropriateness of various tasks for men and women, and that such values encourage or inhibit the sharing of domestic tasks. Whether one has "traditional" or "liberal" attitudes is considered a product of childhood learning as well as adult experience, although the extent to which such attitudes can change, and the ways in which people might move from one category to the other, are not often addressed. Survey items assessing attitudes toward men's and women's work and family activities are typically used to measure the extent to which people think men and women are different and should do different things. For instance, questionnaires often ask whether one agrees that "women should stay home and take care of children while men go out and earn money for the family." Answers to various questions of this sort are combined into "sex-role traditionalism" scales that are often assumed to measure relatively stable personality traits or deeply held personal values.[19] Leaving aside the question of how stable such values or traits might be, these scales do tend to capture the extent to which people express agreement or disagreement with conventional gender stereotypes.

Not surprisingly, some survey researchers using large random samples find that people with "traditional" gender attitudes share significantly less housework and child care than those with "nontraditional" attitudes.[20] Reviewing studies on men's contributions to family work, Joseph Pleck concluded that while the magnitude of the relationship is sometimes small, "studies yield relatively consistent evidence of a relationship between men's sex-role attitudes and their level of family work."[21] What is more remarkable, however, is that many other studies investigating this issue fail to find a significant or strong relationship between gender attitudes and the division of household labor.[22] One comprehensive review of household labor literature concluded "in spite of all the talk about egalitarian ideology, abstract beliefs about what women and men 'ought' to do are not connected with the division of family work."[23]

One of the areas of ambiguity in past research on gender ideology and housework concerns whose attitudes are being measured. Some researchers link both spouses' attitudes to domestic task sharing, but most find that husbands' attitudes are more strongly associated with sharing family work than wives' attitudes.[24] This is related to the finding, reported earlier, that many wives do not demand help from husbands, and that even those who request assistance have low expectations for compliance. A few researchers, in contrast, have found that wives' attitudes are more likely to influence task sharing than husbands', perhaps because family work is considered by default to be women's work, and if change is to occur, it might need to be initiated by the woman.[25]

Time Availability

The use of time availability to explain who does what around the house can hardly be called a full-blown theory of labor allocation, but it does reflect how most people refer to practical issues when they discuss family labor. This general approach assumes that couples will assign household tasks to the person with the most "free" time, although it is often unclear how people end up with free time in the first place.[26] To measure the concept of available time, researchers have relied on measures of employment status or number of hours employed, assuming that any hours not spent in paid labor are available for use in family labor. This approach accounts for divisions of household labor by considering time demands as well as constraints on one's time. Household *demands,* such as more children or a bigger house, require more household labor, but the extent to which people can perform it is subject to *constraints* such as the amount of time spent in paid employment.[27]

As noted in Chapter 3, most studies conducted in the 1970s and early 1980s found that husbands of employed women spent little or no more time in housework than husbands of housewives, suggesting that time availability of husbands and wives was not being traded in equal fashion.[28] Because so many men did so little family work, and because the vast majority of men were employed full time, the relationship between husband's paid work time and family work time has tended to be small or nonsignificant.[29] In contrast, wife's employment hours and housework hours have usually been found to be significantly related.[30] Perhaps the most consistent finding from two decades of research about this issue is that when women increase their time in employment, they tend to reduce their time in housework. There are, after all, only twenty-four hours in each day, and when women work eight hours a day, it leaves less time for doing all the other things that one does to run a household and raise a family. Men, for their part, often increase their involvement in response to women's increased hours on the job.[31] Even if men don't do more at home when they work fewer hours, or when their wives are employed longer hours, things become more equal between spouses, because the men end up doing a larger proportionate share of the family work.

Although divisions of labor have been found to become more equal, on average, when women are employed more hours, this varies considerably between families, and this variation has made large-scale tests of the time availability hypothesis difficult to confirm. As noted above, the economy of gratitude is different in every family, so that some husbands of full-time employed wives do little housework and think they are doing their wife a favor by simply "letting" her work. In those families we would find no significant relationship between paid work hours and family work hours. Other husbands with full-time employed wives, in contrast, are extremely grateful for their wives' earnings, and feel compelled to "help out" by doing more household chores. In those households, we would find a significant association between paid work hours and family work hours for both spouses, even if the husband still did only a small percentage of all household tasks. Hours of market labor are also subject to constant change as economies of gratitude influence peoples' choices to increase or decrease their work hours. Decisions about who should work more hours and who should care for home and children are definitely tied up with gender ideology and social prescriptions about proper behavior for mothers and fathers. As noted earlier, research shows that there is no simple or straightforward trade-off of wage and family work hours between wives and husbands, and questions remain as to why and when partners would allocate family work on the basis of time availability.[32]

The demand aspect of time availability reflects how long various tasks take, which, in turn, is related to the size of the house, the number of household members, the kind of care they require, the amount of help received from others, and standards for such things as meal preparation and cleanliness. These issues are hard to get at with short survey questions, so researchers using larger samples often measure the size of the household workload with reference to how many children of various ages are in the household. The underlying assumption, which should seem reasonable to most parents, is that more children require more time, and that younger children take the most time of all. In a related issue, we are just beginning to study systematically the assumption of household labor by children themselves, with preliminary findings suggesting that older children's contributions often substitute for those of fathers.[33]

Many studies find that the presence, number, or youth of children are linked to men's participation in family labor, with more and younger children often associated with husbands (and wives) doing more hours of housework and child care.[34] Nevertheless, results concerning the impact of child-care demand are also mixed, with other researchers finding that husbands contribute more if children are absent or there are fewer of them.[35] It may be that even if men increase their absolute levels of child care or housework when there are more or younger children, because their wives are also increasing their domestic contributions, the men's overall share decreases.

Even though researchers tend to set up these three predictors (relative resources, gender ideology, time availability) as competing contributors to sharing housework, it is important to remember that they operate simultaneously and can only be analytically separated by oversimplifying real world processes. Rather than assuming that one of these factors can fully "explain" how household work gets divided, it is more fruitful to ask questions about their relative mix and the social contexts that might privilege one factor over the others. The same might be said for debates between human capital theory and social structural theory, for neither provides a full explanation for how family work is divided. But by looking at how all these factors interrelate, we will be in a better position to predict future patterns of family work. Toward that end, I turn to a recent nationwide survey of American families.

The National Survey of Families and Households

To test some of the ideas described above, I used my own and others' analyses of data from the National Survey of Families and Households (NSFH).[36] This survey confirmed that women's overall household labor time is far greater than men's, and tends to be concentrated in repetitive and time consuming indoor tasks, whereas men's time tends to be concentrated in less frequently performed outdoor tasks. As measured in the 1987 NSFH, men spent an average of 22 hours per week on nine types of household labor, compared to an average of 38 hours each week for women (including preparing meals, washing dishes, cleaning house, washing/ironing, outdoor maintenance, shopping, paying bills, car maintenance, and driving).

Because the NSFH surveyed both married and unmarried people, we can get a rough idea of the impact of being married on the number of hours spent in household labor. Being married has little overall influence on men's average contributions to housework, whereas being married is associated with 10 more hours of household labor per week for women. Married women, in general, do about twice as much household labor as married men. This finding lends support to social-structural theory because it suggests that the institution of marriage has unequal costs and benefits for women and men. We need to be careful about what is causing this difference, however, since married people are much more likely to have children than unmarried people.

For both women and men, having children is associated with more household labor time, but the differences are much greater for women.[37] Men with one child spend about seven more hours a week on household labor than men with no children. Women with one child spend 14 more hours a week than those with no children. For employed women, each additional child increases women's weekly household labor time by over four hours per week, whereas for men the increase per child is two hours per week.[38] And these nine household tasks do not even include direct child care, discussed later, that takes up even more of women's time than of men's. Men and women also tend to adjust their paid work time differently when children are involved. Having a child means working about three more hours on the job per week for men, but for women it is associated with spending about an hour less in the paid labor force each week. Thus, children, like marriage, represent different types of demands on most men and women, with men spending more time on the job, and women spending more time in domestic labor when they have children. As the sociologist Beth Anne Shelton puts it, "The gender gap is present even with no children, but it is exacerbated by the presence of children in the household."[39]

The amount of time one spends on the job is also associated with how much household labor one does, but, again, the link is stronger for women than for men. Women who are employed part time (less than 30 hours per week) spend an average of 15 more hours per week on household labor than women who are employed full time (more than 30 hours per week). Men who work part time also do more household labor, but only about five hours more per week than those who are employed full time. Among couples with two full-time workers, the gap between men's and women's time spent in all forms of household labor is smallest, though women still perform about 63 percent of the total. Each hour a woman spends on the job reduces her contributions to household labor significantly more than an hour on the job does for men.[40]

As noted earlier, the data show that women's contributions to household labor are concentrated in tasks such as meal preparation, meal clean-up, and house cleaning, whereas men's contributions are concentrated in outdoor tasks. For the most time-consuming task of meal preparation, men contribute about one-fourth of the 12 hours spent each week in the average household. Employment status and time at work definitely influence this. Full-time employed women spend about two hours less each week preparing meals than women working part time, and about three hours less than non-employed women. Probably to compensate, husbands of full-time employed wives contribute about an hour more per week to meal preparation than husbands of non-employed wives. Similarly, for most indoor household tasks, employed women do less, and their husbands more, when compared to non-employed women. Whether or not their wives are working outside the home, men's contributions are lowest for washing and ironing, where they contributed an average of less than a fifth of the total weekly time spent. Overall, men do about two-thirds of the outdoor chores, and over three-quarters of the auto maintenance, the least time consuming of the nine tasks.

When all households in the survey are considered, time availability, household labor demand, and gender ideology are associated with respondents doing more household labor as measured by the nine domestic tasks. More time spent on family work is also associated with more family work being performed by one's spouse. Contradicting human capital theory, neither men nor women substite for each other in a zero-sum trade of hours. Instead, if one spouse spends more hours on household labor, so does the other. As noted below, using a proportionate measure of husband's share of housework, I also discovered that wives' share of income makes a difference. When women earn more of the family's earnings, men do more of so-called "women's" tasks.

Before these tentative conclusions can be used to assess the potential for changes in family work, we need to delve a little deeper into the survey data. First, the findings reported above are for the number of hours spent in nine household tasks and do not consider the segregation of household tasks into women's and men's domains, the performance of child care, or the share of the couple's total performed by each spouse. Especially because spouses tend to perform more family work if their spouse does more, an absolute number of hours tells us little about fairness or balance within the couple. To learn about such matters, I rely on a relative measure, representing the percentage of the total hours spent by husbands on tasks usually performed by wives (which I call housework).[41] I also use the percentage of total hours spent by the husband on child-related tasks (labeled child care).[42] The preceding analyses also used estimates from only one respondent. Since, as we've seen, people tend to overestimate their own contributions, averaging estimates from both husbands and wives provides a more balanced assessment of who does what. Using data from both respondents also enables us to ask questions about whose ideology or time availability is more important in shaping divisions of family work.[43]

Child Care versus Housework

As noted in earlier chapters, both men and women tend to talk much more about children and child care than about housework. When mothers and fathers discuss the importance of their family involvements, they usually focus on directly caring for them, sharing leisure time with them, disciplining them, teaching them skills, or instilling in them the morals that they consider to be most important. Mothers, more than fathers, also focus on the intangible aspects of emotional support and caring associated with child care that provide them with a sense of fulfillment. Usually left in the background of these conversations are the indirect domestic tasks associated with raising children or maintaining households. These are the housework tasks normally (and normatively) handled by mothers: meal preparation and clean-up, shopping, housecleaning, and laundry. Leaving housework in the background perpetuates the assumption that it is "naturally" women's work.

Counting the number of hours spent on household labor, as in the analyses above, focuses our attention on chores typically performed by women, but artificially abstracts these tasks from the family and child-centered contexts in which they are performed. Not only are activities like cooking a meal or comforting a child tied to what it means to be a wife and mother (or a husband and father), but the two activities are often intertwined and overlapping. Child care, in particular, is difficult to measure because it is typically performed in conjunction with other household tasks and because the sorts of care given differ between families and vary according to the age of each child. If we want to understand why and how families divide their labor, we need to be clear about the similarities and differences between child care and housework.

Researchers studying household labor usually employ theoretical models and research techniques that treat the allocation of housework and the allocation of child care similarly. In most approaches, both child care and housework are tacitly assumed to be onerous activities that are avoided by more powerful family members — men — and relegated to less powerful family members — wives and daughters. Not only are cooking, cleaning, and child care considered equal inputs into the overall household economy, but who washes dishes and who washes young children are assumed to result from the same causal forces.[44] Yet we need to consider the possibility that child care and housework might be shared in response to different social processes, or that men and women might vary their contributions to each based on different factors. For example, in the interview studies, I found that many men were motivated to spend time with their children because of emotional and practical reasons and so rearranged their schedules to spend more time in the home. Once there on a regular basis, and often in response to reminders from their wives, these men also came to notice more about housework and performed more indoor chores. This is only one of many possible connections between the two domestic activities, but if a similar process was occurring in other families as well, then the performance of child care would be a strong predictor of the performance of housework in national survey data. To investigate some of the possible interrelationships between child care and housework, and to see if they respond to the same hypothetical causal forces, I used a subset of the NSFH sample composed of married couples with children under the age of five. These parents were asked detailed questions about their housework and child-care practices and gave estimates of time spent in each activity.[45]

A related area of ambiguity in past household labor research concerns the relative influence that each spouse has over the allocation of domestic responsibilities. Although most researchers agree that women typically act as household managers and gatekeepers to husband's involvement in child care and housework, the question remains whether more egalitarian arrangements result from husbands' or wives' initiative. As noted above, disagreement exists between researchers on the overall impact of ideology, resources, or time availability on divisions of household labor, as well as conflicting findings about the relative importance of each spouses' inputs to these three factors. For example, some researchers suggest that the husband must take the initiative if he is to assume a greater share of family work. Lending support to this hypothesis is the frequent finding that husbands' attitudes toward appropriate family and gender roles are a better predictor of household labor sharing than wives' attitudes.[46] This would suggest an individualistic model of behavior change: as men adopt more progressive attitudes toward appropriate gender and family roles they will be motivated to assume a greater proportion of housework and child care.

Assuming a conflict model of household task allocation, in contrast, other researchers have suggested that more equitable divisions of labor are dependent on explicit scheduling and overt bargaining by wives.[47] This approach grants wives a pivotal causal role in household labor sharing and is consonant with descriptive research detailing the ways in which wives and mothers act as gatekeepers, regulating men's involvement in child care by setting standards, keeping schedules, and facilitating father–child interaction.[48] Supporting this position, one recent study using a representative sample found that wives' attitudes were more important than husbands' attitudes in predicting more equal divisions of household labor.[49]

Taken together, these findings show that competing hypotheses regarding the differential impact of wive's gatekeeping and husband's initiative on men's assumption of child care and housework have both received support. While representative samples have been employed in some of these studies, results remain contradictory, and we do not yet understand the interplay of forces that might privilege one spouse's ideology, income, education, or time availability over the other's in allocating either housework or child care. In the following analysis, I separate child care from housework in an attempt to clarify which causal forces may be most important for each.[50]

In a series of statistical analyses, I discovered that men's share of child care and of housework best predicted each other. Many variables predicting the sharing of housework differed from those predicting child care, but they were both the strongest predictors for each other. Following the findings from the interviews, I interpret these results to mean that when men get more involved in caring for their young children, they also get more involved in doing housework.[51]

In general, men did a larger percentage of the housework when they were employed fewer hours; when their wives were employed more hours; when wives had less traditional attitudes; and when wives earned a greater percentage of the family income.[52] There was also some suggestion that men shared more housework if they had fewer children or if their preschool children were younger. The results for child care followed a different pattern. Men did a larger percentage of the direct care of preschoolers if they were employed fewer hours, held less traditional attitudes, and their wives were employed more hours. Men also did significantly more of the child care if there were more children in the family, or if their preschool children were older (closer to five years old).

These findings imply that the wife's gatekeeper role may be more influential than the husband's individual initiative for housework, but that the husband's initiative may be more important than the wife's in the performance of child care. The data also support the idea that parents with young children share housework primarily in response to the wife's initiative. Wives who earn more of the household income, those with more education, and those who have less traditional attitudes are more able to bargain effectively for greater participation from husbands, especially when their husbands work fewer hours. Wives with higher relative resources also tend to be less attached to the homemaker role and more readily share the tasks associated with it. This interpretation supports a conflict model of household labor allocation that conceives of the sharing of housework as resulting from a power dynamic: A wife's economic and educational resources and less traditional ideology enable her to do less around the house and encourage her husband to do more.

In the statistical analysis of survey data, wives' employment characteristics were also strongly related to men's share of child care, supporting social structural theory's suggestion that mothers will do the child care unless time constraints prohibit it. In addition, husbands contributed more when children were older and presumably less dependent on their mothers, and when there were two or more children in the home. Although the wife's time availability serves to regulate the husband's participation in child care, this analysis shows that the husband's time availability and gender ideology are also extremely important to his assumption of responsibility for children. In fact, these results suggest that a father's feelings about appropriate family and gender roles may be relatively more consequential for the assumption of routine parenting than his wife's attitudes.

Resource and exchange theories acknowledge power imbalances within families, but they tend to oversimplify what goes on in most households by assuming that men and women follow similar reasoning processes when allocating domestic tasks. Although relative resources and time availability were strong predictors of labor sharing for both men and women, we need not assume that these are gender-neutral commodities with fixed value as resource theories often imply. Rather, they operate in the context of a symbolic system that defines men and women as essentially different and "naturally" responsible for specific tasks. In other words, relative resources do not exist apart from, nor stand in opposition to, gender ideology as our theoretical and statistical models often imply. The theory that best fits these findings, social structural theory, considers both ideology and resource exchange, recognizes both cooperation and conflict within marriage, and acknowledges the primary role of job market inequities in the creation and perpetuation of women's double workday.

Human capital theory also predicts that housework will be shared in response to job resources and time availability. Nevertheless, unlike social structural theory or resource theory, human capital theory erroneously assumes that the family, as a unit, maximizes the utility of all family members. Whereas resource theory tends to ignore gender, human capital theory acknowledges that domestic work can carry different meanings for men and women through the introduction of the concept of "tastes" for certain types of tasks. I have always reacted negatively to the use of this term as a description of peoples' tendencies to favor market work or family work. I can sometimes envision a "taste" for tasks like gardening or decorating, but I still have a hard time seeing someone having a "taste" for cleaning toilets, doing laundry, or scrubbing floors. I am especially troubled by the assumption that these so-called tastes are predetermined and fixed ("exogenous" and "stable" in econometric terms). By basing tastes on underlying biological predispositions, human capital theory removes them from the realm of social life, where I think they belong. This makes the gendered division of labor seem inevitable and masks gender inequality.

By combining some of the features common to resource theory and human capital theory, and by moving beyond them to consider the importance of gender ideology, social structural theory does a better job of explaining why asymmetric divisions of household labor are so common. The social structural factors promoting unequal divisions of labor in this sample were relatively easy to isolate: women earned an average of only about a quarter of what the men did, and were employed fewer than half as many hours per week. Coupled with peoples' ideas about appropriate activities for men and women, and the needs of children, most employed mothers ended up working a double shift.

Despite inequality in the division of household labor in most of these families, domestic relations were neither predetermined nor static. On the contrary, I found that a substantial minority of men were assuming significant responsibility for household labor, probably in response to some women's enhanced bargaining positions and their willingness to negotiate for change. Unlike the prediction of human capital theory that women with young children would specialize in household labor while their husbands would forsake it, the men were doing a larger share of the household labor than most men in the survey. In addition, men's involvement with young children, driven by both ideological and practical factors, was the best predictor of sharing housework. This prompted me to turn the analysis of survey data toward some of the issues that might motivate men to become more involved with their children. As we saw in Chapter 5, the men I interviewed who shared the most child care tended to have waited longer to have their first child, so the next analysis focuses on whether birth timing makes a difference for divisions of labor in this nation-wide sample of families.

Delayed Childbirth

Demographers have shown that delayed childbearing, more common in the early part of this century, has increased dramatically in the last two decades, and is more common in the United States today than at any time since figures were collected.[53] Delayed childbearing is variously defined as occurring after age 25, after age 28, or after age 30.[54] In the absence of a theoretical warrant for selecting either extreme, I used the middle figure of age 28 as a hypothetical, and admittedly arbitrary, dividing line between "early" and "delayed" transitions to parenthood. In this analysis, I was interested in seeing if early and delayed parents develop similar or different patterns of household labor allocation. In particular, I was concerned with whether the three most commonly tested predictors of household labor—ideology, resources, and time availability—applied equally to both early and delayed parents.

The timing of the onset of parenthood can affect the lives of all family members in a variety of ways. Demographers find that delayed childbearers, compared to others, have more education, enjoy higher occupational status, have higher incomes, are more likely to have planned the birth of children, eventually have fewer children, and spend more money on those children.[55] Researchers studying these trends in birth timing are primarily interested in longer-term structural and demographic variables such as maternal labor force participation, fertility, and wage rates, often using explanatory models that ignore housework and individual level social psychological variables.[56] Using economic models, some have argued that a "role hiatus" between the role of daughter and traditional roles of wife and mother gives young women an opportunity to develop "tastes" for employment.[57] Using longitudinal data, others have found that if young women spend more time living in nonfamily households before marriage, they are less likely to develop traditional attitudes about wive's work and family roles.[58] As noted in the last chapter, more fine-grained interview studies using small samples have also suggested that delaying the birth of a first child can have profound influences on later marital life. Based on the interviews, I assumed that early transitions to parenthood would lead to more conventional divisions of family labor and that later transitions would lead to more cross-gender sharing of household labor. For men, I reasoned that early transitions to parenthood would be more likely to be accompanied by financial insecurity, limited occupational seniority, and low levels of "readiness" for parenting.[59] Such factors might discourage men from assuming responsibility for housework, whereas later transitions to parenthood, with greater financial security, higher motivations for fathering, and more long-standing patterns of spousal labor sharing, might encourage sustained sharing of domestic labor. As noted in Chapter 5, one of the underlying hypotheses regarding wives was that early childbearing would promote women's dependence on family roles and kinship networks for social identity, whereas delayed childbearing would promote independence and more bargaining about the allocation of domestic work.

Using the NSFH data, Masako Ishii-Kuntz and I found significant differences between early and delayed parents.[60] Delayed-birth husbands spent only slightly more time on housework than early-birth husbands, but the later-birth husbands performed a significantly larger share of the couple total.[61] For early-timed parents, wife's greater resources, wife's less traditional gender/family values, husband's greater time availability, wife's lesser time availability, and younger children were significantly associated with husbands doing more housework. For delayed parents, the pattern was similar, except that wife's earnings were nonsignificant and husband's values were significantly associated with husbands doing more. Contrary to the prediction of human capital theory, for both groups, the presence of younger children was associated with more sharing of routine housework. As in the previous analyses, who does what around the house was related to all three of the common predictors: time availability, relative resources, and ideology.

Our findings show that factors associated with the mother were particularly important to divisions of labor in early-birth families. Fathers who had a first child before age 28 were likely to do more of the couple's housework if their wives contributed more to the household income and if their wives held less conventional values. Men's own attitudes about appropriate gender and family roles, in contrast, did not significantly influence the housework allocation in early-timed families. Taken together, these findings suggest that early-timed parents may share household labor if the wife makes it happen. A wife's increased earnings and her less traditional values encourage her to negotiate and bargain for more participation by her husband. Concomitantly, these factors are likely to facilitate her relinquishing a portion of the homemaker role to her husband. This interpretation supports both the relative resources and ideology hypotheses and conceptualizes the sharing of housework as the result of a power dynamic—a wife's ideals and marital power allow her to do less around the house and encourage her husband to do more.

Wives' relative economic resources and ideology may be especially salient in early-birth families for an economic reason related to the timing of the transition to parenthood. Those couples who become parents in their teens or early-to-mid twenties are likely to have lower total earnings than those who become parents in their late twenties or thirties. A lower household income is apt to make wive's higher percentage contributions more important. Thus, wives in early-birth families may be more able to translate higher earnings into shared housework, either by encouraging husbands to help, or by doing less themselves.

In contrast to the early-timed fathers, men who had children after turning 28 were significantly more likely to share housework in response to the husband's ideology and time availability. In delayed-birth families, the husband's less traditional gender/family ideology and fewer employment hours were strong predictors of his performing more mundane and routine housework traditionally considered to be "women's work." For couples who deferred childbirth, wife's earnings did not make a significant contribution to the husband's share of routine household labor.

Although I could not directly analyze the couples' decision-making, I would guess that the husband's ideology and time availability were more important in later birth families because of several life course factors. Those who have children later have a longer history of negotiating household divisions of labor and have accumulated experiences and observations of others from which to make social comparisons. Early birth couples, in contrast, are more likely to use their own families for models of domestic labor and purposes of self-evaluation. Because of cohort effects, most of the parents in this sample are likely to have experienced gender-segregated divisions of labor in their families of origin. Thus, delaying the transition to parenthood might have the effect of making household labor decisions more individualistic, and more likely to be influenced by personal ideology instead of by kin or other less cosmopolitan social networks. In addition, the better overall economic position of couples who delay childbirth may make the wife's financial contributions somewhat less important.

Delayed-birth fathers were also found to be employed slightly longer each week than early-birth fathers which, in the absence of countervailing factors, would lead to *less* housework by delayed-birth husbands. In fact, delayed fathers contribute slightly more hours to housework, and because delayed-birth wives are performing fewer hours of housework, husband's proportionate contributions ended up being significantly higher. The net impact of men's employment hours on their share of housework was also found to be significantly greater among the delayed group. In other words, *when they were available, delayed-birth fathers were more likely to do more of the housework.* Delayed-birth fathers were also significantly more likely than early-birth fathers to agree that housework should be shared when both spouses are employed full time.[62]

Delaying the transition to parenthood might have even more important consequences for women than for men. Instead of moving directly from being a daughter in one family to being a mother in another, women who postpone childbearing have more opportunities to establish independent—usually employment-related—identities. This can influence the extent to which they derive a sense of self-worth from being a wife, mother, and homemaker. Such processes can enhance wives' willingness to lower housecleaning standards or cut back on housework, and probably also contribute to their ability to negotiate with husbands for increased contributions to domestic labor. To test these hypotheses more directly, we will need to study interaction in representative samples of families and follow them for many years as they make decisions about having children and making commitments to paid and family work.

Even though it seems that birth timing has a significant impact on household labor, the timing of parenthood does not occur independently from other social influences. This analysis also showed that men who have children later in life are likely to be more highly educated, have higher incomes, have less conventional values, have fewer children, and live in more metropolitan regions of the United States. These factors combine to produce patterns of sharing household labor that differ for early and late-timed parents. The timing of a first birth is itself the result of a combination of these influences, and should not be considered a separate and unique contributor to divisions of family labor.

Divorce and Remarriage

With divorce and remarriage increasingly common, we need to consider what happens in marriages with one or both partners who were previously married. Fortunately, the NSFH contains enough of these households to conduct a comparative analysis using different types of two-parent households with children. Before turning to the results of that analysis, however, I briefly review past studies to identify some possible influences of divorce and remarriage on family work.

Contemporary trends show that Americans are increasingly likely to divorce. If current rates continue, 60 percent of recent first marriages will be disrupted.[63] Significantly, however, most Americans remarry. While this trend is evident in many industrialized nations, the remarriage rate is higher in the United States than anywhere in the world. Over 40 percent of U.S. marriages are remarriages for one or both partners and most divorced people remarry within about three years.[64] Divorces and remarriages frequently involve children as well, with 35 percent of children born in the early 1980s expected to live with a stepparent before the age of 18.[65] Giving birth in remarriage is also quite common. Fifty-four percent of women who remarry are expected to have a child in that marriage.[66] (For a more complete discussion of current and future trends in marriage, divorce, and remarriage, see Chapter 8.)

Recent studies on remarried families have contributed to our knowledge of child development, marital satisfaction, and divorce likelihood, but we still know little about how and why various stepfamily forms are similar or different from one another.[67] One of the most often cited hypotheses used in remarriage studies, though difficult to measure, is Cherlin's "incomplete institution" hypothesis. According to this view, remarriages and stepfamilies are under stress because they lack normative prescriptions for role performance, institutionalized procedures to handle problems, and easily accessible social support.[68] Some suggest that such role ambiguity in stepfamilies can lead to stress and conflict and produce less satisfying family relationships.[69] Despite such predictions, however, most studies find that marital satisfaction differences between first and remarriages, remarried men and women, stepmothers and stepfathers, and various child living arrangements, are generally small and of little practical meaning.[70] Because we don't yet know what differences to expect, in this analysis I test whether the common predictors of household labor apply equally to married and various remarried household types.

Again using the NSFH data and relying on the statistical expertise of Masako Ishii-Kuntz, I discovered that more household labor is shared in remarried households than in first married households.[71] Although there were some differences between different types of remarried households, they shared significantly more of the five household tasks of cooking, meal clean-up, laundry, shopping and housecleaning than first-married households. Husbands in remarried families with only biological children contributed more absolute and relative hours of housework than husbands in any other household type. Regardless of whose children were present in the remarried household, however, remarriage was a significant predictor of greater contributions from men, even after controlling for the factors discussed above, as well as a few additional ones, such as contributions to household labor by children and other adults. As in the previous analyses, significant predictors of more sharing included both spouses' employment hours and ideology, wife's share of earnings, fewer children, and younger children. In an unanticipated finding, fathers did a greater percentage of the housework if their children performed more hours of housework, and this was especially so for remarried families with stepchildren. Human capital theory predicts that the labor of older children will substitute for the labor of husbands, but we found just the opposite: when children did more housework, so did fathers.

Another significant finding concerning stepfamilies was that wives were spending more hours in paid employment than wives in remarriages or first marriages with biological children. Since wives' hours spent in housework did not vary significantly across the different family types, this means that women in stepfamilies were likely to put in more total hours on paid and unpaid labor combined. Although they were not relieved of the overall time burdens of work, their allocation of labor was nonconventional in two ways. First, they were spending more time in paid employment, and probably maintaining more financial independence and career advancement potential. Second, their husbands were doing more of the tasks conventionally performed by women. Husbands in remarried households with only biological children were also performing a greater share of these stereotypical "feminine" chores.

The incomplete institutionalization hypothesis and other approaches to research on remarriage and stepfamilies have tended to view these families as somehow deficient because they were not governed by precise norms and role prescriptions. Although ambiguity about the roles of family members in these households may indeed increase conflict and negotiation, this may have some positive impacts. Insofar as "incomplete institutionalization" or fluid role conceptions allow for more experimentation and bargaining over housework and parenting, remarriages and stepfamilies probably provide more opportunities for change in the gender-basis of household labor allocation. We should remember that one of the things that has been institutionalized in traditional family structure and practice is a heavy dose of male dominance. As Goldschieder and Waite point out, women have been using their newfound economic resources to buy out of marriage, whereas wealthier men have been using their superior resources to buy in.[72] Instead of lamenting continued high levels of divorce and romanticizing bygone days of "stable" families, we should acknowledge some of the advantages of being able to end marriages that are not supportive and entering new marriages as so many Americans now do. Remarriages and stepfamilies are often more complicated than the old model, and probably contain more bargaining and negotiation between and among spouses and children. The question then arises, are high divorce rates such a bad thing, particularly when most people remarry and when many new families do a more equitable job of dividing labor between all family members?

What Do We Know?

What simple lessons can we learn from the different theories and empirical findings summarized in this chapter? First, there is an element of truth in each of the theories presented above, as most couples use a combination of practicality, power, and ideology to divide household labor and market labor. None of these factors, in itself, is able to predict who does what in any particular family. Even when we consider all three together, we cannot predict very well what the division of labor will be in any one family, because a multitude of personal and social factors shape economies of gratitude and influence countless subtle negotiations over who does what. The problem is that family life is complicated and constantly changing, with individual choices and couple decisions often overriding simple tendencies to follow social forces described by abstract theories. Couples do consider efficiency and sometimes trade one form of labor for another, but often they divide household labor inefficiently and without regard to how much labor the other spouse is performing. Couples also appear to divide housework in response to underlying power relations, but many refrain from using superior resources to avoid unpleasant tasks. Couples also regularly conform to gender stereotypes and espouse traditional attitudes, but sometimes ideology and practice do not coincide, and sometimes beliefs appear to be after-the-fact justifications for practices that couples have already adopted.

Just as we cannot isolate one primary causal factor in the allocation of housework within individual families, we cannot finally resolve debates between human capital and social-structural theories about the underlying causes of labor divisions in the larger society. Both are plausible explanations for observed patterns of labor, and both rely on the significant predictors of relative resources and time availability to predict who does what around the house. Social-structural theory places considerably more emphasis on gender ideology, and highlights institutional and structural aspects of gender inequality rather than relying on market forces and individual choices. Hypotheses from both theories received support in the above analyses, but social-structural theory received more empirical support than human capital theory. Because ideology was a consistent significant predictor of housework sharing in these analyses, and because couples did not specialize in one form of labor to the extent that human capital theory predicted, social-structural theory's predictions were more often confirmed.

Rejecting human capital theory as a complete explanation for why men do little around the house does not mean that we should reject all aspects of exchange or rational choice perspectives. For example, people do evaluate many of their choices about paid and unpaid labor in terms of bargains (exchanges), trade-offs (labor substitution), foregone advantages (opportunity costs), and who's "good" at it (efficiency and specialization). These concepts and practices are helpful in understanding the practical features of allocating labor in households. Exchange and resource theories, with their explicit consideration of power, also provide us with an underlying reason why women might be expected to do more, and give us some insight into possibilities for change. As noted above, however, we also need to include gender ideology in our models, for we must understand family obligation and patterns of gratitude if we are to understand who does what for the family. Most people resist thinking about their lives as structured by oppressive forces outside their control. Nevertheless, many report being frustrated by restricted choices, and women, in particular, find their life chances limited in ways predicted by social-structural and conflict theories. Nor do people generally think about their children or their homes in the terms used by human capital theory. When women assume the majority of household tasks, they do not usually report that this is a decision based on efficiency. People act as if they are in total control of their lives and simultaneously see only a narrow range of choices open to them. Complete information is impossible, and rarely are we the efficient rational maximizers that economic theories imply. We do, however, focus on the meaning of what we are doing, and that meaning is often shaped by gender ideology.

One of the most significant findings reported above is that people's views of what they "ought to" be doing constrain their choices and shape their behaviors. Couples do not arrive at divisions of household labor simply because they always sit down and figure out how they can spend the least amount of time to complete the most tasks with the least financial loss. Out of necessity, couples take practical matters into account, but their willingness to spend extra time with a sick child, to cook a special family dinner, or to put flowers on the dining room table, are dependent on the special rewards that these tasks carry for them. These rewards are not gender-neutral, because they are shaped by how people think women (or men) *should* act and what actions express that one is a *good mother* (or father). In short, doing household labor is doing gender, and we cannot hope to understand why people do what they do unless we understand how they conceive of gender. This means we cannot avoid gender ideology, and must rely on theories of household labor allocation that explicitly take gender ideology into account. This is not the same as saying that "sex-role attitudes" cause people to divide labor in certain ways or that ideas are more important than material factors in producing a gendered division of labor. On the contrary, as we saw in reviewing the history of separate spheres, larger economic and demographic shifts typically accompany and often precede shifts in gender ideology. The conclusion to be drawn from this analysis is that gender ideology matters, and that it ought to be considered in conjunction with other social and economic factors. If our theories ignore or minimize the influence of gender ideology, we run the risk of misrepresenting what is going on and masking gender inequality.

Most economic, human capital, and rational choice approaches include ideology in their theoretical models only through the concept of individual preferences or tastes. This contradicts many of the findings presented here, slights the impact of ideology on peoples' lives, and understates the possibilities for social change. Tastes are not predetermined and stable and, while some aspects of household labor can be purchased, most family work is not allocated like other market goods and services. In fact, both individual tastes and labor markets are products of multiple social forces and, as my analysis suggests, are subject to rapid shifts depending on historical changes in material and ideological conditions. Whatever their specific underpinnings, gender relations and gender ideology are social creations, not biological givens, and it is misleading to assume that having breasts and a uterus gives women a "taste" for housework, or that having a penis makes men inattentive parents or lousy housekeepers.

Our social theories of family work should pay attention to the ways that gender is socially constructed and how it shapes power and influence. Once we acknowledge that gender is a social creation, we can focus our attention on the social institutions and practices that create narrow definitions of what it means to be a man or a woman, and the differential rewards and limitations that go with gender. Families and labor markets structure our daily interactions and encourage us to divide labor on the basis of biological sex. This division of labor, in turn, shapes our individual and cultural identity. But, as we will see in the next chapter, there is an enormous range of variation in what is humanly possible.

These long theoretical discussions tend to mask the simple and important findings about family work from national survey data presented in this chapter: First, relative resources, ideology, and time availability are all important to divisions of household labor. Second, housework and child care influence each other, and respond to different pressures for sharing between husbands and wives. Third, people who wait longer to have children achieve more equal divisions of household labor. Finally, remarried households are more likely to share household labor than others. I rely on these findings, among others, when I venture out on a limb to make some predictions about the future in the last chapter.

7

Gender, Culture, and Fatherhood

Earlier chapters recounted stories from American parents struggling to balance job and family obligations, traced the historical ebb and flow of separate spheres for men and women, and offered some theoretical explanations for why modern parents might share family work. Momentarily stepping back from our own culture, however, we can evaluate whether it makes any difference how mothers and fathers divide family work and predict how the sharing of parenting might affect gender relations in the 1990s and beyond. In this chapter I delve into these questions by drawing on the research of anthropologists and sociologists who look at civilizations and societies seemingly far removed from our own.[1] Using examples from Africa, Asia, the Middle East, and the South Pacific, and summarizing the results of two worldwide statistical studies, I ask how fathering, masculinity, and women's status are mutually intertwined in pre-modern societies. I then consider some contemporary views of manhood that glorify masculine ritual and essentialize gender differences. Rejecting mythopoetic separatism, I focus on how cooperation in parenting and productive labor leads to the cultural patterning of gender equality.

The Legacy of Margaret Mead

In a series of famous studies on South Pacific Islanders conducted more than half a century ago, Margaret Mead provided us with insights that continue to

guide our thinking about gender, culture, and family work.[2] Mead demonstrated that the specifics of what it means to be a man or woman differ from
culture to culture, but that biology puts limits on these differences. Noting that
women's natural ability to bear and nurse children provides them with a sense
of purpose unavailable to men, she described how men tend to construct their
identities in opposition to women. Mead was one of the first scholars to focus
on men's preoccupation with maintaining exclusively masculine pursuits.
Because Mead's ideas help explain how parenting and gender are related, I
begin this chapter with a brief review of her fieldwork in New Guinea.

In 1931, Mead and her husband, Reo Fortune, found themselves unexpec-
tedly stranded on a mountaintop of one of the largest islands in Melanesia.
They were on their way to study another New Guinea tribe, but when they
were abandoned by their guides and carriers, they decided to live with and
study the mountain Arapesh. In her compelling autobiography, *Blackberry
Winter,* Mead tells about living among the Arapesh, hobbling around on a bad
ankle, trying in vain to keep up with her restless and volatile husband. Mead
and Fortune were like oil and water, and their differences were reflected in how
they reacted to the mountain Arapesh. Whereas Fortune characterized the
Arapesh as formless and unattractive, Mead was respectful of their gentle
lifestyle and congeniality. Setting out to understand gender-linked temperamental differences among "primitives," Margaret Mead eventually came to see
her own marital difficulties as resulting from temperamental differences
between her and her husband.[3]

Mead and Fortune moved on to study the Mundugumor, a neighboring
New Guinea tribe who were extremely aggressive and exploitive. After considerable difficulty trying to work together studying these two groups, Mead and
Fortune met Gregory Bateson, who introduced them to a third New Guinea
tribe, the Tchambuli. Mead, Fortune, and Bateson spent countless hours in a
tiny mosquito tent while studying the Tchambuli, discussing how human
temperaments differ, and how culture shapes those temperaments. In these
discussions, they drew heavily on Ruth Benedict's idea that every culture is a
product of selective emphasis and discouragement of specific human traits and
her popular conceptualization of culture as "personality writ large."[4]

The most compelling intellectual product of this fieldwork was Mead's *Sex
and Temperament in Three Primitive Societies.* In it, Mead compared the temperaments of people in these three societies with stereotypical behaviors and
personalities of American men and women. Among the docile Arapesh, both
men and women tended to conform to Westerners' expectations for feminine
behavior. They were a gentle people who cherished children, and both men
and women were sensitive and nurturing. The Mundugumor, in contrast, were
very competitive and antagonistic. According to Mead, both men and women
of the Mundugumor conformed to Westerners' expectations for masculine
behavior: they were independent, callous, and rejecting of children.

The third group, the Tchambuli, were perhaps the most interesting, be-cause in many ways they reversed the gender expectations of Westerners. Tchambuli women were brisk and coolly cooperative, whereas Tchambuli men were markedly sensitive and flighty. Mead described how the business-like women made choices that affected the men's lives, and how the men's subservience was associated with masculine personality traits that Westerners would think of as feminine. According to Mead, the men were preoccupied with trivial gossip, tended to be moody, and were subject to fits of jealousy. Mead concluded that "many, if not all, of the personality traits which we have called masculine or feminine are as lightly linked to sex as are clothing, the manners, and the form of head-dress that a society at a given period assigns to either sex."[5] This view is remarkably similar to the modern social construc-tionist position distinguishing sex from gender. Today, most social scientists use sex to refer to biological factors, and gender to refer to those personal and social characteristics that are constructed differently in each culture.[6]

Margaret Mead was one of the few widely respected women intellectuals of her time, and her own struggles against those with preconceived notions about women's "rightful place" helped shape her choice of research topics and her perceptions of those she studied. Mead's personal insights and emotions are woven into her research on these three New Guinea cultures (she eventually divorced Fortune and married Bateson, with whom she later had a child). Her engaging narratives, and her meshing of subjective and objective approaches to gender issues earned her a loyal following and more than a few critics over the years. A product of her times, she never moved beyond labeling those she studied as "primitives," but her personal and interpretive observa-tions foreshadow postmodern feminist critiques of pure rationality and scien-tific objectivity. It is now commonplace to observe that all social science research, though it purports to be studiously objective, is biased by the preconceived notions, measurement procedures, and topic selection of its (predominantly male) investigators.[7]

Although some anthropologists have disputed Margaret Mead's interpreta-tions or questioned her field methods, her work in New Guinea remains one of the most insightful and thought-provoking studies of gender ever conducted.[8] Although Mead contended that gender was culturally constructed, she also occasionally privileged biological over cultural explanations.[9] This tended to drive critics wild. In response to her critics' attempts to force her into choosing *only* biological or *only* cultural explanations for gender differences, Mead replied, "we not only can have it both ways, but many more than both ways."[10]

By looking at the types of societies Margaret Mead studied, we can better understand how parenting, gender, and power are linked. Stepping back to examine some of the broad outlines of human societies allows us to ask questions about what is natural, how much change is possible, and what might happen if mothers and fathers shared family work. Using tribal and peasant societies from all over the world also allows us to investigate questions about biological versus cultural patterning of gender and parenting.[11] Biological theories suggest that genetic programming, hormones, and differences in size, strength, and aggressiveness dictate that men will dominate women. In their most extreme form, these theories argue for the inevitability of patriarchy.[12] Other theories focus on subsistence practices, technological development, property control, descent systems, residence patterns, warfare, ideology, societal complexity, and colonialism to understand how and why men come to dominate women.[13] Rather than testing the relative merits of various theories, in this chapter, I focus on how nurturing fatherhood and gender equity are linked in these pre-modern societies.

Gender Relations in Pre-Modern Societies

Missionaries, traders, anthropologists, and ethnographers of all sorts have provided rich detailed descriptions of myths, rituals, and everyday life in societies that used to be called "primitive." Some of these nonindustrial societies seem preoccupied with separating men and women, while others are relatively unconcerned with gender differences.[14] The Mundurucu tribe of the central Amazonian rain forest are a classic example of a hunting and gathering society that symbolically separates the sexes.[15] Men and women both make substantial contributions to subsistence, but they do so separately, and women are formally excluded from all religious offices and positions of public leadership. Young women are expected to sit in the back, walk in the rear of a file, and eat after the men do. Every Mundurucu woman must have an adult male protector, and women band together in all activities to guard against the forced sexual intercourse that is expected if a woman is discovered alone outside the village. Mundurucu babies are totally dependent on their mothers and then cared for exclusively by women, with fathers showing little or no interest in children until they are able to walk.

Mundurucu men participate in elaborate male rituals related to their two favorite activities: hunting and warfare. The taking of trophy heads was regarded by the Mundurucu as the ultimate goal of all warfare, and their repeated attacks on other tribes earned them the reputation of being the fiercest of all the tribes in the central Amazon. As late as the 1950s, ethnographers reported that men still spent considerable time in ceremonial activities related to warfare, with plentiful physical contests, vociferous oratory, exclusive men's houses, and various all-male rituals.

According to several anthropologists' accounts, however, Mundurucu men's bravado serves to mask their fear of women. The men's vulnerability is evident in male-oriented Mundurucu myths such as the "cult of the sacred trumpets." According to legend, the trumpets, which are believed to contain spirits of their ancestors, were expropriated by the men from the original custody of the women. The trumpets are kept in special chambers in the men's houses, where women are forbidden to see them, under threat of gang rape. In order to please the trumpet spirits, men used to bring back trophy heads of non-Mundurucu. Yolanda and Robert Murphy, who lived among the Mundurucu, describe the myth of the sacred trumpets as "an allegory of man's birth from woman, his original dependence upon the woman as the supporting, nurturant and controlling agent in his life, and of the necessity to break the shackles and assert his autonomy and manhood."[16]

While this description fits nicely with what some claim is the universal need of males to break the mother-son bond, we must remember that not all tribes exhibit these patterns of male solidarity and gender antagonism. Even tribes in the same geographical area, such as the Amazonian Machinguenga, provide a stark contrast to the hypermasculine Mundurucu. Machiguenga men cooperate with their wives in subsistence activities, take part in child care, and do not formally initiate boys into exclusive men's houses or rituals. The ideal man in Machiguenga culture is soft-spoken and nonviolent. He is honest, hardworking, loyal to his family, has some shamanistic healing skills, behaves decorously, and is respectful of others' independence. Unlike the Mundurucu, Machiguenga men are not expected to be violent or aggressive, and men who become enraged or have trouble controlling their aggression are described as *tovaiti iseraritake*—literally, "plenty of he-male-is." Instead of being honored or respected, such men are avoided, and if they cause too much fear in the community, they are driven off.[17]

Societies that are relatively unconcerned with demarcating men from women may be less common than those concerned with affirming men's masculinity, but comparatively egalitarian societies have existed in every major region of the world.[18] Some of the most prominent examples of tribes with little gender demarcation come from islands in the South Pacific, the same region of the world that has produced fanatically hypermasculine tribes.[19] For example, when Europeans first encountered the people of Tahiti, they were surprised by the lack of differentiation between genders. A woman could do almost anything a man did, including conversing with whomever she pleased, initiating sex, participating in men's sports, occasionally wrestling with men, and even becoming a chief. Later fieldwork among the Tahitians revealed that gender differences were still "blurred" or "blended": Men were no more aggressive than women and women did not seem "softer" or more "maternal" than the men. Men routinely cooked and prepared food, showing little concern for defining themselves as essentially different from women. For example, Tahitian men often assumed the role of women when explaining local customs to visitors:

Teri'i Tui [a Tahitian informant] demonstrated the traditional method of giving birth to men and to his youngest children by pretending he was pregnant and sitting down on the floor in the proper position. He then asked his oldest sons to pretend to help him with the delivery. Other men when talking about the nursing of a baby, showed how it was done by holding an imaginary baby to their own breasts.[20]

The Tahitian language also reflects the society's lack of concern with gender difference: pronouns and nouns do not indicate the gender of subject or object.

Reflecting the patriarchal assumptions of European cultures, Western missionaries described Tahitian men as passive and timid. In actuality, they are gentle and mild tempered and show little concern for expressing or protecting their manliness. This is so even though Tahitian boys are initiated with rites of passage that include a minor superincision of the penis. Unlike hypermasculine tribes, however, Tahitian men perform rituals that are relatively simple and unstressful, and no onus is attached to crying out, showing fear, or fainting during their ceremonies. Since there is no concept of "male honor" to defend, when Tahitian men are provoked, they rarely become aggressive.[21]

As these examples illustrate, substantial variation exists in the extent to which men display stereotypical "macho" behavior. According to my cross-cultural analysis, about one in four nonindustrial societies placed little or no emphasis on men being aggressive, strong, or sexually potent. Included in this category are societies like the Tahitians who are relatively unconcerned with defending male honor. At the other end of the spectrum, about a third of societies are like the Mundurucu, with their marked emphasis on competitive and boastful displays of masculinity.

Macho displays are part of the overall pattern of power and privilege between men and women in any culture, but women's deference toward men can be considered separately. In about two-thirds of pre-modern societies, wives defer to their husbands in domestic decisions; in about a quarter, wives are explicitly prohibited from disputing their husbands; and in a few societies wives are routinely required to kneel or bow when greeting their husband. In about half of societies, women are excluded from most public gatherings or rituals and, in some, the women must give up their seat to any man who wants it, or seat themselves behind their husbands.

Aloofness and Intimacy of Husbands and Wives

After many years of studying families from cultures around the world, John and Beatrice Whiting described two basic societal types that can help us understand the sorts of gender displays just described. They suggest that marital and family relationships in nonindustrial societies follow a pattern of being either intimate or aloof. In the former, a man is highly involved in the domestic life of his family. He eats and sleeps with his wife and children, gossips with them at the evening meal, helps his wife care for their infant children, and is present and helps her at childbirth. In the other pattern, a man stays aloof from his wife and children and is not directly involved in domestic affairs. He spends his leisure time gossiping with other men and often eats and sleeps with other men as well. He does not help his wife with infant care and stays away from her while she is giving birth.[22]

Although the simple contrast between intimate and aloof societies may be overdrawn by the Whitings, their research suggests that men's involvement in domestic life is an important source of difference between cultures. Sex segregated and hypermasculine societies like the Amazonian Mundurucu fit the aloof pattern, whereas the Tahitians exemplify the intimate and egalitarian pattern. Why does the more hostile and combative pattern emerge? The Whitings propose that husbands and wives tend to room apart in societies where warriors are needed to protect property and that rooming apart has the psychological effect of promoting belligerence and defensiveness in men.

Compensatory Masculinity

The Whitings' descriptions of aloofness and intimacy fit nicely with Margaret Mead's ideas about gender and power in nonindustrial societies. According to Mead, men and women tend to perform different activities and occupy somewhat different social positions in all cultures, but, regardless of the specific content of these activities or positions, the things that the men do in any particular society are likely to be considered (at least by the men) the most important.

Mead, along with later feminist theorists like Nancy Chodorow and Mary O'Brien, suggest that men's propensity to exclude and devalue women stems from their tenuous role in childbearing and childrearing. Mead saw women's maternal identity and their nurturing ties to their children as so deeply rooted in biological conditions that "only fairly complicated social arrangements can break it down entirely."[23] Men, on the other hand, had to overcome a weak link to children and family by creating exclusive male activities and devaluing female activities.

> In a great number of societies men's sureness of their sex role is tied up with their right, or ability, to practice some activity that women are not allowed to practice. Their maleness, in fact, has to be underwritten by preventing women from entering some field or performing some feat. Here may be found the relationship between maleness and pride; that is, a need for prestige that will outstrip the prestige which is accorded to any woman.[24]

Although some later theorists reject Mead's claims for the universality of such patterns, many support Mead's central insight that men exclude women from public pursuits because they feel excluded from the birth process.

Reversing the typical Freudian idea that women envy men ("castration complex" and "penis envy"), Mead and others focus on men's "womb envy" stemming from their peripheral role in the magical processes of human reproduction.[25] Masculinity is thus seen as a compensatory reaction to men's insecurity.

Although men in nonindustrial societies usually exercise direct authority over women, they also legitimate and justify their power through elaborate masculinity rituals and symbolic separation from women. These practices are often supported through elaborate systems of myth and religion that symbolically express tensions between men and women. For example, almost every culture has tales about the way the world began that are passed from generation to generation through oral story telling. These origin myths provide insight into how the society values women's and men's contributions to society. Whereas many culture's creation stories portray only mythical males as important to the beginning of the world, others glorify both males and females. The anthropologist Peggy Sanday suggested that cultures that glorified women as well as men in myth would be more likely to include men in childrearing.[26] In my own cross-cultural analysis, I found that societies with fathers who were physically close to their children, who cared for them on a routine basis, and who were warm and affectionate toward them, were the most likely to have both male and female gods.

Although these results are tentative, we can speculate that the mythical symbolism of a culture is intimately tied up with patterns of childrearing and gender relations. Ideologies and myths serve to legitimate, justify, legalize, and symbolically codify existing patterns of social relations, but rarely is there a simple correspondence between the two. In this case there are at least two possible interpretations of the observed association between myth and practice, and both could be true simultaneously. In the first, following the social psychological reasoning of Margaret Mead and Nancy Chodorow, we would predict that father-present societies produce both men and women with internalized nurturing capacities. Because from an early age they had received love and care from both male and female caregivers, we would expect them to conceive of the beginning of the world in gender-balanced terms. A second interpretation reverses the causal order and assumes that egalitarian gender mythology promotes men's involvement in child care. Miriam Johnson suggests this approach, claiming that societies governed by a "maternal paradigm" would value mothering and be more likely to encourage males to participate in nurturing activities.[27]

However one conceives of the causal ordering of the two, a strong correspondence exists between gender-balanced mythical portrayals and gender-balanced parenting. In the following analysis, I explore this correspondence further, suggesting that gender-balance in parenting is also related to gender-balance in everyday ritual and gender-balance in social power.

Fatherhood in Pre-Modern Societies

How involved with babies and children are fathers in pre-modern societies, and what sorts of limits are set by the biological factors referred to by Mead and others? Contrary to the 1950s American stereotype of mothers being primarily responsible for the daily care and supervision of their own young children, child care has predominantly been a shared enterprise in nonindustrial societies. In about eight of ten nonindustrial societies, young children between the ages of 18 months and five years have spent less than half of their time with their own mothers. While the children's other caretakers are often women, about half of all societies have been documented as having close father–child relationships.[28] A few contrasting examples of how parents relate to children and men relate to women in these pre-modern societies show how our stereotypes of innate gender differences do not always fit.

Cultures with fathers who take an active part in child care are common in every major region of the world, but some of the most nurturant fathers have been observed among pygmy tribes of central Africa. For example, in *Intimate Fathers,* the anthropologist Barry Hewlett presents a detailed account of Aka pygmy fathers, who do less child care than Aka mothers, but sleep with their infants, have physical contact with them throughout the day, feed and soothe them, and habitually show them affection.[29] Even more well known are the Mbuti tribe, of the African Ituri forest, who were popularized by Colin Turnbull in his book *The Forest People.*[30] The Mbuti, like other pygmies, are hunters and gatherers who depend on and worship the forest in which they live. Few Mbuti occupations are strictly reserved for either men or women. Both gather the plentiful mushrooms, roots, berries, nuts, herbs, fruits, leafy vegetables, and bark that grow in the forest, and hunting is frequently a joint effort. Both men and women make hunting nets, although a man will usually attend to his own net, repairing it and adding to it as the need arises. Men help maintain and alter the huts, though this is usually done by the women because the dwellings are considered the woman's property. In general, women and men have equal say in family and group decisions, and no one attempts to dominate either the natural or the human environment.

Similar to the Tahitians, the Mbuti system of kinship terminology lacks terms that distinguish between male and female, except at the parental level. Even here, Colin Turnbull describes a significant point in the life of every young Mbuti when he or she accepts the father as a "kind of mother."

> The adult male who has been sharing the familiar leaf bed with its mother, and whose body smell, sound, taste, appearance, and rhythm it knows almost as well, and which has been found to be every bit as secure and safe, begins to fondle the child as its mother does. He takes it to his breast and holds it there. With everything else so familiar, the child explores for milk, but instead of milk is given its first solid food.[31]

In contrast to Mbuti or Tahitian men, for whom masculinity flows peace-fully and effortlessly from daily interaction with both men and women, other cultures insist on defining men as fundamentally different from, and in opposition to, anything female. In contrast to the intimacy and shared activ-ities of the Mbuti, the Rwala Bedouins of the Middle East reflect the more aloof and aggressive style of parenting as suggested by the Whitings. Before modern times, the Rwala, who live in the North Arabian Desert, frequently engaged in warfare and raiding among clans. Because the men were deeply con-cerned with displaying fierceness and maintaining honor, they had little time for babies. Women's work was sharply divided from that of men, who were waited on by wives and daughters, and men ate separately from both women and children. Bedouin dwelling tents were divided into separate compart-ments for men and women, with the public men's side used for entertaining guests, conducting business, and defending honor.[32] Bedouin women had no formal legal or political roles and were technically the property of their husbands or fathers.[33]

Childrearing patterns among the Rwala promoted the individual autonomy and toughness that were the hallmarks of masculinity in that culture. No baby was put to the breast until it yelled and one year olds took responsibility for feeding themselves from a communal dish, with no one checking to see if they got enough. If a toddler fell over a tent rope and cut its knee, its mother would reprimand it for shameful crying. By the time children were three or four they would have stopped showing emotion simply because of physical pain, though crying with rage was sometimes tolerated as a show of spirit. Mothers, grand-mothers, and aunts taught generosity with teasing or by asking two year olds to hand over precious objects, such as sweets, which, if not freely given, would be snatched away with mock seriousness. By the time children reached the age of about six or seven, direct teaching stopped, and children learned from experi-ence. They assumed adult-like duties at an early age and were responsible for maintaining the family's honor. For example, a seven-year-old girl would be expected to make guests comfortable by providing tea or coffee and an eight-year-old boy would be expected to avenge the killing of his father. Gender segregation was also evident in sibling relationships, with girls encouraged to serve their brothers and boys taught to look after and protect their sisters.[34]

Rwala Bedouin fathers had almost no responsibility for the routine care of young children and only paid attention to them when they were old enough to assume adult-like roles. Whereas Rwala mothers were treated by children with affection, fathers were treated with deference and respect. Since a father and his children were physically separated most of the time, it was said that before the age of seven, boys would go to their father "only for an occasional talk." Fathers used a saber or dagger to instill obedience and bravery in their sons. Boys between the ages of three and seven were circumcised with a knife by their fathers during ceremonies lasting several days.[35]

What difference does it make that Mbuti and Rwala fathers have such different relationships to their wives and their children? As noted earlier, some childrearing theories suggest that if men are relatively absent from early childhood socialization, young men grow up with a need to vehemently separate themselves from women.[36] There is little consensus among scholars about the specific ways that childrearing arrangements produce sexist men, but many agree with the basic idea that when men do not participate in infant and early child care, it produces men who are insecure in their masculinity. Chodorow, Mead, and others suggest that men form a rigid sense of self and that masculine identity is fundamentally oppositional and insecure. Boys raised in father-absent cultures are expected to fear women and continually reaffirm their superiority by restricting women's access to power, exhibiting threatening or violent behavior, and performing daring acts of physical strength or athletic prowess.[37] Other neo-Freudian researchers have focused on all-male rituals in pre-modern societies, suggesting that circumcision, initiation rites, bloodletting, and the couvade (simulating pregnancy symptoms) symbolically resolve men's gender-identity problems that stem from father-absent childrearing.[38]

If these ideas are basically correct, we would expect societies with involved fathers to produce males with few psychological needs to form all-male collectivities and devalue women. If fathers regularly participated in domestic life, young children would identify with men as well as with women. In these father-involved societies, the status of women, as measured by women's participation in community decision-making and women's access to positions of authority, should be higher than in societies in which fathers or other men were uninvolved in childrearing. Father-involved societies should also have fewer public displays of bravado and fewer ritualized displays of male superiority.

Both psychoanalytic and social learning versions of theories about the formation of gender identity and the acquisition of masculine or feminine personality traits postulate not just a "present" father, but also a father who is affectionate and emotionally supportive. If fathers are present, but violent or abusive, we would not expect their presence to promote gender equality. If, on the other hand, fathers were available in the way that mothers often are, we would expect young children to model and learn from men as well as women. Thus, we need to focus on whether fathers are likely to touch and hold infants, feed young children, and interact with them in nurturing ways. What is "nurturing" is, of course, subject to cultural definition, but if men are generally present for children in physically and emotionally supportive ways, we would expect children to identify with, and internalize, aspects of the father as well as the mother.

This is exactly what my statistical analysis of societies from around the world revealed. At all levels of societal complexity, distant father–child relationships were significantly associated with a general belief that women were inferior to men and an exclusion of women from public rituals.[39] Conversely, societies with close father–child relationships were unlikely to treat men as superior or women as inferior, and women exercised authority over most aspects of their lives. Regardless of the ultimate reasons for fathers being involved with their children, when they are it has important consequences for a social psychology of gender equality. In societies where men develop and maintain close relationships with young children, hypermasculine displays and competitive posturing are rare. These societies rarely require wives to publicly pay homage to their husbands and, as we will see below, are also much more likely to allow women to hold positions of power.[40]

Women's Status in Pre-Modern Societies

Most early cross-cultural researchers considered the status of women to be universally inferior to that of men and invoked biological and moral arguments to support their views.[41] In recent years, sociologists and anthropologists have challenged the idea of universal male dominance by showing how women have exercised control over important political, economic, and social processes in almost all societies. These more recent researchers have called our attention to a variety of social forces that contribute to women sharing power and authority with men.

In many societies, women maintained control over resources by producing food, owning property, or managing trading networks. In some societies, women held high public office such as chief or queen, maintained powerful leadership positions such as shaman or family leader, and participated in tribal councils or community forums. The distinction between public and private is not clearly drawn in many cultures, but women in societies from all major regions of the world have held powerful positions and participated in community decisions.[42] As for marriage and parenting, a few contrasting examples can help to dispel the illusion that biological factors predetermine who should rule and who should follow.

The Negrito Semang of the Malay Peninsula provide a good example of a society that affords women high status in community affairs. The Semang were a foraging society with little gender differentiation when they were first described by Westerners in the early twentieth century. Because most European observers were men with Victorian-era prejudices about women's frailty and subservience, the full extent of female authority in so-called primitive societies like the Semang is undoubtedly underestimated. Nevertheless, in 1925, one outside observer noted that a woman was "the ruler of the Negritos." Another European observer of that era described a Semang woman named Isan as "a very alert and voluble woman who has the ability to assert herself even with men."[43]

As described by these early twentieth century observers and later anthropologists, Semang men and women participated jointly in most activities of everyday life. Men did not band together for hunting or warfare, did not congregate in separate male houses, and were closely involved in all family and childrearing activities. Women, as well as men, could own property and both contributed to collective discussions about important matters facing the community. The anthropologist Peggy Sanday describes decision-making among the Semang as open and egalitarian. "To the extent that leadership exists, it is based on the ability to be assertive. This women can do as well as men."[44]

We can contrast the egalitarian and intimate Semang with the sex segregated and aloof Azande of Africa. The British anthropologist Evans-Pritchard studied the Azande in the late 1920s, at which time he estimated that the diverse peoples of the Azande state numbered over two million. Although the local governing structures had been altered by European and Arab influences, Evans-Pritchard reconstructed the politics of the region through extensive field and historical research. He characterized the Azande state, which ranged from savannah forest in the north to dense tropical rain forests in the south, as ruled by a complex system of male-dominated provinces. There was usually a paramount king and semi-autonomous princes, who ruled through various governors, deputies, and military leaders. Royal power and authority controlled all judicial and military functions. Dynastic rivalries, wars, and assassinations were common in the Azande state, in part because allegiance was established over subjects, rather than over set geographical territories, and because male rulers sent sons away to rule over their own domains. Evans-Pritchard describes Azande history as "a chronicle of parricides, fratricides, and the slaughter of sons and cousins on a Visigothic scale."[45]

Many of the institutions of Azande society were male controlled. Descent was reckoned through the father's line, newly married couples typically moved near the husband's kin, and daily life was extremely sex segregated. Fatherhood was defined in terms of procreation rather than by any direct participation of men in child care. Authoritarian fathers were treated with utmost respect by their sons, and daughters were relegated to the background where they worked and ate separately with other female members of the household. Even though Azande women made significant contributions to subsistence by producing and processing food, their status was extremely low. Wealthier men had many wives, and female slaves and concubines were commonplace. Women were considered childbearers and domestic servants, and were given no part in public life. Evans-Pritchard alludes to Azande women's subordinate political position by commenting that it was considered "highly improper" for any woman, even one of wealth and noble lineage, to have a public status requiring her to exercise authority over men.[46]

As noted in the above examples, there is wide cross-cultural variation in the ability of women to exercise authority. Societies in which women participate, along with men, in discussing and deciding important issues in public arenas are fairly common. In almost half, women can speak up and be listened to, and, like the Semang, are rated as high on female public participation. Societies like the Azande, in which women are excluded from important community forums, are also common, as almost 30 percent in my studies have followed this pattern. In general, women are less likely to hold leadership positions (chief, family, leader, shaman, etc.) than they are to participate in general community decision-making.[47] In two-thirds of the societies, like the Azande, the same political positions were either not open to both men and women, or women almost never held them (even if there was no official prohibition against their doing so). In the other third of the societies, like the Semang, women frequently or occasionally held the same leadership positions as men.[48]

The social structure of the society, as measured by marital residence rules, descent patterns, fraternal interest groups, and property control, tends to shape whether or not women can hold office and participate in community decisions.[49] But if fathers are present and affectionate, the society is more likely to afford women a substantial public role. Close father–child relationships are associated with greater public power and prestige for women in virtually all types of societies. Whether the society is densely populated with an elaborate bureaucracy and written records, or a simple preliterate band of nomads, if fathers are close to children, women are likely to exercise authority. Whether the society is warlike or peaceful, the sharing of child care and the sharing of public authority tend to go hand in hand. Similarly, whether the society has a developed agricultural resource base or subsists by gathering and hunting wild edibles, the association between these two realms remains important.[50]

To test whether the sharing of child care with people other than the father might actually be accounting for the observed results, I looked at the extent of non-maternal care and non-parental care.[51] In over half the societies, non-parents were rated as important caregivers, but their presence did not account for women's enhanced position. Thus, the sex of child caregivers appears to be especially important. When aunts, grandmothers, and other female neighbors share child care, the mother gets a break, but the society is *not* more likely to provide women with access to public power. In contrast, when fathers are intimately involved in the routine care of children, the status of women is higher.

Cultural Patterning of Gender and Fatherhood

As noted above, my studies of pre-modern societies suggest that fatherhood and gender relations are inextricably linked. Using statistical modeling techniques, I found that nurturant fathering was the most consistent predictor of gender equity, though property control and institutional forces were also found to shape gender relations in this worldwide sample of nonindustrial societies. If fathers were absent from childrearing, there was more male dominance and more gender antagonism throughout the society. If fathers participated in childrearing, in contrast, and if women controlled wealth and property, men were less prone to macho displays and wives were not required to offer ritual deference to husbands or other men.

Although displays of manliness are more common in smaller and less differentiated societies, ideologies of women's inferiority were most common in more complex societies. Societies tend to have internally consistent patterns of gender dominance so that the presence of hypermasculine rituals is also usually associated with a general belief that men are superior to women. Conversely, societies with little emphasis on men demonstrating their strength and sexual prowess are unlikely to consider women inferior. Nevertheless, it is smaller societies that tend to rely on chest pounding rituals to maintain male dominance whereas more complex societies rely on ideology to accomplish the same end. What is acted out in ritualized daily interactions in less complex societies is institutionalized in more general cultural belief systems in larger and more stratified societies.

The most important conclusion from my cross-cultural studies is that when fathers are more involved with child care, men are less misogynist and women have more social and political power. But questions remain as to how we should interpret these findings. Most scholarship focuses on how childrearing shapes adult personalities, and the theories mentioned above similarly give weight to the potential influence of men's childrearing on the development of balanced masculine identities in the younger generation. If we take a more fluid view of personality, however, we might also focus on the ongoing socialization of adults, especially the impact of routine child caregiving on men's identities. In addition, women's social power can be viewed as causally prior to the involvement of men in child care. If women have substantial public prestige and authority, they will be more likely to put pressure on men to increase their contributions to childrearing and other domestic activities.

Whichever way the causal arrows run, we need to acknowledge the interplay between parenting and overall gender relations in the society. Given women's biological capacity to bear and nurse children, men's participation in early child care necessarily entails a minimum level of cooperation between men and women. Sharing childrearing tasks probably creates expectations for cross-gender cooperation in other, more public, activities, which would make it easier for women to exercise public authority. Conceptualized in this way, task sharing between genders becomes the most important focus of concern, and we can begin to analyze the ways in which cooperative activities between men and women contribute to the organization of social life on nonbiological bases. This approach de-emphasizes biological differences by focusing on the ways in which men and women respond similarly to the structural features of daily activities such as parenting. Unfortunately, this approach runs counter to recent popular calls for a return to "traditional family values" and to the visions of fatherhood and masculinity promoted by new age masculinists like the poet Robert Bly.

Wild Men and Father Hunger

Ever since Bill Moyers' PBS special *A Gathering of Men,* it has been fashionable to discuss (or ridicule) the current state of American manhood in terms of Robert Bly's mythopoetic ideas. The problem with modern man, according to Bly, is "father hunger," which can be cured by bonding with other men in ancient masculinity rites.[52] Across the nation, men — mostly white and middle-aged — have been drumming, dancing, and sharing their feelings at mythopoetic weekend retreats reminiscent of boy scout campfires.[53]

Using "hearth stories," Bly weaves together myth, poetry, and social commentary to convince men that they should toughen up and stop being wimps. In the best-selling *Iron John,* he retells the story of a "hairy man" who becomes mentor to a young boy. Through a series of adventures that are interpreted as stages in male growth, Bly reflects on the importance of initiation for proper masculine development and invokes idyllic images of ancient male bonding rituals. Although it is easy to lampoon the antics of Bly and his followers, the rapid and widespread popularity of his teachings reveals that a growing number of American men are experiencing an unsettling sense of insecurity driven by the recent modest gains of some American women.

What motivates Bly to retell masculinity stories from ancient societies and delve into the supposed mythical roots of manhood? The problem, as he sees it, is that modern American society is producing too many boys and too few real men. (On this point, Bly sounds like many popular politicians — Ronald Reagan, Oliver North, Newt Gingrich — or movie stars — Bruce Willis, Sylvester Stallone, Arnold Schwarzenegger.) Bly thinks that since the 1970s, men have become more thoughtful and gentle, and he worries that the new "soft male" is trying too hard to please his mother or girl friend and is spending too much energy trying to be a nice boy. Bly notes that the movement toward "harder women" and "softer men" seemed like a nice arrangement for a while, but he tells us that we've lived with it long enough to see that it "just doesn't work."[54]

What has caused the sorry state of contemporary American manhood? According to Bly, the major culprits are women. He claims that a "mother–son conspiracy" is keeping sons at home for too long and producing far too many mamma's boys. He also chides the "separatist wing" of the feminist movement for trying to breed the natural fierceness out of men.[55] According to Bly, passive and naive soft males are blindly taking abuse from women who enjoy dominating them.

The naive man feels a pride in being attacked. If his wife or girlfriend, furious, shouts that he is "chauvinist," a "sexist," a "man," he doesn't fight back, but just takes it. He opens his shirt so that she can see more clearly where to put the lances. He ends with three or four javelins sticking out of his body, and blood running all over the floor.[56]

I have yet to find a woman whose experience metaphorically corresponds to this scenario, but I think Bly is describing a fear that many men share. It is a fear born of a sense of slipping power and authority over women, and it makes men receptive to a mythical resconstruction of history and anthropology. The mythopoetic solution proposed by Bly assuages men's fears of emasculation, even if his chest-pounding and moon-howling rituals are a bit too arcane for most. Rediscovering the instinctual and timeless male warrior within, men are encouraged to overcome "psychic incest" between mother and son and reclaim their lost power. With a rhetorical flourish, Bly urges American men to emulate Australian aboriginal initiators who use a sword to cut the "psychic umbilical cord" that binds boys to their mothers and keeps them from growing into full-fledged adult men.[57] (Never mind that Aborigines had not discovered metal.)[58]

Putting aside the details of factual accuracy, Bly's symbolic solution to the modern soft male predicament is to adopt and adapt old world bonding rituals. By reclaiming the ancient art of male initiation, we might bring vitality to our declining culture and reinstate respect for "masculine integrity." In this view, only other men can turn boys into men, by welcoming them into the "ancient, mythologized, instinctive male world." It is the wild men's job "to teach the young man how abundant, various, and many-sided his manhood is." In this way the boy's body "inherits physical abilities developed by long-dead ancestors, and his mind inherits spiritual and soul powers developed centuries ago."[59] Thus, Bly invokes millions of years of "natural" male dominance, suggesting that embracing it will lead us out of our current confused state.

Like many so-called traditionalists and much of popular culture, Bly celebrates men's bravado and women's admiration of it: "Men and women alike once called on men to pierce the dangerous places, carry handfuls of courage to the waterfalls, dust the tails of the wild boars. . . . Men have been loved for their astonishing initiative: embarking on wide oceans, starting a farm in rocky country from scratch, imagining a new business, doing it skillfully, working with beginnings, doing what has never been done."[60] These images of take-charge men fit nicely with the rugged individualist masculine ideal that permeates our culture. Whether an explorer, an entrepeneur, an inventor, an athlete, or a soldier, the real man knows no boundaries and is always willing to take risks.

The image of the real man is supported by a complimentary, but altogether different, image of the homebound real woman—kind, sensitive, caring, and sometimes sexy in a flirtatious or receptive manner. These images of timeless essential differences between men and women might be harmless, but for their resonance with violent portrayals of male-dominated sexuality.

> Male and female make up one pair, the light and the dark another, the one and the many another, the odd and even another.
> . . . Rejoicing in the opposites means pushing the opposites apart with our imaginations so as to create space, and then enjoying the fantastic music coming from each side. . . . One can feel the resonance between opposites in flamenco dancing. Defender and attacker watch each other, attractor and refuser, woman and man, red and red. Each is a pole with its separate magnetic charge, each is a nation defending its borders, each is a warrior enjoying the heat of extravagant passion, a distinguished passion which is fierce, eaglelike, mysterious.[61]

What intrigues me here is not that Bly portrays men and women as different, but that he elevates whatever differences might exist to the level of spiritual essence and violent opposition. He appreciates this difference only as opposites, as nations defending their borders, and implies that *the male* is the active principle, the fierce initiator, fighting to penetrate the receptive female. The mythopoetic tendency is to celebrate a primordial opposition between masculinity and femininity that is fixed and eternal and to simplify the Jungian notion that male and female forms of energy reside in all individuals.

The Dangers of Celebrating Difference

Unfortunately for Bly and the many popular pundits that celebrate gender differences as natural and unchanging, recent research shows just how much effort it takes to create the impression that men and women are fundamentally different. For instance, the anthropologist Gayle Rubin notes: "Men and women are, of course, different. But they are not as different as night and day, earth and sky, yin and yang, life and death. In fact, from the standpoint of nature, men and women are closer to each other than either is to anything else."[62] Even for a topic as widely accepted as the putatively natural sex differences in math and verbal skills, we are learning that most of the gender disparity is socially created.[63]

Unfortunately for the rest of us, however, Bly's pseudo-biological and poetic pronouncements are seen as a promising new direction in gender studies and in "men's studies." The sociologist R. W. Connell comments, "For those of us who have been trying to get questions about masculinity on the intellectual agenda, it is deeply embarrassing to see such material publicized as the latest word about men. It is not just that *Iron John* is a little cavalier with the facts. By any intellectual standards, the book is appallingly bad: overgeneralized, under-researched, incoherent, and at times self contradictory."[64] Although we can easily dismiss Bly's faulty scholarship, we cannot ignore the fact that many men (and women) want to believe what he is saying, and *that* seems to be the topic most worthy of future study.

Mythopoetic arguments about emasculated men and the need for male validation are remarkably similar to rhetoric heard in Victorian America. Around the turn of the century, influential public figures proclaimed their vigorous support for fraternal organizations that would promote male bonding and solidarity. From about 1880 to 1920, hundreds of fraternal orders like the Odd Fellows and Freemasons gained thousands of members by putting them through an elaborate sequence of male initiation rituals. Whereas gentlemen in the early nineteenth century tended to avoid physical exertion, the later part of the century saw an enormous growth in outdoor sports and camping that were idealized for their contributions to masculine character. Popular magazine depictions of male heroes at the turn of the century shifted from earlier praise of piety, thrift, and industry to appreciation for vigor, forcefulness, and mastery. This was also the era in which the Boy Scouts, with their emphasis on turning boys into "red blooded, moral, manly men" grew to unprecedented size.

Men's preoccupation with masculine validation was also accompanied by public debates about the "proper" role of women. As noted in Chapter 2, the "cult of true womanhood" encouraged women to fulfill their moral destiny through motherhood and wifely deference, and discouraged them from participating in the traditional male preserves of business and politics. Not incidentally, this was the era when unprecedented numbers of women entered the labor force, swelling the ranks of formerly all-male occupations such as clerks, typists, bookkeepers, cashiers, and sales personnel.[65]

The lesson we can learn from this brief historical comparison is that an ideological belief system always reflects a complex interplay of social and economic forces. As women began to perform jobs that men had previously performed, and as men's jobs became increasingly "feminized," romantic visions of halcyon days arose. In the late nineteenth and early twentieth centuries, women's "nature" turned pure and men became preoccupied with affirming their manliness. It is precisely at such times that conservative movements to return to "natural" gender roles gain force. In response to direct economic competition from women, men defend their privileged position by asserting their "inherent" ruggedness and suitability for "men's work." A corollary ideology of women's purity and virtue, championed by elite men and their wives, can thus be seen as a backlash against women's economic achievements, however modest.

Concern for American men's toughness and individualism can be traced throughout our history, but fears of emasculation are especially strong during times when women have achieved gains in the marketplace and the legal arena.[66] Since we have just passed through two decades of growth in female labor force participation, a resurgence of the women's movement, and some modest legal reforms to protect women, it is not surprising that calls for reasserting "masculine integrity" have lately achieved prominence. We must remember, however, that claims about the essential nature of men and women carry some profound intellectual and political dangers.

Oversimplified gender dichotomies, and calls for "fierce" initiation ceremonies, tend to resurface whenever men feel challenged by women. What troubles me about the mythopoetic and fundamentalist religious ideas about gender is that they ignore cross-cultural and historical diversity and reify essentialist notions of what it means to be a man or a woman. Will reinstituting ancient male initiation rites or emulating feudal patterns of patriarchal privilege heal modern men and rescue a declining culture? Definitely not. In fact, re-enacting ancient chest-pounding rituals is likely to increase gender antagonisms rather than promoting some idyllic balance between fierce men and yielding women. Similarly, attempting to honor fundamentalist notions of husbands as undisputed rulers and wives as naturally subservient will only lead to trouble for most modern families.

Underlying both mythopoetic and fundamentalist beliefs is the assumption that mothers and fathers are inalterably different. This notion is also perpetuated by many scientists, counselors, and social service providers. Given the link between gender dominance and a belief in gender difference, we ought to rethink the idea that fathers are incapable of nurturing like mothers. Instead of assuming, like Bly and others, that the natural role of the father is to break the mother-son bond, we ought to begin expecting fathers to create their own bonds with children early in their lives.[67]

Iron John, for all its shortcomings, struck a chord among American readers. Over a year on national best-seller lists is a significant accomplishment for the retelling of a Grimm Brothers' fairy tale about a hairy man who lives at the bottom of a pond. Mythopoetic books about masculinity like Robert Bly's *Iron John* or Sam Keen's *Fire in the Belly* are popular, in part, because they tell men that it is OK to feel grief, anger, and resentment. These books speak to men's sense of powerlessness and counsel them to reclaim their "natural" masculine strength by symbolically and emotionally separating themselves from women. What is disturbing, however, is that conventional "masculine" responses to feelings of powerlessness — whether in the home or in global politics — tend to be violent.

While Bly writes large the image of the overly passive soft male, it is the "hard male" that captures the imagination of most American men. A neverending barrage of popular action movies continues to celebrate a violent and fiercely independent masculinity. For example, Arnold Schwarzenegger's "iron man" — *Terminator 2* — came out about the same time as *Iron John* and grossed over $100 million after just 15 days in theaters. While the brave heroes in these movies usually have a tender side, images of their masculinity are anything but soft. Rambo-like heroes are tough and aggressive and never let anyone push them around. The underlying message is that nice guys, when victimized by crooks and bullies, unleash a just and violent masculinity that has been lying dormant within them.

Accepting the notion of a natural masculine fierceness or an inborn "need" for masculine validation can have negative consequences for women because it contributes to men's sense of superiority. Ritual separation from women carries the very real danger of perpetuating the abusive treatment of women and other men. Men already objectify women and use aggression against females and "unmasculine" males. Providing such men with symbolic justification for their aggression will only make matters worse.

My emphasis on the dangers of overstating differences between men and women is not new among scholars who investigate gender inequality. Nevertheless, there are many inside and outside of academia who dismiss such warnings as naive or disingenuous. From new right conservatives quoting Biblical passages about the "rightful" place of the father to avant garde French feminists celebrating a unique consciousness that flows from the female body, there are many popular images of fundamental, timeless, and natural gender difference. Many of these accounts call up primordial images of tribal societies to verify their version of natural gender differences. Savage males and nurturing females from ancient times come to stand for some underlying deep structure of masculinity or femininity. Unfortunately, the imagery resonates so closely with our own culture's gender ideology that most people accept the tribal portrayals as evidence for the inevitability of patriarchal power and feminine frailty. As I hope I have shown in this chapter, this is a fundamentally false assumption based on an inaccurate reading of human history and cross-cultural variability.

Studying patterns of parenting, deference, and gender display in nonindustrial societies helps us understand how power and control operate in everyday life. Who eats first, sits last, or talks back reflects a sort of "micropolitics" of gender that operates in tribal societies as well as in modern industrial ones. If daily practices allow men to dominate women and define themselves as essentially different, they can more easily maintain their privileged status. Seen from this perspective, mythopoetic calls for reinstituting ancient male initiation rites carry regressive more than progressive potential. The practices that accompany all-male initiation rites and everyday affirmations of masculine strength and fortitude typically work to the disadvantage of women, children, gay men, and others who are excluded. While ritual gender segregation and celebration of difference may not theoretically or inherently imply male domination, in practice this is what happens. Hypermasculine societies tend to require that women show deference to men and that wives do their husbands' bidding. This unequal distribution of personal service is also typically accompanied by an unequal distribution of material goods, with men monopolizing resources and accumulating wealth. Societies that segregate men and celebrate masculinity are also the most likely to be misogynist.

According to the cross-cultural analysis in this chapter, the key to minimal gender dominance and deference is ongoing gender cooperation in childrearing and property control, not carving out separate domains for men and women. When men help take care of young children and women control property, boys are apt to grow up with fewer needs to define themselves in opposition to women, and men are less inclined toward antagonistic displays and boastful posturing. When wives are not required to defer to husbands, and men are not encouraged to brag and be macho, then cultural ideologies are unlikely to portray men as superior and women as inferior. Parenting and gender equity are thus inalterably linked.

New Cultural Models

Bly and others are probably right to identify "father hunger" as a malaise of late twentieth century American society, though most of the recent policies proposed to remedy the situation appear misguided. Chasing down fathers who do not pay child support may keep a few more men involved with their children and would help divorced mothers cope financially, but cutting single moms off welfare and giving custody rights to unwed fathers will make women's and children's lives even more difficult than they are now. Recreating male initiation ceremonies to symbolically sever mother–son bonds (as Bly proposes) is no solution either, because it would only increase the level of gender antagonism in the society. The answer is not to invoke symbolic images of past gender segregation, but to reinforce images of gender equality and cooperation wherever we can find them.[68]

Generalizing my analysis of nonindustrial societies to the modern era yields the following conclusion: The way to minimize masculine insecurity and bravado is not to separate men from women, but to ensure that they cooperate in both childrearing and productive work. Instead of rejecting the mother and ritually accepting the father at puberty, men need to get involved much earlier in children's lives. This would not be a separatist involvement that rejects women and initiates adolescents into an anti-woman fraternity of men. Instead, it would entail a nurturing masculinity based on cooperation with, and acceptance of, mothers. It would also entail the active involvement of fathers with *daughters,* not just sons.

This is not some far-out dream that is unattainable because of some underlying biological sex difference. In fact, it is a fairly typical pattern among human societies, as illustrated by the cross-cultural examples in this chapter. This is not to say that it will be easy to accomplish anything close to equal parenting or true gender equity. Once intitiated, male dominance is extremely resistant to change, and the cross-cultural record is littered with examples of violence and exploitation used to protect masculine privilege. Nevertheless, as indicated in the next chapter, larger social and economic trends may set the stage for some significant changes in gender and parenting in the coming decades.

8

The Future

The sociological analysis in the previous chapters suggests that when men and women share family work, the entire society benefits. My review of recent research also shows that American mothers and fathers are slowly moving in that direction. Underlying social forces are pushing us toward a blending of gender and family roles and away from older patterns of authoritarian fathers and subservient wives.

At the same time, a reactionary backlash threatens recent efforts to promote gender equity in the home and in the workplace. Clarion calls for family values have grown louder and nostalgic visions of mythical families have gained popularity. These conservative ideologies have gained strength because the so-called "traditional" family of a breadwinner-father and a homemaker-mother has become more rare.

The controversies and tensions surrounding gender and family changes affect virtually all Americans. Disagreements over family and work are increasingly common between husbands and wives. Older parents are having a hard time understanding the motivations and behaviors of their grown children. Younger parents are having a hard time coping. And politicians, religious leaders, and everyday people are pontificating about what's wrong with THE AMERICAN FAMILY.

In this climate of contradictory rhetoric about families, it is extremely important to be able to place recent changes in a larger social context. I focus on some underlying economic and cultural trends in this final chapter to move away from the vitriolic rhetoric and romantic imagery that surrounds debates about changes in family life. In so doing, I hope to capture a glimpse of future patterns of parenting and work in American households. I end with with some surprisingly optimistic projections about how and why we will continue down the road toward greater gender equity.

Family Work

Because family work is so tied up with what it means to be a man or a woman in our society, changes have been personal and difficult. Household divisions of labor have been slow to respond to the realities of family life in the age of employed mothers. Interviews with two-job families showed that some changes are underway, although truly equal sharing of child care and housework is still a rarity.

When men do take on more of the mundane domestic tasks of cooking, cleaning, and child tending, however, the balance of power in a household begins to shift. If husbands assume a larger share of the housework, employed wives escape total responsibility for the second shift, and women enjoy better mental health.[1] In addition, when fathers take on significant responsibility for children, they begin to develop sensitivities that have been assumed to come with being a mother.[2] When fathers share in routine parenting, children thrive intellectually and emotionally, and they grow up with less rigid gender stereo-types.[3] Sharing household labor thus carries the potential for transforming the meaning of gender in this and future generations.[4] Perhaps more important, if men took responsibility for family work and performed more of the everyday tasks that it takes to run a household, there are strong indications that gender inequality and discrimination against women would decrease substantially.[5]

What factors might encourage the sharing of family work? In my inter-views, people mentioned many reasons for attempting sharing, and I grouped these under the general headings of gender ideology, relative income, practical necessity, provider identity, social networks, and birth timing. I used these motivating and constraining forces, along with others from previous research, to develop hypotheses for testing on a nationwide survey of American house-holds in Chapter 6. In that analysis, various social factors and personal characteristics encouraging American couple to share household labor were isolated and compared to one another. In general, I confirmed that more domestic labor is shared when resources and constraints are divided equally between husbands and wives and when they believe in gender equity.

Summarizing the specific findings from that research, we can conclude that husbands share more housework and child care when their wives are employed more hours. This occurs when women have careers and identify strongly with their work, but also when they put in long hours at relatively menial working-class jobs. Men also do more if their wives earn more of the total household income, especially if they are defined as economic co-providers. More sharing is evident when wives negotiate for change, delegate responsibility for various chores, and relinquish total control over managing home and children. Sharing of family work is also common when husbands' and wives' attitudes and ideology support gender equity. When husbands are employed fewer hours and value family time over rapid career advancement, they do a greater proportion of the housework and child care. Finally, more tasks are shared when fathers get involved in infant care, take responsibility for the mundane aspects of parenting, and move beyond the role of household helper.

Several social and demographic factors are also associated with more sharing of family work. Husbands do more when the couple has a more cosmopolitan and less dense social network, which means that they tend to move around and have less frequent contact with their parents and other kin. Parents who delay the transition to parenthood until their late twenties or thirties also share more of the housework and child care. This seems to be the case, even after controlling for the factors mentioned above, such as relative income or time spent on the job. Individuals who have divorced and remarried, especially those giving birth to a child in a second marriage are also especially likely to share family work. Finally, those parents who have fewer and older children appear to share more domestic labor than others.

Some of these motivations for sharing family work are linked together, and others are missing, but this list is a good starting point for making predictions about the future. Extrapolating recent social and economic trends, we can use this list to estimate how larger forces will shape divisions of family work in the next century. Toward that end, I document Americans' changing attitudes about gender and family, review marriage and birth patterns, summarize recent economic trends, and make projections about future developments. This exercise in sociological crystal-ball gazing, however uncertain, serves as an important corrective for the nostalgic rhetoric that passes for social analysis about the future of families.

Social Trends

Changing Attitudes

Social scientists debate endlessly about whether changes in attitudes cause changes in behavior or whether changed behaviors force us to adjust our attitudes. Either way, attitudes give us a glimpse into potential social changes and our possible reactions to them. From studies conducted a decade or two ago, we know that most American wives did not feel it was unfair that they were required to do virtually all the family work.[6] Husbands generally concurred, though most surveys neglected to ask them about such matters, assuming that housework and child care were out of their purview. More recently, fewer men and women are willing to accept unequal divisions of family work as natural or inevitable, and we are likely to see even more attitude changes in the future.

Using nationwide survey data from the late 1970s and early 1980s, Joseph Pleck reported that only about a third of American wives wanted their husbands to do more around the house. At the same time, over half the husbands reported thinking that their wives expected more from them. This indicates that husbands may be expecting more of themselves than their wives are expecting of them, even if they fail to follow through. As noted in Chapter 3, Pleck also suggests that mothers want their husbands to be more involved with the children, not so the women will have less work to do themselves, but because the father's participation is seen as benefiting the children.[7]

Focusing on these three attitudes, we can predict even more change in the future. If more wives want help from husbands to make things more fair, if more men feel pressure from wives to do more, and if more mothers want fathers to be involved for the children's benefit, we will see more actual sharing of family work. All three attitudes have become more prevalent in the past decade, and all are likely to increase even further.

Underlying these three views about men and women sharing family work are more general shifts in Americans' attitudes about marriage, divorce, and the appropriate roles of husbands and wives. In addition, a fourth important motivation — that men themselves will want to share child care and housework — is also likely to shape future divisions of household labor. To see what has been happening with American's attitudes on these issues, I turn to recent opinion polls.

The most important attitude shifts in the past three decades can be summarized by saying that there has been a weakening of the rules surrounding family behavior and an expansion of the range of acceptable behavior. The normative imperative to marry, remain married, have children, restrict intimate relations to marriage, and maintain separate roles for men and women has deteriorated significantly according to various national surveys.[8] The increased acceptance of individual choice in these matters has occurred in spite of (and as a precursor to) all the rhetoric about the need for a return to "traditional" family values.

These shifts in attitudes about marriage and family have occurred in the context of a growing individualism in the United States and other industrialized nations of the world. Surveys of childrearing values from the 1920s to the 1970s show that American parents have placed decreasing emphasis on obedience, loyalty to church, and conformity, while putting increased emphasis on autonomy, tolerance, and thinking for one's self.[9] The gradual increase in tolerance and independence go hand in hand with the loosening of normative prescriptions about family life.

Between the 1960s and late 1970s, significantly fewer Americans expressed a belief in the idea that everyone should marry and have children. Similarly, the proportion of Americans who disapproved of cohabitation, extramarital affairs, and divorce decreased dramatically during this time. Even though these attitude shifts suggest that people are more likely to accept nonconventional family behaviors, the vast majority of Americans continue to say that they value and desire marriage, parenthood, and family life.

The trend toward accepting all sorts of family arrangements rose dramatically in the 1970s but leveled off during 1980s and into the 1990s. In only one area have attitudes continued to change as fast, or faster, than they did in the 1970s: gender roles. Even though attitudes were relatively liberal by the end of the 1970s, they became even more so during the 1980s and 1990s. In answer to questions about who should make family decisions, who should work, who should take care of children, and who should be involved in politics or other extra-family activities, Americans continued to become more accepting of women's increasing independence and opportunities. This was especially so for younger people, as indicated by surveys of high school seniors.[10] In addition, Americans became less worried about the negative impacts of maternal employment or day care on children, an attitude change that paralleled the dramatic increase in both these activities during the same time period. Overall, we saw a marked deterioration of the ideal of separate spheres for men and women between the 1960s and the early 1990s, at least as measured by responses to opinion polls.

In 1977, two out of three Americans answering the General Social Survey agreed that "it is better for everyone involved if the man is the achiever outside the home and the woman takes care of home and family." By 1991, the proportion agreeing had fallen to 41 percent, with only about one in three baby boomers concurring.[11] Another traditional view is that "it is more important for a wife to help her husband's career than to have one herself." More than half of all Americans agreed with this statement in 1977. In 1985, 36 percent agreed, and by 1991, just 29 percent agreed that the man's job was most important. We can see that support for separate spheres and the automatic dominance of men has weakened dramatically in the past few decades, though a substantial minority of Americans still clings to the so-called traditional view.

Yet even the most traditional Americans are getting less conservative about women's roles. Of those who identify themselves as political conservatives, and of those who identify as Protestant fundamentalists, the proportion who agreed that the husband's career was more important than the wife's fell from about 60 percent to under 40 percent.[12] Overall, most Americans are also less worried about the well-being of children of working mothers than they were in the past. In 1977, half of Americans agreed that "a working mother can establish just as warm and secure a relationship with her children as a mother who does not work." By 1991, two-thirds of Americans agreed. Large scale opinion polls also confirm that younger people are less traditional in their attitudes than older ones, and that those with more education, especially those who went to college, tend to approve of women working and sharing most of the rights enjoyed by men.

Most attitude surveys have focused on changing attitudes about women, but there is some indication that attitudes about men are also changing. For example, national surveys of young people show an upward trend from the mid-1970s into the 1980s in the number who agree that men should share housework. In 1985, 76 percent of female high school students and 71 percent of male high school students agreed that husbands should take on more of the housework and child care if their wives were employed.[13] Perhaps even more important, these percentages tend to go up once the young people move out on their own. In a panel study that followed a group of families over time, daughters and sons were asked if a wife should expect her husband to help around the house after he comes home from a hard day's work. In 1980, when they were 18 years old, about 75 percent said yes, but by the time they were 23 in 1985, 86 percent of the women and 88 percent of the men said that the wife should expect help from her husband.[14] Other surveys of college students suggest that even the most traditional men are willing to help out with household chores, and that even the most traditional women expect this of them.[15]

The educational and career expectations of young Americans are also fast converging. In the 1960s, boys had higher educational and occupational aspirations than girls.[16] By the 1980s, however, there were few if any gender differences in youth aspirations, and some surveys even found that girls had higher occupational aspirations.[17] Over 90 percent of adolescent girls expect to be employed after they marry, and virtually all of those expect to be working after they become mothers, although most plan to be out of the labor force for a year or two after giving birth. Most adolescent boys similarly expect their future wives to work, though many express uncertainty about whether their wives will continue to be employed after having children.[18] The fact that girls see their labor force participation to be more continuous than boys expect of them shows that women's attitudes have changed faster than men's and portends future marital conflict over employment and family work once they become parents.

Although boys are much less likely than girls to expect to take time off from work after having a child, we can see some recent changes in young people's attitudes about this issue as well. A survey of youth conducted from 1988–90 found that one out of four eleventh grade boys planned to take a year or more of leave from employment after having a baby.[19] It is likely that, as the boys mature, they will become increasingly aware of the costs that career interruptions might entail, but it is significant that many initially desire to take an active role in parenting. As we saw in earlier chapters, a man's motivation to become a nurturing parent is one of the best predictors of his assuming responsibility for a range of domestic tasks.

The polls show that more than ever before, young American women and their potential husbands expect to have both careers and children. Women, more than men, anticipate that they will be forced to make career sacrifices when they have children, but neither are very realistic about the future. Survey questions measuring youth attitudes cannot tell us what divisions of labor will actually look like as people mature, marry, and become parents, because everyone adjusts behavior to shifting circumstances. Adolescents' expectations about their adult lives are especially unstable as they respond to the pressures and constraints of their own rapidly changing lives.[20] For example, some women who initially want to have careers turn toward homemaking because they discover that working conditions, pay, and the intrinsic satisfactions of employment are less than they had expected. Others plan on working only temporarily until they have children, but find that a career is more satisfying than expected, or that they cannot make ends meet without a job. Similarly, men who expect to be career-oriented sometimes shift to becoming family men, and some who have few career ambitions become absorbed in their work because of changing circumstances.[21] Still, that both young women and young men initially want to share employment and family work is likely to favor more explicit bargaining strategies and influence both spouse's perceptions of fairness in divisions of household labor.

The trend toward men valuing family involvement is not just limited to adolescents. A large number of studies show that men in the United States, and in many other industrialized countries, rank fatherhood as more important than paid work.[22] A majority of fathers say they should be directly involved in their children's lives, even though they do not necessarily follow through by spending significant amounts of time with them or performing more routine chores. The most common justification for limited father–child contact is that the men's jobs require them to be away from home.[23] The status of economic provider is still central to men's self-concept, so it is not surprising that employment obligations would be seen as limiting their parenting. Nevertheless, as the labor force participation of men and women becomes more similar, and especially if we continue to see men's and women's wages converging, we can expect some gradual changes in attitudes toward the exclusiveness of the provider role.[24] In general, these shifts in attitude signal that men will be less able to use employment as an excuse to escape domestic responsibilities than they have in the past.

The shift toward accepting working mothers and expecting more from fathers is also played out in American popular culture. Many researchers suggest that media portrayals of fatherhood changed dramatically in the past few decades as images of the "new" expressive and caring father became commonplace.[25] Others suggest that changes in popular culture have been more modest and contradictory.[26] In recent television commercials, for instance, fathers represented two-thirds of the parents shown, and most were pictured as sensitive and kind. Simultaneously, however, television images of aggressive and domineering men were even more prevalent, and the contradictory media images were difficult to reconcile.[27]

Some researchers conclude that rhetoric and imagery surrounding the "new" father far outstrip any observable change in the allocation of daily responsibility for children. In contrast, my research suggests that it may be the media imagery that lags behind behavioral change, since most fathers on situation comedies are still shown as well-meaning but comicly inept.[28] No matter how positive such portrayals are, however, visions of fathers have captured the attention of advertisers and their potential consumers (most of whom are women). These images provide us with representations of men who spend time with their families rather than being gone all the time. Although we should be cautious about assigning a causal role to such imagery, its presence adds to the growing body of evidence that men want to be more involved with their children.

Most men now claim that they want to parent differently from their own fathers. Most, in fact, will spend significantly more time in the day-to-day activities of parenting than the generation that preceded them. Starting with their presence in the delivery room, men who become fathers in the future will be less resistant to changing diapers, preparing bottles, and actively caring for their growing children than past fathers. The attitude changes and personal motivations noted above will play a part in this, but practical necessity will likely play and even more important role in bringing about family changes. Most men will end up participating in hands-on parenting because of the many unerlying demographic, economic, and social forces that continue to shape their lives.

Demographic Trends

Demographic trends are important because they represent broad patterns of regularity in people's lives. The frequency, likelihood, and timing of marriages, births, divorces, and deaths tell us something about how families change over time. Demographers sometimes claim that population dynamics are the primary force behind societal change and that if we monitor cycles of fertility (births) or mortality (deaths) we will understand the most important processes shaping our future. Like neo-classical economic theories that rely on the "unseen hand" of free market forces, such analyses focus on overarching biological and ecological processes to explain why and when individuals form or dissolve families. For example, some focus on the large size of the baby boom cohort (those born between 1946 and 1964) to make predictions about fertility rates, employment patterns, or consumption preferences.[29]

One of the problems of using only large scale demographic factors (like cohort size) to explain family-related demographic factors (like fertility rates) is that it ignores the feelings and actions of family members who are making countless daily decisions as they respond to a variety of social pressures. In fact, the larger structures and the individual feelings and actions are intimately linked. Abrupt population shifts like the baby boom are often unanticipated, because demographic models cannot acknowledge the power of local situations, shifting attitudes, and individual choices. As peoples' personal experiences show, gender strategies influence the allocation of family work, and are equally important in shaping decisions about whether and when to marry, divorce, or have a child. Because family members are constantly adjusting their attitudes and expectations during the course of their everyday lives, the choices they make, when considered in the aggregate, constitute the makings of the next wave of demographic trends. Consequently, demographic factors should be considered in tandem with other social and psychological influences when predicting the future.

Rates and trends derived from government documents like marriage licenses or birth certificates ignore the rich texture of peoples' everyday lives, but they do tell us about the changing contexts in which people make family-related decisions. An annual figure for median age at first birth, for example, does not convey the individual events and traumas that led up to a decision to give birth to an unplanned child or to have an abortion, yet both these personal paths are reflected in the demographic statistic. The median age at first birth succinctly summarizes the outcomes of many individual choices and situational constraints, and tells us what the average tendency is among the population in any given time period. By stepping back from the particulars of individual lives to focus on the level of aggregate demographic trends, we can better understand how the range of choices available to family members has shifted over time. By documenting how the broad demographic outlines of family life have changed in the past few decades, we are in a better position to predict what families might look like in the twenty-first century.

Marriage Trends

As outlined in Chapter 2, dramatic changes have been occurring in U.S. marriage patterns in the last few decades. The most significant trends are that people are waiting longer to get married and that they are increasingly likely to divorce. This has not, however, threatened the institution of marriage.

Contrary to backlash rhetoric about the disappearance of families, the number of married people in the United States continues to increase. Between

1970 and 1995, that number actually increased by more than 20 percent. Primarily because people marry later and divorce more, the proportion of all adults who are married has declined, but the vast majority of Americans still marry.[30] This trend is not likely to change in the coming decades. The Census Bureau estimates that at least 90 percent of Americans will marry in the future.[31]

Marriage Timing

These days, most people wait until their mid-twenties to marry. In the United States at the turn of the century, men were likely to marry at about age 26 and women at about age 22. The median age at first marriage gradually fell, until it was about 23 for men and about 20 for women during the 1950s and 1960s. Since that time, people have been waiting longer to marry. During the early 1980s men tended to marry, on average, by the time they were 25 and women by the time they were 23. Soon, the average figure for men will reach 27 and for women, 25.[32] These trends are similar to those of other modern industrialized countries throughout the world. In Denmark, for example, the median age at first marriage for men is now 29 and for women is 27.[33]

Although women in the United States waited about as long to marry in 1890 as they do today, they did so for somewhat different reasons. A century ago, most families lived on farms, few women were employed, and divorce was extremely rare. Today, few American families live on farms, most women are employed, and divorce is common.

Modern reasons for postponing marriage are many and varied, but most studies find that later marriage is now associated with women attending college, working full time, and living on their own for awhile. In contrast, women who marry early usually make an abrupt transition from being a child in one family to being a wife and mother in another, and their husbands typically act as primary breadwinners. Early marriage thus tends to be associated with more segregated roles for men and women within the family. Delayed marriage, on the other hand, tends to be associated with more similar life experiences for men and women, which can lead to more equal resources and marital power. Older ages at first marriage are also associated with reduced chances for divorce, and some demographers predict that as delayed marriage continues, the divorce rate will edge downward.[34]

We can use demographic trends in age at marriage to highlight another interesting change that has been occurring over the past century: the relative ages of men and women in marriages have been converging. In 1890, the median age at first marriage for men was over four years higher than it was for women (26 vs. 22), reflecting the typical pattern of grooms being significantly older than their brides. With some fluctuations, the age gap between spouses has narrowed gradually over the years, and by the 1990s it was down to about two years.[35] That husbands tend to be older than wives both reflects and reproduces male dominance. The older person tends to have more experience and higher earnings than the younger, so age differentials reveal something about the relative distribution of power or status in marriages. Though overall age differences are a poor measure of specific marital resources, the weakening of the male older norm suggests that a shift toward more equal marital power has been occurring.[36]

To summarize, there have been two basic shifts in marriage timing: People now wait longer to marry and men are marrying women closer to their own age. According to demographic projections, both trends are likely to continue. These changes, as noted above, have the potential to enhance women's bargaining position within the marriage. More equal marital relationships will, in turn, put more pressure on men to do more around the house. I return to this issue below.

Divorce and Remarriage

The increased likelihood of divorce is another major demographic change that has occurred during this century. At the turn of the century, only about one in 10 marriages could be expected to end in divorce. Since then, the likelihood that a marriage would end in divorce has gradually increased, except for a slight anomalous dip around 1950.[37] By the 1970s, the chances of a marriage ending in divorce were about 50 percent. Since then, the rate has leveled off or even dropped slightly, especially for younger cohorts and for those who delay marriage.[38] Divorce rates are higher for blacks than whites, and lowest of all for people of Hispanic origin, but the general trend has been similar for all groups.[39]

People are more likely to divorce than they used to be, but they are also likely to marry again, often leading to the creation of blended or stepfamilies. Remarriage rates in the United States are higher than any other large industrialized nation in the world, with over 40 percent of marriages involving at least one spouse who was formerly married.[40] About three-quarters of all divorced Americans eventually remarry, with men more likely to remarry than women.[41] Whether we rely on low or high estimates of remarriage rates, we can expect continued high levels of remarriage and a large number of reconstituted and blended families in the future.[42]

Putting these marriage trends together, we can see that the biggest historical change has to do with duration: marriage just doesn't last as long as it used to. People are waiting longer to marry, they are more likely to divorce, and they tend to remarry (even if many wait awhile before remarrying). Because of this waiting around and switching partners, even though people live much longer, the proportion of a person's life spent in marriage has been gradually decreasing.[43]

As you might imagine, this has implications for the nature of married life and the allocation of family work. One way that marital relations are affected is that marriage is seen as more contingent. This has the potential for making divisions of labor within marriage more open for negotiation, and raises the chances that equity in household labor allocation will be considered when deciding about continuing or ending a marriage. The fact that people are spending less time married also influences the ways that they understand and perform household labor. When one assumes responsibility for housework or child care before getting married or remarried, expectations for future divisions of family work can change. Presumably, men are more likely to learn to cook and clean for themselves when they live on their own. Women, on the other hand, may gain insight and leverage in future relationships if they experience living situations in which they are not responsible for feeding and cleaning up after men. Thus, continuing trends in the timing and duration of marriage, in the absence of countervailing forces, are likely to favor more sharing of household labor in the future.

Fertility

The major fertility trends of the last few decades include having children later in life and eventually having fewer of them. American women born before 1940 had an average of over three children, whereas women born since then have averaged only about two. Childlessness has also increased, but the vast majority of married women still become parents. The latest predictions assume that only about 15 percent of women born in the 1950s will ultimately remain childless, and that the statistically average woman will have two children.[44]

Although most women still have children after they are married, a significant recent change has to do with the fact that marriage and parenting are no longer automatically linked. The number of births to unmarried women has increased dramatically in the past few decades, with the highest percentages for young black women, who are now as likely to give birth outside of marriage as in it. Nevertheless, the rate of increase in nonmarital births has been greater for whites than blacks in recent years.[45]

As a result of increases in out-of-wedlock birth and divorce, the number of single-parent households in the United States more than doubled between 1970 and 1990.[46] Single-parent households are usually headed by mothers, but the rate of growth for single-father households has been even higher than for single-mother households.[47] About half of all recently born children can expect to spend some time in a single-parent family before they reach the age of 18.[48] Although many single-parents do not remarry (or marry for the first time), most do. As a result, a third of all American children born in the 1980s are expected to spend some time in a stepparent household and rates are expected to be similar for those born in the 1990s.[49]

Birth Timing

Adults in the United States are not only waiting longer to marry and remarry, but most are also waiting longer to have children. The tendency to delay the transition to parenthood is most pronounced for married people, but is offset, in part, by the trend toward more births outside of marriage, many to younger mothers. When births to all American women are considered, the average tendency is to wait longer to bear children.

In the 1950s and 1960s, it was rare for a woman to wait until her mid-twenties to have her first child. Since the 1980s, however, the majority of women have postponed becoming parents at least until they reach the age of 25. Births to women over 30 have risen even faster than those to women in their mid-twenties, and births to women over 30 now constitute a full one-third of all U.S. births.[50] Delayed birth is linked to higher levels of employment for women, and tends to be more common in economic hard times, such as during the depression of the 1930s.[51] Demographers predict that recent trends toward delaying parenthood will continue, or perhaps increase, in the coming decades.[52]

What difference does it make that women are waiting longer to have children? As we saw in Chapters 5 and 6, women who delay having children spend more of their early adult years in school and in the labor force than others. They are also less likely to give up their jobs when they become mothers and take less time off from work leading up to and following the births of their children.[53] As noted below, this dramatic departure from previous patterns of maternal labor force participation will undoubtedly influence future divisions of household labor.

Working Mothers

Women's labor force participation has increased so dramatically over the past few decades that it is arguably the most important social or economic trend in recent history.[54] Although labor force participation rates for all women have risen sharply, the most significant changes have occurred for mothers. Even though the Census Bureau did not even begin collecting statistics on working mothers until 1976, the proportion of mothers in the paid labor force almost doubled in 20 years and is projected to increase even further.[55]

In the early '60s, most first-time mothers quit their jobs when they became pregnant, but by the 1980s, most pregnant women stayed employed. And the characteristics of those who kept working also changed. In the 1960s, employed expectant mothers tended to be young and poor (teenage mothers, high school drop-outs, part-time workers, etc.). By the 1980s, most pregnant women who stayed employed were over the age of 25 and college-educated. The economic need for two workers drove many new mothers to hold onto jobs that they would have abandoned in the earlier era and the middle-class pattern came to resemble the earlier working-class one.[56]

Women not only stay employed longer into their pregnancies than they used to, but they also return to work more quickly after they have children. Over half of new mothers in the United States return to their jobs before their first child is one year old, with most coming back to work within three months of the birth, and most working full-time.[57] Regardless of income or educational levels, returning to work rapidly after childbirth is becoming the norm. As we've seen, this trend is likely to encourage the sharing of family work, insofar as the unavailability of the mother puts increased pressure on the father to do more.

An important factor that will influence maternal employment patterns and household labor allocation in the future has to do with the availability of parental leave. One of the best predictors of whether a woman returns to work soon after having children is whether she receives maternity benefits.[58] The assurance of job security after childbirth, coupled with financial need, prompts most women with maternity benefits to return to work rapidly. If increasing numbers of employers offer parental leaves and benefits, we would expect women to be even more likely to stay in the labor force both before and after giving birth. Whether this is likely to happen depends on larger economic and social trends as outlined below.

Gendered Job Markets

The steady rise in women's labor force after World War II corresponded to a restructuring of the national and global economy. In the United States, there was dramatic growth in service industries and occupations and a decrease in the relative importance of employment in agriculture and manufacturing.[59] Women entered the labor force in record numbers because the demand for secretaries, typists, clerks, and other so-called women's jobs increased rapidly.[60] This gendered structuring of the labor market had important implications for the division of family work.

Jobs become stereotyped as appropriate for one or both genders in response to changing economic, cultural, and historical contexts, and the existence of stereotyped jobs helps mold career opportunities and shape family roles. At present, occupations with especially high concentrations of women include secretaries and other office workers, retail clerks, maids, electronics assembly-line workers, school teachers, nurses, real estate agents, and social workers.

Despite some entry by women into traditionally "male" occupations in recent years, men continue to predominate in management, higher status professions (e.g., doctors and lawyers), skilled crafts (e.g., carpentry, plumbing), manufacturing, and jobs involving outdoor labor. Although men's and women's jobs require roughly equivalent amounts of formal education prior to entry, women's occupations have less on-the-job training, offer fewer opportunities for advancement, and are less likely to entail supervising other workers (especially men).

Occupational segregation by gender has weakened somewhat over the past several decades as more women have become managers and jobs like reporter, bus driver, bartender, pharmacist, and insurance adjustor have opened up to women. Nevertheless, the jobs women hold are typically less prestigious than corresponding men's jobs. For example, school bus drivers tend to be women whereas metropolitan transit drivers are usually men.[61] Decreasing job segregation is therefore both real and illusory.[62] Current estimates are that approximately 60 percent of men or women would still have to change occupations in order to achieve a gender-balanced workforce in the United States.[63]

Not only do men and women tend to do work in different industries and hold different jobs within an industry or organization, but women's jobs continue to pay less than men's. White women's median annual earnings in the United States are still between 65 and 75 percent of white men's. Both Afro-American and Hispanic women earn less, on average, than white women, but they earn closer to the men's earnings within those ethnic groups.[64] Even though women's earnings continue to lag behind those of men, there are some indications that the gap is narrowing. In the United States, women's wages have shown steady increases since the 1970s, while men's wages have remained stagnant or even declined. And in virtually every other modern industrialized democracy in the world, women have been able to substantially increase their earnings relative to those of men. For example, in the industrial and government sectors of the economy, women workers in Sweden earn about 90 percent of what Swedish men earn.[65] Thus, although the gender gap in pay remains substantial, there is a clear and consistent trend toward a narrowing of that gap, especially among minorities and younger adults.

Why does the labor market remain biased against women? In a popular modern version of the ideology of separate spheres, job segregation and the gender gap in pay are rationalized by claiming that women are naturally predisposed to care for children and tend homes.[66] This assumption is usually accompanied by claims that women are paid less or assigned to "female" jobs because they are not temperamentally suited for the competitive business world, or that they are poor risks for job training because they exert less effort on the job and are likely to quit work to have babies.[67] In contrast, most empirical studies find that if there are differences between men's and women's efforts on the job, it is women who expend more effort than men, in part to overcome stereotyped notions of female incapacity.[68]

Some also argue that occupations are segregated because of self-selection — that is, women prefer female-dominated jobs because they are less demanding and allow more time off for family responsibilities. Although women *do* tend to work part-time more often than men, the general trend is toward more women working full-time, and evidence suggests that most women's jobs have closer supervision and *less* schedule flexibility than men's jobs.[69] The claim that women earn less because they frequently quit work to have babies is contradicted by the finding that women do not have higher turnover rates than men when the wage level of the job is considered.[70] Similarly, some suggest that women favor lower paying gender-typed jobs because they like the kind of work involved. Self-selection into occupations such as nursing or teaching may indeed occur because the work bolsters one's self-image as a caring woman. This illustrates that paid work, like family work, provides opportunities for "doing gender." Nevertheless, the gendered meaning of work can change, and young women today are much more likely than ever before to say they would like to pursue jobs that are stereotyped as men's work. There has also been a decline in the overall gender segregation of college majors in the past decades, and women now outnumber men in colleges across the country.[71] This does not mean that women will necessarily fulfill their non-traditional career goals, because discrimination in the job market, blocked career mobility, and individual choices about marriage and children will intervene in later years.[72]

Job segregation and unequal pay, along with women's unemployment, are associated with marriage bargains that include wives' obligation to perform domestic labor and husbands' sense of entitlement to receive unpaid domestic services. If job markets were to become less segregated, pay scales were to equalize, and more women were employed, we would expect more sharing of domestic work. To see how likely these female employment scenarios might be, we need to look briefly at even larger economic trends and future projections.

Overall Economic Trends

The overall economic outlook on the global and national level has the potential for significantly altering the direction or magnitude of some of the demographic and employment influences noted above. A complete analysis of future economic trends is beyond the scope of this chapter, but it is helpful to sketch some broad potential influences to provide a context for predicting future divisions of family work.

Most observers agree that a worldwide economic transformation is taking place, although there is disagreement over what is changing, the pace of change, the reasons for change, and the expected outcomes.[73] Some researchers focus on the importance of technological innovation, comparing recent developments in computers and information processing to the first industrial revolution.[74] Others concentrate on the need for new skills and the reorganization of work.[75] Still others focus on the changing nature of global markets and rapidly accelerating international competition.[76] All these processes are part of the global transformation of finance, business, and industry, and all are elaborately interconnected. Most observers concur that capital is becoming more internationalized and that competitive markets around the world are more closely linked than ever before.

Employers in the United States and throughout the world have attempted to maximize profits and increase efficiency through restructuring, technological innovation, and reduction of labor costs. They have often moved production from factory and office to private homes; from older urban areas to less expensive rural areas; and from industrialized countries to less developed countries. These changes in the global division of labor have occurred as the general economy has shifted away from large scale manufacturing, particularly in the male-dominated "smokestack industries." The movement of capital and employment has been toward "tertiary sector" or service industries that are the bedrock of the information economy.[77] Almost 80 percent of the new jobs created in the 1970s and 1980s were in the service sector (finance, real estate, insurance, transportation, public utilities, retail and wholesale trade, legal and social services, and government). Additional service *jobs* exist within manufacturing, but most service job growth has been in the service *sector,* especially in the lower paying and less skilled jobs. Although the U.S. service sector has two tiers, women are the majority of workers in both tiers and, in both, their wages continue to lag behind those of men. Similarly, minority men and women are also disproportionately found in the lower tier of the service sector and earn lower wages.[78]

These trends and tendencies have also been accompanied by what has been labeled "downsizing" and "deskilling." Fueled by economic recession and aided by dramatic changes in technology, many workers have been asked to do more in less time, and to take over functions previously performed by someone else. In many cases, this restructuring has also been accompanied by reductions in middle-level management. Technological innovation has also produced increased demand for certain kinds of highly skilled labor, much of which has been defined as men's work. Job skills, it seems, carry gendered meanings that are quite resistant to change. For example, Cynthia Cockburn shows that when new technologies are introduced into various work processes, men tend to retain control over them, thereby defining skill as masculine and attempting to exclude women from the more skilled positions.[79] As one recent study put it, "Men get the hardware to play with, women get the software; men form the computer companies, women work the assembly lines; men do more of the military-funded artificial intelligence work, women do the routine program-ming in the banks and insurance companies."[80]

Economic restructuring has also been aided by the "triumph" of neoclassical economics and an unquestioned belief in the superiority of the "free" market. As Joan Acker and others have noted, however, the most successful economies in the recent global transformation—Japan and Germany—do not follow many of the laissez faire precepts of free-market philosophy.[81] Nonetheless, belief in the wisdom of unrestrained markets led to various political actions and inactions during the 1980s and 1990s, including deregulation of business and industry, erosion of labor regulations, reduction in nonmilitary state spending, and privatization of social programs and state-owned production. Most analysts predict more of the same in the near future.

Governmental policies and global economic transformation—including tech-nological change, internationalization of markets, employment restructuring, and deskilling—had mixed consequences for American men and women. In general, real income growth faltered between the late 1970s and the mid-1990s, with the only income gains among those at the upper end of the income distribution.[82] Incomes of those families and households in the lower half of the income pyramid remained stagnant, with significant negative consequences for children. Record numbers of children fell into the ranks of the poor as the real median income of young families with children declined by about a third: from $23,705 in 1970 to $16,219 in 1990 (both in 1990 dollars).[83]

In the face of this rising poverty and increasing inequality, as noted above, women's labor force participation increased dramatically. The gender wage gap narrowed slightly, as women made gains and men slipped backwards. Women entered many fields once dominated by men and began to assume a larger share of professional and managerial jobs. Despite these gains, however, most women still occupied low paying, gender-typed jobs with limited upward mobility and few benefits.

Economic Projections

Although economic projections are fraught with uncertainty, we can extrapo-late from these recent trends to predict the future. The rate of overall economic growth, as measured by the gross national product (GNP), will likely continue to slow over the coming decades. Whether the GNP climbs steadily or moves in fits and starts, however, most economists predict substantial new growth in service jobs and relative decline in manufacturing ones.[84] Federal military expenditures and related defense industries are also projected to continue their decline, though future political gains by Republicans could slow this trend. These forces should result in a continuation of the mixed trends in income and employment that we have seen during the past decade.

The fastest rates of employment growth are predicted for occupations that require higher levels of education or training, although there will continue to be more college graduates entering the labor force through 2005 than there will be openings for jobs that call for college degrees.[85] Even though some higher-level jobs will grow at a fast rate, the bulk of new jobs will be at the lower end of the occupational pyramid. This will continue a trend in which jobs are polarized into routine, low-wage, highly controlled work and non-routine, relatively autonomous, higher-wage jobs.[86] Both the number and proportion of workers earning near the minimum wage increased during the 1980s, especially among women and people of color, and this trend is expected to continue.[87] If there is weakness in the overall U.S. economy, we might expect even more restructuring of employment, and a higher percentage of low wage jobs in virtually every sector of the economy, but even modest growth is likely to continue these trends. How this will differentially affect men and women is still an open question.

Women's recent employment gains are expected to continue, even in the face of declining economic growth, but their earnings and employment hours will not rival those of men. By the year 2005, women will constitute nearly half of the labor force.[88] Women are a majority of workers in the three occupational categories that are projected to have the most job openings between 1995 and 2005: (1) service; (2) administrative support (including clerical); and (3) professional specialty. Health and personal service occupations, both composed primarily of women, are projected to have extremely high growth rates in the coming decades as well.[89] Especially in fields like this, where women are already significantly represented, the proportions of women in higher paying jobs (e.g., professional specialties, executive, administrative, and managerial jobs) is expected to increase.[90] Others predict that gains for women in management will level off as restructuring eliminates significant numbers of middle-level management positions and favors the incumbency of men.[91]

Part-time positions, which accounted for about 20 percent of all workers in 1991, are also projected to increase substantially.[92] Part-time and flexible work situations typically allow for integrating family work and paid work, but such positions also tend to lack benefits (health insurance, vacation pay, parental leave, etc.) and few offer opportunities for career advancement. Women hold almost two-thirds of current part-time jobs, and growth in this area will mean employment for many more women in the near future. Nevertheless, because of financial necessity, job availability, and personal preference, most employed women will continue to work full-time.

We can thus expect more women in the labor force in the next decade, even if the economy falters or overheats. Some women will continue to enter higher paying management and professional positions, but the majority will occupy lower paying second-tier positions. Aggregate projections for minority women and men are even more pessimistic, with continued overall decreases expected in their earning power.[93] With decreases in manufacturing jobs, however, the relative positions of men and women will continue to converge. Men's pay is likely to continue its downward slide and, in the more bleak projections, unemployment for men is expected to increase significantly. Equality of employment is definitely not just around the corner, but we can expect a continuing narrowing of the gap between men and women's labor force participation rates and pay scales. This will occur in the context of increasing income inequality in the population at large, and increasing pressure on both spouses in married couples to be employed. Thus, we should guard against thinking of near-term economic developments as simply a movement toward labor market equity for women. These developments represent new forms of shared job limitations as much as they represent new patterns of shared job opportunities.

The ideal of a single wage supporting the family will become even less of a reality for married couples in the coming decades, as dual-earner couples will outnumber single-earner couples by more than two to one. Divorce rates may decline slightly, as economic pressure will encourage couples to stay together. The major economic dividing line between families will be the number of earners in the household, with two-job couples faring better, on average, than single-breadwinner families or single-parent families. For subgroups with high rates of male underemployment and increasing earnings for women, there will be less incentive to stay married or to marry in the first place. Single mothers and their children will continue to struggle economically, and most will be at risk for living in poverty.

These economic developments and employment opportunities are also linked to changes in labor relations. For example, labor unions declined in membership and influence in the United States during the past two decades, and they are likely to continue that downward trend in the face of government cutbacks and global economic restructuring, especially in the heavy manufacturing industries. This will disproportionately affect workers who are men, but all employees will be threatened with less job security, lower wages, and fewer benefits. The few unions with continued growth are likely to have large numbers of women members, including teachers, garment workers, and government service employees.

Ironically, because some unions historically advocated a single family wage for men workers and excluded women from their ranks, the declining significance of unions may speed the process of wage equality between men and women. Since unions strive for better pay and benefits for all workers, however, their declining influence will mean that both men and women will be working for less in the future, even if they are treated more equally. Though not likely, it is also possible that a resurgence of union influence will be seen in the future. This could take us in two different directions. One possibility, which I consider unlikely, would see unions continuing to advocate a family wage system by protecting men's jobs and wages at the expense of women's.

This would replicate the pattern observed following World War II, and would increase gender antagonism and inequality in the workplace. More likely however, are combined union and feminist political efforts to move toward "pay equity" or "comparable worth." Progress here is also likely to be limited in the next decade, as recovery from economic recession continues slowly and as free-market ideology continues to exert pressures for deregulation and cutbacks in government employment. Nevertheless, as more women enter and stay in the labor market, wage differentials and employment discrimination will become salient to more workers, and, if popular support for the idea of equal pay for equal work increases, there may be some limited governmental attempts to integrate the labor market and further standardize pay scales between men and women. This, of course, will depend on the ability to mobilize resources and organize effective national reform efforts, enterprises that fell far short of expectations during the past decades.

Trends in Family Policies and Programs

In addition to the economic factors discussed above, a number of institutional and political trends will undoubtedly affect family life and gender relations in the coming decades. In the face of an increasing federal deficit and a sluggish economy, government-supported financial aid programs are likely to be cut back or remain limited in the near-term. For instance, the size of direct welfare payments to families (e.g., Aid to Families with Dependent Children — AFDC) is likely to decrease, even as the need for this type of support will expand. Future reforms are expected to tighten qualification guidelines and force single mothers to enter job training programs and take minimum wage jobs to receive modest benefits. The Family Support Act of 1988 took the first steps toward transforming AFDC from an income support scheme to a workfare program and future reforms will continue that trend. Critics claim that job training programs are of dubious merit and argue that forcing mothers to leave their young children to work at menial jobs does not promote family values.[94] The Family Support Act also required States to establish guidelines for child support payments that are now deducted from the absent parent's wages. In an era of shrinking governmental resources, workfare reforms and enforcement of private child support will become even more popular. Levels of support for educational programs, child care, and medical care, on the other hand, are likely to remain stagnant or decline in the coming decade, though there will be some opportunities for reform or restructuring.

The Family Leave Act of 1993 is a good example of the type of governmental family support that is possible in the United States in the 1990s. This bill, originally vetoed by President Bush, was re-passed by Congress and signed into Law by President Clinton in 1993. It mandates just 12 weeks of *unpaid* leave to care for a new baby or a seriously ill family member, and only applies to companies with more than 50 employees. That it took a decade to pass this law, with its minimal benefits for parents, does not bode well for future significant government reforms or for the development of a coherent family policy at the federal level.

Most other modern industrial nations make much larger contributions to the welfare of their families and children. In contrast to the minimal unpaid family leave that some U.S. parents now enjoy, Canadian workers receive 15 weeks of family leave at 60 percent pay.[95] Virtually every European nation provides at least that much support to individual parents, and most provide significantly more. For example, Swedish workers receive 90 percent pay for 36 weeks and prorated paid leave for the next 18 months.[96] In addition, many European nations provide direct cash payments to parents when a child is born and most also fund the construction and operation of group child-care facilities. The difference is that in Europe, child care is viewed as a public responsibility, and social welfare programs have a long history. Some European countries justify child support programs because they are trying to enhance women's employment in order to boost national productivity. Other nations focus on the well-being of future generations and stress the need for programs that promote optimal child development.[97] Either way, these countries invest heavily in the future by subsidizing their children's care. In the United States, we continue to assume that families are private and that parents are individually responsible for the well-being of children.

The Child-Care Shortage

Over two-thirds of all U.S. children under 18 now have mothers who are employed, and over two-thirds of these mothers are employed full-time.[98] As noted above, the trend toward maternal employment has been marked in the last decade, and is likely to continue. Fathers are even more likely to be employed than mothers. In two-job families, parents often work nonday shifts, so that care can be shared. In about one out of five two-job families, at least one parent works a nonday shift, so that parents can alternate child care between them.[99] Alternative employment scheduling—or flextime—is also used by some workers, so they can adjust their work hours to cover child care needs. For example, DuPont has between 10,000 and 15,000 employees who are working flextime.[100]

Besides sharing care between parents, families also care for younger children by having older siblings watch over them, especially after school. Many parents feel forced to leave school-aged children unattended until they return home from work, leading some commentators to suggest that there is an epidemic of "latch-key" children. While some children fare well in self-care, others suffer, and research suggests that unattended children are more at risk for delinquency and drug use. Although exact estimates are difficult, most parents continue to need some form of help with child care, especially during the morning hours of employment.

Forms of nonparental (and nonsibling) child care in the United States have been changing recently. Care by relatives, while declining, is still the most common form of nonparental child care for preschool-aged children, especially among the working class. Among the middle and upper classes, in-home sitters, nannies, and housekeepers are still common, but decreasing in significance compared to the 1950s and 1960s. The flap over President Clinton's first choice for Attorney General, Zoe Baird, brought the issue of immigrant women caregivers into media prominence, and there are indications that this is an increasingly prevalent solution to the child-care problems of upwardly mobile dual-career professional couples. Nevertheless, the percentage of preschool children cared for by in-home sitters has actually declined by more than one-half since 1965. The use of family day-care homes (usually an unlicensed working-class mother watching extra children in her own house) has increased slightly in the past two decades, but the use of larger day-care centers has seen the biggest increase in recent years. Between 1965 and 1985, the percent of preschool children served by child care centers increased almost 400 percent, and is now the second most common form of nonparental child care, following care by relatives.[101]

American child-care centers and family day-care homes tend to be low-budget operations. Despite various laws attempting to regulate them, most family day-care homes are unlicensed and the quality of care they provide varies greatly. Day-care centers, in contrast, must meet numerous government health and safety standards, including teacher licensing, adult–child ratios, indoor and outdoor space requirements, nutrition programs, health maintenance, and building upkeep. Most day-care centers are run by nonprofit organizations such as schools, churches, or community service agencies. A new trend is toward franchised for-profit day-care centers (facetiously labeled "McKids"), but these businesses still serve only a small portion of the child-care "market." Some businesses have begun to offer on-site child care in response to employee demands. Such centers have been found to increase worker productivity, reduce absenteeism, and minimize turnover and subsequent retraining costs. Presently, only about 2,000 employers out of 6 million businesses nationwide provide some form of child-care assistance, and few provide on-site care. As late as the 1980s, only about 500 corporations or hospitals provided child-care centers at or near the workplace.[102] Taken together, the different forms of day care available in the United States provide care to only a fraction of the children whose parents need it.

The child-care shortage is not likely to improve much in the coming years, because more and more mothers are working, and because substantial child-care subsidies from the government are unlikely. Another demographic factor is compounding the problem — the large size of the baby boom cohort born between 1946 and 1964. Baby boomers are not having as many children as previous generations, and they are waiting longer to have them, but because there are so many adults in the cohort, the number of preschool children is on the rise. As of 1980, the number of preschool children in the United States began to grow, and, in 1990, there were about 23 million children under the age of six. Similarly, the number of school-aged children (5 to 17 years old) started to increase in 1986 and will exceed 45 million by 1996.[103] Because maternal employment is not just a passing fad, and because there are increasing numbers of children, there is likely to be continuing pressure on businesses to provide job leaves, flexible scheduling, and on-site child care, and on governments to regulate businesses and offer community day-care facilities. In the face of economic stagnation and the dominance of a free-market ideology, however, it is unlikely that we will see anything like a European-style commitment to child care in this country.

The lack of commitment to child care in the United States is both cause and consequence of American parents' troubles finding quality care for their children. Most day-care homes and centers are woefully understaffed with poorly paid and underqualified personnel. Even though most people say they support "quality" day care, the people who are paid to care for children have trouble making enough to support themselves. Ninety-eight percent of U.S. child-care workers are women, and, on average, they earn much less than janitors or zookeepers. That we should pay the adults who tend our children less than we pay those who park our cars, take care of our pets, or haul our garbage is seen by many as a national disgrace, but that has not yet motivated us to upgrade the child-care industry via governmental subsidy.

Child-care workers are in the lowest tenth of all wage earners, with an average pay of only about five dollars per hour. Nine out of 10 child care providers who work in private homes earn below poverty-level wages, and even those who work in educational and social service positions in larger day-care centers earn a median income of just $9,204 per year.[104] Even though we pay child care workers very little, we expect them to create cheerful family-like environments and work wonders with our children. Faced with extremely high expectations, low wages, and poor benefits, many child-care workers leave the field for less stressful and higher paying employment. The average day-care center in the United States has an employee turnover rate of over 40 percent per year.[105]

The child-care arrangements of American parents change frequently because of dissatisfaction with caregivers, because children grow older, and because of the changing availability of care.[106] Shifts from relative care to some form of group care are the most common. In order to keep working on a continuous basis, most American parents rely on multiple forms of child care and make adjustments when one form of care fails, when they gain flexibility at their workplace, or when their family income goes up or down.[107] What seems to be consistent across these trends, however, is the increasing likelihood that fathers are expected to contribute to primary care. The pressure for fathers to assume more of the routine child care is not just a fad that will reverse itself in a few years. The demographic, economic, and political factors discussed above will continue to provide the impetus for fathers to do more.

Predicting Future Sharing

The social, demographic, and economic trends described above can now be combined with the general predictors of household labor sharing discussed throughout the book and summarized at the beginning of this chapter. The effects of various trends will undoubtedly be mixed for both men and women, and many will both encourage and discourage the sharing of family work. For example, specific effects will differ according to age, family composition, life cycle stage, employment, ethnicity, social class, area of residence, and other factors. In the interests of brevity, however, I focus the ensuing discussion on the general effects of prominent trends among the average married couple household with children. After listing 10 predictors of father invovlement derived from my previous research, I speculate on how each factor will be affected by the major trends and how each will influence future divisions of family work. The 10 factors include (1) wives' employment, (2) wives' earnings, (3) wives' initiative and home management, (4) ideology, (5) husbands' employment, (6) fathers' attachment to parenting, (7) social networks, (8) delayed parenting, (9) divorce and remarriage, and (10) family size and age of children.

1. **Wives' Employment.** *As wives are employed more hours and become more attached to their jobs, couples will share more housework and child care.*

The trends in this area are unequivocal. More women will be employed in the future, and mothers will tend to remain in the labor force. Women's employment will seem less optional and more women will move into management and professional careers. Women's continuous employment and job attachment will have the effect of increasing pressure on men to do more with the children and around the house.

2. **Wives' Earnings.** *As wives earn more of the total household income and become defined as co-providers, couples will share more housework.*

Trends in this area are tied to overall growth in the economy and possibilities for state intervention. In the near term, the wage gap is expected to shrink, and the labor market to become less segregated, but gains will be limited and we will not approach pay equity or gender-neutral job markets. Men will continue to make more money and work longer hours than women. Most women will continue to be seen as secondary providers, though two incomes will be considered even more essential than they are today. To the extent that earnings of husbands and wives will converge, we can expect more sharing of household labor. Insofar as men's wages will remain above those of women, however, we can expect only modest changes.

3. **Wives' Initiative and Home Management.** *More wives will negotiate for change, delegate responsibility for various chores, and relinquish total control over managing home and children.*

We can expect more bargaining and delegation on the part of wives because two-job families will become even more common, women will work more hours, child-care options will remain limited, and the ideology of separate spheres will continue to decline in influence. This does not mean that most women will relinquish responsibility or control over housework and child care, as the majority of women will continue to assume that these activities are primarily women's duty. Nevertheless, more wives will press husbands into service as household and child-care helpers, and, in an increasing percentage of couples, men will exercise significant responsibility for a few tasks previously considered "women's work." The most change is likely to come in child care, for mothers will continue to value father involvement for the sake of the children, and men will be delegated relatively easier child-tending duties. Significant participation of men in shopping, cooking, and meal clean-up is also expected.

4. **Ideology.** *More husbands and wives will believe in gender equality, leading to more sharing of child care and housework.*

Change in this area is also predominantly unidirectional and uninterrupted. Most people, especially if they are younger, already say they subscribe to the ideal of equality of opportunity for men and women, and growing numbers will endorse such concepts in the future. Likewise, as two-job families become more common and most children spend some time in the care of others, fewer people will publicly proclaim that working mothers are negligent or that their children will be damaged. Most people will continue to assume that women are better equipped for parenting, though a growing proportion will subscribe to the idea that men can nurture as well as women. Both women's and men's attitudes will continue to shape divisions of labor in the future, as they rely on family tasks and paid employment to define themselves. Changing attitudes about the gender appropriateness of certain tasks will affect both spouse's expectations, influence bargaining strategies, and shape perceptions of fairness. Both women and men will become less rigid in defining specific activities as solely the province of one gender, which, in turn, will propel even more change in attitudes and behaviors. This is not to say that change will be swift or uniform. Men's attitudes on gender issues will remain more conservative than those of women, and many will continue to maintain their privileged position by not noticing when certain things need doing or by remaining incompetent at some tasks.[108] Nevertheless, some household tasks, like shopping, cooking, and washing dishes, will become less tied to gender identity in the future, at least in a substantial minority of American households. Changes in attitudes about men's role in child care will continue to lead the way, as two-parent families will become even more convinced that children need to have frequent contact with their fathers. Whether men assume significant responsibility for the day-to-day care of their children, however, will depend on more than just attitude change.

5. **Husbands' Employment.** *As husbands are employed fewer hours and value family involvement over rapid career advancement, couples will share more routine child care and housework.*

Projections concerning husbands' employment are mixed. Despite predictions of decline or limited growth in men's employment hours and wages, most men will continue to be employed more hours than their wives. Since employment hours are the strongest and most consistent predictors of household labor performance, we can expect most couples to allocate the majority of housework and child care to wives. Nevertheless, because the gap between men's and women's employment hours will continue to narrow, we can expect that practical factors like time availability will motivate many couples to share more. Insofar as scheduling flexibility, nonday shifts, and part-time work among men persist or increase, we can expect that couples will share more aspects of domestic labor.

With continuing growth in the service sector of the economy and cutbacks in the manufacturing sector, we can also expect higher unemployment rates among men than women. Although men's unemployment is not automatically associated with assumption of more responsibility for housework and child care, some studies of egalitarian couples reveal that unemployment or underemployment was indeed central to the process of husbands adopting tasks previously performed by wives.[109] When unemployment among men is coupled with growing employment among women, we can expect more sharing of family work, and increases in the small number of role-reversed couples.

In general, men will continue to be defined in terms of their provider status, and women will continue to be considered secondary providers, even when they are employed full time. Nevertheless, we will continue to see a weakening in the normative prescription for men to be only breadwinners. The trend toward men defining success in personal terms (as well as career terms) is likely to persist or even accelerate in the next two decades.[110] This will also have costs, as those who elect to pursue the "daddy track" of reduced employment hours will continue to be labeled as less serious and will be less likely to receive promotions and other benefits.

6. **Fathers' Attachment to Parenting.** *As fathers become more involved in baby care, they will begin to take more responsibility for routine child care, and a significant minority will move beyond the role of household helper.*

As noted above, in the next few decades, men in two-parent families are expected to place more value on spending time with their children. A large number of new fathers will be motivated to compensate for a perceived lack of emotional connection with their own fathers, but in the next generations, more men will be emulating their own fathers' parenting behaviors. Although many men will be relatively uninvolved in the day-to-day aspects of child care, most signs point toward greater involvement of fathers. Expectant fathers will continue to participate in birth preparation classes and most will attend their children's births. With higher rates of employment among women with infants, more fathers can be expected to perform early child care. More solo time spent in baby care will lead to greater attachment to the father role and more involvement in later child care. Increased participation in child care will also lead to more performance of other routine household labor. In the population at large, a counteracting force discouraging men's involvement with children will be continued high levels of out-of-wedlock birth and marital dissolution (discussed below in 9).

7. **Social Networks.**   *Couples embedded in loose-knit cosmopolitan social networks will share more household labor. Those in more dense, localistic, kin-centered networks will share less.*

The projections for this factor are contradictory, with many economic trends encouraging contact with kin and low geographic mobility, but other trends encouraging more cosmopolitanism. One the one hand, a stagnating or slow-growing economy would continue recent trends toward fixity of residence. When people live on limited incomes, they are less likely to move long distances and more likely to share households with kin. During times of economic hardship, young couples with children are not likely to move far away from their families of origin, and may even move back into a parent's house, which tends to promote more traditional divisions of household labor. A counteracting tendency is for renters to move more frequently than homeowners, and for those under age 30 to move more frequently than older persons. This means that families with young children have many occasions to leave their local neighborhoods, though most moves are local.[111]

Working against local residence and frequent contact with kin are general patterns of schooling, employment, and cultural homogenization, particularly among the middle class. College attendance is expected to remain high or increase in the next two decades, which often draws young people away from hometowns before they have children of their own. Employment trends can also encourage moves to new areas, with net in-migration to the "sun-belt" areas of the United States increasingly common. For example, 1970s steel mill closings in the northeast, 1980s farm foreclosures in the midwest, and 1990s defense industry layoffs on the West Coast drove many families away from their local social networks. In addition, continuing trends toward "modernization," including the spread of compulsory schooling, movement to the suburbs, and proliferation of popular national media, have promoted individualism, encouraged cosmopolitanism, and diluted the impact of localistic kin networks. These forces are quite general, but, on the whole, can be said to have weakened traditional gender-based divisions of labor.

8. **Delayed Parenting.** *More parents will delay the transition to parenthood until their late twenties or thirties and will likely share more child care and household labor.*

The trend toward delaying the transition to parenthood will continue. This trend is related to several factors mentioned above, including growing individualism, changing family and gender ideology, increased education and employment for women, increased co-habitation and divorce, delayed marriage, high levels of divorce, and the increasing reliance of couples on two incomes. Delayed parenting, in conjunction with these and other factors, will encourage more sharing of child care and housework among American couples.

9. **Divorce and Remarriage.** *High rates of divorce, remarriage, and giving birth in second marriages will encourage the sharing of household labor.*

Although the divorce rate has stabilized or dipped recently, it will stay at relatively high levels for the foreseeable future. Remarriage rates are also expected to stay at high levels. This will influence divisions of labor in at least two general ways. First, there will be more remarried couples, who have different forms of labor allocation, but who tend to share more than others. Second, and related to the first point, the bargaining position of wives and husbands is changing, because marriage is perceived as more contingent.

A growing individualism has promoted a weakening of normative standards to be married, stay married, remarry, or raise children outside marriage. In the face of increased opportunities for women outside the home, the economic incentives for women to be married have decreased. Women are more economically dependent on marriage than men, but men's economic incentives for marriage have risen because two incomes are increasingly important. Women's obligatory performance of domestic chores used to be part of the marriage bargain, just as men's financial providing once was. Now, however, since women are becoming at least partial economic providers, there are more expectations for men to assume a share of the domestic work. Because ending a marriage or starting a new one is less stigmatized than it once was, the possibility of divorce will influence new marital bargains. The balance of providing and homemaking will increasingly enter into both spouses' implicit calculations regarding the desirability of marriage partners and the likelihood of remaining together as parents.

After divorce, women tend to suffer downward mobility, especially if they have children. This will change little in the next decade. Although child support enforcement will be more consistent, more absent fathers will be unemployed or underemployed. Women will continue to be awarded custody in most divorce cases, and the number of single mother households will remain

high. Nevertheless, the incidence of joint custody will increase, keeping more
fathers in touch with their children. The enforcement of child support orders
through automatic wage withholding will also tend to encourage more contact
between noncustodial fathers and their children.[112] Thus, in addition to
increased father participation in two-parent families, we will have a continuation of substantial levels of father absence, but we may see slightly more post
divorce father–child contact.

10. **Family Size and Age of Children.** *Fertility will edge downward and
couples with fewer and older children will share more housework and child care.*

The trend toward smaller family size is likely to have minimal impacts on
overall divisions of household labor, but the direction of influence is expected to
be toward more sharing. If a couple has one or two children, it is less likely that
the mother will become the child-care expert, giving up her job and focusing
exclusively on caring for children. In contrast, if couples have many children, it is
more likely that the mother will be out of the labor force for longer periods of
time and perform most of the household labor. Also, when children are younger,
mothers tend to be more responsible for child care and housework, and, as
children age, fathers tend to become more involved in their care. Although the
variation in household labor sharing between families of various sizes is so great
as to render this factor almost inconsequential, there is a statistically significant
relationship that is expected to continue into the next century. Insofar as delayed
childbirth, lower levels of fertility, and an aging population will combine to
produce smaller families with older children, we can expect the aggregate level
of household labor sharing to increase slightly.

Putting It All Together

Considering all ten factors together, I predict that more American husbands and
wives will share child care and housework. Changes in family work allocation
will not occur for all families, and the pace of change will be different for people
living under different circumstances. Perhaps the most important future development is that inequality will persist as family diversity increases. In general,
two-job couples will enjoy even greater relative advantage over single-job families, single-parent families, and other household types.

The type of family in which one lives—including how many parents and
how many earners—will become the most important basis of class standing in
the United States. Outside of a small privileged elite, it will take two secure,
well-paying jobs to ensure that a family stays in the upper middle class. Even
many families with two earners will hover around the poverty level as more
jobs become low paying and sporadic. Women and minorities will be disproportionately affected by problems of low pay, underemployment, and limited
resources. Tragically, more American children will live in poverty.

How will families respond? Out of necessity, single parents and adults in lower income households will share substantial child care and housework with older children, kin, and others. When husbands are present in limited income households, they will also share in more domestic tasks than they have in the past. New opportunities will be available to some, and women at all class levels and in all ethnic groups will continue to narrow the gap between their own and their husband's earnings. Within the new patterns of increasing stratification, we can thus expect to see some movement toward more gender equality.

For relatively privileged dual-career couples, there will also be enormous variation among families. In the middle class, those without children will enjoy relative economic advantage and will devote more time and energy to their careers. At all economic levels, couples with children will be forced to make some career sacrifices, and because of continuing gender inequality in the job market, more of these sacrifices will be made by women than by men. Still, we will see more men tailoring their employment to fit their family needs. More fathers will select jobs on the basis of compatibility with child-care arrangements, more will elect to work flexible or nonday shifts, and fewer men will unquestioningly assume that they owe their employers overtime or take-home work. Even though more men will thus opt for a "daddy track," changes in work culture will come slowly. Although normative sanctions are expected to weaken, men who choose to spend time with their children instead of working will continue to be thought of as less serious and risk being passed over for promotions. Still, as more men treat employment as women have tended to in the past, we can expect a slight weakening of gender discrimination on the job. As women work more hours and earn more money, they will become accepted as *necessary* providers, even if most will not be considered fully equal *co*-providers. As discussed throughout this book, this will have major impacts on future divisions of household labor.

Not everyone will move toward gender equality in household labor, and the changes noted above will often work at cross purposes. Some couples will continue to follow conventional gender-segregated divisions of labor, while others will opt for virtual role reversal. Most, however, will fall somewhere in between, sharing some tasks and dividing others on the basis of gender. Some families will lament the changes and fight them at every turn. Others will accept and applaud them, attempting to divide tasks evenly and to move away from manager/helper dynamics. We can predict, however, that the general direction of change will be toward more sharing and more acceptance of different types of sharing.

Women's employment and men's assumption of family work are not temporary fads that will soon fade. Many men and women will continue to resist by harkening back to halcyon images of separate spheres. This backlash will not stem the flow of historic change. Even if we see a limited revival of fundamentalist morality like we had in the early 1980s, there will be continuing pressures on women to work for wages and men to do more family work. In fact, a public renewal of appreciation for family and children will only serve to hasten some of the changes that are already underway. This is because new government income support programs that might reduce women's incentives for employment are extremely unlikely, as are government subsidies for child care that might reduce pressure on men to do more. The conservative trend toward limiting government and privatizing services thus reaches into families as much as any liberal social welfare program, and men will be expected to pick up at least some of the slack at home. As the analysis presented above indicates, most of the pressures for sharing family work are related to underlying demographic, economic, and ideological trends that have been building for many decades. While not impervious to change, these trends will not abruptly reverse themselves in the near future.

What does it matter that men will feel more pressure to contribute to the daily activities that it takes to run a household? As noted above, some men will resist more than others. Some women will also resist change in the allocation of responsibility for household labor. In the older, historically bounded version of separate spheres that still governs many aspects of family life today, women were forced to shoulder virtually all the housework and child care. But the cult of true womanhood that legitimated the separate spheres ideal also celebrated mothers' unique sensitivity, subservience, and purity. These traits supposedly made women ideally suited to care for home and children. Since the home came to be defined as the wife's domain, she gained a certain measure of power, albeit a power that carried a cost of dependence on husbands and limited authority in more public realms. This ambivalent experience of home as haven continues today. Women, more than men, find the tasks of tending houses, caring for children, and serving spouses to be uniquely fulfilling. Wives and mothers often report that feeding or comforting family members gives them intense pleasure and a sense of purpose in life. Given the lack of respect accruing to women outside the home, families remain one of the few domains where women's knowledge and authority are accepted and women's activities celebrated. Sharing the intimate details of housework and child care with husbands thus entails a potential loss of control and esteem for some women.

As we saw in earlier chapters, when husbands take on some of the household duties that have traditionally been performed by wives, arguments over standards usually arise. The subtle and overt negotiations over how often a task should be performed, or the best technique for its performance, are often accompanied by increased tension and conflict. Many women want to avoid this tension and so choose not to bargain for more contributions from their husbands. Men also tend to feel incompetent (or feign it), further limiting their responsibility for certain tasks. Often, men remain in a helper role, having to be reminded to do chores, or to maintain the wife's standards of cleanliness.

But as more men are faced with having full responsibility for various domestic tasks, more of them can be expected to move out of a dependent helper role.

As men begin to assume more responsibility for housework and children, we can expect mixed results. To begin with, more women will be relieved of full responsibility for domestic activities. If women desire help, this has positive impacts on their health, strengthens marital satisfaction, and allows them more time to pursue their careers. For most women, sharing the physical burden of housework is an enormous relief, and, for others, sharing the emotional burden of worrying about the children can be liberating. On the other hand, trying to share with a husband who is a lousy housekeeper or an inattentive parent can raise a wife's anxiety to unacceptable levels. If women do not want more help, and do not want to give up control over home and children, being forced to share can have negative impacts on their health and marital satisfaction. Some women continue to feel that asking their husbands to do housework demeans their masculinity and represents a failure of their manhood. For these women, increased sharing is experienced as troublesome, and whenever possible, they try to get back to gender-segregated patterns of household labor. Nevertheless, since people's consciousness tends to be shaped by their routine activities, for some who initially resist, even unwanted sharing, if moderately successful, can have the effect of diluting the influence of gender on future patterns of family labor allocation.

Conflicts between husbands and wives, but also between fathers and children, are likely to increase as more men begin taking at least partial responsibility for the stressful day-to-day operations of households. Although this will provide opportunities for fathers to develop closer relationships with their children, it will also afford them more opportunities to have negative interactions. Proportionately more fathers than mothers physically and sexually abuse children, so the effects of more participation by fathers cannot automatically be assumed to have positive effects on children or their families. Men also tend to pay more attention to sons than daughters, and to maintain more rigid gender stereotypes than mothers. Bringing such men into more active contact with children could therefore reinforce gender differences, rather than working toward their demise. It is also true that fathers who take sole or equal responsibility for children depart from the patterns exhibited by more traditional fathers. Although it is unclear what causes what, it appears that highly participant fathers adopt a more gender-neutral style of parenting that resembles mothers' styles more than traditional fathers'. Children of highly participant fathers tend to perceive them as more punitive than children with less involved fathers, a pattern that reflects the involvement of fathers in routine limit setting.[113] In general, shared parenting fathers must give up the privileged status of outsider and hence tend to develop less romanticized and more realistic relationships with their children. Mothers usually consider this to be a positive development, whereas fathers seem to be more ambivalent about it.[114]

Fathers who take on responsibility for child care often report that the experience makes them more complete people. That is, fathering provides them opportunities to develop the more caring and emotional sides of themselves. To survive the daily trials and tribulations of child care, many parents find that they must develop clarity about what is most important, patience with the uneven pace of children's development, and sensitivity to subtle differences in feelings and actions. What's more, good parenting strikes a balance between guidance and service. Aloof, authoritarian, and judgmental styles of interaction do not work well in baby care, and tend to create more problems than they solve. Because men cannot rely on no-nonsense, directive, "masculine" styles of interaction, they are forced to develop more gentle and expressive ways of relating. In fact, some of the new fathers I interviewed told me that infant care forced them to recognize, label, and talk about their own and their children's feeling.

Child care provides men a relatively safe opportunity to explore these new ways of relating. Caring for young children has a different quality from interactions with other adult men, which tend to be restricted to set patterns of concern for work, sports, and "things" (tools, cars, equipment, adventure, etc.). For most men, child care is also qualitatively different from their interactions with women, particularly in romantic and marital relations. In these close relationships with women, men often exhibit major ambivalence and fears of intimacy. With their children, in contrast, men can enthusiastically enter into a relationship predicated on unconditional love, emotional vulnerability, and innocence. This is a profound experience for many men, and although it sometimes makes their wives jealous because the men cannot give the same type of love to them, it tends to change the men. In their own words, it begins to "open them up" to various expressive possibilities, including sadness and loss surrounding their relationships with their own fathers. Caring for young children also frequently demands that fathers serve their children. The position of having to be sensitive to and responding to the spoken and unspoken needs of others makes many men uncomfortable. After all, men are not used to being in subservient positions where they must wait on others. The experience of this, however, helps men develop an attentiveness and caring that they come to appreciate.

As reported in earlier chapters, children with actively participant fathers tend to enjoy a number of social, emotional, and intellectual advantages over other children. It is not clear that this is because of the fathers' unique contribution, or simply because the children enjoy the benefits of having two adults give them the kind of care, love, and attention that promotes optimum development.[115] For most families, there are some definite advantages to having fathers intimately involved in the care of children. When fathers care for infants, toddlers, and older children, the men tend to develop more caring and supportive relationships with other adults around them.[116] Particularly if fathers do the kinds of tasks we associate with mothering, the potential for longer-term change in gender relations also increases. This is so for several reasons.

First, active fathering will produce children with fewer psychological needs to distance themselves from the "opposite" sex. If a man is actively involved in infant care, he will be incorporated more fully into the internal psychic life of the growing child. If Chodorow and other psychoanalysts are correct, shared parenting will thus change typical emotional dilemmas and "heterosexual knots" that drive men to reject women and denigrate the feminine in other men and in themselves.[117] If both men and women took care of babies on a routine basis, then both boys and girls would internalize aspects of both parents in their innermost selves. Instead of developing fluid ego boundaries and experiencing the world through others, girls would be able to assert their individuality without threatening their sense of self. Instead of developing rigid ego boundaries and objectifying women, men would be more able to tolerate ambiguity and experience intimacy with others. This has the potential for reducing high levels of violence, abuse, and other forms of instrumental domination. The cross-cultural analysis presented in Chapter 7 lends support to this view, and shows that societies with close father-child relationships afford women higher status and show less gender antagonism.

The second reason that shared parenting can promote longer term gender equality also concerns its impacts on children, but broadens the focus to include more than just hypothesized unconscious processes. Whether they intend it or not, what parents do in the presence of their children shapes the goals, ideals, and understandings of those children. At all ages and stages, children observe and emulate role models, the most important of whom are family members. Socialization also occurs in schools, peer groups, and through the media, but virtually all researchers acknowledge the importance of parents in the formation of gender identity and the understanding of what it means to be a man or woman. If boys are exposed to men nurturing and doing housework, they will have a larger repertoire of masculine behaviors to draw from in developing their own style of masculinity. If girls are exposed to women who have careers and identity supports outside the home, they will likewise have more options in defining themselves. Both boys and girls will also see a wider range of gender possibilities and preferences that will help shape their selection of friends and romantic partners. Children will also develop cognitive frameworks that will be less organized around fundamental differences between men and women.

A third reason that involved fathering can change gender relations concerns its impact on adults. What people learn about gender in childhood is important, but it is necessary to have some other routine processes to sustain and confirm the meaning of gender. Boys are taught to play with trucks and girls are taught to play with dolls, and both come to think that this is natural. But these preferences would soon fade if we did not have other ritualized forms of interaction that perpetuated and reinforced the notion that men and women were essentially different and that they should do different things. By performing different tasks in our everyday lives, we literally construct and resconstruct the meaning of gender.

In conventional divisions of labor, woman cook and men don't. Nevertheless, if a man cooks steaks on a barbecue grill, we have no trouble reinterpreting this activity as masculine. Similarly, a man can wear an apron while doing carpentry work, but if he wears an apron while dicing scallions or arranging fresh-cut flowers, we begin to worry about his masculinity. Thus, the tasks he does, the clothes he wears, and the place where the labor occurs, all enter into our implicit calculations about the gender-appropriateness of his actions. In performing appropriate gender tasks, men construct their masculinity (and women construct their femininity). What happens, then, when men do women's work?

There is nothing intrinsic to cleaning house or tending children that makes it UNmasculine. It is just that we have labeled and accepted these activities as appropriate for women and inappropriate for men. As more men do them, the meaning of gender will begin to change. We will not abandon gendered categories, but the fact that men perform such tasks will slowly alter our concepts about what is appropriate for men and women. We can already see this for a few activities. Men used to get embarrassed if they were seen pushing a baby carriage in public, but now fathers show off their strollers and baby-backpacks as status symbols. Shopping, cooking, and washing dishes are other family work activities that are slowly coming to be seen as activities appropriately shared by husbands and wives. Whether doing the laundry, vacuuming the floors, or cleaning the toilets will also move into the potentially shared category remains to be seen. Nevertheless, we can see that the simple fact of routine performance of housework and child care by men will alter our definitions of what it means to be a man. This does not guarantee that gender relations will become equal, only that the content and meaning of gender will be transformed.[118]

Finally, the erosion of separate spheres will fundamentally alter future relationships between men and women in the larger society. As men take on more responsibility for housework and child care, it will begin to change the nature of employment and influence the overall distribution of resources. Although most women now work for wages, they have not been accepted as full economic providers. As women's wages increase, and as men take on more household duties, the distinctions between men's work and women's work will blur. Men and women workers who are parents will share the same sorts of limitations from employment obligations, but as more men take their family obligations seriously, employers will feel pressure to change the structure and timing of work. As women's earnings and employment hours increase, men will be less able to define providing as their sole and primary duty, and they will be under more pressure to share domestic duties. Thus, changes in housework and market work are reciprocal, and we can expect further change in both as men finally begin to shoulder more family work.

The changes that I see on the horizon are neither revolutionary nor inevitable. They will depend on many individual people making countless piecemeal decisions as they go about living their daily lives. Nevertheless, the general direction of change is moving toward more sharing of labor. This will not come easily, as most men and women will resist as much as they embrace the changes. Men will eagerly take on some tasks, but bitterly resist the imposition of others. Women will eagerly delegate responsibilities for some forms of family work, but at the same time will ferociously guard others. The shifts we will witness will be both painful and fulfilling. Women, as well as men, will be ambivalent about many of the these changes and countless contradictions will emerge. Nevertheless, there will be more sharing of family work and most men and women will find some rewards in the changing patterns of labor allocation.

Ultimately, these changes in the gender division of labor will propel us toward more equality between men and women. For this reason, recent and future conflict over parenting and housework are positive developments. Instead of seeing the glass as half-empty because changes in family work are slow and difficult, I see it as half-full, with a rising water level. As my analysis shows, more fathers will become family men in the future, and as American households forge new ways of dividing family work, we will move closer to true gender equity.

Notes

Chapter 1

1. Nancy Chodorow and Susan Contratto, "The Fantasy of the Perfect Mother," in Barrie Thorne with Marilyn Yalom (eds.), *Rethinking the Family: Some Feminist Questions* revised edition (Boston: Northeastern University Press, 1992), 191–214.

2. See, for example, Martin O'Connell, *Where's Papa?, Father's Role in Child Care* (Washington, DC: Population Reference Bureau, 1993); Barbara Vobejda and D'Vera Cohn, "Dad's Help Seen Reducing Need for Day Care," *Los Angeles Times,* May 21, 1994.

3. Nancy Chodorow, *The Reproduction of Mothering: Psychoanalysis and the Sociology of Gender* (Berkeley: University of California Press, 1978); See also Dorothy Dinnerstein, *The Mermaid and the Minotaur: Sexual Arrangements and Human Malaise* (New York: Harper & Row, 1976).

4. For reviews of research on fathers by psychologists, see Ross Parke, *Fathers* (Cambridge, MA: Harvard University Press, 1981); Michael Lamb, *The Role of the Father in Child Development* (New York: Wiley, 1981); and Henry B. Biller, *Fathers and Families: Paternal Factors in Child Development* (Westport, CT: Auburn House, 1993). For recent sociological studies of fathers, see Kathleen Gerson, *No Man's Land: Men's Changing Commitments to Family and Work* (New York: Basic Books, 1993); Shirley M. H. Hanson and Frederick W. Bozett (eds.), *Dimensions of Fatherhood* (Beverly Hills, CA: Sage, 1985); Jane C. Hood (ed.), *Men, Work, and Family* (Newbury Park, CA: Sage, 1993); Robert A. Lewis and Robert E. Salt (eds.), *Men in Families* (Beverly Hills, CA: Sage, 1986); William Marsiglio (ed.), *Fatherhood: Contemporary Theory, Research, and Social Policy* (Newbury Park, 1995. For an excellent history of U.S. fatherhood, see Robert L. Griswold, *Fatherhood in America* (New York: Basic Books, 1993).

5. Kyle Pruett, *The Nurturing Father* (New York: Warner, 1987); Norma Radin, "Caregiving Fathers in Intact Families," *Merrill-Palmer Quarterly* 27 (1981): 489–514; Norma Radin, "The Influence of Fathers upon Sons and Daughters and Implications for School Social Work," *Social Work in Education* 8 (1986): 77–91; Barbara Risman, "Can Men Mother?" in B. Risman and P. Schwartz (eds.), *Gender in Intimate Relationships* (Belmont, CA: Wadsworth, 1989); E. Williams, N. Radin, and T. Allegro, "Children of Highly Involved Fathers: An 11 Year Follow-up" (University of Michigan, Ann Arbor, 1991), cited in *Babies and Briefcases,* Hearings before the Select Committee on Children, Youth, and Families, House of Representatives, One Hundred Second Congress, First Session, June 11, 1991, U.S. Government Printing Office, Washington DC, pp. 78–85.

6. For exceptions to this pattern, see Griswold, *Fatherhood in America,* Gerson, *No Man's Land,* and others listed in note 4.

7. Mike Clary, *Daddy's Home* (New York: Seaview Books, 1982); Bob Greene, *Good Morning, Merry Sunshine: A Father's Journal of His Child's First Year* (New York: Atheneum, 1984); Gary. B. Trudeau, *Doonesbury* (Universal Press Syndicate, 1985).

8. Pruett, *The Nurturing Father;* Geoffrey Greif, *The Daddy Track and the Single Father* (Lexington, MA: Lexington Books, 1985). For an account of middle-age sons longing for contact with their fathers, see Samuel Osherson, *Finding our Fathers: The Unfinished Business of Manhood* (New York: Free Press, 1986).

9. For a more nuanced and critical look at shared parenting from a practicing feminist therapist, see Diane Ehrensaft, *Parenting Together* (New York: Free Press, 1987).

10. Robert Bly, *Iron John: A Book About Men* (Reading, MA: Addison-Wesley, 1990).

11. On the subject of men's reactionary responses to women's modest gains, see Scott Coltrane and Neal Hickman, "The Rhetoric of Rights and Needs: Moral Discourse in the Reform of Child Custody and Child Support Laws," *Social Problems* 39 (1992): 40–61; and Susan Faludi, *Backlash: The Undeclared War Against American Women* (New York: Crown, 1991).

12. For a review of historical trends and social forces affecting family life, see Randall Collins and Scott Coltrane, *Sociology of Marriage and the Family: Gender, Love, and Property,* 4th ed. (Chicago: Nelson Hall, 1995); Robert Griswold, *Fatherhood in America* (New York: Basic, 1993); Steven Mintz and Susan Kellog, *Domestic Revolutions: A Social History of American Family Life* (New York: Free Press, 1988); Joseph Pleck, "American Fathering in Historical Perspective," in Michael S. Kimmel (ed.), *Changing Men: New Directions in Research on Men and Masculinity* (Newbury Park, CA: Sage, 1987), pp. 83–97.

13. See Joanne Miller and Howard Garrison, "Sex Roles: The Division of Labor at Home and in the Workplace," *Annual Review of Sociology* 8 (1982): 237–262; Alexander Szalai (ed.), *The Use of Time: Daily Activities of Urban and Suburban Populations in Twelve Countries* (The Hague: Mouton, 1972); Kathryn E. Walker and Margaret E. Woods, *Time Use: A Measure of Household Production of Family Goods and Services* (Washington, DC: American Home Economics Association, 1972).

14. Arlie Hochschild with Anne Machung, *The Second Shift: Working Parents and the Revolution at Home* (New York: Viking, 1989).

15. Informants have been given pseudonyms to protect their identities. Interviews were conducted individually with each spouse. Subsequent follow-up interviews were conducted with some couples on a return visit to their home. (see Chapters 3 to 5).

16. O'Connell, *Where's Papa?*

17. See Elizabeth Bott, *Family and Social Network* (New York: Free Press, 1957); Scott Coltrane, "Social Networks and Men's Family Roles," *Men's Studies Review* 8 (1991): 8–15; Laura Lein, "Male Participation in Home Life," *Family Coordinator* 28 (1979): 489–495; Dave Riley, "Network Influences on Father Involvement in Childrearing," in Cochran et al. (eds.), *Extending Families* (Cambridge: Cambridge University Press, 1991).

18. For a more complete description of the interview and card sort methodology employed in the case studies, see Coltrane, "Household Labor and the Routine Production of Gender," *Social Problems* 36 (1989): 473–490.

19. Ross D. Parke, "Fathers and Families," in M. Bornstein (ed.), *Handbook of Parenting* (Hillsdale, NJ: Erlbaum, in press).

20. Williams, Radin, and Allegro, *Children of Involved Fathers.*

21. For examples, see Phyllis Schlafly, *The Power of the Christian Woman* (Cincinnati: Stanford Publishing, 1981); Geroge Gilder, *Sexual Suicide* (Quandrangle, 1973); Rush Limbaugh, *The Way Things Ought to Be* (New York: Pocket Books, 1992).

22. See, for example, Letty Pogrebin, *Family Politics: Love and Power on an Intimate Frontier* (New York: McGraw-Hill, 1983); Barbara Ehrenreich, *The Hearts of Men: American Dreams and the Flight from Commitment* (New York: Anchor, 1984).

23. See, for example, David Popenoe, "American Family Decline, 1960–1990: A Review and Appraisal," *Journal of Marriage and the Family* 55 (1993): 527–542; Norval Glenn, "A Plea for Objective Assessment of the Notion of Family Decline," *Journal of Marriage and the Family* 55 (1993): 542–544; Judith Stacey, "Good Riddance to The Family: A Response to David Popenoe," *Journal of Marriage and the Family* 55 (1993): 545–547; Philip Cowan, "The Sky Is Falling, But Popenoe's Analysis Won't Help Us Do Anything About It," *Journal of Marriage and the Family* 55 (1993): 548–553; and David Popenoe, "The National Family Wars," *Journal of Marriage and the Family* 55 (1993): 553–555.

24. For insightful analyses of such processes, see Stephanie Coontz, *The Way We Never Were: American Families and the Nostalgia Trap* (New York: Basic Books, 1992) and Arlene Skolnick, *Embattled Paradise: The American Family in an Age of Uncertainty* (New York: Basic Books, 1991). For a constrasting view, see David Blankenhorn, *Fatherless America: Confronting Our Most Urgent Social Problem* (New York: Basic Books, 1995).

Chapter 2

1. The label "traditional" is misleading insofar as the good provider role is a relatively recent invention. See Jessie Bernard, "The Good-Provider Role: Its Rise and Fall," *American Psychologist* 36 (1981): 1–12; Jane C. Hood, "The Provider Role: Its Meaning and Measurement," *Journal of Marriage and the Family* 48 (1986): 349–359.

2. Collins and Coltrane, *Sociology of Marriage and the Family.*

3. *Mass Mutual American Family Values Study* (1989), Washington, DC; Mellman and Lazarus, cited in David Popenoe, "American Family Decline, 1960–1990," *Journal of Marriage and the Family* 55 (1993), p. 531; Jane Riblett Wilkie, "Changes in U.S. Men's Attitudes Toward the Family Provider Role, 1972–1989,: *Gender & Society* 7 (1993): 261–279.

4. Lisa Belkin, "Bars to Equality of Sexes Seen as Eroding, Slowly," *New York Times* (August 20, 1989), cited in Kathleen Gerson, *No Man's Land: Men's Changing Commitment to Family and Work* (New York: Basic, 1993), p. 181; James A. Levine, cited in Nancy R. Gibbs, "Bringing Up Father," *TIME* (June 28, 1993), p. 55.

5. For a discussion of changing attitudes about families, see Arland Thornton, "Changing Attitudes toward Family Issues in the United States," *Journal of Marriage and the Family* 51 (1989): 873–893. On the double bind of trying to "have it all," see Pogrebin, *Family Politics* (New York: McGraw-Hill, 1983); Kathleen Gerson, *Hard Choices: How Women Decide About Work, Career and Motherhood* (Berkeley: University of California Press, 1985). On women being held responsible for family matters, see Hochschild, *Second Shift,* Linda Thompson and Alexis Walker, "Gender in Families," *Journal of Marriage and the Family* 51 (1989): 845–871, and Shari Thurer, *The Myths of Motherhood* (Boston: Houghton Mifflin, 1994). For some of the ways that women are

sanctioned when they transgress narrow cultural norms, see Edwin Schur, *Labeling Women Deviant* (New York: Random House, 1984).

6. Wilkie, "Men's Attitudes," Table 3, p. 269.

7. See Arland Thornton, "Changing Attitudes Toward Family Issues in the United States," *Journal of Marriage and the Family* 51 (1989): 873–893; Karen Peterson, "Today's Man Loves Family, Being a Dad," *USA Today* (March 24, 1988), cited in Kathleen Gerson, *No Man's Land*, p. 181; Judith Stacey, "Backwards Toward the Post-Modern Family," in Alan Wolfe (ed.), *America at Century's End* (Berkeley: University of California Press, 1991), pp. 17–34; Nancy R. Gibbs, "Bringing Up Father," *TIME* (June 28, 1993).

8. Gibbs, "Bringing up Father," p. 56.

9. Joseph Pleck, "Are 'Family-Supportive' Employer Policies Relevant to Men?" in Jane C. Hood, *Men, Work, and Family* (Newbury Park: Sage, 1993), pp. 217–237.

10. For example, see Coltrane, "Household Labor"; Gerson, *No Man's Land*; Ralph La Rossa, "Fatherhood and Social Change," *Family Relations* 37 (1988): 451–457. Charlie Lewis and Margaret O'Brien (eds.), *Reassessing Fatherhood* (London: Sage, 1987).

11. For a ground-breaking feminist analyses of how women's oppression is supported by a belief in separate spheres and women's performance of unpaid domestic labor, see Christine Delphy, *Close to Home: A Materialist Analysis of Women's Oppression*, translated by Diana Leonard (Hutchinson: London, 1984). For reviews of research on separate spheres and the household division of labor, see Christine Bose, "Dual Spheres," in Beth Hess and Myra Marx Ferree (eds.), *Analyzing Gender* (Newbury Park, CA: Sage, 1987); Myra Marx Ferree, "Beyond Separate Spheres: Feminism and Family Research," *Journal of Marriage and the Family* 52, (1990): 866–884; Joanne Miller and Howard Garrison, "Sex Roles: The Division of Labor at Home and in the Workplace," *Annual Review of Sociology* 8 (1982): 237–262; and Thompson and Walker, "Gender in Families."

12. Bose, "Dual Spheres"; Myra Marx Ferree, "She Works Hard for a Living: Gender and Class on the Job," in Beth Hess and Myra Marx Ferree (eds.), *Analyzing Gender* (Newbury Park, CA: Sage, 1987); Alice Kessler-Harris, *Out to Work: A History of Wage-earning Women in the United States* (New York: Oxford University Press, 1982).

13. Cynthia Fuchs Epstein, *Deceptive Distinctions* (New Haven: Yale University Press, 1988); Barbara F. Reskin and Patricia A. Roos, *Job Queues, Gender Queues* (Philadelphia: Temple University Press, 1990); Barbara F. Reskin and Heidi Hartmann, *Women's Work, Men's Work: Sex Segregation on the Job* (Washington, DC: National Academy Press, 1986).

14. For debates on this issue, see Michelle Rosaldo, "The Use and Abuse of Anthropology," *Signs* 5 (1980): 389–417; Sharon Tiffany, *Women, Work, and Motherhood* (Englewood Cliffs, NJ: Prentice-Hall, 1982); Miriam Johnson, *Strong Mothers, Weak Wives* (Berkeley: University of California Press, 1988).

15. For an insightful discussion of the role of physical separation in constructing and maintaining male dominance, see Daphne Spain, *Gendered Spaces* (Chapel Hill, University of North Carolina Press, 1992).

16. Robert Griswold, *Fatherhood in America: A History* (New York: Basic Books, 1993).

17. Kessler-Harris, *Out to Work*.

18. Jeane Boydston, *Home and Work: Housework, Wages, and the Ideology of Labor in the Early Republic* (New York: Oxford University Press, 1990); Bose, "Separate Spheres";

Kessler-Harris, *Out to Work;* J. Matthaei, *An Economic History of Women in America* (New York: Schocken, 1982).

19. Elizabeth Pleck, "A Mothers' Wages: Income Earning Among Married Italian and Black Women, 1896–1911," in Michael Gordon, *The American Family in Socio-Historical Perspective* (New York: St. Martin's Press, 1983), p. 490; Stephanie Coontz, *The Social Origins of Private Life* (London: Verso, 1988), p. 256.

20. Carl Degler, "At Odds: Women and the Family in America from the Revolution to the Present" (New York: Oxford University Press, 1980); Pleck, "American Fathering"; Anthony Rotundo, *American Manhood* (New York: Basic Books, 1993).

21. Coltrane and Hickman, *Rhetoric of Rights.*

22. Collins and Coltrane, *Sociology of Marriage and the Family;* John Demos, "The Changing Faces of Fatherhood," in Stanley Cath, Alan Gurwitt, and John Ross (eds.), *Father and Child: Developmental and Clinical Perspectives* (Boston: Little, Brown, 1982), pp. 425–450; Pleck, *American Fathering;* Anthony Synnott, "Little Angels, Little Devils: A Sociology of Children," *Canadian Review of Sociology and Anthropology* 20 (1983): 79–95.

23. Griswold, *Fatherhood,* p. 13.

24. Griswold, *Fatherhood,* p. 11. See also Steven Mintz and Susan Kellog, *Domestic Revolutions: A Social History of American Family Life* (New York: Free Press, 1988), and E. Anthony Rotundo, *American Manhood.*

25. Griswold, *Fatherhood,* p. 18. See also Daniel Blake Smith, *Inside the Great House: Planter Family Life in Eighteenth-Century Chesapeake Society* (Ithaca: Cornell University Press, 1980).

26. Griswold, *Fatherhood,* pp. 10–33.

27. Griswold, *Fatherhood,* p. 19.

28. Mark Carnes and Clyde Griffen (eds.), *Meanings for Manhood: Constructions of Masculinity in Victorian America* (Chicago: University of Chicago Press, 1990); Michael Kimmel and Michael Messner (eds.), *Men's Lives* (New York: Macmillan, 1994); Carl Degler, *At Odds: Women and the Family in America from the Revolution to the Present* (New York: Oxford University Press, 1980); Michael Kimmel, "The Contemporary 'Crisis' of Masculinity," in Harry Brod (ed.), *The Making of Masculinities* (Boston: Unwin Hyman, 1987).

29. Carnes and Griffen, *Meanings for Manhood;* Jeffery Hantover, "The Boy Scouts and the Validation of Masculinity," in Michael Kimmel and Michael Messner (eds.), *Men's Lives (New York: Macmillan, 1989); Degler, At Odds;* Kimmel, "Masculinity."

30. Demos, *Changing Faces;* Pleck, *American Fathering.*

31. Nancy Cott, *The Bonds of Womanhood* (New Haven: Yale University Press, 1977); Mary Ryan, *The Empire of the Mother: American Writing About Domesticity, 1830–1860* (New York: Haworth Press, 1982); Arlene Skolnick, *Embattled Paradise: The American Family in an Age of Uncertainty* (New York: Basic Books, 1991); Barbara Welter, "The Cult of True Womanhood: 1820–1860," *American Quarterly* 18 (1966).

32. See Griswold, *Fatherhood.*

33. Phillipe Ariès, *Centuries of Childhood* (New York: Random House, 1962). For a contrasting view, see Linda Pollock *Forgotten Children* (Cambridge: Cambridge University Press, 1983).

34. Peter Uhlenberg, "Death and the Family," *Journal of Family History* 5 (1980): 313–320.

35. Synnott, "Little Angels," p. 29. For a more contemporary cross-cultural example, see Nancy Scheper-Hughes, *Death Without Weeping* (Berkeley: University of California Press, 1992).

36. Frank Muir and Simon Brett, *On Children* (London: Heinemann, 1980); Synnott, "Little Angels."

37. Skolnick, *Embattled Paradise;* Coontz, *Social Origins;* Christopher Lasch, *Haven in a Heartless World* (New York: Basic Books, 1977).

38. Skolnick, *Embattled Paradise,* p. 32.

39. Coontz, *Social Origins,* p. 262.

40. Viviana Zelizer, *Pricing the Priceless Child: The Changing Social Value of Children* (New York: Basic Books, 1985).

41. Skolnick, *Embattled Paradise,* p. 31; Bose, "Separate Spheres."

42. Griswold, *Fatherhood,* Chapter 5.

43. Griswold, *Fatherhood,* p. 117.

44. See Kimmel, "Crisis of Masculinity"; Rupert Wilkinson, *American Tough* (New York: Harper & Row, 1984); Robert Bellah, Richard Madsen, William Sullivan, Ann Swidler, and Steven Tipton, *Habits of the Heart* (New York: Harper & Row, 1985).

45. Bose, "Separate Spheres."

46. Bose, "Separate Spheres"; Coontz, *Social Origins;* Matthaei, "Economic History"; Natalie J. Sokoloff, *Between Money and Love: The Dialectics of Women's Home and Market Work* (New York: Praeger, 1980); J. M. Jensen, "Cloth, Butter and Boarders: Women's Household Production for the Market," *Review of Political Economics* 12 (1980): 14–24.

47. Bose, "Separate Spheres," p. 268.

48. Skolnick, "Embattled Paradise"; Lawrence Stone, *The Family, Sex and Marriage in England, 1500–1800* (New York: Harper & Row, 1977).

49. See Collins and Coltrane, *Sociology of Marriage and the Family,* pp. 380–386; Mariarosa Dalla Costa and Selma James, *The Power of Women and the Subversion of the Community* (Briston, England: Falling Wall Press, 1972); Heidi Hartmann, "Capitalism, Patriarchy, and Job Segregation by Sex," *Signs* 1 (1976): 137–169; Sokoloff, *Between Money and Love.*

50. It is estimated that about 25 percent of the GNP would have to be devoted to the activities of reproducing and maintaining the labor force if the workers had to be cared for at market rates instead of by unpaid wives and mothers (Sokoloff, *Between Money and Love,* p. 130). If women received salaries for housework comparable to the relatively low rates paid to restaurant, housekeeping, and child-care workers, their labor would be worth over $20,000 per year (Dalla Costa and James, *Power of Women*).

51. Collins and Coltrane, *Sociology of Marriage and the Family,* p. 383.

52. Joann Vanek, "Time Spent in Housework," *Scientific American* 231 (1974): 116–120; Ruth S. Cowan, *More Work for Mother: The Ironies of Household Technology from the Open Hearth to the Microwave* (New York: Basic Books, 1983).

53. Collins and Coltrane, *Sociology of Marriage and the Family.*

54. Collins and Coltrane, *Sociology of Marriage and the Family,* pp. 70, 366–367.

55. Evelyn Nakano Glenn, "Gender in the Family," in Beth Hess and Myra Marx Ferree (eds.), *Analyzing Gender* (Newberry Park, CA: Sage, 1987), p. 363.

56. Lenore Weitzman, *The Marriage Contract* (New York: Free Press, 1981).

57. For a more complete discussion of the history of domestic violence, see Elizabeth Pleck, *Domestic Tyranny* (New York: Oxford University Press, 1987).

58. T. Davidson, "Wifebeating," in M. Roy (ed.), *Battered Women* (New York: Van Nostrand Reinhold, 1977); Jan E. Stets, *Domestic Violence and Control* (New York: Springer-Verlag, 1988).

59. Weitzman, *Marriage Contract,* p. 1189.

60. Arlene Skolnick, *The Intimate Environment* (Boston: Little, Brown, 1987), p. 279.

61. Diane Crispell, "Myths of the 1950s," *American Demographics* 14 (1992): 38–43.

62. Bose, "Separate Spheres," p. 280.

63. See Collins and Coltrane, *Sociology of Marriage and the Family,* pp. 154–185.

64. Bernard, "The Good Provider Role," reprinted in Michael Kimmel and Michael Messner, *Men's Lives* (New York: Macmillan, 1992), p. 206.

65. Skolnick, *Intimate Environment.*

66. Rose Laub Coser, "Authority and Structural Ambivalence in the Middle-Class Family," in Rose Coser (ed.), *The Family: Its Structure and Functions* (New York: St. Martin's, 1964), pp. 370–383; R. D. Laing, *The Politics of the Family* (New York: Random House, 1971); Carol Warren, *Madwives: Schizophrenic Women at Mid-Century* (New Brunswick, NJ: Rutgers University Press, 1987).

67. Skolnick, *Intimate Environment.*

68. Pleck, "American Fathers," p. 91.

69. Ross D. Parke, *Fathers* (Cambridge, MA: Harvard University Press, 1981), p. 4.

70. Figures are from the year 1965. John Robinson, "Who's Doing the Housework?," *American Demographics* 10 (1988): 24–28, 63.

71. 6 Robinson, "Who's Doing the Housework?"

72. U. S. Bureau of the Census, *Current Population Reports,* Series P-23, No. 146 (Washington DC: U.S. Government Printing Office, 1986), Table 5.

73. Dennis A. Ahlburg and Carol J. DeVita, "New Realities of the American Family," *Population Bulletin* 47 (1992): 1–43; Collins and Coltrane, *Sociology of Marriage and the Family;* Crispell, "Myths."

74. Ahlburg and De Vita, "New Realities," p. 2.

75. U. S. Bureau of the Census, *Current Population Reports,* Series P-20, No.458, Household and Family Characteristics (Washington DC: U.S. Government Printing Office, 1992).

76. Ahlburg and De Vita, "New Realities."

77. Jay Belsky, Graham B. Spanier, and M. Rovine, "Stability and Change in Marriage Across the Transition to Parenthood," *Journal of Marriage and the Family* 45 (1983): 567–577; Jay Belsky, M. Lang, and M. Rovine, "Stability and Change in Marriage Across the Transition to Parenthood: A Second Study," *Journal of Marriage and the Family* 47 (1985): 855–866; Philip A. Cowan, "Becoming a Father," in Phyllis Bronstein and Carolyn Cowan (eds.), *Fatherhood Today* (New York: Wiley, 1988); Carolyn Cowan, Philip Cowan, G. Heming, E. V. Garrett, W. S. Coysh, H. Curtis-Boles, and A. J. Boles, "Transitions to Parenthood: His, Hers, and Theirs," *Journal of Family Issues* 6 (1985): 451–481; Ralph LaRossa and Maureen LaRossa, *Transition to Parenthood* (Beverly Hills, CA: Sage, 1981); Scott South and Glenna Spitze, "Housework in Marital and Nonmarital Households," *American Sociological Review* 59 (1994): 327–347.

78. Sarah Fenstermaker Berk, *The Gender Factory: The Apportionment of Work in American Households* (New York: Plenum, 1985); Joseph Pleck, "Husbands' Paid Work and Family Roles: Current Research Issues," in H. Lopata and J. Pleck (eds.), *Research in the Interweave of Social Roles* (Greenwich: Jai, 1983); Robinson, "Who's Doing the Housework"; Thompson and Walker, "Gender in Families."

79. Miller and Garrison, "Sex Roles," p. 242.

80. Michael E. Lamb, *The Role of the Father in Child Development* (New York: Wiley, 1981); Ross D. Parke, "Perspectives on Father-infant Interaction," in J. Osofsky (ed.), *The Handbook of Infant Development* (New York: Wiley, 1979); Ross D. Parke and Barbara R. Tinsley, "Fatherhood: Historical and Contemporary Perspectives," in K. A. Mc-Cluskey and H. W. Reese (eds.), *Life-Span Developmental Psychology: Historical and Generational Effects* (New York: Academic, 1984), pp. 429–457.

81. Belsky, Lang, and Rovine, "Stability and Change"; Cowan, "Becoming a Father"; Ralph La Rossa and Maureen LaRossa, "Baby Care: Fathers vs. Mothers," in Barbara Risman and Pepper Schwartz (eds.), *Gender in Intimate Relationships* (Belmont, CA: Wadsworth, 1989).

82. Robinson, "Who's Doing the Housework?"

83. Heidi I. Hartmann, "The Family as the Locus of Gender, Class, and Political Struggle: The Example of Housework," *Signs* 6 (1981): 366–394.

84. Ronald Kessler and James McRae, "The Effects of Wives' Employment on the Mental Health of Married Men and Women," *American Sociological Review* 47 (1982): 216–227; Catherine E. Ross, John Mirowsky, and Joan Huber, "Dividing Work, Sharing Work, and In-Between: Marriage Patterns and Depression," *American Sociological Review* 48 (1983): 809–823.

85. Berk, *Gender Factory;* Catherine Berheide, "Women's Work in the Home: Seems Like Old Times," *Marriage and Family Review* 7 (1984): 37–55; Pleck, "Husbands' Paid Work"; Walker and Thompson, "Gender in Families."

86. Grace K. Baruch and Rosalind C. Barnett, "Consequences of Fathers' Participation in Family Work: Parents' Role Strain and Well-Being," *Journal of Personality and Social Psychology* 51 (1986): 983–992; Berheide, "Old Times"; Hochschild, *Managed Heart;* Susan Shaw, "Gender Differences in the Definition and Perception of Household Labor," *Family Relations* 37 (1988): 333–337; Walker and Thompson, "Gender in Families."

87. See Berk, *Gender Factory;* Collins and Coltrane, *Sociology of Marriage and the Family,* Chapter 10.

88. Berheide, "Seems Like Old Times"; Marjorie L. DeVault, "Doing Housework: Feeding and Family Life," in Naomi Gerstel and Harriet E. Gross (eds.), *Families and Work: Toward Reconceptualization* (Philadelphia: Temple University Press, 1987), pp. 178–191; Myra Marx Ferree, "Family and Job for Working-Class Women: Gender and Class Systems Seen from Below," in Naomi Gerstel and Harriet E. Gross (eds.), *Families and Work: Toward Reconceptualization* (Philadelphia: Temple University Press, 1987), pp. 289–301; Thompson and Walker, "Gender in Families."

89. For an example of a recent argument about the biological deficiencies of fathers, see Alice S. Rossi, "A Biosocial Perspective on Parenting," *Daedalus* 106 (1977):1–31; and Alice S. Rossi, "Gender and Parenthood," *American Sociological Review* 49 (1984): 1–19. For a review of literature on fathering by psychologists, and examples

of those who assume that gender differences in parenting are primarily socially constructed, see Lamb, *The Role of the Father.*

90. Ross D. Parke and Douglas Sawin, "The Father's Role in Infancy: A Reevaluation," *Family Coordinator* 25 (1976): 365–371.

91. M. Kotelchuck, "The Infant's Relationship to the Father: Experimental Evidence," in Lamb, *The Role of the Father,* pp. 329–344.

92. see Ross D. Parke and Barbara Tinsley, "The Father's Role in Infancy: Determinants of Involvement in Caregiving and Play," in Lamb, *The Role of the Father;* Parke, "Perspectives"; T. G. Power and Ross D. Parke, "Play as a Context for Early Learning: Lab and Home Analyses," in I. E. Sigel and L. M. Laosa (eds.), *The Family as a Learning Environment* (New York: Plenum, 1982).

93. Katharyn A. May and Steven P. Perrin, "Prelude: Pregnancy and Birth," in Shirley Hanson and Frederick Bozett (eds.), *Dimensions of Fatherhood* (Beverly Hills, CA: Sage, 1985) pp. 64–91.

94. Parke and Tinsley, "Fatherhood," p. 211.

95. Nancy R. Gibbs, "Bringing Up Father," *TIME* (June 28, 1993, p. 58); Debra Klinman and Rhiana Kohl, *Fatherhood U.S.A.* (New York: Garland, 1984).

96. For an elaboration of this insight, see Frank F. Furstenberg, "Good Dads—Bad Dads: Two Faces of Fatherhood," in Andrew Cherlin (ed.), *The Changing American Family and Public Policy* (Washington, DC: The Urban Institute, 1988).

97. Scott Coltrane, "Birth Timing and the Division of Labor in Dual-Earner Families," *Journal of Family Issues* 11 (1990):157–181.

98. Candace West and Donald Zimmerman, "Doing Gender," *Gender & Society* 1 (1987): 125–151.

99. Berk, *Gender Factory.*

100. Norval D. Glenn, "What does family mean?," *American Demographics,* 14 (1992): 30–37.

Chapter 3

1. Arlie Hochschild with Anne Machung, *The Second Shift: Working Parents and the Revolution at Home* (New York: Viking, 1989).

2. Hochschild (*Second Shift,* p. 272) cites a study by Greg Duncan and James Morgan (*Five Thousand American Families: Patterns of Economic Progress.* Vol. 6, Ann Arbor: Survey Research Center, University of Michigan, 1978) illustrating the extra hours of work that marriage costs women and saves men: Married women do 1,473 hours of housework per year, compared to 886 hours for single women, 468 hours for single men, and 301 for married men. More recent studies calculate lower disparities between men and women, but married men contribute only about half the hours that married women do to all forms of housework (18 hrs/wk vs. 37 hrs/wk) South and Spitze, "Housework," p. 327. Presser estimates that the total weekly workload in dual-earner married couple households (paid work hours plus hours on nine housework tasks) is 68.8 hours for women and 63.4 hours for men for a gap of over 5 hours per week (Harriet Presser, "Employment Schedules Among Dual-Earner Spouses and the Division of Household Labor by Gender," *American Sociological Review* 59 (1994): 348–364. Because Presser did not include measures of child care or other more hidden home

management time, it is likely that the gap in dual earner households is closer to 10 hours per week or over 500 hours per year.

3. Hochschild's book did not come out until after I had completed my own study of shared parenting in 1987–88, but I did meet and correspond with her before and after I conducted my interviews. I was also able to talk extensively with Lynet Uttal, a friend and fellow graduate student who helped code and analyze some of the interviews for *The Second Shift*. Both offered useful suggestions, provided encouragement, and helped me understand some of the complexities of interviewing couples about paid work and family work. Although my results occasionally depart from the findings of *The Second Shift*, I am indebted to Arlie Hochschild's insightful analysis of what she called "the stalled revolution at home."

4. Kathleen Gerson illustrates this point well in *Hard Choices: How Women Decide About Work, Career, and Motherhood* (Berkeley, University of California Press, 1985) and in *No Man's Land: Men's Changing Commitments to Family and Work* (New York: Basic Books, 1993).

5. See Karen Pyke and Scott Coltrane, Entitlement, Obligation, and Gratitude in Remarriage, Paper presented at the Pacific Sociological Association Annual Meetings, 1995.

6. Hochschild, *Second Shift*.

7. See, for example, Pleck ("Family Supportive Employer Policies," pp. 219–22) who questions Hochschild's calculations and suggests that more change has occurred than she estimates.

8. Myra Marx Ferree, "The Gender Division of Labor in Two-Earner Marriages: Dimensions of Variability and Change," *Journal of Family Issues* 12 (1991): 158–180; John Robinson, "Who's Doing the Housework?" *American Demographics* 10 (1988): 24–28, 63; but see Presser, note 3.

9. Rosalind C. Barnett and Grace K. Baruch, "Determinants of Fathers' Participation in Family Work," *Journal of Marriage and the Family* 49 (1987): 29–40. Myra Marx Ferree, "Beyond Separate Spheres: Feminism and Family Research," *Journal of Marriage and the Family* 52 (1990): 866–884; Linda Thompson and Alexis J. Walker, "Gender in Families," *Journal of Marriage and the Family* 51 (1989): 845–871.

10. Ferree, "The Gender Division"; Robinson, "Who's Doing the Housework?"; Beth Anne Shelton, *Women, Men, and Time: Gender Differences in Paid Work, Housework and Leisure* (New York: Greenwood, 1992); Thompson and Walker, "Gender in Families."

11. See Miller and Garrison, "The Division of Labor"; Thompson and Walker, "Gender in Families." For an example focused on changes in fathering, see Ralph LaRossa, "Fatherhood and Social Change," *Family Relations* 37 (1988): 451–457.

12. For example, see Pleck, " 'Family-Supportive' Employer Policies."

13. Ferree, "Gender Division"; Jonathan Gershuny and John Robinson, "Historical Changes in the Household Division of Labor," *Demography* 25 (1988): 537–552; Robinson, "Who's Doing the Housework"; Shelton, *Women, Men, Time*.

14. Majorie DeVault, *Feeding the Family: The Social Construction of Caring as Gendered Work* (Chicago: University of Chicago Press, 1991); Micaela di Leonardo, "The Female World of Cards and Holidays: Women, Families, and the Work of Kinship," *Signs* 12 (1987): 440–453, reprinted in Barrie Thorne, *Rethinking the Family: Some Feminist*

Questions (Boston: Northeastern University Press, 1992), pp. 246–261: Pamela Fishman, "Interaction: The Work Women Do," *Social Problems* 25 (1978): 398–406; Thompson and Walker, "Gender in Families."

15. Berk, *Gender Factory;* Diane Ehrensaft, *Parenting Together* (New York: Free Press, 1987).

16. Frances K. Goldscheider and Linda J. Waite, *New Families, No Families? The Transformation of the American Home* (Berkeley: University of California Press, 1991); Joseph H. Pleck, "American Fathering in Historical Perspective," in Michael Kimmel (ed.), *Changing Men: New Directions in Research on Men and Masculinity* (Newbury Park, CA: Sage, 1987), pp. 83–97.

17. One in five infants of U.S. working mothers are cared for by their fathers, and one in four preschoolers of mothers employed part-time receive primary care from fathers while their mothers are at work. See Lois W. Hoffman, "Effects of Maternal Employment in the Two-Parent Family," *American Psychologist* 44 (1989): 283–292; Phyllis Moen, *Women's Two Roles* (New York: Auburn House, 1992), pp. 77–79; O'Connell, *Where's Papa;* Harriet B. Presser, "Shift Work among American Women and Child Care," *Journal of Marriage and the Family* 48 (1986): 551–564; Presser, "Shift Work and Child Care among Dual-Earner American Parents," *Journal of Marriage and the Family* 50 (1988): 133–148; Presser, "Can We Make Time for Children?," *Demography* 26 (1989): 523–554.

18. Ehrensaft, *Parenting Together;* Hochschild, *Second Shift.*

19. Some of the findings in this chapter were presented in "Household Labor and the Routine Production of Gender," *Social Problems,* Vol. 36, No. 5, December 1989. Wendy Wheeler helped with interviewing for the couples reported on in Chapter 3, all of whom were residents of suburban California communities. Funding for transcription of interviews was provided by the Business and Professional Women's Foundation and the University of California.

20. I selected couples with children because they have been found to be the least likely to share family work. Others have documented how couples in the "childless" or "empty nest" stages of the family life cycle share more housework (Cynthia Rexroat and Constance Shehan, "The Family Life Cycle and Spouses' Time Spent in Housework," *Journal of Marriage and the Family* 49 (1987): 737–750). Previous studies of egalitarian marriages and dual-career couples also focused more on childless couples than on parents. For example, the authors of *Role Sharing Marriage* reported in 1986 that couples without children in the home were the most likely to attain approximately equal divisions of household labor (Smith and Reid, *Role-Sharing Marriage*). Similarly, Gayle Kimball (*50-50 Marriage,* Boston: Beacon, 1983, p. 137) noted that among self-professed egalitarian couples, children were the most difficult factor in attempting to balance family work, and that having two children impeded role sharing more than having just one.

Some previous research had looked at couples who shared child care, but most of these couples had younger children and only one child. See Bonnie Carlson, *Shared vs. Primarily Maternal Childrearing: Effects of Dual Careers on Families with Young Children* (Unpublished Doctoral Dissertation, University of Michigan,1980); Rick Sapp, *Shared Parent Fathers: Role Entry and Psychological Consequences of Participation in a Nontraditional Male Parent Role* (Unpublished Doctoral Dissertation, The Wright Institute, 1984); Kyle Pruett, *The Nurturing Father* (New York: Warner, 1987)]. Because I wanted to focus on how patterns of shared parenting were sustained over time, not just how they were initiated, I turned to families with more and older children.

Two previous studies helped me decide to focus on parents of school-aged children. A study in Michigan and one in Australia included parents who were sharing the care of preschoolers, and then, two years later, interviewed them again to see what had changed. [See Michael Lamb, "The Changing Role of Fathers," in Michael Lamb (ed.), *The Father's Role: Applied Perspectives* (New York: Wiley, 1986); Norma Radin and R. Goldsmith, "Caregiving Fathers of Preschoolers: Four Years Later," *Merrill-Palmer Quarterly* 31 (1985): 375–383; Graeme Russell, "Primary Caretaking and Role Sharing Fathers," in Michael Lamb (ed.), *The Father's Role: Applied Perspectives* (New York: Wiley, 1986); Graeme Russell and Norma Radin, "Increased Paternal Participation: The Father's Perspective," in Michael Lamb and Abraham Sagi (eds.), *Fatherhood and Family Policy* (Hillsdale, NJ: Lawrence Erlbaum, 1983)]. Both studies reported that social and economic pressures caused at least half of the couples to switch to more traditional parenting arrangements, prompting the researchers to conclude that early patterns of shared infant or toddler care were very unstable. I found the explanations for this conversion to be unsatisfying, especially because earlier studies by psychologists had shown that fathers were likely to *increase* interaction with children as they grew older. To discover what might be contributing to the instability of alternative arrangements, and to explore how some parents continue to share as children mature, I narrowed my referrals down to just those parents with older children. To limit the possible confounding effects of different styles of parenting for older children, I also limited the sample to those with preteen children.

21. The majority of couples referred, including many of those with the most involved fathers, were first-time parents with infants or toddlers. Because they did not fit the sampling criteria established in the beginning of the study, they were not interviewed.

22. For a general discussion of this sampling technique, see Patrick Biernacki and Dan Waldorf, "Snowball Sampling," *Sociological Methods and Research* 10 (1981): 141–163.

23. A few studies published before I began interviewing had relied on paid advertisements to recruit couples who shared parenting—a practice I worried would draw too heavily from those who wanted to show off or be spokespeople for "politically correct" parenting. In an effort to reach relatively "average" shared parenting couples, I chose more discrete sampling techniques, though at the time I did not quite know what "average" shared parenting would look like.

24. Other important sampling issues I considered were the employment, social class, and incomes of those I wanted to interview. I selected only couples with both husband and wife employed at least half-time because I saw wives' employment as potentially the most important precursor to change in the separate spheres ideal. Because past studies of egalitarian couples had tended to interview upscale professional couples, I also avoided talking to doctors, lawyers, or corporate managers. Among those interviewed, mothers were more likely than fathers to hold professional or technical jobs, although most of them were employed in female-dominated occupations with relatively limited upward mobility and moderate pay. Over three-quarters held jobs in the "helping" professions: seven mothers were nurses, five were teachers, and four were social workers or counselors. Other occupations for the mothers were

administrator, laboratory technician, film maker, and bookbinder. Sample fathers held both blue-collar and white-collar jobs with concentrations in construction (3), maintenance (2), sales (3), business (3), teaching (3), delivery (4), and computers (2). Like most dual-earner wives in the United States, sample mothers earned, on average, less than half of what their husbands did, and worked an average of eight fewer hours per week. Eleven mothers, but only five fathers, were employed less than 40 hours per week. In about half the families, mothers were employed at least as many hours as fathers, but in only four families did the mother's earnings approach or exceed those of her husband.

Although higher income couples were willing to be interviewed for this study, I tried to select only couples with moderate to middle incomes. Because in all cases both spouses were employed, most of the couples I interviewed were relatively financially secure, but most were in the bottom half of the income distribution for dual-earner couples in the United States. The average (median) combined annual income for the twenty families was $40,000, with three families under $25,000 and three over $65,000. The parents were primarily in their late thirties when we interviewed them and had been living together for an average of 10 years. Most had attended some college and most were married before they were 25. On average, the mothers gave birth to their first child when they were 27 years old. Sixteen of the couples had two children and four had three children. Over two-thirds of the families had both sons and daughters, but four families had two sons and no daughters, and two families had two daughters and no sons.

25. I coded transcribed interviews using constant comparative techniques as described by Barney Glaser and Anselm Strauss, *The Discovery of Grounded Theory: Strategies for Qualitative Research* (New York: Aldine, 1967).

26. Quotes presented in this chapter are from transcribed interviews unless otherwise noted. Minor grammatical editing was done, in rare instances, to clarify the meaning of a passage.

27. Papers cited by Parke and Tinsley, *Fatherhood*, pp. 208–210 from the International Conference on Infant Studies, New Haven, CT, April 1980, including Frank A. Pedersen, R. Cain, M. Zaslow, and B. Anderson, "Variation in Infant Experience with Alternative Family Organization"; and M. Vietxe, R. H. MacTurk, M. E. McCarthy, R. P. Klein, and L. J. Yarrow, *Impact of Mode of Delivery on Father- and Mother-Infant Interaction at 6 & 12 Months.*

28. Response categories for the question "Who does this task?" were: (1) Self mostly or always; (2) Self more than spouse; (3) Both about equally; (4) Spouse more than self; and (5) Spouse mostly or always (see Coltrane, 1988). Alternate methods of assessing contributions to household labor including time reconstruction methods and activity logs have been found to produce estimates similar to the relative distribution approach used in this study, provided that data are collected from both husbands and wives. See Rebecca Warner, "Alternative Strategies for Measuring Household Division of Labor," *Journal of Family Issues* 7 (1986): 179–195.

29. Following Smith and Reid (*Role Sharing Marriage*, pp. 72–74), I computed a mean score for each couple using the "strict" criteria of 2.5 to 3.5 to represent shared activities. As others have suggested, differences in subjective assessments about family work are themselves worthy of study, for they reveal interesting dynamics concerning

reality construction, power, and gender difference. For a recent discussion, see Herbert L. Smith and S. Philip Morgan, "Children's Closeness to Father as Reported by Mothers, Sons and Daughters: Evaluating Subjective Assessments with the Rasch Model," *Journal of Family Issues* 15 (1994): 3–29.

30. The majority of ratings on 90 percent of the tasks were at least as high as the spouse's self-rating for that task. When mothers and fathers disagreed on their relative contributions to specific tasks, they tended to rate themselves one point higher than their spouse did. This slight egocentric bias is evident in a mean difference score for the 64 tasks of .20. Relatively high self-estimates (mean difference scores over .50) were made for vacuuming, making beds, cleaning porches, baking, wiping kitchen counters, putting food away, and running errands. Sample parents tended to rate their spouse higher than their spouse did (negative mean difference scores) on 11 of 64 tasks, including cleaning bathtubs, preparing dinner, ironing, repairing the car, doing yard work, interior and exterior painting, paying bills, handling insurance, corresponding with relatives and friends, and helping children dress. I discuss differences in men's and women's perceptions of household tasks in Chapter 4.

31. For comparison see Berk, *Gender Factory;* Shelley Coverman and Joseph Sheley, "Change in Men's Housework and Child Care Time, 1965–1975," *Journal of Marriage and the Family* 48 (1986): 413–422; Michael Geerken and Walter Gove, *At Home and At Work: The Family's Allocation of Labor* (Beverly Hills, CA: Sage, 1983); Dana Vannoy Hiller and William Philliber, "The Division of Labor in Contemporary Marriage: Expectations, Perceptions, and Performance," *Social Problems* 33: 191–201; Sharon Nickols and E. Metzen, "Impact of Wife's Employment upon Husband's Housework," *Journal of Family Issues* 3 (1982): 199–216.

32. For an example of similar processes in a group of Scottish families in the 1970s, see Kathryn Backett, *Mothers and Fathers* (London: Macmillan, 1982).

33. For discussions of bargaining strategies to share housework, see Jane Hood, *Becoming a Two-Job Family* (New York: Praeger, 1983); Gayle Kimball, *50–50 Parenting: Sharing Family Rewards and Responsibilities* (Lexington, MA: Lexington Books,1988); Maximilliane Szinovacz, "Changing Family Roles and Interactions," *Marriage and Family Review* 7 (1984): 163–201.

34. I am indebted to Jane Hood (*Two-Job Family,* p. 176) for this way of interpreting the taken-for-granted character of how most couples talk about their household arrangements.

35. Thompson and Walker, "Gender in Families."

36. Karen Fox and Sharon Nickols, "The Time Crunch: Wife's Employment and Family Work," *Journal of Family Issues* 4: (1983): 61–81; John P. Robinson, "The Time Squeeze," *American Demographics* 12 (1990): 30–33.

37. For similar findings about reciprocal influence of employment decisions and family commitments, see Gerson, *No Man's Land.*

38. Joseph H. Pleck and Graham L. Staines, "Work Schedules and Family Life in Two-Earner Couples," *Journal of Family Issues* 6 (1983): 61–82; Harriet B. Presser, "Employment Schedules Among Dual-Earner Spouses and the Division of Labor by Gender," *American Sociological Review* 59 (1994): 348–364.

39. Myra Marx Ferree, Negotiating Household Roles and Responsibilities: Resistance, Conflict, and Change, Paper presented at the Annual Meeting of the National

Council on Family Relations, Philadelphia, 1988; Thompson and Walker, "Gender in Families."

40. Thompson and Walker, "Gender in Families," p. 856; Baruch and Barnett, "Consequences of Father's Participation."

41. See Coltrane, "Routine Production of Gender"; Candace West and Sarah Fenstermaker, "Power, Inequality, and the Accomplishment of Gender," in Paula England (ed.), *Theory on Gender, Feminism on Theory* (Chicago: Aldin, 1992), pp. 151–174.

42. This section of the chapter draws its insight from sociologists who focus on how marriage is socially constructed through ongoing talk and interaction. Because marriage is one of the "least scripted" (Goffman) or most "undefined" (Blumer) interaction situations, the "marital conversation" (Berger and Kellner) is particularly important to a couple's shared sense of reality. See Erving Goffman, *The Presentation of Self in Everyday Life* (New York: Doubleday /Anchor, 1959); Herbert Blumer, "Society as Symbolic Interaction," in Arnold Rose (ed.), *Human Behavior and Social Processes* (Boston: Houghton Mifflin, 1962); Peter Berger and Hansfried Kellner, "Marriage and the Construction of Reality," *Diogenes* 46 (1964): 1–23.

43. Ida Harper Simpson and Paula England, "Conjugal Work Roles and Marital Solidarity," in Joan Aldous (ed.), *Two Paychecks: Life in Dual-Earner Families* (Beverly Hills, CA: Sage, 1981), pp. 147–172.

44. Thompson and Walker, "Gender in Families," p. 856.

45. Ehrensaft, "Parenting Together"; Thompson and Walker, "Gender in Families"; and see references in note 22.

46. West and Zimmerman, "Doing Gender."

47. Sara Ruddick, *Maternal Thinking* (Boston: Beacon, 1989).

Chapter 4

1. Some of the findings in this chapter were presented in Coltrane and Valdez, "Reluctant Compliance: Work/Family Role Allocation in Dual-Earner Chicano Families," in Jane C. Hood (ed.), *Work, Family, and Masculinities* (Newbury Park, CA: Sage, 1994); Valdez and Coltrane, "Work, Family, and the Chicana: Power, Perception and Equity," in *Employed Mothers and the Family Context* (New York: Springer, 1993); and "Stability and Change in Chicano Men's Family Lives," in Michael Kimmel and Michael Messner (eds.), *Men's Lives* (New York: Macmillan, 1994). Partial funding for this research was provided by the University of California, Riverside.

2. For reviews of literature on Latin American Families and projections on their future proportionate representation in the population, see Randall Collins and Scott Coltrane, *Sociology of Marriage and the Family* (Chicago: Nelson Hall, 1994); William A. Vega, "Hispanic Families in the 1980s," *Journal of Marriage and the Family* 52 (1990): 1015–1024; and Norma Williams, *The Mexican American Family* (New York: General Hall, 1990).

3. Maxine Baca Zinn, "Employment and Education of Mexican-American Women," *Harvard Educational Review* 50 (1980): 58–79.

4. William Madsen, *Mexican-Americans of South Texas* (New York: Holt, Rinehart and Winston, 1973), p. 22.

5. Alfredo Mirande, "Chicano Fathers: Traditional Perceptions and Current Realities," in Phyllis Bronstein and Ruth Cowan (eds.), *Fatherhood Today: Men's Changing Role in the Family* (New York: Wiley, 1988), pp. 93–106.

6. V. Crommwell and R. Crommwell, "Perceived Dominance in Decision-Making and Conflict Resolution Among Anglo, Black, and Chicano Couples," *Journal of Marriage and the Family* 40 (1978): 749–760; Glenn R. Hawkes and Minna Taylor, "Power Structure in Mexican and Mexican-American Farm Labor Families," *Journal of Marriage and the Family* 37 (1975): 807–811; Lea Ybarra, "When Wives Work: The Impact on the Chicano Family," *Journal of Marriage and the Family* (1982): 169–178.

7. Betty Garcia-Bahne, "La Chicana and the Chicano Family," in R. Sanchez (ed.), *Essays on La Mujer* (Los Angeles: University of California, L.A., Chicano Studies Center, 1977); Kaye Hartzler and Juan N. Franco, "Ethnicity, Division of Household Tasks, and Equity in Marital Roles: A Comparison of Anglo and Mexican American Couples," *Hispanic Journal of Behavioral Sciences* 7 (1985): 333–344. Norma Williams, "Role Making Among Married Mexican American Women: Issues of Class and Ethnicity," *The Journal of Applied Behavioral Science* 24 (1988): 203–217; Patricia Zavella, *Women's Work and Chicano Families: Cannery Workers of the Santa Clara Valley* (Ithaca, NY: Cornell University Press, 1987).

8. Maxine Baca Zinn, "Qualitative Methods in Family Research: A Look Inside the Chicano Families," *California Sociologist* (1982): 58–79.

9. Maxine Baca Zinn, "Family, Feminism, and Race in America," *Gender & Society* 4 (1990): 68–82. For an excellent discussion of the ways that gender, class, and ethnicity simultaneously influence men in Chicano families, see Pierrette Hondagneu-Sotelo and Michael Messner, "Gender Displays and Men's Power: The 'New Man' and the Mexican Immigrant Man," pp. 200–218 in Harry Brod and Michael Kaufman (eds.), *Theorizing Masculinities* (Newbury Park, CA: Sage, 1994).

10. Vega, "Hispanic Families," p. 1019; Ybarra, "When Wives Work."

11. Frank D. Bean, Russell L. Curtis, Jr., and John P. Marcus, "Familism and Marital Satisfaction Among Mexican Americans: The Effects of Family Size, Wife's Labor Force Participation, and Conjugal Power," *Journal of Marriage and the Family* 38 (1977), 760.

12. Charles H. Mindel, "Extended Familism Among Urban Mexican-Americans, Anglos and Blacks," *Hispanic Journal of Behavioral Sciences* 2 (1980): 21–34.

13. Most interviews were conducted by my research assistant, Elsa Valdez, since she was best able to establish rapport quickly with both mothers and fathers in the sample. Transcriptions were performed by me, Elsa Valdez (then a graduate student, now Assistant Professor of Sociology and Chicano Studies at California State University, San Bernardino), and Hilda Cortez (an undergraduate research intern, then a student at Pitzer College). I am indebted to Ms. Valdez and Ms. Cortez, to Chicana and Chicano undergraduate students in my family sociology classes at UC Riverside, and to colleagues from sociology, all of whom helped me to interpret, understand, and summarize material from the interviews. Interviews were tape recorded, and portions were later transcribed for coding. We used purposive snowball sampling techniques to select 20 Chicano couples living in southern California in which both parents were employed at least 20 hours per week.

14. We recruited families with at least one child of school age (later relaxed to include four year olds) and, as in the previous sampling, purposely excluded childless

couples, new parents, or couples with older children. For dual-career studies, see Robert Rapoport and Rhona Rapoport, *Dual-Career Families* (Baltimore, MD: Penguin, 1971); Robert Rapoport and Rhona Rapoport, *Dual-Career Families Re-examined: New Integrations of Work and Family* (London: Martin Robertson, 1977); Margaret Poloma, "Role Conflict and the Married Professional Woman," in Constantina Safilios-Rothschild, ed., *Toward a Sociology of Women* (Lexington, MA: Xerox, 1972); Lynda L. Holmstrom, *The Two-Career Family* (Cambridge, MA: Shenkman, 1973). For studies of working-class Latino families, see Lewis, *La Vida: A Puerto Rican Family in the Culture of Poverty* (New York: Random House, 1966); Vicki L. Ruiz, *Cannery Women/Cannery Lives* (Albuquerque: University of New Mexico Press, 1987); Zavella, *Women's Work*.

15. On the job experiences of Chicanos, see Denise Segura, "Labor Market Stratification: The Chicana Experience," *Berkeley Journal of Sociology* 29 (1984):57–91.

16. All husbands and 15 wives were employed at least 40 hours per week, and five wives spent between 20 and 30 hours per week on the job. Unlike their own parents and Latinos in general, informants were relatively well educated: 15 husbands and nine wives had at least a B. A. degree; three husbands and seven wives had attended some college; and just two husbands and four wives had just a high school diploma. In contrast, 78 percent of all Hispanics in dual-earner couples in the United States had a high school education or less (U.S. Bureau of the Census, *Current Population Reports*, Series P-20, No. 431 (Washington, DC: U.S. Government Printing Office, 1989). Annual family incomes for the sample families ranged from $26,000 to $79,000, with a median of $53,400, well above the national median for Hispanic dual-earner families of $32,185 (U.S. Census, *Current Population Reports*, P-20, 431). Individual incomes also varied widely; from $4,000 to $48,000. Ninety-five percent of the men, but only 25 percent of the women earned at least $25,000 per year. Five husbands were employed in blue-collar jobs such as painter, laborer, and mechanic; 11 in semi-professional white-collar jobs such as teacher, administrator, or technician; and four in more prestigious professional jobs such as lawyer or agency director. Six wives were employed in low status, low paying jobs such as teacher's aides or day-care providers; eight worked in skilled female-dominated jobs including secretaries, bookkeepers, and clerks; and six wives had professional or semi-professional careers as social workers, teachers, administrators, nurses, or technicians. Many of the women's jobs—like clerks and secretaries—offer modest wages, limited autonomy, and few chances for advancement. Because of this, they might more accurately be classified as white-collar working-class rather than middle-class. Others we interviewed—like teachers and administrators—tend both to give and take orders on the job, and can thus appropriately be labeled white-collar middle-class. For a discussion of classifying spouses and jobs by class, see Randall Collins, "Women and Men in the Class Structure," *Journal of Family Issues* 9 (1988): 27–50.

17. For the interviews reported on in Chapter 3, we recruited couples by asking if they shared child care. In talking with Chicano couples, few used terms like sharing, so we based our initial screening on the basis of having two paid jobs. We began our interviews with staff employees of a university, but soon had referrals to couples far removed from it (over three-quarters of the final sample of 40 individuals were not connected with the university). The final sample varied from what might be termed lower middle class (or "comfortable" working class), to upper middle class. These

terms, however, are too simple to capture the complexity of the class and status positions of the husbands and wives we interviewed. See also Judith Stacey, *Brave New Families* (New York: Basic Books, 1990).

18. Husbands in the sample ranged in age from 26 to 43 years old, with two-thirds between the ages of 35 and 38. Wives tended to be slightly younger, with most between the ages of 33 and 36. Spouses' ages in 14 of 20 couples were within two years of each other, but four husbands were at least three years older than their wives, and one wife was four years older than her husband. At the time of the interviews, couples had been married an average of 13 years, with five couples married less than 10 years, and eight couples married for 15 years or more. Four couples had one child, nine couples had two children, five couples had three children, and two had four children. The ages of the children ranged from 1 to 14 years old, with a median age of seven. Two-thirds of the couples had at least one child in the family who was five years old or younger, but only four couples had youngest children under three years old. Nine of ten identified their current religion as Catholic, with most reporting that they went to church at least once a month.

19. Just one of the husbands and four of the wives spent some time growing up in Mexico; the rest were all born and raised in the United States.

20. Of the 40 husbands and wives interviewed, none had a parent with more than a high school education, and the average educational attainment of the parents was eighth grade. Most of the informants' fathers worked in menial jobs in agriculture or construction. Roughly half of informants' mothers were employed at least seasonally, most in low paying agricultural jobs.

21. This pattern of disagreement was also observed in the first study (results reported in Chapter 3), though differences between spouses' estimates were less pronounced.

22. Jessie Bernard, *The Future of Marriage* (New York: World, 1972).

23. R. Nisbett and L. Ross, *Human Inference: Strategies and Shortcomings of Social Judgement* (Englewood Cliffs, NJ: Prentice-Hall, 1980).

24. S. C. Thompson and H. H. Kelley, "Judgement of Responsibility for Activities in Close Relationships," *Journal of Personality and Social Psychology* 41 (1981):469–477.

25. We followed Smith and Reid's "strict criteria" in computing which tasks were shared by taking the mean of husband's and wife's ratings. Scores in the 2.5 to 3.5 range (of a 1–5 scale) were considered to be shared. See Audrey Smith and William Reid, *Role-Sharing Marriage* (New York: Columbia University Press, 1986), pp. 72–74. Using the mean score for each couple corrects for bias from differential individual perception, but ignores the importance of gender differences in those perceptions.

26. Gary Becker, *A Treatise on the Family* (Cambridge, MA: Harvard University Press, 1981).

27. Heidi Hartmann, "The Family as the Locus of Gender, Class, and Political Struggle," *Signs* 6 (1981): 366–394.

28. Joseph Pleck, "The Work-Family Role System," *Social Problems* 24 (1977): 417–427.

29. Jane Hood, "The Provider Role: Its Meaning and Measurement," *Journal of Marriage and the Family* 48 (1986): 349–359.

30. See Jane Hood, *Becoming a Two-Job Family* (New York: Praeger, 1983); John Scanzoni, *Sex Roles, Women's Work, and Marital Conflict* (Washington, DC: Lexington, 1978).

31. See Hood, "The Provider Role."

32. Hood, "The Provider Role."

33. The mean total amount of time per week that couples spent in paid labor for the ambivalent group was 78 hours, and for the co-provider group was 87 hours.

34. Men's average annual income for full co-providers was $30,000, a full $9,000 less than for ambivalent co-provider husbands. Similarly, co-provider wive's incomes averaged $24,000, which was $6,000 less than for wives in the ambivalent co-provider couples. The average percentage income contribution from wives was similar in both groups: 43–44 percent.

35. Co-provider couples' mean scale score was 2.5, just inside the shared range. Main/secondary provider couples' mean score was 1.7. Main providers with failed aspirations' mean couple score was 2.2. Ambivalent co-provider couples' mean score was 1.9.

36. Hood, *Two-Job Family*, p. 131.

37. For a discussion for the ways that economies of gratitude are shaped by past events see Karen Pyke and Scott Coltrane, Entitlement, Obligation, and Gratitude in Remarriage (paper presented at the Annual Meeting of the Pacific Sociological Association, San Francisco, California, April 1995), and Karen Pyke, *Gender & Society* (1992).

38. Stacey, *Brave New Families*, p. 17.

39. Donna H. Berardo, Constance Shehan, and Gerald R. Leslie, "A Residue of Tradition: Jobs, Careers, and Spouses' Time in Housework," *Journal of Marriage and the Family* 49 (1987): 381–390; Catherine E. Ross, "The Division of Labor at Home," *Social Forces* 65 (1987): 816–833.

40. Zavella, *Women's Work;* Stacey, *Brave New Families*.

41. See, for example, Hochschild, *Second Shift;* Hood, *Two-Job Family*.

Chapter 5

1. Some of the findings in this chapter were presented in "Social Networks and Men's Family Roles," *Men's Studies Review,* vol. 8, no. 3, Summer 1991, pp. 8–15: "Birth Timing and the Division of Labor in Dual-Earner Families," *Journal of Family Issues,* vol. 11, no. 2, June 1990, pp. 157–181; and "Men's Housework: A Life Course Perspective," *Journal of Marriage and the Family,* vol. 54, no. 1, February 1992, pp. 43–57.

2. Erik H. Erikson, Identity and the Life Cycle, *Psychological Issues* 1 (1959).

3. Philip A. Cowan, "Becoming a Father: A Time of Change, An Opportunity for Development," in Phyllis Bronstein and Carolyn Cowan, *Fatherhood Today* (New York: Wiley, 1988); Alan J. Hawkins and Jay Belsky, "The Role of Father Involvement in Personality Change in Men Across the Transition to Parenthood," *Family Relations* 38 (1989): 378–384; Alan J. Hawkins, K. Sargernt, and E. Hill, "Rethinking Fathers' Involvement in Child Care," *Journal of Family Issues* 14 (1993): 531–549.

4. See, for example, Theodore F. Cohen, "What Do Fathers Provide?," pp. 1–22 in Jance C. Hood (ed.), *Men, Work, and Family* (Newbury Park, CA: Sage, 1993); Hawkins et al., "Rethinking Fathers' Involvement"; William Marsiglio, "Contemporary Scholarship on Fatherhood: Culture, Identity, and Conduct," *Journal of Family Issues* 14 (1993):

484–509; John Snarey, *How Fathers Care for the Next Generation* (Cambridge, MA: Harvard University Press, 1993).

5. For examples and a discussion of some possible psychoanalytic roots of this pattern, see Ehrensaft, *Parenting Together.*

6. For an early discussion of fatherhood modeling versus compensation, see Abraham Sagi, "Antecedents and Consequences of Various Degrees of Paternal Involvement in Child Rearing: The Israeli Project," in Michael Lamb (ed.), *Nontraditional Families: Parenting and Child Development* (Hillsdale, NJ: Erlbaum, 1982). For more elaborate syntheses of men's potential motivations for becoming involved parents, see Hawkins, "Rethinking Fathers' Involvement," and Marsiglio, "Scholarship on Fatherhood." For a discussion of how Canadian men lack explicit fatherhood models and blend divergent ones, see Kerry Daly, "Reshaping Fatherhood: Finding the Models," *Journal of Family Issues* 14 (1993): 510–530.

7. Samuel Osherson, *Finding Our Fathers: The Unfinished Business of Manhood* (New York: Free Press, 1986), p. 161.

8. Stone, *Family, Sex, and Marriage.*

9. Zelizer, *Pricing the Priceless Child,* Collins and Coltrane, *Sociology of Marriage and the Family.*

10. For a discussion of current trends in family life, see Collins and Coltrane, *Sociology of Marriage and the Family.*

11. Ehrensaft, *Parenting Together,* p. 157.

12. Mike Messner, " 'Changing Men' and Feminist Politics." See also R. W. Connell, "The Big Picture: Masculinities in Recent World History," *Theory and Society* 22 (1993): 597–624,

13. Bernard, "The Good Provider"; Mike Messner, " 'Changing Men' and Feminist Politics in the United States," *Theory and Society,* 22 (1993): 723–738, and Pirette Hondagneu-Sotelo and Mike Messner, "Gender Displays and Men's Power: The 'New Man' and the Mexican Immigrant Man." In J. Hood (ed.), *Men, Work, and Family* (Newbury Park, CA: Sage, 1994), pp. 200–218.

14. For example, see Melvin Kohn, *Class and Conformity* (Chicago: University of Chicago Press, 1977). See also Griswold, *Fatherhood,* and Eli Zaretsky, *Capitalism, The Family and Personal Life* (New York: Harper & Row, 1976).

15. Kohn, *Class and Conformity.*

16. Kohn, *Class and Conformity.*

17. The housework variable is derived from the card sorting procedures described in Chapter 3 and represents the mean of 5-point couple scores on 30 cooking, cleaning, and clothes care tasks. It excludes all direct child-care and household tasks conventionally performed by men such as home repair and yardwork. A mean score of 2.5 to 3.5 on the housework or child care variables is considered shared.

18. U.S. Bureau of the Census, *Current Population Reports,* Series P-20, No. 153, Households, Families, Marital Status and Living Arrangements (Washington, DC: U.S. Government Printing Office, 1986), Table 3.

19. U.S. Bureau of the Census, *Current Population Reports,* Series P-20, No. 461, Marital Status and Living Arrangements (Washington, DC: U.S. Government Printing Office, 1992).

20. U.S. Center for Health Statistics, *Vital Statistics of the United States, 1980, Vol. 1* (Washington, DC: U. S. Government Printing Office, 1984), Table 1-11.

21. U.S. Center for Health Statistics, *Vital Statistics, 1980,* Table 1-56.

22. Erving Goffman, *Encounters* (Indianapolis: Bobbs-Merrill, 1961), p. 89.

23. See, for example, Daniel Levinson, *The Seasons of a Man's Life* (New York: Alfred A. Knopf, 1978); R. L. Gould, *Transformations: Growth and Change in Adult Life* (New York: Simon & Schuster, 1978); G. E. Vaillant, *Adaptation to Life* (Boston: Little, Brown, 1977).

24. Vaillant, *Adaptation to Life,* p. 220.

25. M. W. Riley, M. Johnson, and A. Foner (eds.), *Aging and Society: A Sociology of Age Stratification* (New York: Russell Sage Foundation, 1972); Jeylan T. Mortimer and Roberta Simmons, "Adult Socialization," *Annual Review of Sociology* 4 (1978): 421–454; Bernice Neugarten (ed.), *Personality in Middle and Late Life* (New York: Atherton, 1964); Orville Brim, "Theories of Male Mid-Life Crisis," *The Counseling Psychologist* 6 (1976):2–9; Levinson, *Seasons;* Vaillant, *Adaptation to Life.*

26. Alice Rossi, "Life-Span Theories and Women's Lives," *Signs* 6 (1980): 1–31.

27. Ross D. Parke, Families in Life-Span Perspective: A Multilevel Developmental Approach, in E. Mavis Hetherington, R. Lerner, and M. Perlmutter (eds.), *Child Development in Lifespan Perspective* (Hillsdale, NJ: Erlbaum, 1988), pp. 151–190.

28. Valerie Kincaid Oppenheimer, "The Life-Cycle Squeeze: The Interaction of Men's Occupational and Family Life Cycles," *Demography* 11 (1974): 227–245; Harold Wilensky, "Family Life Cycle, Work, and the Quality of Life," in B. Gardell and G. Johansson (eds.), *Working Life* (London: Wiley, 1981), pp. 235–265.

29. K. A. May, "Factors Contributing to First-Time Fathers' Readiness for Fatherhood: An Exploratory Study," *Family Relations* 31 (1982): 353–361.

30. This finding is similar to those reported by Pamela Daniels and Kathy Weingarten, *Sooner or Later: The Timing of Parenthood in Adult Lives* (New York: Norton, 1982).

31. See also Carolyn A. Walter, *The Timing of Motherhood* (Lexington, MA: Lexington Books, 1986).

32. Elizabeth Bott, *Family and Social Network* (New York: Free Press, 1957]).

33. Randall Collins, *Conflict Sociology* (New York: Academic Press, 1975).

34. Bott, *Family and Social Network.*

35. Lydia Morris, "Local Social Networks and Domestic Organizations," *The Sociological Review* 33, (1985): 327–342.

36. Laura Lein, "Male Participation in Home Life," *Family Coordinator* 28 (1979): 489–495.

37. Bott, *Family and Social Network;* C. Feiring and D. Coates, "Social Networks and Gender Differences in Life Space of Opportunity," *Sex Roles* 17 (1987): 611–620; M. D. Hill, "Class, Kinship Density, and Conjugal Role Segregation," *Journal of Marriage and the Family* 50 (1988):731–741; Lein, "Male Participation"; L. H. Rogler and M. E. Procidano, "The Effect of Social Networks on Marital Roles," *Journal of Marriage and the Family* 48 (1986): 693–701; Carol Stack, *All Our Kin* (New York: Harper & Row, 1974).

38. Bott, *Family and Social Network;* Alice Rossi and Peter Rossi, *Of Human Bonding: Parent-Child Relations Across the Life Course* (Chicago: Aldine de Gruyter, 1990); Barry Wellman, "Domestic Work, Paid Work, and Net Work," in Steve Duck and Daniel Perlman (eds.), *Understanding Personal Relationships* (London: Sage, 1985), pp. 159–191; Barry Wellman, "The Place of Kinfolk in Community Networks," *Marriage and Family*

Review 15 (1990): 195–228; Beverly Wellman and Barry Wellman, "Domestic Affairs and Network Relations," *Journal of Social and Personal Relationships* 9 (1992).

39. Mark Granovetter, *Getting a Job* (Cambridge: Harvard University Press, 1974); Lydia Morris, "Local Social Networks"; Lynn Smith-Lovin and J. Miller McPherson, "You Are Who You Know: A Network Approach to Gender," in Paula England (ed.), *Theory on Gender, Feminism on Theory* (New York: Aldine de Gruyter, 1993), pp. 223–251.

40. Lein, "Male Participation," p. 491.

41. Bott, *Family and Social Network.*

42. Wellman and Wellman, "Domestic Affairs."

43. Hill, "Conjugal Role Segregation"; David Riley, "Network Influences on Father Involvement in Childrearing," in M. Cochran, M. Larner, D. Riley, L. Gunnarsson, and C. R. Henderson (eds.), *Extending Families* (Cambridge: Cambridge University Press, 1990).

44. Nadine F. Marks and Sara S. McLanahan, *Brave New Families and Their Kin: Who Gives and Who Gets?* (Paper presented at the Annual Meeting of the American Sociological Association, Pittsburgh, August 1992).

45. Riley, "Network Influences."

46. B. J. Hirsch, "Social Networks and the Coping Process: Creating Personal Communities," in B. H. Gottlieb (ed.), *Social Networks and Social Support* (Beverly Hills, CA: Sage, 1981); Sara S. McLanahan, N. V. Wedemeyer, and T. Adelberg, "Network Structure, Social Support, and Psychological Well-Being in the Single-Parent Family," *Journal of Marriage and the Family* 43 (1981): 601–612.

47. See, for example, Robert K. Merton and Alice Rossi, "Contributions to the Theory of Reference Group Behavior," in Paul Lazarsfeld (ed.), *Continuities in Social Research* (Glencoe: Free Press, 1950), pp. 40–105; Thomas F. Pettigrew, "Social Evaluation Theory," in D. Levine (ed.), *Nebraska Symposium on Motivation* (Lincoln: University of Nebraska Press, 1967), pp. 241–311; C. D. Gartrell, "Network Approaches to Social Evaluation," *Annual Review of Sociology* 13, (1987): 49–66.

48. D. Prentice and F. Crosby, "The Importance of Context for Assessing Deservingness," in J. Masters and W. Smith (eds.), *Social Comparison, Social Justice, and Relative Deprivation* (Hillsdale, NJ: Erlbaum, 1987), pp. 165–182.

49. Sandra Stanley, Janet Hunt, and Larry Hunt, "The Relative Deprivation of Husbands in Dual-Earner Households," *Journal of Family Issues* 7 (1986), p. 3. For a discussion of how women make comparisons about family work, see "Linda Thompson, Family Work: Women's Sense of Fairness," *Journal of Family Issues* 12 (1991), pp. 181–196.

50. For a similar finding, see David Steinberg, *Fatherjournal: Five Years of Awakening in Fatherhood* (Santa Cruz, CA: Times Change Press, 1977).

51. Patricia Bourne and Norma Wikler, "Commitment and the Cultural Mandate," *Social Problems* 25 (1978): 430–440.

52. Pleck, "Family Supportive Employer Policies."

53. Stanley, Hunt, and Hunt, "Relative Deprivation."

Chapter 6

1. Some of the findings in this chapter were presented in "Remarriage, Stepparenting and Household Labor," *Journal of Family Issues,* vol. 13, no. 2 (June 1992), pp. 43–57;

"Predicting the Sharing of Household Labor: Are Parenting and Housework Distinct?" *Sociological Perspectives,* vol. 35, no. 4 (Winter 1992), pp. 629–648; and "Men's Housework: A Life Course Perspective," *Journal of Marriage and the Family,* vol. 54, no. 1, February 1992, pp. 43–57.

2. I base my discussion of human capital theory on Becker, Treatise (1981). I am indebted to Berk, *Gender Factory;* England and Farkas, *Households, Labor, Employment;* and Ferree, "Beyond Separate Spheres"; for their critique of human capital theory, and to Peterson and Gerson, "Determinants of Responsibility," for their succinct formulation of contrasts between human capital theory and social-structural theories.

3. Becker draws on the findings and controversial interpretations of sociobiologists such as E. O. Wilson, *Sociobiology* (Cambridge, MA: Harvard University Press, 1975), as well as the "biosocial" arguments of the sociologist Alice Rossi (ed.), *Gender and the Life Course* (New York: Aldine, 1977), to argue that women have intrinsic comparative advantage in child care and household labor. Becker's theory does not exclude the possibility of gender discrimination in the job market leading to differences in efficiency at various tasks, but he presupposes an initial segregation of household and market labor on the basis of biological sex.

4. I am referring to numerous individual theories under the label of social-structural theory, many of which have differences in emphasis or predictions. For example, see Fenstermaker Berk, *Gender Factory;* England and Farkas, *Households, Employment Gender;* Ferree, "Beyond Separate Spheres"; Peterson and Gerson, "Determinants of Responsibility."

5. Berk, *Gender Factory;* Coverman, "Explaining Husbands' Participation"; Peterson and Gerson, "Determinants of Responsibility."

6. Peterson and Gerson, "Determinants of Responsibility."

7. Yoshinori Kamo, "Determinants of Household Labor: Resources, Power, and Ideology," *Journal of Family Issues* 9 (1988): 177–200; Joseph Pleck, "Husband's Paid Work and Family Roles," in H. Lopata and J. Pleck (eds.), *Research in the Interweave of Social Roles* (Greenwich, CONN: Jai Press, 1983), pp. 251–333; Glenna Spitze, "Women's Employment and Family Relations: A Review," *Journal of Marriage and the Family* 50 (1988): 595–618.

8. The theories providing the basis for this approach are many and varied, but for early influential formulations, see Robert O. Blood and Donald M. Wolfe, *Husbands and Wives* (New York: Free Press, 1960); Peter M. Blau, *Exchange and Power in Social Life* (New York: Wiley, 1964); Dair L. Gillespie, "Who Has the Power? The Marital Struggle," *Journal of Marriage and the Family* 33 (1971): 445–458; and John Scanzoni, *Opportunity and the Family* (New York: Free Press, 1970).

9. See, for example, Rae Lesser Blumberg and Marion T. Coleman, "A Theoretical Look at the Gender Balance of Power in the American Couple," *Journal of Family Issues* 10 (1989): 225–250; Heidi Hartmann, "The Family as the Locus of Gender, Class, and Political Struggle," *Signs* 6 (1981): 366–394; Nancy Hartsock, *Money, Sex, and Power* (London: Longman, 1983).

10. S. Model, "Housework by Husbands: Determinants and Implications," *Journal of Family Issues* 2 (1981): 225–237; Catherine E. Ross, "The Division of Labor at Home," *Social Forces* 65 (1987): 816–833.

11. D. H. Berardo, C. L. Shehan and G. R. Leslie, "A Residue of Tradition: Jobs, Careers, and Spouses' Time in Housework," *Journal of Marriage and the Family* 49 (1987): 381–390.

12. For a discussion of the various ways that class position is determined in status-equal and status-discrepant marriages, see Randall Collins, "Women and Men in the Class Structure," *Journal of Family Issues* 9 (1988): 27–50.

13. E. Maret and B. Finlay, "The Distribution of Household Labor Among Women in Dual-Earner Families, *Journal of Marriage and the Family* 46 (1984): 357–364; Spitze, "Women's Employment."

14. George Farkas, "Education, Wage Rates, and the Division of Labor Between Husband and Wife," *Journal of Marriage and the Family* 38 (1976): 473–483; Joan Huber and Glenna Spitze, *Sex Stratification: Children, Housework, and Jobs* (New York: Academic Press, 1983).

15. Arlie Hochschild with Anne Machung, *The Second Shift* (New York: Viking, 1989). See also Karen Pyke, "Women's Employment as a Gift or Burden? Marital Power Across Marriage, Divorce, and Remarriage," *Gender & Society* 7 (1993); Maxine Atkinson and Jacqueline Boles, "WASP (Wives as Senior Partners)," *Journal of Marriage and the Family* 46 (1984): 861–870.

16. See Karen Pyke and Scott Coltrane, "Entitlement, Obligation, and Gratitude in Remarriage." Paper presented at the annual meeting of the Pacific Sociological Association, San Francisco, April 1995.

17. Shelley Coverman, "Explaining Husbands' Participation in Domestic Labor," *Sociological Quarterly* 26 (1985): 81–97.

18. Berardo et al., "Residue of Tradition"; Huber and Spitze, "Sex Stratification"; Kamo, "Determinants"; Joanne Miller and Howard Garrison, "Sex Roles: The Division of Labor at Home and in the Workplace," *Annual Review of Sociology* 8 (1984): 237–262; Ross, "Labor at Home."

19. Using the term "traditional" is misleading, insofar as tradtions are constantly undergoing change and what is now called traditional was not widely practised in peasant or other traditional societies as defined by anthropologists and historians. Using traditional to define typical contemporary gender behaviors also tends to essentialize or even glorify relations of dominance, and encourages the labeling of egalitarian relations as deviant. In addition, reifying "sex roles" or "gender roles" with a role theoretic paradigm carries some political and epistemological dangers. See, for example, Connell, "Gender and Power"; Marie Osmond and Barrie Thorne, "Feminist Theories: The Social Construction of Gender in Families and Society," in *Sourcebook of Family Theories and Methods,* Pauline Boss, William Doherty, Ralph La Rossa, Walter Schumm, and Suzanne Steinmetz (eds.), (New York: Plenum, 1992).

20. Dana Vannoy Hiller and William Philliber, "The Division of Labor in Contemporary Marriage: Expectations Perceptions and Performance," *Social Problems* 33 (1986): 191–201; Kamo, "Determinants; Model, Housework by Husbands"; Carolyn Perucci, H. R. Potter, and D. L. Rhoads, "Determinants of Male Family-Role Performance," *Psychology of Women Quarterly* 3 (1978): 53–66.

21. Pleck, "Husbands' Roles," p. 275.

22. Michael Geerken and Walter Gove, *At Home and at Work* (Beverly Hills, CA: Sage, 1983); Ann Crouter, Maureen Perry-Jenkins, Ted Huston, and Susan McHale,

"Processes Underlying Father Involvement in Dual-Earner and Single-Earner Families," *Developmental Psychology* 23 (1987): 431–440; Coverman, "Explaining Husbands' Participation."

23. Linda Thompson and Alexis J. Walker, "Gender in Families: Women and Men in Marriage, Work, and Parenthood," *Journal of Marriage and the Family* 51 (1989), p. 857.

24. See, for example, Hiller and Philliber, "The Division of Labor"; Huber and Spitze, *Sex Stratification;* Kamo, "Determinants"; Ross, "Division of Labor."

25. Constance Hardesty and J. Bokemeier, "Finding Time and Making Do: Distribution of Household Labor in Non-Metropolitan Marriages," *Journal of Marriage and the Family* 51 (1989): 253–267; Maximilliane Szinovacz, "Changing Family Roles and Interactions," in Beth Hess and Marvin Sussman (eds.), *Women and the Family: Two Decades of Change* (New York: Haworth, 1984), pp. 164–201.

26. See, for example, Gary S. Becker, *A Treatise on the Family* (Cambridge, MA: Harvard University Press, 1981); Geerken and Gove, *At Home and at Work.*

27. For example, see England and Farkas, *Households, Employment Gender;* Spitze, *Household Labor.*

28. K. D. Fox and S. Y. Nickols, "The Time Crunch: Wife's Employment and Family Work," *Journal of Family Issues* 4 (1983): 61–82; Spitze, "Women's Employment"; K. E. Walker and M. E. Woods, *Time Use: A Measure of Household Production of Family Goods and Services* (Washington, DC: American Home Economics Association, 1976).

29. Rosalind Barnett and Grace Baruch, "Determinants of Fathers' Participation in Family Work," *Journal of Marriage and the Family* 49 (1987): 29–40; Coverman, "Explaining Husbands' Participation"; Hardesty and Bokemeier, "Finding Time."

30. Barnett and Baruch, "Fathers' Participation"; Geerken and Gove, *At Home and at Work;* Joseph H. Pleck, *Working Wives/Working Husbands* (Beverly Hills: Sage, 1985); Spitze, Women's Employment.

31. Barnett and Baruch, "Fathers' Participation"; Geerken and Gove, *At Home and at Work.*

32. England and Farkas, *Households, Employment, Gender;* Richard Peterson and Kathleen Gerson, "Determinants of Responsibility for Child Care Arrangements Among Dual-Earner Couples," *Journal of Marriage and the Family* 54 (1992): 527–536; Thompson and Walker, "Gender in Families," p. 856.

33. Jacqueline Goodnow, "Children's Household Work," *Psychological Bulletin* 103 (1988): 5–26.

34. Sarah Fenstermaker Berk, *The Gender Factory* (New York: Plenum, 1985); Richard Berk and Sarah Fenstermaker Berk, *Labor and Leisure at Home: Content and Organization of the Household Day* (Beverly Hills, CA: Sage, 1979); Coverman, "Explaining Husbands' Participation"; Farkas, "Education, Wage Rates"; Geerken and Gove, *At Home and at Work;* Frances K. Goldscheider and Linda Waite, *New Families, No Families? The Transformation of the American Home* (Berkeley: University of California Press, 1991); Pleck, *Working Wives/Working Husbands.*

35. Samson L. Blair and Daniel T. Lichter, "Measuring the Division of Labor: Gender Segregation of Housework among American Couples," *Journal of Marriage and the Family* 49 (1991): 91–113; Cynthia Rexroat and Constance Shehan, "The Family Life Cycle and Spouse's Time in Housework," *Journal of Marriage and the Family* 49 (1987): 737–750; Perrucci et al., "Male Family Role Performance."

36. Sweet, Bumpass, and Call, *National Survey of Families and Households.* This survey was conducted in 1987–88 by the Center for Demography and Ecology at the University of Wisconsin, Madison. Fieldwork was conducted by the Institute of Survey Research at Temple University. The main sample for the survey is a national, multi-stage area probability sample drawn from 100 sampling regions in the conterminous United States. The main sample includes over 9,000 households, with over 3,000 additional households selected to represent under-studied groups such as single parents, minority groups, and nonmarried couples who are living together (cohabitors). These groups were over-sampled in order to obtain enough households to make valid statistical comparisons between groups, but by weighting the overall results to reflect the distribution of the original main sample the randomness and representativeness of the sample are main-tained. This is extremely important, because only with a random sample of U.S. families and households can we be reasonably sure that the results we discover reflect what is going on in households across America. The NSFH is the most detailed national survey of families ever conducted in the United States, and contains a wealth of information on a wide variety of topics, including employment, marital relations, child-rearing patterns, and divisions of household labor. The sample is a good cross section of the country's households, representing the diversity in family and household types that we now take for granted. The average age for adult main respondents was 43 years old. Over half of the households did not have children under 18 living in the home, and under two-thirds were currently married. Blacks and other minority groups made up 20 percent of the sample. Most respondents were employed and most had at least a high school education, with just under one in five holding a college degree. Adult respondents were asked (among many other questions) to estimate the average time they spent on nine individual household tasks in a week, including preparing meals, washing dishes, cleaning house, shopping, washing and ironing, paying bills, driving, outdoor tasks, and auto maintenance. See also Beth Anne Shelton, *Women, Men, and Time: Gender Differences in Paid Work, Housework, and Leisure* (New York: Greenwood, 1992).

37. Shelton, *Women, Men, Time,* p. 97.

38. Shelton, *Women, Men, Time,* p. 104. Shelton rightly pointed out that this differential influence reflects the societal notion that women and men ought to do different kinds of work associated with children. Nevertheless, it is also helpful to view these increases within the context of an already unequal division of labor in most of these households. That is, a two-hour increase in men's domestic labor time represents an increase of 9 percent in the amount of time they spend in household labor. Similarly, married women's increase represents a percentage increase of 11 percent, only slightly higher than that for men.

39. Shelton, *Women, Men, Time,* p. 69.

40. Shelton, *Women, Men, Time.*

41. Men's percentage of housework includes the five items from the NSFH conven-tionally performed by wives: preparing meals; washing dishes and meal cleanup; shopping; washing and ironing clothes; and cleaning house. Wives and husbands made independent estimates of the number of hours per week that they and their spouse spent in these five activities. I guarded against potential inconsistency problems and minimized reporting biases by computing mean scores on each task for husbands and wives using both spouses' reports. Mean scores for each spouse were then summed

to compute the total hours spent on each activity for each couple and the husband's mean score was divided by the couple total to yield the husbands' proportional contribution. Although one husband did 99 percent of the housework, only one in 20 husbands did as much housework as their wives. A third contributed less than 10 percent of the time devoted to housework, with the average contribution from husbands about nine hours per week, representing 19 percent of the total hours devoted to the five housework tasks.

42. If a child under 5 was living in the home, the main respondent in the NSFH was asked: "About how many hours in a typical day do you spend taking care of this child's physical needs, including feeding, bathing, dressing, and putting (him/her) to bed?" I label this measure "child care" below, even though it does not include care given to older children. In my sample, for households with children, the mean child age was six, with an average of 2.2 children per household. See Sweet, Bumpass, and Call, *National Survey of Families and Households,* and note 48 for a discussion of "Focal Child."

43. Relative resources were measured by the wife's percentage of family earnings. Wives without paid employment were included in a zero earning category. Average family income was just under $40,000 per year and the average contribution of wives to the household income was 23 percent. Time availability was measured by employment hours for both husbands and wives, and, in order to refine the measure further, if the respondent's paid work hours during the reporting week were unusual (15 percent of sample), I substituted the respondent's estimate of the *usual* number of employed hours per week. Non-employed respondents were included in a zero-hour category. The mean number of hours worked for husbands was 41 hours per week, and for wives, 19 hours per week.

Gender and family ideology was assessed separately for wives' and husbands' with five survey items constituting an additive index. Respondents were asked how much they agreed or disagreed with the statements (1) "It is much better for everyone if the man earns the main living and the woman takes care of the home and family," (2) "Preschool children are likely to suffer if their mother is employed," and how much they approved or disapproved of (3) "Mothers who work full-time when their youngest child is under age 5," (4) "Mothers who work part-time when their youngest child is under age 5," and (5) Children under 3 years old being cared for all day in a day-care center." Higher scores on this composite measure indicate more traditional or conservative attitudes toward gender and family roles, and lower scores indicate more liberal or progressive attitudes.

44. For reviews, see Thompson and Walker, "Gender in Families"; Ferree, "Beyond Separate Spheres."

45. In the NSFH, a "focal child" was randomly selected from the roster of household members, and the main respondent was asked questions about this child. Since the analysis relies on information about direct child care, and these questions were only asked of respondents whose focal child was under five years old, the available sample was reduced to 640 households. Because of random selection techniques, this smaller sample is also representative of married couple households with preschool children in the United States. Main respondents were asked to estimate the number of hours spent in direct child care (feeding, bathing, dressing, putting child to bed, or meeting other physical needs) for themselves and their spouses. Since about half of the main

respondents were men (53%) and half women (47%), the potential for systematic gender bias is reduced. Housework estimates are means of both spouses' estimates for self and other. See Sweet, Bumpass, and Call, *National Survey of Families and Households.*

46. Hiller and Philliber, "Division of Labor"; Huber and Spitze, "Sex Stratification"; Ross, "Labor at Home."

47. Aafke Komter, "Hidden Power in Marriage", *Gender & Society* 3 (1989): 187–216; Szinovacz, "Changing Family Roles."

48. Ehrensaft, *Parenting Together;* Lamb, *Role of the Father;* LaRossa and LaRossa, *Transition.*

49. Hardesty and Bokemeier, "Finding Time."

50. This subsample of the NSFH with preschool children is similar to the larger sample of married couples, but these parents of preschoolers were somewhat younger than the others and tended to earn less than the average for all couples. The typical couple in this subsample had two children, with the younger child under two years old. These are exactly the couples that human capital theory predicts will segregate household labor the most, because wives are assumed to cut back on employment and concentrate their efforts on baby care and housework, whereas husbands are assumed to increase their time on paid work and decrease their time on family work. In the couples of this subsample, wives contributed a slightly greater share of the family income than in the full sample (26 percent vs. 23 percent), and husbands tended to contribute more hours and a greater percentage of time devoted to the five housework tasks (21 percent versus 19 percent). Men's proportionate contributions to direct child care were slightly higher than their proportionate contributions to housework, averaging 26 percent of the total hours spent by the two parents. These differences suggest less labor specialization among families with younger children, rather than more, as predicted by human capital theory. Nevertheless, as suggested by both social-structural theory and human capital theory, mothers of young children were putting in three or four hours on housework and child care to every hour contributed by their husbands, and husbands were putting in three hours to every hour contributed by their wives in paid employment.

51. This type of sampling and statistical analysis cannot tell us whether child care or housework comes first, but it does confirm that the two are integrally connected. The significant association between the two is consistent with the idea that the performance of either direct child care or housework places men in the home for more hours and encourages them to take responsibility for the other form of family work. My assumption is that fathers who do child care end up doing more housework.

52. Using a statistical modeling technique that allows for multiple simultaneous effects, the influences of all variables were considered simultaneously. Masako Ishii-Kuntz and I used LISREL VII [K. G. Joreskog, "A General Method for Estimating a Linear Structural Equation System," in A. S. Goldberger and O. D. Duncan, eds., *Structural Equation Models in the Social Sciences* (New York: Seminar, 1973); K. G. Joreskog and D. Sorbom, *LISREL VI Users' Guide.* Mooresville, IN: Scientific Software, 1986)] to analyze the non-recursive model. This type of analysis (covariance structure modeling) allows the simultaneous specification of a measurement model linking latent variables to indicators and a structural equation model stating the causal relationships among latent variables. The specification and estimation issues of this model have been

extensively discussed by Joreskog, "General Method"; K. G. Joreskog and D. Sorbom, "Statistical Models and Methods for the Analysis of Longitudinal Data," in D. J. Aigner and A. S. Goldberger (eds.), *Latent Variables in Socioeconomic Models* (Amsterdam: North-Holland, 1977); J. Scott Long, *Covariance Structure Models: An Introduction to LISREL* (Quantitative Applications in the Social Sciences, Series No. 07-034, Beverly Hills: Sage, 1983); B. Wheaton, "Assessment of Fit in Overidentified Models with Latent Variables," in J. S. Long (ed.), *Common Problems/Proper Solutions: Avoiding Error in Quantitative Research* (Newbury Park: Sage, 1988), pp. 193–225.

53. Wendy Baldwin and Christine Nord, "Delayed Childbearing in the U.S.: Facts and Fictions," *Population Bulletin* 39 (1984): 1–37.

54. Age 25, see Baldwin and Nord, "Delayed Childbearing"; Age 28, see M. W. Roosa, "The Effect of Age in the Transition to Parenthood: Are Delayed Childbearers a Unique Group?," *Family Relations,* 37 (1988): 322–327; Age 30, see Sandra L. Hofferth, "Long-term Economic Consequences for Women of Delayed Childbearing and Reduced Family Size," *Demography* 21 (1984): 141–155.

55. Baldwin and Nord, "Delayed Childbearing"; David E. Bloom, "Putting off Children," *American Demographics,* 6 (1984): 30–33, 45; Larry L. Bumpass, Ronald R. Rindfuss, and R. B. Janosik, "Age and Marital Status at First Birth and the Pace of Subsequent Fertility," *Journal of Marriage and the Family,* 40 (1978): 75–86. Thomas J. Espenshade, *Investing in Children: New Estimates of Parental Expenditures* (Washington, DC: Urban Institute Press, 1984); Hofferth, "Long-term Economic Consequences"; Ronald R. Rindfuss, S. Philip Morgan, and Gray Swicegood, *First Births in America* (Berkeley: University of California Press, 1988); A. Vanden Heuvel, "The Timing of Parenthood and Intergenerational Relations," *Journal of Marriage and the Family* 50 (1988): 483–491.

56. Theodore Greenstein, "Human Capital Marital and Birth Timing, and the Postnatal Labor Force Participation of Married Women," *Journal of Family Issues* 10 (1989): 359–382.

57. Karen O. Mason, *Women's Labor Force Participation and Fertility* (Research Triangle Park, NC: Research Triangle Institute, 1974).

58. Linda J. Waite, Frances K. Goldscheider, and C. Witsberger, "Nonfamily Living and the Erosion of Traditional Family Orientations Among Young Adults," *American Sociological Review* 51 (1986): 541–554.

59. K. May, "Factors Contributing to First-time Fathers' Readiness for Fatherhood: An Exploratory Study," *Family Relations,* 31 (1982): 353–361.

60. The subsample used for this analysis contained the 1,087 two-parent households in the NSFH who were in their first marriage, with natural children under the age of 18 living in the home, with data available from both main respondent and secondary respondent. By using the cutoff age of 28, men who became parents the first time when they were 27 or younger were classified as "early" and those 28 or older are classified as "delayed." As a subsample of the NSFH, these couples are representative of U.S. households. In the "average" couple, both husband and wife had high school diplomas, and they had their first child when the husband was 25 and the wife 23. Most had two or more children at the time of the interview, and had been married for over a decade. Eight out of ten husbands were employed full time, with a majority of wives also employed, but many working part-time. Men made an average of five times more

per year than their wives, and median combined couple earnings in 1987 were $32,500.

The primary method of data analysis used to test the proposed relationships between causal variables and household labor for early and delayed parents is the covariance structure model, sometimes referred to as the LISREL model. Using an unobserved variable specification of the relationship between exogenous variables and men's house-work results in three distinct analytical advantages: (1) It is possible to conceive of housework and traditional values as unobserved constructs with multiple indicators. Housework, in particular, is considered a latent construct of gender equity. That is, unlike some previous research, we are concerned not only with who does the mundane and routine housework but, more important, with how gender inequity is routinely perpetuated in the household. By using a latent construct, we address the underlying and wider concept of gender equity in the household domain. (2) The true relationship between exogenous variables and men's housework can be estimated after taking into account random error in the measures. For example, unless we can assume that the measurements for gender/family ideology tap the same concepts between two subsam-ples, we are not certain whether the effect of ideology on men's sharing housework is due to measurement difference or to the effects of ideology. (3) When doing simultaneous analysis of various subgroups, that is, early and delayed parents, comparisons of different models can be made easily. See Coltrane and Ishii-Kuntz, "Men's Housework."

61. Early-timed husband's mean contribution to the five housework tasks was 18 percent of the household total compared to a mean contribution of 21 percent from delayed husbands. The difference in men's proportionate contribution was primarily the result of wives in late-timed families doing less. Wives of early-timed husbands performed an average of 40 hours of housework per week, significantly more than the 33 hours performed by wives of delayed husbands.

62. This survey item asked for the extent of agreement/disagreement with the idea that housework should be shared if both spouses are employed full time. As expected, this item was strongly correlated with measures of the division of household labor. We did not include this item in our family/gender ideology scale, as some others have done, because I worried about the causal ordering of the variables. That is, I thought that many people who were already sharing housework would answer that housework should be shared, whereas those sharing little would justify their current arrangements by indicating that they disagreed that housework would be shared. We chose to include items for the ideology measure that were less likely to be self-justifications about existing patterns of housework (i.e., attitudes toward employment and the use of outside child care).

63. Larry L. Bumpass, "What's Happening to the Family: Interactions Between Demographic and Institutional Change," *Demography* 27 (1990): 483–498.

64. Marion Coleman and Lawrence Ganong, "Remarriage and Stepfamily Research in the 1980s: Increased Interest in an Old Family Form," *Journal of Marriage and the Family,* 52 (1990): 925–940.

65. Paul Glick, "Remarried Families, Stepfamilies, and Step-children — A Brief Demographic Analysis," *Family Relations* 38 (1989): 24–27.

66. H. Wineberg, "Childbearing After Marriage," *Journal of Marriage and the Family,* 52 (1990): 31–38.

67. Coleman and Ganong, "Remarriage and Stepfamily Research"; Lawrence Ganong and Marion Coleman, "Effects of Remarriage on Children: A Review of the Empirical Literature," *Family Relations,* 33 (1984): 389–406; K. Pasley and Marilyn Ihinger-Tallman (eds.), *Remarriage and Stepparenting* (New York: Guilford, 1987).

68. Andrew Cherlin, "Remarriage as an Incomplete Institution," *American Journal of Sociology* 86 (1978): 634–650.

69. G. Clingempeel, "Quasi-kin Relationships and Marital Quality," *Journal of Personality and Social Psychology,* 41 (1981): 890–901. Lynn White and Alan Booth, "The Quality and Stability of Remarriages: The Role of Stepchildren," *American Sociological Review,* 50 (1985): 689–698; Lynn White, Alan Booth, and John Edwards, "Children and Marital Happiness," *Journal of Family Issues,* 7 (1986): 131–147; Lynn White, David Brinkerhoff, and Alan Booth, "The Effect of Marital Disruption on Child's Attachment to Parents," *Journal of Family Issues,* 6 (1985): 5–22.

70. E. Vermer, M. Coleman, L. Ganong, and H. Cooper, "Marital Satisfaction in Remarriage," *Journal of Marriage and the Family* 51 (1989): 713–725; Coleman and Ganong, "Remarriage and Stepfamily Research"; Masako Ishii-Kuntz and Marilyn Ihinger-Tallman, "The Subjective Well-being of Parents," *Journal of Family Issues,* 12 (1991): 58–68.

71. See Ishii-Kuntz and Coltrane, "Remarriage, Stepparenting, and Household Labor."

72. Goldschieder and Waite, *New Families, No Families* (Berkeley, University of California Press, 1991).

Chapter 7

1. Some of the findings in this chapter were presented in "Father-Child Relationships and the Status of Women: A Cross-Cultural Study," *American Journal of Sociology,* Vol. 93, No. 5 (March 1988), pp. 1060–1095; and "The Micropolitics of Gender in Nonindustrial Societies," *Gender & Society* 6 (1992): 86–107. These studies, in turn, were based on the research of many scholars as noted throughout the chapter.

2. Margaret Mead, *Sex and Temperament in Three Primitive Societies* (New York: William Morrow and Company, 1963; originally published 1935); and *Male and Female* (New York: William Morrow and Company, 1949).

3. Margaret Mead, *Blackberry Winter* (New York: Simon and Schuster, 1972). See also Peggy Reeves Sanday, "Margaret Mead's Views of Sex Roles in Her Own and Other Societies," *American Anthropologist* 82 (1980): 340–348.

4. Ruth Benedict, *Patterns of Culture* (Boston: Houghton Mifflin, 1934).

5. Mead, *Sex and Temperament,* p. 280.

6. See, among others, Peggy Reeves Sanday and Ruth Gallagher Goodenough (eds.), *Beyond the Second Sex: New Directions in the Anthropology of Gender* (Philadelphia: University of Pennsylvannia Press, 1990); and Candace West and Donald Zimmerman, "Doing Gender," *Gender & Society* 1 (1987): 125–151.

7. For a critique of male bias in the natural and social sciences, see Ruth Bleier (ed.), *Science and Gender* (New York: Pergamon, 1984); Donna Haraway, "Animal Sociology and a Natural Economy of the Body Politic." *Signs* 4 (1978): 21–54; Sandra Harding, *The Science Question in Feminism* (Ithaca, NY: Cornell University Press, 1986);

Shulamit Reinharz (ed.), *Feminist Methods in Social Research* (New York: Oxford University Press, 1992); for background arguments, see Thomas Kuhn, *The Structure of Scientific Revolutions* (Chicago: University of Chicago Press, 1970). Margaret Mead, as well as some modern feminist scholars, have also been criticized by some for selectively using non-Western societies to argue about issues that have little relevance to indigenous peoples. For example, see Ifi Amadiume, *Male Daughters, Female Husbands: Gender and Sex in an African Society* (London: Zed Books, 1987).

8. Derek Freeman, *Margaret Mead and Samoa: The Making and Unmaking of an Anthropological Myth* (Cambridge, MA: Harvard University Press, 1983).

9. See especially Mead, *Male and Female.*

10. Preface to 1950 edition of *Sex and Temperament;* see also Sanday, "Margaret Mead's Views," note 2, p. 340.

11. For a more complete description of the samples used in this chapter, see "Father-Child Relationships and The Micro-Politics of Gender." See also Martin K. Whyte, *The Status of Women in Preindustrial Societies* (Princeton, NJ: Princeton University Press, 1988). The societies used in the two studies summarized here are all non-industrial, but they range from small nonliterate hunting and gathering bands to peasant communities within complex agrarian societies. Most of the societies were relatively small in scale with about half representing autonomous communities with populations of under 1,500. About half of the societies had limited state structures, as in the case of a paramount chief ruling over a number of local communities. Most also had class or caste distinctions, hereditary slavery, or important status differences based on the possession or distribution of wealth. About one-third of the societies had relatively undeveloped resource bases — that is, subsistence economies primarily reliant on gathering, hunting, or fishing. The remaining societies had more developed resource bases with primary reliance on various forms of agriculture or animal husbandry. While trade was common to most of the societies, the goods that were exchanged typically contributed only marginally to the overall subsistence needs of the people.

12. See, for example, Daniel Amneus, *Back to Patriarchy* (New York: Arlington House, 1979); Steven Goldberg, *The Inevitability of Patriarchy* (New York: William Morrow, 1973); George Gilder, *Sexual Suicide* (New York: Quadrangle, 1973).

13. For reviews see Coltrane, "Micropolitics," Coltrane, "Father-Child Relationships"; Janet Chafetz, *Sex and Advantage* (Totowa, NJ: Rowman & Allanheld,1984); and Randall Collins, Janet Chafetz, Rae Lesser Blumberg, Scott Coltrane, and Jonathan Turner, "Toward an Integrated Theory of Gender Stratification," *Sociological Perspectives* (1994).

14. For examples of ethnographies, see Marilyn Gelber, *Gender and Society in the New Guinea Highlands* (Boulder, CO: Westview, 1986); Gilbert Herdt, *Guardians of the Flutes: Idioms of Masculinity* (New York: McGraw-Hill, 1981); Richard Randolph, David Schneider, and Mary Diaz (eds.), *Dialectics and Gender: Anthropological Approaches* (Boulder, CO: Westview, 1988); Marilyn Strathern (ed.), *Dealing with Inequality: Analyzing Gender Relations in Melanesia and Beyond* (Cambridge: Cambridge University Press, 1987); Sherry Ortner and Harriet Whitehead, *Sexual Meanings* (Cambridge: Cambridge University Press, 1981).

For discussions of the concept of male dominance in nonindustrial societies, and its cross-cultural variation, see Ernestine Friedl, *Women and Men: An Anthropologists View*

(New York: Holt, Rinehart, and Winston, 1975); Eleanor Leacock, *Myths of Male Dominance* (New York: Monthly Review Press, 1981); Peggy Reeves Sanday, *Female Power and Male Dominance* (Cambridge: Cambridge University Press, 1981); Alice Schlegel, *Male Dominance and Female Autonomy* (New Haven, CT: HRAF, 1972); Sharon Tiffany, *Women, Work, and Motherhood* (Englewood Cliffs, NJ: Prentice-Hall, 1982); Martin King Whyte, *The Status of Women in Nonindustrial Societies* (Princeton, NJ: Princeton University Press, 1978).

15. For descriptions of the Mundurucu, see Yolanda Murphy and Robert Murphy, *Women of the Forest* (New York: Columbia University Press, 1985); Robert F. Murphy, *Headhunter's Heritage* (Berkeley: University of California Press, 1960); Peggy Reeves Sanday, *Female Power and Male Dominance* (Cambridge, England: Cambridge University Press, 1981).

16. Murphy and Murphy, *Women of the Forest*, p. 121.

17. Orna Johnson and Allen Johnson, "Oedipus in the Political Economy: Theme and Variations in Amazonia," in Randolph, Schneider, and Diaz, *Dialectics and Gender*.

18. Martin King Whyte, *The Status of Women in Preindustrial Societies* (Princeton, NJ: Princeton University Press, 1978). For a modern example of an egalitarian society, see Maria Lepowsky, "Gender in an Egalitarian Society: A Case Study from the Coral Sea," in Peggy Sanday and Ruth Goodenough (eds.), *Beyond the Second Sex* (Philadelphia: University of Pennsylvannia Press, 1990). Lepowsky describes the sexually egalitarian Vanatinai who live on a large island 225 miles southeast of mainland New Guinea. As with the contrast between the sex segregated Mundurucu and the more egalitarian Machiguenga of the Amazon region, the Vanatinai live close to some of the most male-dominant and gender antagonistic societies ever described by anthropologists. Among the Vanatinai, there is no ethic of male dominance, no organized rituals of male separation or initiation, and no belief in female pollution. People value the activities of men and women equally, and considerable overlap exists in what they do. Even in traditional exchange relationships and in the influential mortuary ritual context, women are able to gain personal prestige and exercise authority over others. If they earn the respect of others, women as well as men may be referred to as strong, wise, or generous (see Sanday and Goodenough, Introductory note, *Beyond the Second Sex*, p. 169).

19. For descriptions of hypermasculinity in the New Guinea Highlands, see Herdt, *Guardians of the Flutes*, and Gelber, *Gender and Society in New Guinea*.

20. Robert Levy, *Tahitians: Mind and Experience in the Society Islands* (Chicago: University of Chicago Press, 1973), p. 235.

21. David Gilmore, *Manhood in the Making: Cultural Conceptions of Masculinity* (New Haven: Yale University Press, 1990).

22. John Whiting and Beatrice Whiting, "Aloofness and Intimacy of Husbands and Wives," *Ethos* 3 (1975): 183–207.

23. Mead, *Male and Female*, p. 191.

24. Mead, *Male and Female*, p. 159–160.

25. Mead, *Male and Female*. See also Bruno Bettleheim, *Symbolic Wounds: Puberty Rites and the Envious Male* (New York: Free Press, 1954). Michelle Rosaldo, Sherry Ortner, Mary O'Brien, Nancy Chodorow, Dorothy Dinnerstein, Isaac Balbus, Jessica Benjamin, Evelyn Fox Keller, Brian Eslea, Miriam Johnson, and other scholars have written about men's feelings of exclusion as related to the psychodynamics of childrearing. For

discussions of men's ritual attempts to be part of the birth process (as in couvade), see Roger Burton and John Whiting, "The Absent Father and Cross-Sex Identity," *Merrill-Palmer Quarterly* 7 (1961): 85–95; Herdt, "Guardians"; Robert Munroe and Ruth Munroe, *Psychological Interpretation of Male Initiation Rites: The Case of Male Pregnancy Symptoms," Ethos* 1 (1973): 490–498; Robert Munroe, Ruth Munroe, and John Whiting, "Male Sex Role Resolutions," in Robert Munroe, Ruth Munroe, and John Whiting (eds.), *Handbook of Cross-Cultural Human Development* (New York: Garland, 1981).

Most of these discussions are dependent on Freudian theoretical models, wherein men are responding to a deeply submerged ambivalence toward their own mothers. Since infants are completely dependent on mothers, both boy and girl infants experience the mother as omnipotent, and eventually come to symbolically internalize the mother in the normal process of development. As girls develop their own sense of self, they can stay attached to the mother and those parts of themselves that are mother-like. Boys, in contrast, must reject both mother and the feminine self within, if they are to establish a masculine identity. Some psychoanalytic theorists, like Chodorow and Dinnerstein, see boys' identification with the father and repudiation of the mother in personal intrapsychic terms, whereas other postulate a more positional identification see Philip Slater, "Toward a Dualistic Theory of Identification," *Merrill-Palmer Quarterly* 7 (1961), pp. 113–126. John and Beatrice Whiting, for instance, conceptualize the boys' identification with the father as reflecting a desire to possess power as exercised by men in the society. There are important differences between "phallocentric" and "gynocentric" accounts of the process of gender identity formation and men's insecurity. Phallocentric theories tend to focus on the father and inequities in the institution of marriage (see Miriam Johnson, *Strong Mothers, Weak Wives* (Berkeley: University of California Press, 1988), whereas gynocentric accounts tend to focus on the mother and the importance of childrearing during the preoedipal period (Chodorow, Dinnerstein, Balbus).

26. Sanday, *Female Power*, p. 245.

27. Miriam Johnson, *Strong Mothers, Weak Wives* (Berkeley: University of California Press, 1988), p. 225.

28. To capture the type and extent of father-child contact among the societies in this study, I relied on three general numeric measures. The first item was originally coded as physical proximity between father and young children (see Herbert Barry and Lenore Paxson, "Infancy and Early Childhood: Cross-Cultural Codes," *Ethnology* 10 (1971): 466–505). After a review of the source materials, Katz and Konner noted that the Barry and Paxson scale "is a global measure of the father-child relationship in terms of both emotional warmth and physical proximity" ["The Role of the Father: An Anthropological Perspective," in M. Lamb (ed.), *The Role of the Father in Child Development* (New York: Wiley, 1981), p. 172]. The full measure has five different levels ranging from no close proximity to regular, close relationship or companionship. I used these father–child closeness ratings for infancy (roughly 0–24 months) and early childhood (roughly 2–5 years) because both periods are theoretically important for identity formation and social learning.

I wanted to make sure that this measure was not just measuring the tendency of fathers to sleep or work near children, so I turned to two additional measures that had been constructed for these societies. Anthropologists Ronald and Evelyn Rohner reviewed ethnographies to code the societies on two additional dimensions of parenting: routine care and emotional warmth or expressiveness. A seven-point routine childcare measure represents the extent to which fathers assumed significant responsibility for regular care, supervision, and discipline of children aged 3 to 6. Unfortunately, many ethnographers did not record information about men's (or women's) involvement in such tasks, so many societies have missing data for this measure. The other measure is a seven-point paternal affection scale that represents the extent to which the father–child relationship is characterized by emotional warmth. Instead of focusing on routine or obligatory care, this measure reflects spontaneous physical and verbal expressions of warmth and affection. The three father–child measures are significantly but only moderately correlated with each other, indicating a tendency for proximate fathers to be emotionally warm and involved in routine child care, but allowing for mixed patterns such as close-by fathers who are rarely affectionate.

29. Barry S. Hewlett, *Intimate Fathers: The Nature and Context of Aka Pygmy Paternal Infant Care* (Ann Arbor: University of Michigan Press, 1991).

30. Colin Turnbull, *The Forest People* (New York: Simon & Schuster, 1961).

31. Colin Turnbull, *The Human Cycle* (New York: Simon & Schuster, 1983), p. 40.

32. William Lancaster, *The Rwala Bedouin Today* (New York: Cambridge University Press, 1981). For a discussion of the spatial aspects of gender segregation, and their impacts on access to information and the maintenance of male dominance, see Daphne Spain, *Gendered Spaces* (Chapel Hill: University of North Carolina Press, 1992).

33. Some note that the exclusion and protection of women among the Rwala and some other groups in the Middle East or Northern Africa provides them with a measure of autonomy and power See Ifi Amandiume, *Male Daughters, Female Husbands: Gender and Sex in an African Society* (London: Zed Books Ltd., 1987); and Lancaster, *Rwala Beduoin*]. Authority can be exercised through segregated systems of power and prestige, but in most such instances, including the Rwala, women remain subservient to men in marital relations and community decision-making. It is not that women are without power in such societies, for men typically must have wives in order to exercise public authority themselves, and women have ways of shaming or undermining men's authority. Nevertheless, women's public status is indirect and an ideology of male superiority is maintained. While I acknowledge women's exercise of influence in all societies, in this analysis I am concerned with the overt sharing of public status and power between men and women.

34. Lancaster, *Rwala Bedouin*, pg. 67.

35. Katz and Konner, *Role of Father*, pp. 170–171; Lancaster, *Rwala Beduoin*. For a discussion of the political purposes of public circumcision rituals see Karen Paige and Jeffrey Paige, *The Politics of Reproductive Ritual* (Berkeley: University of California Press, 1981).

36. I use the term father–child relationship to describe the relationship between a significant male figure and children. This figure is usually, but not necessarily, the biological father of the child.

37. See Mead, *Male and Female*; Beatrice Whiting, "Sex Identity Conflict and Physical Violence," *American Anthropologist* 67 (1965): 123–140; John and Beatrice Whiting, "Aloofness and Intimacy of Husbands and Wives," *Ethos* 3 (1975): 183–207; Slater, *Glory of Hera*; Chodorow, *Reproduction of Mothering*; Dinnerstein, *Mermaid and Minotaur*; Isaac Balbus, *Marxism and Domination* (Princeton, NJ: Princeton University Press, 1982);

Brian Easlea, *Science and Sexual Oppression* (London: Weidenfeld & Nicolson, 1981); Jeff Hearn, *The Gender of Oppression* (Brighton: Wheatsheaf, 1987).

38. Burton and Whiting, "The Absent Father"; Herdt, "Guardians"; Munroe and Munroe, "Male Initiation Rites"; and Munroe, Munroe, and Whiting, "Male Sex Resolutions."

39. As suggested by some materialist theories, women's lack of control over property (including limited opportunities to inherit wealth, own dwellings, or use the fruits of productive labor) was also associated with men displaying more belligerence and bravado. This finding suggests that men's macho displays often confirm and reinforce existing property relations rather than compensating for a lack of control over valued resources. Men in societies engaged in frequent warfare were also more likely to be preoccupied with boastful and antagonistic displays than those in societies where warfare was rare. Finally, in societies that were more complex, as evidenced by factors like population density, technological development, and political integration, there was less emphasis placed on men displaying strength, aggression, and sexual prowess.

40. Another important issue, however, is whether it is the specific contribution of fathers that makes a difference, or whether something else about childrearing patterns might account for the fact that women exercise public power. For instance, there is a general association between style of childrearing and fathers' closeness to children. Societies with indulgent patterns of childrearing, like the African pygmies, tend to include fathers in the routine aspects of children's upbringing. Not only do mothers have frequent and prolonged nurturing contact with children, but father–child interactions also tend to be warm and affectionate. In contrast, societies with less indulgent childrearing customs, like the Rwala Bedouins, tend to have harsh and distant father–child relationships. To investigate the possibility that overall lenience in childrearing might account for the associations that I was attributing to nurturing from fathers, I added a measure of child indulgence (Barry and Paxson, "Infancy and Early Childhood," col. 16b.). This five-point parenting practices scale ranged from consistently lenient and indulgent to persistently harsh, severe, and punishing. Adding this variable into the statistical analysis did not predict higher status for women and did not change the relationship between fathering and women's power.

41. Edward E. Evans-Pritchard, *The Position of Women in Primitive Societies and Other Essays in Social Anthropology* (New York: Free Press, 1965).

42. Janet Chafetz, *Sex and Advantage* (Totowa, NJ: Rowman & Allanheld, 1984); Leacock, *Myths of Male Dominance;* Michelle Rosaldo, "The Use and Abuse of Anthropology," *Signs* 5 (1980): 389–417; Marc Howard Ross, Female Political Participation, *American Anthropologist* 88 (1986): 843–858; *Whyte, Status of Women.*

43. Sanday, *Female Power*, p. 21.

44. Sanday, *Female Power*, p. 21.

45. E. E. Evans-Pritchard. "The Zande State," in E. E. Evans-Pritchard (ed.), *The Position of Women in Primitive Societies and Other Essays in Social Anthropology* (New York: Free Press, 1965).

46. Evans-Pritchard, "Zande State," p. 129.

47. See Marc Howard Ross, "Political Decision Making and Conflict," *Ethnology* 22 (1983): 169–192; Ross, "Female Political Participation." The measure I used for women's access to leadership in this analysis was originally labeled "gender differences

in political or quasi-political positions" and refers to the extent to which official leadership positions were open to, and actually held by, both women and men.

48. It should be noted that some societies have separate female organizations or positions, and in some societies women exercise authority in exclusive or private decision-making, rather than in more public arenas. Women's exclusion from public decisions and offices does not necessarily mean that they have no power, and it is important to acknowledge women's resistance to male dominance, even in gender-segregated societies. In those societies where the "public" world of men is sharply divided from the "private" world of women, there are various ways for women to exert some influence, especially in the "feminine" sphere of domestic activities. It is incorrect to label these societies as completely male dominated, because even when women are subservient to men, as among the Azande or the Mundurucu, mothers and wives are able to assert some privilege or control, usually based on notions of complementarity between male and female realms. Nevertheless, women in these societies typically must resort to exercising power through the men in their families, and so are constrained in their ability to exercise direct influence over matters of concern to the entire society.

49. For the analysis of women's office holding and participation in community decision-making, a variable measuring women's percent contribution to subsistence was used because there was no direct measure of women's control over the distribution of resources (see Coltrane, "Father-child Relationships"). In some hunting and gathering societies, women contribute as much as 80 percent of the food supply [Herbert Barry and Alice Schlegel, "Cross-Cultural Codes on Contributions by Women to Subsistence," *Ehtnology* 21 (1982): 165–188. 1982]. In about a quarter of societies, women contribute more to subsistence than the men, and in most societies women make significant subsistence contributions. Some theories suggest that when women contribute more to the production of food, they will have more say over important community decisions and be able to exercise public power (Sanday, *Female Power*). In my analyses, entering women's percent contribution to subsistence into the statistical regression equations did not significantly influence the ability to predict women's public status. Like other researchers, I found that the amount of work that women do toward survival does not necessarily guarantee them a say over collective decisions. In fact, in some societies, women do virtually all the daily productive labor, but enjoy little control over the fruits of that labor. Other researchers have suggested that women's status is lowest when they make either very large contributions to subsistence, or when they make only minor contributions (Blumberg, *General Theory*). I coded this variable to see if women's middle-level subsistence contributions might be associated with higher public status for women, but found no significant relationships. The simple fact of women's participation in productive labor does not necessarily increase their public status. Control over the distribution of resources, rather than simple participation in their production, is the determining factor in materialist conceptions of gender inequality (Blumberg, "General Theory"; Chafetz, *Sex and Advantage;* Leacock, "Myths of Male Dominance"; Sacks, *Sisters and Wives*). Culturally specific political and economic structures, along with typically male-dominated prestige systems and ideologies, mediate between production of resources and the exercise of control over them.

Many theories of women's status in nonindustrial societies combine economic factors with some of these cultural and institutional factors. In general, it appears that men's authority over women is legitimated and perpetuated through male-dominated descent systems and residence patterns as noted above, but other marriage institutions are also important. Some focus on how marriage practices like bridewealth (a payment of wealth for a woman at marriage) or brideservice (a payment of labor) act as a way for men to control and exchange women (See Claude Levi-Strauss, *The Elementary Structures of Kinship* (Boston: Beacon, 1969); Rubin, "The Traffic in Women"; Sherry Ortner and Harriet Whitehead, "Introduction: Accounting for Sexual Meanings," in Sherry Ortner and Harriet Whitehead (eds.), *Sexual Meanings: The Cultural Construction of Gender and Sexuality* (Cambridge, England: Cambridge University Press, 1981), pp. 1–27; Jane Collier and Michelle Rosaldo, "Politics in Simple Societies," in Sherry Ortner and Harriet Whitehead (eds.), *Sexual Meanings: The Cultural Construction of Gender and Sexuality* (Cambridge, England: Cambridge University Press, 1981), pp. 275–329). Although bridewealth and brideservice societies differ from one another in important ways, they both represent the treatment of women as valuable property exchanged through marriage. In this analysis, the presence of bridewealth or brideservice was used as a control, but was not significantly associated with less public authority for women. As with the other measures of male-controlled social structure, including patrilineality or patrilocality, the presence or absence of bridewealth service did not significantly change the association between close father–child relationships and higher public status for women.

50. I focused my analyses on the ability to share leadership and decision-making with men because the direct exercise of power entails a different type of authority than that exercised as a wife or daughter. It is this more public and assertive authority that is also of concern to women in modern industrial settings. When I constructed a measure of overall decision-making for the entire sample of societies that counted women's ability to influence decisions in private, such as within the family, along with women's participation in more public decisions, the measure was also significantly associated with father–child relationships. Women's influence on important matters, regardless of where this influence is exercised, is linked to fathers' participation in childrearing. Nevertheless, women's exercise of more public forms of power or authority are more strongly associated with men's involvement in early childhood socialization.

51. Nonmaternal care: Barry and Paxson, "Infancy and Early Childhood," col. 13b; Nonparental care: Ronald Rohner and Evelyn Rohner, "Parental Acceptance-Rejection and Parental Control," *Ethnology* 20 (1981): 245–260; and Ronald Rohner and Evelyn Rohner, "Enculturative Continuity and the Importance of Caregivers," *Behaviour Science Research* 17 (1982): 91–114.

52. Robert Bly, *Iron John: A Book About Men* (Reading, MA: Addison-Wesley, 1990). See also Robert Bly, "Men's Initiation Rites," *Utne Reader* (April-May, 1986).

53. Jerry Adler, "Drums, Sweat and Tears," *Newsweek:* (June 24, 1991).

54. Bly, *Iron John,* pp. 2–3.

55. Bly, *Iron John,* p. 46.

56. Bly, *Iron John,* p. 63.

57. Bly, *Iron John,* p. 165.

58. R. W. Connell, "Drumming up the Wrong Tree," *Tikkun* 7 (1993): 34.

59. Bly, *Iron John,* p. 55.

60. Bly, *Iron John,* p. 60.

61. Bly, *Iron John,* p. 175.

62. Gayle Rubin, "The Traffic in Women: Notes on the Political Economy of Sex," in R. Reiter (ed.), *Toward an Anthropology of Women* (New York: Monthly Review Press, 1974).

63. Doris Entwisle, Karl Alexander, and Linda Steffel Olson, "The Gender Gap in Math: Its Possible Origins in Neighborhood Effects," *American Sociological Review* 59 (1994): 822–838.

64. Connell, Drumming, p. 33.

65. Mark Carnes and Clyde Griffen (eds.), *Meanings for Manhood: Constructions of Masculinity in Victorian America* (Chicago: University of Chicago Press, 1990); Jeffery Hantover, "The Boy Scouts and the Validation of Masculinity," in Michael Kimmel and Michael Messner (eds.), *Men's Lives* (New York: Macmillan, 1989); Carl Degler, *At Odds: Women and the Family in America from the Revolution to the Present,* (New York: Oxford University Press, 1980); Michael Kimmel, "The Contemporary 'Crisis' of Masculinity," in Harry Brod (ed.), *The Making of Masculinities* (Boston: Unwin Hyman, 1987), pp. 121–154.

66. See Kimmel, "Crisis of Masculinity"; Rupert Wilkinson, *American Tough* (New York: Harper & Row, 1984); Robert Bellah, Richard Madsen, William Sullivan, Ann Swidler, and Steven Tipton, *Habits of the Heart* (New York: Harper & Row, 1985).

67. Scott Coltrane and Kenneth Allan, " 'New' Fathers and Old Stereotypes: Representations of Masculinity in 1980s Television Advertising," *masculinities* 2 (1994): 43–66.

68. For a recent example of an attempt to reclaim and celebrate traditional fatherhood, see David Blankenhorn, *Fatherless America* (New York: Basic, 1995). For an example of recreating ancient images of gender equality, see Riane Eisler, *The Chalice and the Blade;* for a discussion of the limited amount of change in media images of masculinity, see Coltrane and Allan, "New Fathers and Old Stereotypes."

Chapter 8

1. For a summary of factors related to women's psychological distress and well-being, see John Mirowsky, and Catherine E. Ross, *Social Causes of Psychological Distress* (New York: Aldine de Gruyter, 1989). In general, if women want help with family work and receive it, they have higher marital satisfaction and lower levels of depresssion. For examples of recent findings confirming this pattern, see Jay Belsky, H. J. Ward, and M. Levine, "Prenatal Expectations, Postnatal Experiences and the Transition to Parenthood," in R. Ashmore and D. Brodinsky (eds.), *Perspectives on the Family* (Hillsdale, NJ: Erlbaum, 1986), pp. 111–146; Carolyn Cowan and Phillip Cowan, *When Parents Become Partners* (New York: Basic Books, 1992); Susan McHale and Ann Crouter, "You Can't Always Get What You Want: Incongruence Between Sex-Role Attitudes and Family Work Roles and Its Implications for Marriage," *Journal of Marriage and the Family* 54 (1992): 538–547.

2. Ross D. Parke, "Fathers and Families," in M. Bornstein (ed.), *Handbook of Parenting* (Hillsdale, NJ: Erlbaum, in press).

3. For recent summaries of research on fathers' impacts on child development, see Henry B. Biller, *Fathers and Families: Paternal Factors in Child Development* (Westport, CT: Auburn House, 1993); and Parke, "Fathers and Families." Using a national survey sample, Amato found that "Regardless of the quality of the mother-child relationship,

the closer children were to their fathers, the happier, more satisfied, and less distressed they reported being" (p. 1039) Paul R. Amato, "Father-Child Relations, Mother-Child Relations, and Offspring Psychological Well-Being in Early Adulthood," *Journal of Marriage and the Family* 56 (1994): 1031–1042.

4. This claim is based on two theoretical approaches briefly summarized in earlier chapters. For a recent summary of a social constructionist and ethnomethodological approach to gender, see Candace West and Sarah Fenstermaker, "Power, Inequality and the Accomplishment of Gender," in Paula England (ed.), *Theory on Gender/Feminism on Theory* (New York: Aldine de Gruyter, 1993), pp. 151–174. For a recent summary of psychoanalytic approaches, see Christine L. Williams, "Psychoanalytic Theory and the Sociology of Gender," in England, *Theory on Gender,* pp. 131–149.

5. For supporting theoretical formulations based on different (but related) models of social change, see Janet Chafetz, *Gender Equity: An Integrated Theory of Stability and Change* (Newbury Park, CA: Sage, 1990); Nancy Chodorow, *The Reproduction of Mothering* (Berkeley: University of California Press, 1978); Nancy Hartsock, *Money, Sex, and Power* (London: Longman, 1983), and the references in note 4.

6. Linda Thompson and Alexis J. Walker, "Gender in Families," *Journal of Marriage and the Family* 51 (1989): 845–871, p. 858.

7. Joseph Pleck, *Working Wives/Working Husbands* (Beverly Hills, CA: Sage, 1985).

8. Unless otherwise noted, trends reported in this discussion are from an analysis of multiple national random sample surveys as summarized by Arland Thornton, "Changing Attitudes Toward Family Issues in the United States," *Journal of Marriage and the Family* 51 (1989): 873–893.

9. Duane F. Alwin, "From Obedience to Autonomy: Changes in Traits Desired in Children, 1924–1978," *Public Opinion Quarterly* 52 (1988): 33–52.

10. Thorton, "Changing Attitudes," p. 875.

11. Jill Grigsby, "Women Change Places," *American Demographics* 14 (November 1992): 48.

12. Grigsby, "Women Change," p. 49.

13. Thornton, "Changing Attitudes," Table 1B, p. 876.

14. Thornton, "Changing Attitudes," Table 1A, p. 876.

15. Anne Machung, "Talking Career, Thinking Job," *Feminist Studies* 15 (1989): 35–58.

16. M. M. Marini and E. Greenberger, "Sex Differences in Occupational Aspirations and Expectations," *Sociology of Work and Occupations,* 5: 147–178.

17. H. S. Farmer, "Career and Homemaking Plans for High School Youth," *Journal of Counseling Psychology,* 30 (1983): 40–45; Katherine Dennehy and Jeylan Mortimer, *Work and Family Orientations of Contemporary Adolescent Boys and Girls in a Context of Social Change,* Paper presented at the 87th Annual Meeting of the American Sociological Association, Pittsburgh, Pennsylvania (August 1992), p. 9.

18. Dennehy and Mortimer, *Work and Family,* p. 16; C. K. Tittle, *Careers and Family: Sex Roles and Adolescent Life Plans* (Beverly Hills, CA: Sage, 1981).

19. Dennehy and Mortimer, *Work and Family,* p. 17.

20. Ronald R. Rindfuss, E. C. Cookey, and R. L. Sutterlin, "Young Adult Occupational Achievement: Early Expectations Versus Behavioral Reality," cited in Dennehey and Mortimer, *Work and Family,* p. 24.

21. Kathleen Gerson, *Hard Choices: How Women Decide About Work, Career, and Motherhood* (Berkeley: University of California Press, 1985), and *No Man's Land: Men's Changing Commitments to Family and Work* (New York: Basic Books, 1993).

22. See, for example, the studies reviewed in Joseph Pleck, "Husbands' Paid Work and Family Roles," in Helena Lopata and Joseph Pleck (eds.), *Research in the Interweave of Social Roles*, Vol. 3 (Greenwich, CT: JAI Press, 1983), and Michael Lamb and Abraham Sagi (eds.), *Fatherhood and Family Policy* (Hillsdale, NJ: Erlbaum, 1983).

23. Theodore Cohen, "Remaking Men," *Journal of Family Issues*, 8 (1987): 57–77; Ralph LaRossa, "Fatherhood and Social Change," *Family Relations* 34 (1988): 451–457.

24. Jessie Bernard, "The Rise and Fall of the Good Provider Role," *American Psychologist* 36 (1981): 1–12.

25. Robert A. Fein, "Research on Fathering: Social Policy and an Emergent Perspective," *Journal of Social Issues* 34 (1978): 122–135, and Ralph LaRossa, "Fatherhood and Social Change," *Family Relations* 37 (1988): 451–457.

26. Family researchers have only recently discovered that interest in fathering has fluctuated for over a century and that symbolism about fatherhood has alternated between providing and nurturing. Images have also alternated between congratulatory and demeaning. See Maxinne Atkinson and Stephen Blackwelder, "Fathering in the 20th Century," *Journal of Marriage and the Family* 55 (1993): 975–986; Scott Coltrane and Kenneth Allan, " 'New' Fathers and Old Stereotypes: Representations of Masculinity in 1980s Television Advertising," *masculinities* (in press); Frank Furstenberg, "Good Dads—Bad Dads: Two Faces of Fatherhood," in Andrew Cherlin (ed.), *The Changing American Family* (New York: Urban Institute, 1988), pp. 193–218; and Pirette Hondagneu-Sotelo, and Michael Messner, "Gender Displays and Men's Power: The "New Man" and the Mexican Immigrant Man," in Jane C. Hood (ed.), *Men, Work, and Family* (Newbury Park, CA: Sage, 1994), pp. 200–218.

27. Coltrane and Allan, " 'New' Fathers"; Scott Coltrane and Ken Allan, *Homemakers and Breadwinners Revisited: Changing Images of Fathers in Television Commercials*, Paper presented at the Annual Meeting of the Pacific Sociological Association Annual Meetings (Portland, April, 1993).

28. For arguments about cultural images exceeding behaviors, see Ralph LaRossa, "Fatherhood and Social Change," *Family Relations* 37 (1988): 451–457; and Charlie Lewis and Margaret O'Brien (eds.), *Reassessing Fatherhood* (London: Sage, 1987). For evidence that cultural images of "new" fathers may not be so new, see Coltrane and Allan, " 'New' Fathers," and Griswold, *Fatherhood in America*.

29. See, for example, Richard Easterlin, *Birth and Fortune: The Impact of Numbers on Personal Welfare* (New York: Basic Books, 1980).

30. About 95 percent of U.S. men and women between the ages of 45 and 54 have been married at least once. Dennis A. Ahlburg and Carol J. De Vita, "New Realities of the American Family," *Population Bulletin* 47 (August 1992), p. 12.

31. U.S. Bureau of the Census, *Current Population Reports*, Series P23-180, Marriage, Divorce, and Remarriage in the 1990s (Washington, DC: U.S. Government Printing Office, 1992).

32. By 1992 the median age at first marriage for men was 26.5 and for women was 24.4, the highest levels recorded since the federal government began keeping such

statistics in the late 1800s. U.S. Bureau of the Census, *Current Population Reports.* P20-468, 1992, p. vii.

33. Constance Sorrentino, "The Changing Family in International Perspective," *Monthly Labor Review* 113, No. 3 (March 1990): 43.

34. James R. Wetzel, "American Families: 75 Years of Change," *Monthly Labor Review* 113 (1990): 4–13.

35. In 1930, the age gap between husbands and wives was 3.0 years; in 1950 it was 2.5 years; in 1970 it was 2.4 years; and in 1990 it was 2.2 years. U.S. Bureau of the Census, *Current Population Reports.* P20-461, 1992. By 1992, the median age at first marriage for men had dropped to 2.1 years older than that of women. U.S. Bureau of the Census, *Current Population Reports.* P20-468, 1992.

36. Candace West and Bonnie Iritani, *The Male Older Norm.* Unpublished manuscript, University of California, Santa Cruz.

37. Andrew Cherlin, *Marriage, Divorce, Remarriage* (Cambridge, MA: Harvard University Press, 1981).

38. Arthur Norton and Jeanne Moorman, "Current Trends in Marriage and Divorce Among American Women." *Journal of Marriage and the Family* 49 (1987): 3–14.

39. U.S. Bureau of the Census, *Current Population Reports.* P20-468, 1992, p. 5.

40. U. S. National Center for Health Statistics, *Monthly Vital Statistics Report,* vol. 40, no. 4, Supplement, DHHS Pub NO. (PHS) 91-1120 (Hyattsville, MD: Public Health Service, 1991).

41. Not only do men remarry more frequently than women, but different groups of women also show different remarriage rates. About two-thirds of divorced white women remarry, whereas about half of divorced black or Hispanic women do so. *Family Planning Perspectives,* Vol. 187 (May/June1986), pp. 134–135; and Dennis A. Ahlburg and Carol J. De Vita, "New Realities of the American Family," *Population Bulletin* 47, No. 2. (August 1992), p. 17.

42. Since the timing of marriage and divorce influence the likelihood of remarriage, and because we are not certain about rates of remarriage for women over 50, it is difficult to make precise projections about future remarriage rates. Some continue to claim that near-term levels of remarriage will hover around three-fourths, whereas others predict that the rate will be closer to two-thirds. See Larry Bumpass, James Sweet, and Teresa Castro Martin, "Changing Patterns of Remarriage," *Journal of Marriage and the Family* 52 (1990): 747–756; U.S. Bureau of the Census, *Current Population Reports,* Series P23-180, Marriage, Divorce, and Remarriage in the 1990s (Washington, DC: U.S. Government Printing Office, 1992), p. 5.

43. Thomas J. Espenshade, "Marriage Trends in America," *Population and Development Review* 11 No. 2 (June 1985): 193–245.

44. U.S. Bureau of the Census, *Current Population Reports,* Series P-23, No. 176. Studies in American Fertility. Late Expectations: Childbearing Patterns of American Women for the 1990s (1991), p. 9.

45. U.S. Bureau of the Census, *Current Population Reports Series* P-23, No. 162. Studies in Marriage and the Family (1989), p. 6.

46. U.S. Bureau of the Census, *Current Population Reports Series* P-23, No. 162. Studies In Marriage and the Family. (1989), p. 14.

47. In 1980, ten percent of single-parent households were headed by men, but by 1988, the number had doubled, so that they constituted 13 percent of the total. U.S. Bureau of the Census, *Current Population Reports Series* P-23, No. 162. Studies in Marriage and the Family, (1989), Table C, p. 16. A major reason for the increase in single-father households was the transformation of post-divorce child custody laws. See Scott Coltrane and Neal Hickman, "The Rhetoric of Rights and Needs: Moral Discourse in the Reform of Child Custody and Child Support Laws," *Social Problems* 19 (1992): 401–420.

48. Larry Bumpass, "What's Happening to the Family? Interactions Between Demographic and Institutional Change," *Demography* 27 (1990), p. 485.

49. Although the proportion of African-American children who live in single-parent households exceeds that of all other race/ethnic groups, almost two-thirds of all U.S. children living with one parent are white. Larry Bumpass and James Sweet, "Children's Experiences in Single-Parent Families," *Family Planning Perspectives* 21 (1989): 256–260.

50. In 1960, fewer than 20 percent of first births in the United States were to women 25 years of age or older, but by 1985, the figure had climbed to over 41 percent. In other words, women were twice as likely to wait until their mid-twenties to become parents in the 1980s as they were in the 1960s. In the late 1970s, fewer than one in five births in the United states were to women over 30, but, by 1990, one out of three births were to women in this age group. Birth rates for specific groups of women in the later child bearing ages (e.g., 30–34 years, 35–39 years, and 40–44 years) have all increased significantly since 1980. U.S. Bureau of the Census, *Current Population Reports,* Series P-20, No. 454, Fertility of American Women (1991), p. 12.

51. Ronald Rindfuss, S. Philip Morgan, and C. Gray Swicegood, *First Births in America* (Berkeley: University of California Press, 1984).

52. Rindfuss et al., *First Births;* U.S. Census, Late Expectations, p. 13.

53. In the 1980s, older expectant mothers (and those with more education) were likely to work longer into their first pregnancy, were less likely to quit or be fired from their jobs, and were more likely to receive maternity benefits during pregnancy than younger expectant mothers. For those having their first child during the years 1981–85, about twice as many younger mothers (age 18–22) quit their jobs as older mothers (age 25 +). Regardless of when they had children however, mothers in the 1980s were likely to return to work by the time their babies were three months old.U.S. Bureau of the Census, *Current Population Reports,* Series P-23, No. 165, Work and Family Patterns of American Women, 1990, p. 19.

54. In 1960, only about a third of women over the age of 16 were in the paid labor force, but by the late 1980s, more than half of all women over age 16 were employed. U.S. Census, Work and Family Patterns, p. 13.

55. When the Census Bureau first began collecting data on working mothers in 1976, they found that 31 percent of women who had a child in the last year were in the paid labor force. That figure rose each year, so that by 1980, 38 percent of women 18 to 44 years old with infants under a year were employed. By 1990 (the most recent year for which these statistics are available), 53 percent of mothers with children under one year old were in the labor force. U.S. Bureau of the Census, *Current Population Reports,* Series P-20, No. 454, Fertility of American Women, 1991, p. 4. For college graduates,

the maternal employment rate rose even more sharply, from 44 percent in 1980 to 68 percent in 1990. U. S. Census, Work and Family Patterns, p. 17.

56. For those women who gave birth to their first child in the early 1960s, only 44 percent were employed at any point during their pregnancy. In contrast, two-thirds of those giving birth for the first time in the 1980s were employed during their pregnancy, and 80–90 percent of those were working full time. Older and more highly educated women in the 1980s were not only more likely to keep their jobs when pregnant, but were also more likely to work longer into their pregnancies than their younger and unmarried counterparts from the 1960s. In the early 1960s, when less than one-half of women worked during their pregnancy, almost two-thirds quit their jobs before their first birth. Things had changed by the 1980s, when only about a quarter of women reported quitting their jobs altogether as the result of having a baby. In the earlier period, less than a third of the mothers reported some kind of maternity leave, mostly unpaid. In the early 80s, in contrast, over two-thirds of first-time mothers used some form of leave, with two-thirds of those reporting paid leave (maternity, paid, or sick leave). U.S. Census, Work and Family Patterns.

57. Economic need is the most important factor motivating women to return to work so soon after having a first child. Although pre-birth choices about staying employed during pregnancy are strongly influenced by one's job skills and educational attainment, women at all educational levels are about equally likely to return to work after giving birth. U. S. Census, Work and Family Patterns, pp. 22–24.

58. Over 70 percent of women who had a first birth in the 1980s returned to work within six months if they had received maternity benefits during or after their pregnancy. U. S. Census, Work and Family Patterns, p. 11.

59. Paula England and Irene Browne, "Trends in Women's Economic Status," *Sociological Perspectives* 35 (1992): 17–51; Jennifer Glass, Marta Tienda, and Shelly A. Smith, "The Impact of Changing Employment Opportunity on Gender and Ethnic Earnings Inequality," *Social Science Research* 17 (1988): 252–276.

60. Valerie Kincade Oppenheimer, *The Female Labor Force in the United States: Demographic and Economic Factors Governing its Growth and Changing Composition* (Berkeley: Institute of International Studies, University of California, 1970), cited in England and Browne, "Trends," p. 22.

61. Rapid entry of women into specific jobs has not always increased the relative position of women because it has often been accompanied by a de-skilling and decrease in those jobs' wages relative to other occupations. For professions like medicine and law, training programs now accept and graduate more women than ever before, but the overwhelming majority of doctors and lawyers are still men, and the higher status sub-specialties (i.e., surgery and corporate law) remain largely male dominated. Barbara F. Reskin and Patricia A. Roos, *Job Queues, Gender Queues: Explaining Women's Inroads into Male Occupations* (Philadelphia: Temple University Press, 1990). Jerry Jacobs, *Revolving Doors: Sex Segregation and Women's Careers* (Stanford: Stanford University Press, 1989).

62. Eighty percent of all working women are still employed in 20 of the 420 occupations listed by the Department of Labor. See Barbara Ehrenreich and Frances Fox Piven, "The Feminization of Poverty," *Dissent* 31 (1984): 162–170; Karen Miller-Loessi, "Toward Gender Integration in the Workplace," *Sociological Perspectives* 35 (1992): 1–15.

63. England and Browne, "Trends," p. 25.

64. The differences in estimates of the sex gap in pay result from using different comparison techniques. Comparing the median annual earnings of men and women employed over 35 hours per week results in a sex gap of about 65 percent for whites. Using median weekly earnings shows a sex gap of almost 70 percent, and adjusting for total the number of hours worked each week results in estimates that white women earn about 75 percent of what white men earn. Afro-American and Hispanic women generally earn between 80 and 90 percent of what men of the same race or ethnicity earn. See England and Browne, *Trends,* pp. 24–33.

65. Linda Haas, *Equal Parenthood and Social Policy* (Albany: State University of New York Press, 1992), p. 35.

66. I am indebted to England and Browne ("Trends," pp. 32–36) for their formulation of this issue.

67. Gary S. Becker, "Human Capital, Effort, and the Sexual Division of Labor," *Journal of Labor Economics* 3 (1985): S33–S58.

68. Denise D. Bielby and William T. Bielby, "She Works Hard for the Money," *American Journal of Sociology* 93 (1988) 1031–1059; England and Browne, "Trends," p. 33.

69. Miller-Loessi, "Gender Integration," pp. 8–9.

70. England and Browne, "Trends," p. 35.

71. Margaret Mooney Marini and Mary Brinton, "Sex Typing in Occupational Socialization," in Barbara F. Reskin (ed.), *Sex Segregation in the Workplace* (Washington, DC: National Academy Press, 1984) pp. 192–232; Jacobs, *Revolving Doors.*

72. For example, see Kathleen Gerson, *Hard Choices: How Women Decide About Work, Career and Motherhood* (Berkeley: University of California Press, 1985).

73. In presenting competing economic scenarios, I draw on Joan Acker, "The Future of Women and Work," *Sociological Perspectives* 35 (1992): 53–68.

74. See Ray Marshall, *Unheard Voices: Labor and Economic Policy in a Competitive World* (New York: Basic Books, 1987).

75. Stephen Wood, *The Transformation of Work?* (London: Unwin Hyman, 1989).

76. Michael Porter, *The Competitive Advantage of Nations* (New York: Free Press, 1990).

77. Penelope Ciancanelli and Bettina Berch, "Gender and the GNP," in Beth Hess and Myra Marx Ferree, *Analyzing Gender* (Newbury Park, CA: Sage, 1987), p. 260.

78. Acker, "The Future," p. 58; Eileen Appelbaum and Peter Albin, "Differential Characteristics of Employment Growth in Service Industries," in Eileen Appelbaum and Ronald Schettkat (New York: Praeger, 1990), pp. 36–53.

79. Cynthia Cockburn, *Machinery of Dominance* (London: Pluto, 1985); see also Acker, "The Future," p. 61.

80. Ciancanelli and Berch, "Gender and GNP," p. 261.

81. Acker, "The Future."

82. U.S. Bureau of the Census, *Current Population Reports,* Series P60-183, Studies in the Distribution of Income (1992).

83. By the early 1990s, one in five children under 18 were living in poverty, and about one in four children under six were classified as poor. As a result, more families than ever before received foodstamps (25 million), and Aid to Families with Dependent Children (4.6 million). U.S. Congress, House of Representatives, *America's Families: Conditions,*

Trends, Hopes and Fears, Select Committee on Children Youth, and Families (Washington, DC: U.S. Government Printing Office, February 19, 1992), p. 4.

84. Ronald E. Kutscher, "New BLS Projections," *Monthly Labor Review* 114 (1991): 3–16.

85. Daniel Hecker, "Reconciling Conflicting Data on Jobs for College Graduates," *Monthly Labor Review* 115 (1992): 3–12; Kristina J. Shelley, "The Future of Jobs for College Graduates," *Monthly Labor Review* 115 (1992): 13–20.

86. Acker, "The Future," p. 62.

87. Kevin Phillips, *The Politics of Rich and Poor* (New York: Random House, 1990). Eileen Appelbaum and Peter Albin, "Differential Characteristics of Employment Growth in Service Industries," in Eileen Appelbaum and Ronald Schettkat (eds.), *Labor Market Adjustments to Structural Change and Technological Progress* (New York: Praeger, 1990), pp. 36–53.

88. Over 47 percent of the 2005 labor force will be women, up from about 45 percent in 1990. Kutcher, "BLS Projections," p. 9.

89. Kutscher, "BLS Projections"; George Silvestri and John Lukasiewicz, "Occupational Employment Projections," *Monthly Labor Review* 114 (1991): 64–94.

90. Silvestri and Lukasiewicz, "Employment Projections," p. 92.

91. Acker, "The Future," p. 65.

92. Acker, "The Future," p. 63.

93. Kutscher, "BLS Projections," p. 11.

94. See, for example, David Segal, "Motherload: Should We be Forcing Single Welfare Moms to Work Full Time?" *The Washington Monthly* (October 1992) Reprinted in *Utne Reader* 57 (1993), pp. 56–57.

95. Amitai Etzioni, "Children of the Universe," *Utne Reader* 57 (May/June 1993), p. 60.

96. Linda Haas, *Equal Parenthood and Social Policy: A Study of Parental Leave in Sweden* (Albany: State University of New York Press, 1992). Haas provides an insightful discussion of Sweden's attempts to encourage parental leave taking among fathers, which has met with mixed, but generally limited success. One of the discouraging factors in the Swedish leave program was that the generous benefits available to parents could be taken by either the mother or the father, but not both at the same time. This pitted mothers against fathers during the early leave taking, making them competitors for paid time off from work. Supporting one of the central findings from my research, Haas reported that if Swedish men did take parental leave after the birth, they were more responsible for later child care and were reported to be better at it (p. 158).

97. Sheila Kammerman, "Child Care, Women, Work, and the Family," in Jeffery S. Lande, Sandra Scarr, and Nina Gunzenhauser (eds.), *Caring for Children* (Hillsdale, NJ: Erlbaum), 1989, pp. 105–107.

98. Deborah Phillips, "Future Directions and Need for Child Care in the United States," in Jeffery S. Lande, Sandra Starr, and Nina Gunzenhauser (eds.), *Caring for Children* (Hillsdale, NJ: Erlbaum, 1989).

99. Harriet Presser, "Shift Work and Child Care Among Young Dual-Earner American Parents," *Journal of Marriage and the Family* 48 (1988): 133–148.

100. Etzioni, "Children," p. 60.

101. Phillips, "Future Directions," p. 262.

102. Sandra Hofferth and Deborah Phillips, "Child Care in the United States, 1970–1995," *Journal of Marriage and the Family* 49 (1987): 789–815; Phillips, "Future Directions."

103. Hofferth and Phillips, "Child Care."

104. Phillips, "Future Directions," p. 264.

105. Etzioni, "Children," p. 54.

106. Arleen Leibowitz, Linda J. Waite, and Christina J. Witsburger, "Child Care for Preschoolers," *Demography* 25 (1988): 205–220.

107. Glenna Spitze, "Women's Employment and Family Relations," *Journal of Marriage and the Family* 50 (1988): 595–618.

108. For useful discussions of why men are reluctant to give up privileges, see William Goode, "Why Men Resist," pp. 287–310 in Barrie Thorne and Marilyn Yalom (eds.), *Rethinking the Family,* 2nd ed. (Boston: Northeastern University Press, 1992); and Lynne Segal, *Slow Motion: Changing Masculinities, Changing Men* (New Brunswick, NJ: Rutgers University Press, 1990).

109. See, for example, Gayle Kimball, *50–50 Parenting* (Lexington, MA: Lexington Books, 1988; Norma Radin, *Predictors of Father Involvement in Childcare,* Paper presented at the Meeting of the Society for Research in Child Development, Detroit, Michigan, 1983; Graeme Russell, "Problems in Role-Reversed Families," pp. 161–179 in Charlie Lewis and Margaret O'Brien, *Reassessing Fatherhood;* and Segal, *Slow Motion.*

110. Lamb, Pleck, and Levine, "Paternal Involvement," pp. 116–123.

111. U.S. Bureau of the Census, *Current Population Reports* P20-463, Geographical Mobility (October 1992).

112. Coltrane and Hickman, "Rhetoric of Rights and Needs."

113. Lamb, Pleck, and Levine, "Effects of Paternal Involvement," p. 121.

114. Graeme Russell, *The Changing Role of Fathers?* (St Lucia, Queensland: University of Queensland Press, 1983).

115. In an excellent review of fathers and child development, the psychologist Ross Parke comments:

> A voluminous literature has emerged over the last three decades that clearly demonstrates relations between quality of paternal involvement and children's social, emotional, and cognitive develoment. At the same time, considerable evidence shows a good deal of overlap and redundancy between fathers' and mothers' impact on children. There is less evidence that fathers make a unique contribution to children's development.

Ross D. Parke, "Fathers and Families," in M. Bornstein (ed.), *Handbook of Parenting* (Hillsdale, NJ: Erlbaum, in press). In recognizing that two parents can enhance development, I am not arguing that two parents are always better than one. The quality of care and the "fit" between caregiver and child can override any potential benefits from having two involved parents. Most children in single parent families fare quite well, despite the relative average disadvantage they face in terms of income, neighborhood, schooling, etc.

116. Ross Parke ("Fathers and Families," p. 41) concludes that "although the processes are not yet well understood, it is clear that involved fathering relates in positive ways to other aspects of men's lives." John Snarey, *How Fathers Care for the Next Generation* (Cambridge, MA: Harvard University Press, 1993), notes that "men who are

parentally generative during early adulthood usually turn out to be good spouses, workers, and citizens at mid life" (p. 119).

117. Nancy Chodorow, "Oedipal Asymmetries and Heterosexual Knots," *Social Problems* 23 (1976): 454–467.

118. The process of doing gender is not new. Gender has always been an accomplishment; it is just that in times of rapid social change, it is easier to see how we are actively constructing gender through our everyday activities. See West and Zimmerman, "Doing Gender."

Index

Abuse
  of children, 186, 231
  of wives, 39, 233
Acker, Joan, 216, 281n.73
Adoption, 45
Affective individualism. *See* Individualism
African Americans, 28, 40, 84, 209–10, 213
Aggressiveness, 180–83, 186, 197–98, 206
Aka pygmies, 185
Aloofness, 182–87, 190–91, 269n.22, 270n.25.
  See also Separate spheres
Anger, 118, 120–22, 147, 181, 196. *See also*
  Aggressiveness, Conflict
Arapesh, 178
Attitudes. *See also* Ideology
  recent changes in, 201–6
  toward gender roles, 202, 204, 223–27
  toward individual self-determination, 202–3
Azande, 189–90

Baby. *See also* Infants
  boom, 40, 44, 203, 206–7, 222
  care of, 27, 41–42, 46–48, 57, 59–62, 178,
    180, 183, 185–86, 206, 225–26, 233
Baird, Zoe, 221
Bargaining. *See* Negotiation
Bateson, Gregory, 178–79
Becker, Gary, 152, 281n.67
Benedict, Ruth, 178
Bernard, Jessie, 239n.1
Bias
  in estimates of labor allocation, 92–93

in past research, 267–68n.7
Biology
  as an insufficient explanation for gender, 28,
    48–50, 167, 175, 188, 191, 194, 198
  in theories of labor allocation, 152–54,
    167, 178–80, 183, 185, 188, 244n.89,
    259n.3
Birth. *See also* Fertility
  cesarean, 57, 60–61
  as a conscious decision, 129, 207
  death and, 31
  fathers' presence at, 49, 57–58, 206, 226
  impact on family roles of, 46–47, 57–59,
    227–28, 265–66n.60
  men's avoidance of, 183
  men's experience of, 58–59
  natural, 58–60
  in 1950s, 42, 211
  rates of, 86, 211, 228
  timing of, 21, 40, 44, 49, 126–33, 168–71,
    200, 211, 227, 249n.27, 279n.53
  and women's employment, 211–12
Blumer, Herbert, 251n.42
Bly, Robert, 7, 24, 192–94, 196, 198, 274n.52
Bott, Elizabeth, 133–35, 257n.32
Boy Scouts, 31, 192, 195
Breadwinner. *See also* Provider
  attitudes toward, 26, 41, 95, 99, 201–6
  and family debates, 21, 196
  history of, 28, 33–34, 40–44, 208
  man's duty as, 10, 25, 39, 97
  as a statistical minority, 44

285